PUEBLO STYLE AND REGIONAL ARCHITECTURE

Pueblo Style and Regional Architecture

edited by **NICHOLAS C. MARKOVICH**
Associate Professor and Director of Basic Programs
Louisiana State University

WOLFGANG F. E. PREISER
Professor and Director, Center for Research and Development,
School of Architecture and Planning
University of New Mexico

FRED G. STURM
Professor and Chair, Department of Philosophy
University of New Mexico

VNR VAN NOSTRAND REINHOLD
New York

Cover photograph: Exterior of the Center for Non-Invasive Diagnosis, University of New Mexico, Albuquerque (Westwork Architects). Copyright © 1988 Kirk Gittings/SYNTAX.

Frontispiece: West facade of Zimmerman Library, University of New Mexico, Albuquerque (John Gaw Meem, Architect). Copyright © 1988 Anthony Richardson/SYNTAX.

Library of Congress Card Number 89–30618
ISBN 0-442-31896-0

Printed in the United States of America

Van Nostrand Reinhold
115 Fifth Avenue
New York, New York 10003

Van Nostrand Reinhold International Company Limited
11 New Fetter Lane
London EC4P 4EE, England

Van Nostrand Reinhold
480 La Trobe Street
Melbourne, Victoria 3000, Australia

Nelson Canada
1120 Birchmount Road
Scarborough, Ontario M1K 5G4, Canada

16 15 14 13 12 11 10 9 8 7 6 5 4 3 2 1

D
720.978
PUE

Library of Congress Cataloging in Publication Data

Pueblo style and regional architecture/edited by Nicholas C. Markovich, Wolfgang F. E. Preiser, Fred G. Sturm.
    p. cm.
    Includes index.
    ISBN 0-442-31896-0
      1. Regionalism in architecture—Southwest, New. 2. Pueblo Indians—Architecture.
3. Indians of North America—Southwest, New—Architecture. 4. Pueblo Indians—Architecture—Influence. 5. Indians of North America—Southwest, New—Architecture—Influence. I. Markovich, Nicholas C. II. Preiser, Wolfgang F. E. III. Sturm, Fred Gillette.
NA727.P84 1990
720'.978—dc19   89-30618
                                              CIP

Dm

Contents

Foreword

Architectural regionalism is cultural, climatic, and technological. It should not be thought of as a parochial concern but as a principled attitude no matter where one builds. It must also accommodate change. The task before us is not to revive, but to revitalize style not merely as external decoration but as a response to a life-style, creating places that are particular and distinctive through a creative synthesis linking past and present and leaving its own heritage.

It is unfortunate that the word "regional" has often taken on a derogatory connotation such as in "regional painter" or "regional writer," implying something less than first, or world, class. This is not quite as true in the field of architecture, however, where both in academe and in the profession there recently has been a growing concern with regional issues.

If regionalism is the thesis, then in dialectical terms the antithesis must be cosmopolitanism, internationalism, eclecticism. This is the province of major capital cities. Thesis and antithesis demand a synthesis, creatively linking past and present, developing a new heritage.

In a world of mass consumerism and instant communication, the dichotomy is ever more obvious. On the one hand, our globe as seen from outer space encourages a "one world" view, financial markets are international, technology ("high tech") is cosmopolitan, satellites make television reception possible in the most remote villages of the third world. On the other hand, there is a strong reaction, a revival of fundamental tribalisms, a wish to hold on to deeper cultural, mystical, and religious roots. Dreams of the family tribe abound. Essentially regional, and resisting becoming part of a melting pot, the roots can be Basque, Welsh, Hopi, Armenian, Sikh, Kurd, or Lithuanian. Architecturally this resistance favors so-called appropriate technology (generally "low tech"). In Hungary, regional and historically oriented designs now confront the official governmental style, which is seen as progressive and international.

Germany during its recent unfortunate period straddled both sides, demanded romantic regionalism (*Heimatstil*) for its residential buildings, the "cozy look," yet pompous, cleansed international classicism (à la Speer) for its public edifices, "the impressive look." The word "kitsch" could be applied to both. This shows the importance ascribed to physical images and their effect on the general public.

The dichotomy continues—regionalism rooted in the life and work of many generations against designs and patterns often abstract and rootless, which at worst result in buildings that cannot be distinguished whether they be in Tel Aviv, Chicago, Hong Kong, or London, cities where skyscrapers, an international building style, now dominate the skyline.

New Mexico benefits from romantic regionalism; regional traditions are everywhere evident and continuing. Three architectural styles are clearly dominant: (1) the

Territorial style, an imposition of classical details onto native building forms, (2) the Spanish Mission style, used by the Santa Fe Railroad for its stations and not as prevalent as the other two styles, and (3) the Pueblo Revival style, called Spanish Pueblo by John Gaw Meem, which is the subject of this book. I believe that the power and continuity of these styles is due to the centuries-long isolation of New Mexico, its comparative poverty, the cultural pride of its various ethnic communities, and the wishes of newcomers to participate in its collective memories and myths. It is also now evident, as tourism becomes a major financial resource, that being different and distinctive is beneficial economically.

It is especially in the Pueblo Revival style that there exists a "there" in New Mexican regional architecture. It is, of course, commercially exploited. The Santa Fe style of furniture, clothing, and other artifacts is now fashionable. Santa Fe prides itself on being the "City Different" and controls its architecture to make sure that there is visual continuity even if only skin deep. While I do not like the superficial and cosmetic nature of much that occurs, it is liked generally by the inhabitants, and it is useful as a tourist attraction. The irony is that this tourism may help retain some of the past, even if only as "memory wallpaper." This is probably the best we can ask for at this moment in time.

This book, however, should help in the task of going beyond such superficiality in search of a truly contextual architecture adding to our understanding of what makes New Mexico special, what we were, what we are, and what we can be.

George Anselevicius, FAIA
Dean, School of Architecture and Planning
University of New Mexico

Preface

In a world that is increasingly tending to think alike and look alike, it is important to cherish and preserve those elements in our culture that belong to us and help differentiate us. We are fortunate in this region in that we have a style of architecture that uniquely belongs to us and visually evokes memories of our history and our earth itself. (John Gaw Meem, "Development of Spanish Pueblo Architecture in the Southwest," *New Mexico Architecture*, Sept.–Oct., 1966.)

Within the lexicon of architecture in the Americas, New Mexico possesses a rich and time-honored legacy. The traditions of architecture in this southwestern region of the United States have developed over many centuries, building on the cultural essence of the Anasazi and other peoples of the pre-Hispanic period. After the virtual abandonment of the urban centers of the Anasazi, later Puebloan groups of this region inherited and extrapolated these earlier concepts of space, form, and being, carrying on an already centuries old architectural tradition.

That early concept has survived and was developed further in the architecture of the Spanish, from the time of their arrival in the 1500s. Other European-American groups developed their own concepts of a regional interpretation of architecture from the time of their entrance into the area during the period of U.S. colonization in the 1800s. This historically recent period of settlement has brought about the most change and has placed the regional concept in the greatest state of flux. New Mexican architecture now is at a point of earnest conflict between the evolving tradition of regional architecture and new imported ideologies of architectonic form and image.

The semiarid climate of New Mexico protects and preserves the ancient building tradition, presenting the expressions of meaning from the past to us in the present. A short distance from twentieth century New Mexican towns and cities, we are quickly transported to places still replete with the expressions of meaning left by other cultures and manifesting ancient times. We are, by the nature of the southwestern cultural and geographic landscape, made acutely aware of the meaning of diverse human experience. In this place, the cosmology of the Pueblo World and its ancestry meets directly with the cosmology of the European-American world. The two must confront each other and accommodate each other, presenting a concept of meaning unique to the southwestern United States. The new cosmology formulates what we know as New Mexico and becomes part of our physical and cultural meaning. Here fragments of ancient architecture dot the landscape, and the questions of preservation and the promulgation of tradition are serious ones.

This project effort, which entertains the notion of Pueblo style and regional architecture, was the result of a collaboration among many individuals speaking to the phenomenon of architecture, place, and culture that are so uniquely presented to the world in the region of New Mexico. This humanistic endeavor has brought together archaeologists and anthropologists, artists and historians, as well as architects and philosophers. Native Americans, Hispanic Americans, and Anglos joined together in this project to search for regional meaning in the architectural expression of this region, which is the epicenter of culture and heritage for the American Southwest. Our journey is a search for the evidence of truth in the meaning of our ancient cultures and the new. Our collective intellectual gesture was toward the rediscovery of ancient and continuing myths. Our search, presented in the chapters of this book, is a first attempt at an interdisciplinary understanding of culture, architecture, and place in the American Southwest.

A symposium on Pueblo style and regional architecture was held, and a traveling photographic exhibit was designed to illustrate the evolution and varied interpretation of that style, with photographic examples ranging from Chaco Canyon to modern-day architecture in New Mexico. The project reflects what Paul Horgan stated so aptly in his foreword to Bainbridge Bunting's book, *John Gaw Meem: Southwestern Architect.* It reads as follows:

> People who come to New Mexico in answer to a need—for health, informality in ways of living, livelihood in what seems a surviving frontier—often end up being possessed by the landscape. I use the term most broadly for I mean not only the physical beauty of the plains, the mountains, the quality of the sky with all its variations of color and light: I mean also what the poet Hopkins meants by "inscape"—that lodgement of spirit whose work it is to take the materials of the known world and unify them through an embracing philosphy.
>
> The ancient earth visions made manifest in the American Southwest bear long witness to the way in which the land itself formed ways of living for several laminations of culture; so that prehistoric dwellings and enclosures of ceremony, followed by the town structures of Spanish colonialism and the early Anglo-American plains settlements, all seem like features of the grand landscape itself in their shapes, materials, and survivals of weather. In their turns, generations of new arrivals can see the visible evidence of a particular sequence of social history speaking across many centuries. A recognition of this, often unspoken but powerful, must surely be a stong element in the spell cast upon the newcomer by the *ambiente* of the land of New Mexico.
>
> This, despite the threat against the spell begun in 1880 with the triumphant coming of the transcontinental railroad, and its quickening promise of commercial prosperity. Headlong developments in the technological network of social and commercial exchange have worked for over a century a kind of erosion against old forms of the local heritage. It is not a new process—older cultures everywhere throughout time have been modified or wholly overthrown by the newer. But what has had the dignity of survival can be protected if recognized for what its value really is in the sum of a heritage provided there are those who can see it, respect it, and work, fight if necessary, to keep it for its own sake amidst the tendency of modern commerce to inspire hideous novelties of individual taste in a contest for customer attention that has wrecked much of the visual decorum of clustered America.

Nicholas C. Markovich

Contributors

Tony Anella is an architect working on his apprenticeship in Los Angeles. A native of Albuquerque, he is primarily interested in how man builds in the landscape of the American Southwest. His Master of Architecture thesis was the design of a visitor center and archaeologic research facility for Mesa Verde National Park.

George Anselevicius is Dean of the School of Architecture and Planning, University of New Mexico. He has taught in India, Mexico, and Switzerland, and is the recipient of a number of design awards for his buildings. He is a Fellow of the American Institute of Architects.

T. J. Ferguson is Director of Southwest Programs for the Institute of the NorthAmerican West, Flagstaff, Arizona. Former Tribal Archaeologist for Zuni Pueblo, he is currently a Research Associate of the Zuni Pueblo Archaeology Program. He is co-author of *A Zuni Atlas.*

David Gebhard is Associate Professor of Architectural History and Curator of the Architectural Drawing Collection in the University of California at Santa Barbara.

Ethel S. Goodstein is Associate Professor of Architecture at the University of Southwestern Louisiana. An architectural historian and historic preservation consultant, her research interests and publications focus on comparative study of North American art and architecture. She also serves as chairperson of the Landmarks Preservation Commission of Lafayette, Louisiana.

Louis A. Hieb is Head Special Collections Librarian at the University of Arizona Library. As an anthropologist he has done field work at Hopi and has published articles on the Hopi world view, ritual clowns, masks, and ritual. He also has written on vernacular architecture.

Theodore S. Jojola is Director of Native American Studies and Assistant Professor of Planning in the School of Architecture and Planning at the University of New Mexico. He is an enrolled member of Isleta Pueblo and is involved in examining change and process in tribal community development as related to modernization.

John L. Kessell is Associate Professor of History at the University of New Mexico and director of the *Vargas Project.* He is author of *Cross, Crown, and Kiva*, a historical study of Pecos Pueblo and Mission, and *The Missions of New Mexico Since 1776.*

George Kubler is Professor Emeritus and Senior Research Fellow at Yale University. After publishing *Religious Architecture in New Mexico* he became interested in sixteenth century Mexican architecture. This led to research into Iberian architecture and pre-Columbian art and architecture. He is currently writing a book on the aesthetic recognition of ancient Amerindian art and architecture.

Stephen H. Lekson is an anthropologist on the staff of the Arizona State Museum. He has done field work at Anasazi, Hohokam, and Mogollon archaeological sites. His book on the architecture of Chaco Canyon sites has challenged long-held assumptions about the earliest forms of Pueblo building.

Tsiporah Lipton is a graduate of York University, Toronto, Canada, where she completed a Master of Fine Arts degree in Dance History and Criticism. She is presently in the Southwest, researching issues of space, form, and dance.

Nicholas C. Markovich is Associate Professor at the School of Architecture at Louisiana State University, where he also directs the basic design programs. He was formerly Assistant Dean of the School of Architecture and Planning and Presidential Lecturer at the University of New Mexico. His research interests are in design and architecture theory with an emphasis in regionalism.

Barbara J. Mills worked for the Zuni Pueblo as archaeologist from 1976 to 1981. She is Assistant Professor of Anthropology at Northern Arizona University.

Folke Nyberg is Professor of Architecture and Urban Design at the University of Washington as well as a practicing architect. His articles and papers on architectural design theory are numerous and are currently being gathered for publication in a forthcoming book.

Buford L. Pickens is Professor Emeritus of Architecture at Washington University and past president of the Society of Architectural Historians and the Association of Collegiate Schools of Architecture. He has served as director of the School of Architecture at Tulane and as dean of the School of Architecture at Washington.

Wolfgang F. E. Preiser is Professor of Architecture and Director of the Center for Research and Development of the School of Architecture and Planning of the University of New Mexico. He also directs the Planning Research Institute and is a partner in Architectural Research Consultants. Publications include five books, 15 monographs, and over 60 articles dealing with architecture and planning.

V. B. Price is a poet, editor, political columnist, and architecture writer working in New Mexico. He is former editor of *Century* and *New Mexico Magazine,* and is the architecture editor of *Artspace.* He teaches architectural writing in the School of Architecture and Planning and is a faculty member in the general honors program of the University of New Mexico.

Amos Rapoport is Distinguished Professor of Architecture at the University of Wisconsin, Milwaukee. One of the founders of Environmental Behavior Studies (EBS), he approaches all topics from a cross-cultural, interdisciplinary EBS perspective with emphasis on concepts and theory. Among his many publications are the books *House Form and Culture, The Meaning of the Built Environment,* and *Human Aspects of Urban Form.*

David G. Saile is a member of the faculty at Arizona State University and a noted researcher in Pueblo architecture studies. He has been active for 20 years in built environment research.

Stephen D. Schreiber is a Visiting Professor at the University of Miami School of Architecture, where he teaches design studios and graphics courses. In 1988, he received the school's Woodrow Wilkins Award for Outstanding Teaching. Professor Schreiber graduated from Dartmouth College and the Harvard University Graduate

School of Design. He is also a practicing architect and has been responsible for the design and contruction of numerous commercial structures, housing projects, and private residences. His design work has been published in *Architecture* magazine.

Calbert Seciwa is a native of Zuni Pueblo who has held various administrative and educational positions within Zuni government, most recently as Tribal Administrator. He is with the Indian Studies Program, Arizona State University, Tempe.

Farouk Seif is president of Metadesign & Transplanning Consultants, an architectural firm in Seattle, Washington. He has published several articles and papers and has taught architecture at Louisiana State University, Texas Tech University, and Faculty of Fine Arts in Cairo, Egypt. He is currently writing his doctoral dissertation at the University of Washington.

Carl D. Sheppard is Professor Emeritus at the University of Minnesota. He taught at UCLA and now resides in Santa Fe, New Mexico. His earlier research interest was the art and architecture of the Middle Ages, but since retirement from teaching his focus is on the development of Pueblo style. He is co-author of *Looking at Modern Painting* and *Creator of the Santa Fe Style: Isaac Hamilton Rapp, Architect.*

Glade Sperry, Jr., heads the Albuquerque firm of Westwork Architects, whose works have been featured in *Architecture* and *Architectural Record*. Several of his projects have received honor awards from the American Institute of Architects.

Fred G. Sturm is chair of the Department of Philosophy at the University of New Mexico, Honorary Professor of Foreign Languages and Literatures at Shaanxi Teachers University (Xi'an, China), Editor-in-Chief of the *Journal of Chinese Studies,* and director of the Institute for Pueblo Indian Studies of the Indian Pueblo Cultural Center and its research library and Pueblo archives. He is a philosopher of art and aesthetics, and also publishes extensively in the fields of East Asian and Latin American philosophy.

Rina Swentzell is an architectural consultant in Santa Fe, New Mexico. She is a native of Santa Clara Pueblo. Her M.A. thesis on the history and significance of Santa Clara architecture is well known. Her interest in the relation between built environment and cultural world view and values has been expressed in her doctoral dissertation and recent work.

Michael E. Welsh is Assistant Professor of History at Cameron University. He previously taught at Oregon State University, St. John's College in Santa Fe, and the University of New Mexico. He has published a *History of Army Engineers in the Southwest* and has been commissioned to write the official centennial history of the University of New Mexico.

Chris Wilson is Adjunct Assistant Professor of Architecture at the University of New Mexico. As an architectural historian he has served since 1983 as consultant to the State Historic Preservation Division of New Mexico. His M.A. thesis was a study of the architectural and cultural history of the Plaza of Santa Fe, New Mexico.

Acknowledgments

Sponsors

Planning Research Institute, Inc., Albuquerque
School of Architecture and Planning, University of New Mexico
Institute for Pueblo Indian Studies of the Indian Pueblo Cultural Center, Albuquerque
Native American Studies Program, University of New Mexico
American Institute of Architects, Albuquerque Chapter
New Mexico Society of Architects

Funding Support

New Mexico Endowment for the Humanities
The City of Albuquerque Urban Enhancement Trust Fund
The University of New Mexico Centennial Committee
The Albuquerque Community Foundation
Eastman Kodak Corporation
The Friends of the School of Architecture,
School of Architecture and Planning, University of New Mexico

Symposium Program Committee

Wolfgang F. E. Preiser, Project Director and Symposium Convener
Nicholas C. Markovich, Co-chair
Fred G. Sturm, Co-chair

Exhibition Committee

Nicholas C. Markovich, Coordinator and Director
Wolfgang F. E. Preiser
Van Dorn Hooker
Kirk Gittings
Anthony Richardson

Photography

Kirk Gittings and Anthony Richardson
Historic Photographs:
New Mexico State Photographic Archives
Museum of New Mexico History Library, Santa Fe
University of New Mexico Photographic Archives

Secretarial Assistance

Tina Taylor and Marsha G. Floyd

Logistical Support

Cecilia Fenoglio-Preiser
Nicholas G. Preiser
Agnes Truske
Perry J. Segura

Introduction

As a somewhat conventional historian of the region, I confess to a heady rush every time I dare use a term so patently interdisciplinary as "the built environment." This book, as we shall see, goes far beyond—to emic and etic landscapes, rituals and metaphors of building, earth navels, mythologizing and demythologizing. Together, we are off again, as we should be periodically—anthropologists, archaeologists, architects and planners, art historians, a philosopher and a poet, scholars and observers—on tour through a unique cultural landscape. We share the hope of better understanding the Pueblo world through its architecture and perhaps discovering along the way something of the mystique of New Mexico.

John L. Kessell
Associate Professor of History
University of New Mexico

PUEBLO STYLE AND REGIONAL ARCHITECTURE

V. B. Price

The "mystique of New Mexico," like the spirit of any distinct cultural environment, is an essential quality, a gestalt, that transcends the sum of its parts. In a state that calls itself the land of enchantment, this mystique arises from the chemistry among exotic incongruities. These include majestic land forms; geographic isolation; the remains of a pre-Columbian urban civilization and the cultural survival of its Pueblo descendants; a rich Hispanic history of conquest, adaptation, and nurturing insularity; and a romantic Anglo idealization of the images emerging from this unique cultural and geographic florescence.

This book on Pueblo style and regional architecture brings together some twenty scholars and thinkers of diverse persuasions from many parts of the country to explore the complex interplay of culture and design in New Mexico. The richness of the interdisciplinary mix sees architects and archaeologists, Pueblo Indian scholars, art historians, planners, critics, and cultural investigators come to grips with one of the thorniest architectural problems of our century and the next—the preservation of regional and local identity as it manifests itself in the built environment.

The wealth of perspectives removes scholarly and cultural barriers to permit a stimulating interchange of new information and points of view. These chapters almost defy summary, their range is so wide and multifaceted. What follows, therefore, must be an interpretive and subjective overview. It begins with a few opening remarks, then distills the highlights of the volume, and closes with a brief analysis of its implications.

The synergy created by the diversity of topics reveals an undercurrent of unexpected questions, such as the following.

- Are architecturally traditional Hopi villages more culturally secure than modernized Zuni Pueblo, or, in other words, does architecture not only contain culture but also shape and reinforce it?
- Is there a fundamental discontinuity or a continuity of spirit between ancient and vernacular forms and New Mexico revival styles?
- What are the functional and symbolic differences between vernacular models, high-style regional architecture based on those models, and mass-produced suburban products that allude to them both?
- Is there an inherent conflict, an economic and semantic clash, between the meaning of symbolic and nostalgic forms and the architectural packaging of public relations tourist imagery?
- Can historic preservation conserve cultural iconography without freezing cultural imagery in the past and blocking the design flexibility that financially impoverished cultures must exhibit to survive?
- What are the major differences among archaeological ruins, vernacular building traditions, and regional revival styles with respect to the influence they might have on contemporary architectural practices?
- Is regionalism in architecture irrevocably bound to mass-market tourism, or does it have higher cultural, educational, and psychological functions?

- What are the implications of the differences between architecture as sculptural form and architecture as the moral and cosmological symbol it is among the Pueblos?
- Given its deeply materialistic culture, is it possible for "European" America to develop a cosmologically symbolic architecture as the Pueblos have done? Or, to ask the question another way, can buildings of symbolic significance contribute to the creation of a new social ethos?
- Can the blend of modernism and regionalism such as is found at the central campus of the University of New Mexico serve as a prototype for Pueblo peoples in their battles with the federal government for culturally appropriate and efficient new housing?
- Is architecture as memory doomed to be replaced by architecture as commerce?
- Is there, to quote Eliel Saarinen, a "fundamental form" for the architecture of New Mexico in the twenty-first century?

Such questions arise from the broad social context in which this book takes place, a context that many fear will prove to be on the threshold of a radical transformation of the architectural and human environments on this planet. A world once rich in architectural diversity has become increasingly homogenized—conquered, if you will—by a steady encroachment of international corporate and consumer culture, one in which the creation and consumption of standard products in a standardized and predictable marketplace is the pragmatic end that justifies virtually any means. Cultural variety, not to mention sense of place, is vanishing along with rain forests, stratospheric ozone, healthy oceans, and innumerable plant and animal species.

Yet in the uniform global economy of the twenty-first century, cultural landscapes will be, paradoxically, among the most valuable commodities. Their essential rarity alone will ensure their continued demand. Like the nascent international economy of the nineteenth century, the marketplace of the future will be leavened by tourism and its exotic products. Unique human habitats will be looked upon as antidotes to the miseries of competitive existence. The economy of the future, however, like that of the present, is more likely to devour cultural localities than to preserve them. It is much handier, after all, to create a controllable likeness of a culture than to have to deal with the unpredictable nature of that culture itself.

One of the most pressing environmental issues for architects and planners in the twenty-first century will concern the preservation of unique localities and the people who inhabit them. The overwhelming temptation in the corporate marketplace will be to "Santatize" such places using the temptingly successful Santa Fe model. When it comes to economic development, regionalism as commodity can be based on the manufacture of inauthentic environments—gentrified Disneylands, if you will—or the protection of authentic and evolving cultural landscapes that are at once places to live as well as places to market.

Issues such as these underlie the subject matter of this volume. The authors have sought to come to terms with both the phenomenal survival of Pueblo culture into the twentieth century and the unique process of mutual adaptation that characterizes Anglo, Hispano, and Pueblo culture in New Mexico. It could be said in a backhanded way, for instance, that Pueblo and Hispano cultures have adopted, from time to time, a form of big city, Anglo provincial architecture, a classical or international style, just as Anglo New Mexico has created a Spanish and Pueblo Revival style architecture. In New Mexico, mutual influence is the key.

The twenty-one chapters can be grouped into three broad categories:

1. Assessments of Anasazi and Pueblo architecture, the cultures that produced them, and the influences they have had on regionalism in New Mexico. This includes critical views on scholarly and popular misconceptions of these

vernacular sources as well as sensitive revelations of their mythological and spiritual contexts.
2. Analyses of regionalism as an aesthetic, scientific, political, and cultural phenomenon in America, New Mexico, and the rest of the world.
3. Discussions of both the dangers and the values of regionalist sentiment in New Mexico as it wears its various guises as a revolutionary force, a loving expression, a conservative tradition, and a reactionary institution embodied in rigid zoning codes.

In the first category, archaeologist Stephen Lekson discusses in Chapter 6 his contention that the preoccupations of early archaeologists to help modern Pueblos substantiate land claims led to what he considers misinterpretations of data. Debunking what he calls "Southwestern hyperbole," Lekson sees an Anasazi world "almost perpetually out of balance," characterized not by permanence but by "remarkable" mobility, and although ancestral to the Pueblos also culturally distinct from their settled urban way of life. Using an ethnographic approach to interpret Anasazi architectural artifacts is, he maintains, fraught with intellectual dangers.

In a somewhat similar vein, Yale emeritus art historian George Kubler discusses in Chapter 12 the preoccupations and accomplishments of W. H. Holmes and Adolf Bandelier, two men who did much to establish the mystique of Pueblo and Indian culture in America. Bandelier viewed American Indian culture from an early sociological and anthropological perspective, whereas Holmes approached it from an artistic and natural history point of view. To my mind, it seems that both projected onto the past the biases and ignorance of their day, as we continue to do with ours. Holmes, the first director of the National Gallery of Art, adopted an evolutionary approach of "primitive" art with a hierarchical view that had "savages" at one end of the scale and "civilization" at the other. Bandelier, author of *The Delight Makers*, made often wild, supposedly unromantic, protoscientific observations, such as claiming that Native American religious and social organization was the same for the entire continent and denying that the Pueblos possessed any aesthetic sense. Both, Kubler writes diplomatically, "were precursors of anthropological archaeology, without themselves being able to practice it before its appearance."

In Chapter 5, the historian David Saile presents an overview of the Pueblo built environment, which emphasizes the living quality of Pueblo architecture as a natural and spiritual entity. Saile remarks on the fragmentation of scholarship in the field and discusses the regrettable absence of an integrated gestalt interpretation of Pueblo building and design.

From another viewpoint, in Chapter 7, Theodore Jojola, a Native American scholar, counteracts the image of Pueblo culture as static and frozen in time by showing how "the Pueblo community has undergone significant change over relatively short" periods. His examination of modernization and Pueblo lifeways at Isleta Pueblo argues that it "has been the adaptive behavior of the Pueblo people that has kept their communities vital and progressive." In Chapter 8, anthropologists T. J. Ferguson, Barbara Mills, and Calbert Seciwa of Zuni Pueblo, in their examination of contemporary Zuni architecture and society, support Jojola's views. The Zuni people have, they affirm, "historically chosen function over form as they have rebuilt their village to keep pace with modern times." "Innovation in Zuni architecture," they write, "has been guided by a pragmatic approach that favors cost-effective solutions to basic problems." Although Zuni Pueblo "no longer looks like it did in the past," in important social and ceremonial ways "it continues to function as it always has." Housing built by the U.S. Department of Housing and Urban Development (HUD), on the other hand, has had profound negative effects on Zuni social, cultural, and economic ways of life. HUD housing was called "a Trojan horse," bringing modernizing conveniences to Zuni Pueblo along with a hidden cache of extra social and financial costs.

Unlike Zuni, Hopi villages have maintained a strong connection with traditional building materials and symbolic forms. Among the most conservative of the Pueblos, Hopi is perhaps the most successful at warding off modern influence. Anthropologist/librarian Louis A. Hieb in Chapter 9 discusses the concerns of "symbolic anthropology" and its shifting of analysis from "function" to "meaning." He argues that "Hopis perceive, experience, and describe their architectural forms metaphorically in terms of their conception of the world and their place within it." Vernacular architecture at Hopi is a language, a "cultural construction," Hieb writes, in which physical form is bonded to cultural meaning and value.

In a similar way, dance historian Tsiporah Lipton analyzes Tewa visions of space in Chapter 10. Exploring the relationship between space in settlement patterns, architecture, pottery decoration, and dance, Lipton reveals an affinity between perception, symbolization in pottery, and actualization of space in dance. Tewa cosmology, which emphasizes a "consanguinity between the land and the people, serves to shape consistent patterns." Tewa villages, for instance, "carry out a visual dialogue with the landscape, not simply blending into the background, but also being active participants."

In Chapter 3, Santa Clara Pueblo architect Rina Swentzell writes that Pueblo myths "give a clear description of the nature of the cosmos, as well as the structuring of the house, kiva, and community forms. The Pueblo world . . . is an altogether hallowed place where 'the breath,' or life energy, flows through both the animate and inanimate realms in such a manner that even the house, kiva, and community forms breathe of that breath and are essentially alive." The myths show, she says, how structure at the physical level is integral with structure at the metaphysical level. She concludes by saying that a Pueblo house or structure is "not an object—or a machine to live in—but is part of a cosmological world view that recognizes multiplicity, simultaneity, inclusiveness, and interconnectedness."

In Chapter 19, Folke Nyberg and Farouk Seif explore the relationship between the ritual and architecture of the ancient Egyptians and those of the Hopi, concluding that religious rituals "relate to regional qualities of place," with the Egyptians in "processional" and symbolic architectural space, with the Hopi in "landscape-oriented and antimonumental ceremonial dances."

The lesson of Pueblo architecture for the modern world, Los Angeles architect Tony Anella observes in Chapter 4, is that the modern built environment can come "to complement the land" when we learn "to live with it, and not merely on or in spite of it." Anella contrasts the Albuquerque bedroom community of Rio Rancho and its "bulldozed grid" of roads with the built environments of Taos, Sandia, Santa Ana, and Tesuque pueblos in which natural mountains and man-made buildings are considered to be part of the same urban whole, with natural landmarks completing the urban form.

A major misconception of regionalism in New Mexico concerns the image of harmonious triculturality. Philosopher Fred G. Sturm, in his presentation on the aesthetics of the Southwest, (Chapter 2), writes that to understand the development of the Pueblo Revival style of architecture it is necessary "to take note of the conflicting value systems of the Pueblo societies, Hispanic culture, and Northwest European Anglo culture." "Rather than constituting a modern development of an architectural style that reflects a Pueblo Indian aesthetic," Sturm observes, revival style architecture in Santa Fe, and at the University of New Mexico in particular, reflects "the disparate pluralism of the Southwest in which three separate systems of aesthetic values coexist precariously."

In the second category of presentations analyzing regionalism as aesthetic, scientific, political, and cultural phenomena, Amos Rapoport, from the University of Wisconsin School of Architecture, writes in Chapter 20 that in environmental design a region "is any portion of the earth's surface that stands apart from others in terms of [a] set of perceptible characteristics . . . that produce a cultural landscape with a distinct character or ambience." Such landscapes are "taken to be intimately related to human life and are primarily for living and working in rather than just for looking at. They are also," he emphasizes, "always symbolic; that is, they have *meaning*." He concludes by observing that while the future of "regional architecture seems problematic," regional cultural landscapes, which are "never designed" have "a better chance" for survival in the twenty-first century. In other words, self-sustaining cultures are hardier than economically vulnerable architectural styles.

In prefacing his presentation "Regionalism in American Architecture: A Comparative Review of Roots" (Chapter 18), Buford Pickens sees regionalism in the United States today as having recovered from "a strong pejorative taint" that began in the 1930s. While cautioning against provincialism and stressing inspiration over imitation, Pickens observes that many American architects believe that the "potentials for an 'authentic regionalism'" now exist in "vernacular architecture" rooted in "human ecology." American architecture has evolved "like an ecological experiment, testing the effects of many new environments," he writes. "The seeds from Old World species of architecture and town plans were sown at different places on virgin soil, under conditions of producing vital new characteristics."

New Mexico architectural historian Christopher M. Wilson puts Spanish/Pueblo Revival style architecture in the "soil" of the tradition of romantic reaction and picturesque aesthetic in Chapter 14. "Resistance to cultural homogenization," he observes, "has taken two forms": one, by traditional people such as the Pueblos and Hispanic Americans defending their "local vernacular culture from the pressures of the dominant, industrial culture"; the other by the reaction of the romantic movement against Renaissance classical culture and later against industrial capitalism in the Arts and Crafts movement, in New Deal regionalism, and in the counterculture/environmental movement. "New Mexico and its regional architecture," he writes, "does not represent some backwater that refuses to join the modern age, but instead is a valuable example of a continuing Romantic tradition." He concludes by saying that regional styles have a profound "symbolic and psychological dimension" and that "tourism is not some silly diversion at the fringe of our culture but instead is an integral part of the modern industrial world."

Art historian David Gebhard in Chapter 11 on Hispanic revivalism in the American Southwest quotes California architect preservationist Arthur B. Benton, who argued in 1910 that the "Southwest and California should develop their own regional architectural mode." Gebhard says that Benton contended that the essence of regional architecture in our region was "the sense of romance and of a deep-set desire to return to that which was the natural, the rural, and the rustic." Gebhard sees this desire as bound up not only with the "classic Jeffersonian distrust of the city" but more positively with the Emersonian and Whitmanesque "sentiment of folk nationalism" that "sustained the democratic ideal of returning to the simple and puritanical rural life."

Nicholas Markovich, assistant dean of the University of New Mexico's School of Architecture and Planning, details in Chapter 15 the political and pragmatic realities behind the creation of the Santa Fe style in the capital city just after New Mexico statehood in 1912 when newcomer developers, or "modern conquistadores" as they were called locally, had shown a blatant disconcern for the unique Southwestern architectural context of the city. Markovich analyzes the values, sentiments, political and educational decision making that made revivalism in Santa Fe possible. He takes a positive view of regionalist design politics, seeing the Santa Fe Revival style not only as a statement of continuity with traditional New Mexican culture but also as planning and design strategy that has resulted in a cityscape unique in the nation.

The third category of presentations deal with both the values and the dangers of regionalist sentiment in New Mexico. Two chapters on the University of New Mexico—

which next to Santa Fe is the great bastion of revivalist iconography in the state—discuss the image and the paradoxes inherent in campus design.

Historian Michael Welsh, in his presentation on the social and cultural implications of the University of New Mexico's Revival style architecture (Chapter 16), asks rhetorically what such a style says "about the uniqueness and complexity of New Mexican life. Did acceptance of Southwestern building styles by the recently arrived Anglo population also indicate a willingness to accommodate other aspects of Indian and Hispanic culture, such as language, art, music, cuisine, government, or religion?" Welsh details some of the brutal blindspots and prejudices of Anglo newcomers at the turn of the century regarding traditional New Mexican cultures and the turmoil and bigotry that surrounded the early development of Revival style architecture on campus.

The popularity of regional styles in architecture, especially Southwestern styles, is discussed by University of Minnesota art historian emeritus Carl Sheppard and Miami University's Stephen D. Schreiber. In Chapter 13 they document the far-reaching influence of the Southwest style. Their examples give evidence of Pueblo style in Minnesota and Miami, where developers have capitalized on the romantic nature of faraway places.

When regionalism becomes an ideology ossified in zoning codes, the effect can both damage vernacular forms and inhibit contemporary designers. This occurs when a regional aesthetic ceases to be a reaction against homogenizing influences and becomes instead a force for blind conformity. In writing of Pueblo images in contemporary regional architecture, Albuquerque architect Glade Sperry contends in Chapter 21 that the "Pueblo style is not a style, it is a way of life shaped by reaction to the desert climate, available building materials, and cultural and mythological forces. . . . To replicate the evidence of cultures that came before dooms the culture of the present." Sperry calls for a new kind of regionalism, a "transcendant regionalism," that would expand to include "the region of the mind" and come to "honor the heritage of its place not by replicating its built forms but by capturing the spirit that brought them into being."

For all the sentiment against traditional regionalism—or regional forms as we know them evolving from the turn of the century—those of us who inhabit such buildings and have been influenced by them understand what art historian Ethel Goodstein means in her chapter on Georgia O'Keeffe's New Mexico (Chapter 17) when she writes that "character of place and creation of place are interwoven; vernacular traditions of expression and space have the potential to be conceptional points of departure rather than preconceived esthetic ends."

When viewed as a whole, this volume suggests that the usefulness of regional style architecture in New Mexico is suspended today in a polarity that has at one end an excess of zeal in promoting Revival styles and at the other end a cynical disregard for the emotional and symbolic importance of regional styles in maintaining the unique cultural landscape of New Mexico. Within this "architectural dialectic," to borrow a phrase from UNM Architecture Dean George Anselevicius, an important struggle for a new synthesis is taking place. The battle is between the antitheses of inclusiveness and exclusiveness more than it is between styles and aesthetic theories. On one side is the meaning of regionalism as a symbol of identity, of psychological nurture, as a container and preserver of self-evolving culture, and as an act of homage in gratitude for the wisdom and richness of the Pueblo and Hispanic traditions. On the other side we see regionalism as purely an economic force, as a gentrifying compromiser of vernacular culture, as a marketing device, and, paradoxically, as a chief opponent of the national franchise, fad, and formula architecture that is inundating the rest of the nation's localities, but unfortunately also as an inhibitor of creativity.

Perhaps the synthesis some seek is, indeed, an evolving, organic regionalism. Such a synthesis would be one in which existing vernacular cultures and their people are deemed to be more important than zone-enforced building styles. But regionally sensitive design zoning would in turn be viewed as contributing both to a contemporary architecture respectful of context and to a local expression that neutralizes the homogenizing influences of global aesthetic fashion and architecture as forms of bureaucratic utility and corporate advertising. Such a synthesis would be guided by the spirit of self-respecting open-mindedness that is the hallmark of the best of New Mexico's cultural heritage.

I

Pueblo World Views and Values

When the term "Pueblo style architecture" is used, reference is made to the "Pueblo revival," which began at the first part of the twentieth century, and those building styles that have grown out of that movement. It represents an adaptation of elements appropriated from earlier Hispanic and Indian architectural forms that had been neglected, if not consciously rejected, by Anglo immigrants during the second half of the nineteenth century. The earliest roots of Pueblo style are found in the centuries-old, pre-Hispanic building tradition. Essential to an understanding of the buildings and settlement patterns of the ancestors of the Pueblo Indians are the world views and values upon which they are based and which are expressed through them. The first chapter of part I of the book discusses the conflicting value structures of the three cultures that have been instrumental in the historical evolution of Pueblo style architecture. The conclusion is that present day Pueblo style rests upon a disparate pluralism in which irreconcilable systems of aesthetic values coexist precariously. The second and third chapters address traditional Pueblo Indian world views and values. Rina Swentzell relies on the mythological corpus for a description of the world as sacred and vital, breathing a life energy that enters dwelling units, kivas, and communal forms, making them essentially living entities. Tony Anella contrasts Pueblo Indian settlement patterns where buildings complement the landscape and are viewed as interacting with the land, to Anglo settlements, which are imposed arbitrarily upon the land.

Fred G. Sturm

If a discussion of the aesthetics of the Southwest is to be meaningful, the two terms *aesthetics* and *Southwest* need to be defined at the outset. At least, I need to stipulate the way in which I propose to use them.

AESTHETICS

Aesthetics is a word that is often employed in a very imprecise way, whether it appears in popular literature (newspaper articles by art critics, for example) or scientific discourse (such as treatises on the psychology or sociology of art). There are times when I am inclined to agree with the author who wrote a century and a half ago

> There has lately grown into use in the arts a silly, pedantic term under the name *Aesthetics*. . . . It is however, one of the metaphysical and useless additions to nomenclature in the arts in which the German writers abound. (Gwilt 1842).

The word *aesthetics* can be traced to the Sanskrit root *avia*, which refers to that which is evident, that is, that which appears directly and does not need for its comprehension or grasping any inference or explication. The related Greek root *aisthe-* refers to direct apprehension by and through the senses, as well as the feeling tone that accompanies such apprehension. The word *aesthetics* itself was formulated in the mid-eighteenth century by the German philosopher Alexander Gottlieb Baumgarten.[1] It was the time of the great epistemological polemic concerning the sources and process of knowledge between the rationalists headed by Descartes and the empiricists headed by Locke. The Cartesian position grounded the process of obtaining knowledge in reason and not in sense data. The ideas of the mind that are clear and distinct, that have the characteristic of being "self-evident," are capable of initiating a deductive process through which a body of true and certain knowledge can be erected. In contrast, the Lockean position insists that the mind has no ideas of its own and is empty until the moment in which the senses receive "simple ideas" from outside the body, which today we call, using Hume's terminology, "sense impressions."

Baumgarten was a rationalist in the tradition of Descartes and Leibniz. As a rationalist he gave preference to knowledge obtained through rational processes, but as someone interested in art, and especially in the critical process that judges the value of works of art, determining the degree of "beauty"—or artistic value—that the work possesses, and assuming the sensual nature of works of art, Baumgarten became interested in sense data. He wanted to study carefully this level of human experience. In 1750 he published the first volume of a work entitled *Aesthetik*. He defined this neologism in this way: "*Aesthetics* is the science of sensory knowledge, or inferior gnoseology." The purpose of the new science was to establish that which is beautiful or beauty. The greater part of that volume deals with this problem. In sum, the concept "beauty" is shown to consist not in a quality, but rather in a unity of multiple parts. It is an order of sensed parts established internally that is not thought but merely sensed. There is passive reception of multiple sensations, and then an association of these sensations in a relational unity, and a reaction to that unity, not at the level of reason, but of sensation. The judgment of beauty is not a rational judgment, but rather an immediate and sensory reaction. The study of this process, which Baumgarten designated "aesthetics," "is the youngest sister of logic."

Strongly influenced by Baumgarten's account of aesthetics, Immanuel Kant carried the analysis further in both his *Critique of Pure Reason* and his *Critique of Judgment*. In the former he analyzed the function of reason in the process of obtaining intelligible understanding of sensory experience. The section entitled "Transcendental Aesthetic" describes the process of perception and the a priori conditions of sensory perception through which the spatiotemporal objects of our world of experience are constituted. "Aesthetic" here refers to the method by which we order the objects of our experience by the imposition upon sense data of transcendental forms of space and time. In those pre-Gestaltist days, Kant accepted the Humean version of the nature of sense data: immediate and absolutely discrete sensory elements with no order or relation at all. The epistemological process consisted for Kant in the activity of reason in organizing the data in a reasonable and logical fashion, first relating them spatially and temporally and then relating the spatiotemporal objects within a logical matrix of a "world." "Aesthetics" in the first Kantian critique refers to the way in which we order our experience. In the *Critique of Judgment*, Kant concerns himself with the basis of rational judgments regarding aesthetic value, how reason makes judgments concerning beauty, and the fundamental value of contemplation both of natural objects and of objects of art.

Aesthetics in Baumgarten's usage is primarily passive, although the immediate reaction to direct sensation and perception is included. In Kant's usage, aesthetics becomes active, including the meaningful ordering of sensual experience and judgment regarding the value of that which is experienced. Since the time of Baumgarten and Kant, the word they coined and defined has been employed both in the Baumgarten sense—immediate sensual perception and response—and in the Kantian sense—meaningful organization of sensual experience and judgment of the value of experiential objects and events.

The concept of a special type of experiencing called "aesthetic" that has developed tends to follow the Baumgarten usage in which an object or event is experienced as it appears in and of itself apart from any external or ulterior relationship, without consideration for any possible practical or cognitive utility, and evokes an immediate organic or psychophysiological response. The idea of an act of appreciation designated "aesthetic" tends to follow the Kantian usage. "Appreciation" is derived from the Latin word for "price" or "value." An act of appreciation is that of placing a price on, or better of evaluating the worth of, the term "evaluation" being derived from the Latin that implies drawing value out of or expressing the intrinsic worth of. To appreciate aesthetically is to recognize the intrinsic worth of an object or event, as distinct from any extrinsic value it may possess, and to rank objects and events implicitly in an order of preference according to their values relative to each other.

I shall use the word "aesthetics" with these meanings in mind, referring to the way in which objects and events of the experienced environment are grasped in their immediacy and the responses the grasping evokes, with special attention to the interaction that occurs between that which is experienced and the experiencer, through which the environment is finally constituted meaningfully both in the fashion in which it is interpreted—the perspective we designate as "world view"—and the effort to transform it by giving it those preferred structures that are judged to be of positive value.

It is important to note that the same objects and events can be experienced both aesthetically and nonaesthetically. A tree, for example, can be appreciated for its own sake, attention paid to the form of its trunk and branches, the colors of its bark and leaves, and the way it relates to its setting. It can be appreciated also for its economic value, comparing the potential board feet of lumber it would provide if it were cut down with the damage to the soil through erosion that might occur due to the cutting. In daily experience, these are not necessarily isolated judgments but often occur almost simultaneously, a decision to preserve or cut a tree depending upon a comparison of the aesthetic and economic judgments. This is certainly true when we consider the creative art of architecture, where a "built environment" is superimposed upon a "natural environment" and where both "aesthetic" and "practical" value judgments come into play. This interplay of various kinds of value helps us see the interrelatedness of the various realms of value, and their ordering. Those values that are "practical," "extrinsic," or "instrumental" are determined ultimately by reference to values that are "intrinsic"; and "intrinsic" values are ultimately related to that which is of "ultimate concern"—to use Paul Tillich's phrase—to an individual or a culture. In this way, an intimate relationship can be seen to obtain between the aesthetic and religious values of a given cultural tradition. When we examine the "aesthetics of the Southwest," I believe that this will become quite evident.

SOUTHWEST

To refer to the "aesthetics of the Southwest" is to break with a fundamental assumption of Baumgarten and Kant. Both of them assumed a uniformity in human reasoning that implied common human experience and universal judgments. Kant's analysis of basic logical categories through which intelligibility was obtained is based on the depth-grammar structures of the Indo-European language family. It did not occur to him that there might be other language families with divergent grammatical structures from which alternative logics could be derived—in other words, that not all human thinking, or experiencing, was necessarily alike. Nor was he aware of the evolution of language as its use entered into a dialectic with the historical experience of a society speaking that language, so that the same language spoken by two different societies might over the course of time develop two quite distinct patterns such that the Spanish spoken in Truchas, New Mexico, for example, would come to diverge considerably from the Spanish spoken in Asunción, Paraguay.

Although it may be evident that there is a basic human commonality between the people of twentieth-century Truchas and the people of twentieth-century Asunción, between the people of modern Xi'an, China, and the people of modern Baghdad, Iraq, between the people of thirteenth-century London and the people of twentieth-century London, nonetheless we find that there are significant differences in both world view and aesthetic valuation. It is meaningful, therefore, to speak of eighteenth-century German aesthetics as distinct from Han Dynasty Chinese aesthetics, and it is possible to refer meaningfully to the aesthetics of the Southwest.

But to what do we refer when we mention the American Southwest or the Great Southwest? These designations are not geographically precise. On the one hand I have heard the terms used to include an area encompassing both Louisiana and southern California; on the other hand, I have encountered them in a use restricted to the state of New Mexico. We are here examining an architectural style called Pueblo as a prime example of regional architecture. Therefore, I shall restrict the term Southwest to "greater" New Mexico, that is, the areas, including southern Utah, southern Colorado, and parts of Arizona, where the origins of this style of building developed before the advent of European intruders. It is a geographico-cultural term, therefore, referring to the region inhabited by the twenty present-day Pueblos and their ancestors.

Clearly, the Southwest as thus defined is multicultural and has been for many decades. This means that within the Southwest there are several senses of what is of ultimate concern, several sets of communal tastes and preferences, several ways of constituting and interpreting the world of human experience. Any effort to describe or analyze the aesthetics of the Southwest must take this multicultural nature of the region into serious consideration and be prepared to deal with conflict in tastes and preferences, in value judgments and ideals.

It is common to refer to three constitutive cultures in New Mexico: the Indio, the Hispano, and the Anglo. This is, of course, a gross oversimplification. Each of those designations refers not to a single cultural heritage but to a diversity of traditions that are often in conflict. There are three major Indio cultures, for example: the Apache, the Navajo, and the Pueblo. Among the nineteen distinct Pueblos that continue to exist within New Mexico, five different languages are spoken, and these belong to three language families. If we add the Hopi, the twentieth extant Pueblo society in the Southwest, a sixth language belonging to a fourth language family has to be included. Within the Hispano world of New Mexico one must note a major division between the old families who proudly trace their ancestry back to Spanish colonists under the viceroyalty of New Spain and more recent immigrants from Mexico and other Spanish American countries. The Anglo community includes everyone else: non-Hispanic Caucasians, Blacks, Asian Americans—hardly a homogeneous cultural tradition!

However, despite such diversity, it can be stated with historical and sociological accuracy that three fundamental cultural traditions inform the societies of the Southwest:

1. The culture shared by Pueblo societies, despite their differences, many aspects of which have been adopted by the Navajo and Apache over the course of almost six centuries of interaction through acculturation.
2. The old-family Hispanic culture, rooted in the age of discovery of the "New World," its conquest and colonization in the name of God and King, coinciding with the Counter-Reformation and the revival of Scholasticism in sixteenth-century Iberia.
3. Northwest European, predominantly English, German, and French, after immigration to the Atlantic coastal regions of northern North America at the time of the western European "Enlightenment" with all its implications for new ways of thinking theologically, philosophically, and scientifically and for reordering political and socioeconomic institutions.

Although the latter culture predominates today in its contemporary form, the other two continue to be vital, and there is an uneasy coexistence of the three with an underlying conflict of values including those of aesthetic taste and preference, ways of constituting experience and of viewing the world, and approaches to artistic creativity. To fully understand the development of Pueblo style architecture from its origins among the Pueblo Indians and their ancestors, through its adaptation by the Spanish during the periods of colonization and Mexico's early independence, to its "revival" by the Anglo community in the early twentieth century, it is necessary to take note of these conflicting value systems, both at the level of aesthetics and at the deeper level of that which is taken to be of ultimate concern by each of the informing cultures.

THE QUESTION OF ULTIMATE CONCERN

By using "Pueblo" to designate a Southwestern regional style of architecture, reference is being made back to a tradition of building that is associated with Pueblo culture and has its origins with their ancestors. Historically there has been a continuity of architectural evidence, from the semisubterranean pithouses with their associated storage areas and refuse heaps, proceeding to surface dwellings with blocks of storerooms and residential units together with kivas that serve as ceremonial and communal centers and preserve the pit-house concept, and coming up to the housing of modern Pueblos before the introduction of mobile homes and HUD-financed structures.

It is difficult, if not virtually impossible, to reconstruct with any degree of accuracy the value systems of the ancestors of the present-day Pueblos who initiated Pueblo style architecture, to describe their aesthetics, or to identify what for them was of ultimate concern. When there is an apparent continuity of cultural tradition, there is a great temptation to interpret archaeological data by reference to ethnological information. However, reading modern attitudes back into a reconstruction of the mental attitudes of earlier generations is highly speculative and at best yields interpretations that are merely suggestive. Nonetheless, there does seem to be a good reason for yielding to the temptation in this instance. Coincident with the development of permanent housing was the development of an economy based on settled agriculture. Continuity of material culture, including architectural development, and continuity of agricultural economy would seem to argue for some continuity in thought. Since the traditional value system of the Pueblo societies as expressed through traditional mythology, sacred symbols, and ceremonial observances is closely associated with agriculture and that which is necessary for fertility of the soil and germination of seed, it may be safe to assume that the tradition is one that can be traced back to the time when an agriculture-based economy was first introduced to the region.

It seems evident that for traditional Pueblo culture, that which is of supreme value and ultimate concern is the land. It is the earth that is most sacred, and the spirits of the earth. Referred to often as our Earth Mother, it is seen to be the source of all life, the source of our life, the foundation of our community. The myths of origin vary from Pueblo to Pueblo, but there are common elements. One of these is an origin of the people under the surface of the earth, in an underworld—in the womb, as it were, of the Earth Mother. The history of each people begins with an emergence out of the nether regions up to this plane of existence. The point of emergence plays an important part of symbolism. In the Hopi version, Spider-Woman instructs the people that in building kivas they are to place a small hole of emergence in the floor to remind them of where they originated and what they are looking for (Courlander 1971). After death there is a return to the earth's interior from whence we as humans came. On sacred mountains and hills there are located earth navels, and in the pueblo itself there is located an "Earth Mother Earth Navel Middle Place," which functions as the "center of centers and navel of navels" (Ortiz 1972), the place where medicine men at the end of the winter reach deep into the earth to place seeds in order to reawaken the fertility of the soil. In the Zuni account of origins, the people become very concerned, almost to the point of obsession, to find the Middle Place, the middle of the earth. Finally it is located, thanks to Water-Strider and the Rainbow, both of whom take precise measurements of the earth's surface. Then the myth declares, according to Dennis Tedlock's translations,

> That's where he is. Everything all over the wide earth—well—everything depended on him and on the middle place for fertility. For their part the priests would sit down and ask for rain; when it rained at Zuni it would rain all over the earth.
> When they first started living this way all the village people, at Santo Domingo, at Hopi, all the villagers would anxiously await the time when our priests went into retreat at Zuni. (Tedlock 1978).

Human origins are in the earth. Human destiny is to return to the earth. Life springs from the earth. The people and the land are intimately related. One of the most powerful contemporary statements of this concept is given in the poem by Simon Ortiz, Acoma Pueblo poet and short-story writer, entitled "We Have Been Told Many Things But We Know This To Be True":

The land.   The people.
They are in relation to each other.
We are in a family with each other.
The land has worked with us.
And the people have worked with it.
This is true:
                    Working for the land
and the people—it means life
and its continuity:
Working not just for the people,
But working for the land.

We are not alone in our life;
we cannot expect to be.
The land has given us our life,
and we must give life back to it.

The land has worked for us
to give us life—
breathe and drink and eat from it
gratefully—
and we must work for it
to give it life.
With this relation of family,
it is possible to generate life.
This is the work involved.
Work is creative then.
It is what makes for reliance,
relying upon the relation of land and people.
The people and the land are reliant
upon each other.
This is the kind of self-reliance
that has been—
before the liars, thieves, and killers—
and this is what we must continue
to work for.
By working in this manner,
for the sake of the land and people
to be in vital relation
with each other,
we will have life,
and it will continue.

We have been told many things,
but we know this to be true:
the land and the people. |Ortiz 1980|.[2]

The contrast with his view of the land as being of supreme value with the role that the earth plays in the Hispanic view of the cosmos is very revealing of the fundamental axiological difference that exists between the two cultures. I refer, of course, to the Hispanic culture of the time of colonization, although there is a certain cultural continuity with contemporary Hispanic culture in New Mexico that has been preserved through language, customs, and institutions. Sixteenth-century Spanish culture was consciously Christian, and even more consciously Catholic. The fifteenth century came to a glorious end with the final successful struggle against Muslim rule on the Iberian peninsula and the first voyage of discovery by Columbus under the patronage of the new monarchs of a united Spain. Spanish Catholicism was a militant Catholicism, having been engaged for so long in its struggle against Islam. Spanish nationalism was a fresh and proud nationalism that viewed its mission as linked closely to that of the Church. At the same time two threats were perceived to the Faith from the north: Protestant heresies, and the "New Thought" associated with such names as Descartes and Gassendi. Spanish Catholicism lent its full support to movements initiated to combat these threats: the Counter-Reformation, the Inquisition, the revival of Scholasticism. Truth was revealed through Scripture, preserved and transmitted as a Body of Saving Truth through the agency of the Church. That revelation was very clear as far as the relation between the people and land is concerned:

> In the beginning God created the heavens and the earth. . . . And God said,
> "Let the waters under the heavens be gathered together into one place, and let
> the dry land appear." And it was so. God called the dry land Earth. . . . And
> God said, "Let the earth put forth vegetation. . . ." And it was so. . . . And God
> said, "Let the earth bring forth living creatures according to their kinds. . . ."
> Then God said, "Let us make man in our image, after our likeness; and let them
> have dominion over the fish of the sea, and over the birds of the air, and over
> the cattle, and over all the earth, and over every creeping thing that creeps
> upon the earth. So God created man in his own image, in the image of God he
> created him, male and female he created them. And God blessed them, and
> God said to them, "Be fruitful and multiply, and fill the earth and subdue it,
> and have dominion over the fish of the sea and over the birds of the air and
> over every living thing that moves upon the earth." (Genesis 1:1, 9–11, 24–28).[3]

The earth is not the source of life; the earth is created by the divine, and living things—plants, animals, humans—are created and placed on the earth. The mundane is distinguished from the sacred, the earthly from the heavenly. The human is placed on the earth to have dominion over the earth and all living creatures on the earth. This relationship of human to earth is, of course, almost opposite to the relationship described in Pueblo mythology. The same is the case with attitudes toward agriculture. Instead of being a cooperative enterprise between the human community and the spirits of the earth, it is viewed as hard labor, a punishment for original sin:

> . . . cursed is the ground because of you; in toil you shall eat of it all the days
> of your life; thorns and thistles it shall bring forth to you; and you shall eat the
> plants of the field. In the sweat of your face you shall eat bread. (Genesis
> 3:17b–19a).[3]

A further contrast with Pueblo mythology is the role of the snake and its relation to the human. Because of the serpent's role in the act of original sin, it was punished:

> The Lord God said to the serpent, "Because you have done this, cursed are you
> above all cattle, and above all wild animals; upon your belly you shall go, and
> dust you shall eat all the days of your life. I will put enmity between you and
> the woman, and between your seed and her seed; he shall bruise your head,
> and you shall bruise his heel." (Genesis 3:14f).[3]

Yet in Pueblo mythology and symbolism the snake represents water and the forces of fertility and is the messenger between the human community and the spirits of the earth. Spanish colonial art included many portrayals of the Virgin Mary as the "new Eve," or, better, the mother of the "new Adam," treading on a serpent. The message such paintings and sculptures conveyed to Pueblo Indians was far different from their significance for Spanish colonists! It is highly significant for purposes of contrast that the worst punishment meted out to the snake was to crawl upon the earth and to eat the dust of the earth, and for the human the extreme punishment was to die and be buried in the earth. To the colonists, to return to the earth was to be cut off from life and the divine. When redemption occurs it is achieved through the death and burial of the Savior, followed by his rising from the dead—and the earth—and his ascension from the earth into the heavens. As the Pueblo orientation is toward the earth, which is the source of all life and is sacred, so the Spanish Catholic orientation is toward the heavens, where God dwells and eternal life is to be enjoyed. The divine is associated with the heavens and not the earth. The important events of divine–human encounter are usually on mountaintops, the point at which earth meets sky. Moses climbs a mountain to receive the Torah from God. Jesus is transfigured, his divine nature revealed to his closest disciples on a mountain. The birth of the Savior was heralded by a star in the heavens and the singing of a heavenly choir; and at the time of baptism the voice of God announcing the significance of the man being baptized came from above. "The Tewa," according to Alfonso Ortiz (1972, 23), "are primarily concerned with the middle and the below." The Spanish Catholic, we should say in contradistinction, was primarily concerned with the high and the above.

The Anglos, who became the dominant force in New Mexico during the last half of the nineteenth century, came with a world view and set of values that differed from those of the sixteenth-century Spanish as radically as the Spanish differed from the Pueblos. The original Anglo colonists along the Atlantic coast were, in the main, Protestants who subscribed to the Calvinist theology, which, as Max Weber tried to demonstrate, provided the intellectual basis for the "spirit of capitalism," tempered with the Arminian theology of the Methodist tradition, which replaced the doctrine of double predestination with a more optimistic doctrine of free will and the hope of being made perfect in this life. The conception and birth of the new independent United States of America, however, occurred within the context of the "new thought" of seventeenth-century France and England and the "Enlightenment" of the eighteenth century. John Locke was the leading spokesman for the new way of viewing the world; a secularization of many of the values of the earlier Christian vision, a stress on progress within history through human effort replacing the earlier eschatological vision of the coming of the Kingdom of God through divine intervention, and the replacement of a stress on communalism with an individualism, which was to become a *rugged* individualism in Anglo America, rooted in a new epistemological analysis of how humans order their perceptual experience. The new religion that stemmed from Lockean philosophy, and to which most of the "founding fathers" subscribed, was Deism. God was viewed as a Master Mason who turned his creation over to the care and crafting of human masons, who, trusting in reason alone, were free to manipulate and exploit that creation for their own benefit and happiness. The view of the land, and the relation of human to land, was articulated most clearly in the words of John Locke as appropriated by those who declared independence from British rule and proceeded to constitute a new nation:

> We hold these truths to be self-evident: that all men are created equal; that they are endowed by their creator with certain inalienable rights; that among these are life, liberty, and . . . (*The Declaration of Independence in Congress*, July 4, 1776, para. 2).

"[And] the pursuit of happiness" is the way the revised American version went, but the original Lockean version mentions "property" as the third inalienable right of humans. For Locke, when human labor combines with the earth or natural resources, private property results, and government is instituted through a social contract entered into by sovereign individuals to protect individual life, liberty, and property. Human happiness comes through property, the exploitation of the earth and the resources of the earth.

The dockets of New Mexican courts today include much litigation concerning water rights, land ownership and usage rights, and natural resources rights, which arises from the clashing of these three radically different ways of viewing the relationship between the human and the earth and the very nature of the earth. The Anglo notion of private property, individual ownership of parcels of land, is inconceivable in traditional Pueblo Indian terms. As Rina Swentzell points out, "the notion was common that the people were out of the earth and, hence, belonged to it" (Swentzell 1976, 9), so that the idea that land could belong to people would be unintelligible. Boundaries of Pueblo land were created by earth forces, and at the extreme the four sacred mountain ranges were conceived of as the spatial limits of the four cardinal directions (Ortiz 1972, 18). Cooperation with the land and the forces of the land is the Pueblo notion, rather than ownership of the land and exploitation of its resources.

Ownership of the land by private individuals in fee simple is foreign to the Hispanic view as well. The Promised Land concept views the land as a gift from God to a people. At first it was to Abraham *and his seed*—a familial or communal land grant. Next it was to Moses as the chosen leader of the Chosen People. Then there was the renewal of the communal land grant to the Holy Remnant of Israel promised through the prophets of the Exile. And so the Spanish Crown, basing its action on these scriptural grounds, granted land to families and groups. It is very important to note the Spanish view of the "fourth continent," which had just been discovered. It was seen as a New World, untouched somehow by the corruption that was the result of the Fall. It was a new Eden, given to the Catholic monarch of Spain and his people, in which to restore Paradise. The Spanish conquistadores and colonists were retracing the steps of the Chosen People in Israel. When Fray Angelico Chavez wrote *My Penitente Land: Reflections on Spanish New Mexico* (Chavez 1974), he repeated the parallel between the history of the Spanish people in New Mexico and the history of the Children of Israel in the headings of many of his chapters: "Cross Over Jordan," "Land of Genesis," "Same as Jerusalem's," "Into the Promised Land," "A New World Babel," "The Lost Tribe," "Return From Babylon."

As Israel, the Promised Land, was given to the descendants of Abraham by God through Moses, so the New World was given to the Spanish Crown by God through papal decree and made available through communal land grants for the use of the colonists during their sojourn on the face of the earth until their death and resurrection and journey upward to eternal life in heaven. The Anglo did not share the Pueblo notion of the earth as having produced him and, in the end, laying claim to him. Nor was his attention directed toward heaven. The land was an open frontier, to be conquered and claimed and fenced and exploited. His eyes glanced neither downward nor upward, but outward toward new frontiers of open space where private claims could be staked and ownership titles obtained. This was the "manifest destiny" of the Anglo as he traveled westward and southwestward.

SOUTHWESTERN AESTHETICS AND "PUEBLO STYLE" ARCHITECTURE

The clash of cultures that characterized the Southwest, traceable directly to the irreconcilable differences among the Pueblo, Hispanic, and Anglo traditions concerning view of the world and system of values, has had a profound effect on aesthetics in the Southwest, including the utilization at various times throughout history of "Pueblo style" in southwestern architecture. The original "style," as created by the ancestors of the Pueblos, begins with the semisubterranean pit house, a dwelling that is identified partially with the earth itself—set within the ground, its upper part an obvious extension of the ground level. As surface dwellings evolved from the pit-house stage, there remained an identification with the ground. Not only was there a continuation of the pit house in the kiva, but the surface structures themselves continued the identification. They were not constructed and placed on the ground; rather they appeared to be extensions rising out of the ground. As Rina Swentzell has observed, "the walls defining the structures were extensions of the earth and within the structures the walls lost identity as man-made and rather remained as extensions of the earth" (Swentzell 1976, 25). Both the later cliff dwellings of the Four Corners region and many of the historic Pueblos such as Laguna, Santa Ana, and Zia blend into their natural settings so perfectly that they seem to be mere extensions of the cliffs or mesas where they are situated.

Next to architecture, perhaps the oldest art form created by the ancestors of the Pueblos is ceramics. Again there is a natural identification with the earth. Potters seek out their own clay, considering it to be a living creature, a gift from the earth mother. Without the aid of a manufactured potter's wheel, the pot is fashioned out of coils with shaping stones and sticks. The slip is made of clay. The designs are added using pigments derived directly from clays, stones, berries, and other organic materials collected and ground by the ceramicist. Pueblo artists generally have followed in the line of the ceramicists, preferring to use natural pigments ground from organic materials they themselves gather rather than commercially manufactured paints and oils. Earth tones predominate in traditional paintings. In the most recent art form, sculpture, there is a preference for local alabaster quarried by the sculptor himself. Victor Vigil, well-known in this new Pueblo Indian art form, informed me that he began as an urban Indian in California following the lead of popular Anglo sculpture, where the emphasis was on the sculpted figure in which the stone, or other medium employed, had been completely overcome and virtually "forgotten." The figures he at first created were typical urban Indian romanticized Plains Indian representations. When he returned to Jemez, the Pueblo of his parents and ancestors, to recapture his cultural roots, he told me he began to experiment with figures related to the Jemez story and experience, usually a combination of human and animal, emerging from the stone but still identified with the stone, never completely independent of it (Sturm 1985).

The most obvious adaptation of the Pueblo style by the Spaniard is to be found in the mission churches. In the case of most of them it could be said that the walls are indeed extensions of the ground, and yet the most prominent feature is the towers, which rise upward so that the structure looks not like an extension of the ground, but like a building rising up out of the ground and toward the sky. The only equivalent upthrusting object in the Pueblo is the ladder that rises out of the roof entrance to the kiva, and there the emphasis is downward. One goes down into the kiva by way of the ladder. But the church tower thrusts upward and, as an integral part of the structure, seems to be lifting the building away from the earth toward the heavens. A Spanish contribution to building in the Southwest was the introduction of manufactured adobe bricks, made in forms of mud with straw added as binder, as a substitute for the torrones, natural earthen bricks cut directly from the soil of stream banks containing roots and other organic matter that served as an intrinsic binder.

The advent of Anglo domination in the latter half of the nineteenth century did not witness an adaptation of Pueblo style architecture by the new settlers. Instead, a style to be known as Territorial House developed as a regional adaptation of buildings that were found in the midwestern towns from which the new settlers had come, using the same building materials and similar forms. Fray Angelico Chavez captures the attitude of the first Anglo settlers toward the Pueblo and Hispanic cultures, especially with regard to architecture, in the following passage:

> For the English-speaking American it was then easy in the extreme to begin and continue making New Mexico more and more his own, and in his philistine image. Whatever was "mexican", as he termed the entire regional tradition as if speaking in lower case type, had no place in the new scheme of things. Especially after the railroad came, physical changes openly flaunted this attitude. The plaza of Santa Fe began turning into a replica of the midwestern town of brick and boards with false fronts trimmed with scrolled tin. New towns of the type sprang up by the railway depots . . . consigning the "old towns" to the less privileged natives. (Chavez 1974, 25).

The Anglo-initiated Pueblo style revival did not occur until the early twentieth century, and it seems to have been the result of two quite divergent forces. The first was a desire to promote tourism, a purely commercial and capitalistically driven concern. Restaurants, hotels, railroad rest stops, and souvenir shops adopted the local style of architecture to appeal to a tourist interested in exotic sights and local color. Here was a bit of "foreign" culture within our own national boundaries made fairly easily accessible by public transportation. Affiliated with this drive to "revive" the Pueblo style for commercial ends was the push to revive the traditional Indian art forms—especially ceramics and jewelry—and to encourage Indian artists to adopt an easel painting form, largely sponsored by art dealers.

Somewhat later in the century, certain Anglo artists and writers from the East Coast, disenchanted with what they considered to be increasing decadence in the European and Anglo-American art worlds, consciously abandoned their cultural roots and origins and found in the Pueblo and Hispanic traditions of New Mexico an exciting new "home"—home in two senses: artistic inspiration and dwelling style. It must be said that both the earlier commercial interests and the new art colonists have had a detrimental effect upon the Pueblo Indian artistic tradition. J. J. Brody, in his treatise on *Indian Painters and White Patrons,* has presented a persuasive thesis that

> the categories (for judging Native American art work in competitions) by their very existence force the painting into artificial, predetermined molds, established by the White hierarchy that controls the exhibits and strongly influenced by the donors of prize money, usually collectors or dealers. The molds are formulated by the consumers rather than by the artists.
> (Brody 1971, 194).

On the other hand, when the "expatriate" artists and writers have attempted to remedy this situation in which artistic work by Pueblo Indians and other Native Americans is stereotyped to fit the perception of Anglo consumers, the result has been the imposition of eighteenth-century Anglo values of individualism in which creativity is equated with personal expression and novelty in the use of materials and forms.

Brody quotes at length from a booklet in which the aims of the Institute of American Indian Arts are described, including the following statement, which expresses very clearly these Anglo Enlightenment values:

> . . . you can train a man to be the very best plumber in the world and he will go to Los Angeles and end up a drunk if you have not given him some sense of self worth and a way of facing the world as an individual. This is what we are trying to build through the arts. It is simply a vehicle of self-realization.
> (Brody 1971, 199).

It is also the antithesis of the traditional Pueblo Indian emphasis on communalism, where a negative value judgment is made of the effort of an individual to stand out above or over against the group. The promotion of individual artists by art dealers and art journals continues to cause tension within the home Pueblos of those artists because of this fundamental clash between the Pueblo Indian ideal of communalism and the Anglo ideal of individualism.

The same analysis can be made about buildings designed and constructed in the Pueblo Revival style, whether the architect is Anglo, Hispanic, or Pueblo Indian. Either the building conforms to what has been perceived through Anglo eyes to be "typically Pueblo," or there is an effort to utilize the "traditional style" in a novel way that will add the stamp of the individual architect, or the consumer, in addition to the characteristics that are taken to be essential to the "style." Rather than constituting a modern *development* of an architectural style that reflects the Pueblo aesthetic, these buildings represent a sharp *deviation* from that style in order to reflect the radically different Anglo aesthetic. The city of Santa Fe and the campus of the University of New Mexico, prime examples of the Pueblo style revival, do not give architectural testimony to a continuing southwestern aesthetic in which the values of three cultures have blended harmoniously, but rather reflect the disparate pluralism of the Southwest in which three separate systems of aesthetic values coexist precariously, the Pueblo and the Hispanic threatened by the overwhelming presence of the Anglo.

REFERENCES

BRODY, J. J. 1971. *Indian Painters and White Patrons.* Albuquerque: University of New Mexico Press.

CHAVEZ, FRAY ANGELICO. 1974. *My Penitente Land: Reflections on Spanish New Mexico.* Albuquerque: University of New Mexico Press.

COURLANDER, HAROLD. 1971. *The Fourth World of the Hopis.* New Haven: Fawcett Premier, p. 40.

GWILT, 1842. *Encyclopedia Architectura.* London.

ORTIZ, ALFONSO. 1972. *The Tewa World: Space, Time, Being, and Becoming in a Pueblo Society.* Chicago/London: University of Chicago Press, p. 21.

ORTIZ, SIMON. 1980. *INAD Literary Journal,* I(1):35.

STURM, FRED GILLETTE. 1985. "Victor M. Vigil, Sculptor in Alabaster." *Pueblo Horizons,* 8(9):5.

SWENTZELL, RINA. 1976. "An Architectural History of Santa Clara Pueblo." Thesis submitted in partial fulfillment of the requirements for the degree of Master of Arts in architecture in the Graduate School of the University of New Mexico, Albuquerque, New Mexico. July.

TEDLOCK, DENNIS. 1978. *Finding the Center: Narrative Poetry of the Zuni Indians.* Lincoln: University of Nebraska Press, p. 287.

NOTES

1. Baumgarten's major works dealing with aesthetics are *Meditaciones Philosophicae de Nonnullis ad Poema Pertinentibus* (Halle, 1735), translated as *Reflections on Poetry* by K. Aschenbrunner and W. B. Hoelther (Berkeley, 1954), and *Aesthetica* (two volumes; Frankfurt an der Oder, 1750, 1758).

2. The collection of poems entitled *Fight Back: For the Sake of the People, For the Sake of the Land* constituted the *entire* first issue of vol. I of the *INAD Literary Journal.*

3. The verses from Genesis quoted here are from *The Holy Bible*, Revised Standard Version, published by Thomas Nelson, New York, 1953.

Pueblo Space, Form, and Mythology

Rina Swentzell

Myths and stories of a culture do not tell about subjective human preferences but rather describe the conditions for life implicit in a world with a particular structure. Pueblo myths and stories, specifically, give a clear description of the nature of the cosmos as well as the structuring of the house, kiva, and community forms. The Pueblo world, first of all, is an altogether hallowed place where "the breath," or life energy, flows through both the animate and inanimate realms in such a manner that even the house, kiva, and community forms breathe of that breath and are essentially alive. The myths, stories, songs, and prayers tell about the Pueblo cosmos as a vital and inclusive containment within which opposite forces are brought together and united by that energy, which flows through everything and everybody. Within that cosmos, interaction and communication between all life forms—including house, kiva, and community forms—is recognized. The myths demonstrate how structure at the physical level is integral with structure at the metaphysical level.

The metaphysical assumptions underlying the Pueblo myths, stories, songs, and prayers define a cosmos that can be described as a contained spherical unit. The sky is referred to as a basket in a Tewa song (fig. 3-1): "The blue flower basket on the top of heaven [sky] seems. It gleams and all is done" (Spinden 1933, 79). The references to the earth as a bowl are common and complete the other half of the world-sphere. "'Behold,' said the mother as a great terraced bowl appeared at hand and within it water, 'this is as upon me the homes of my tiny children shall be. On the rim of each world-country, terraced mountains shall stand'" (Cushing 1974, 23). The terraced or serrated bowl is a common Tewa ceremonial item that symbolizes the lower half of the world (fig. 3-2). J. P. Harrington, for instance, in describing the process of consecrating

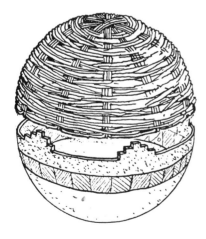

3-1 *Sky-basket (top) and earth-bowl (bottom). (Drawing: Jeremiah Iowa.)*

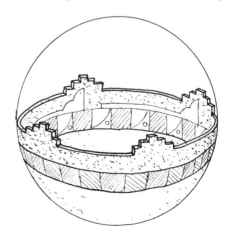

3-2 *Earth-bowl. (Drawing: Jeremiah Iowa.)*

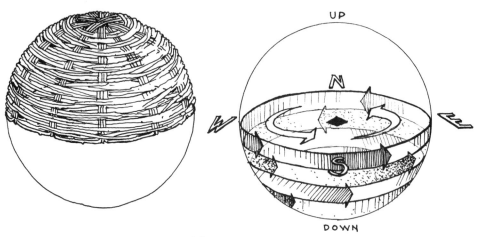

3-3 *Sky-basket. (Drawing: Jeremiah Iowa.)*

3-4 *Four levels and six directions. (Drawing: Jeremiah Iowa.)*

water, talks about the associate who "proceeds to consecrate water in a serrated medicine bowl dipping the water from a water vase with a gourd. He empties six gourdsful of water into the bowl symbolic of rains from the six regions" (Harrington, n.d.). The act is a simultaneous recognition of the six regions located within the medicine bowl.

The basket-sky covers the terraced bowl-earth to complete the spherical world (fig. 3-3). The light basket-sky is associated with coldness, while the heavier bowl-earth is warm. "Warm is the Earth-mother, cold the Sky-father, even as woman is warm, man the cold being" (Alexander 1964, 208). The Zuni talk about the "four-fold Containing Mother-earth and the all-covering Father sky" (Cushing 1974, 379). "The earth is often compared to a woman, with the underworld her womb and the emergence place her vagina" (Taube 1986, 74).

Opposites (sky and earth, light and heavy, male and female, warm and cold) are, then, also part of the contained spherical Pueblo world unit. The idea of the containment of opposites within the inclusive whole is in alignment with the universal Pueblo concept of simultaneity within which many levels of existence are recognized. For instance, within the lower earth-half of that world unit are the horizontal multilevels, worlds, or four planes of existence, which exist simultaneously. An Acoma story mentions these horizontal levels.

> Our mother lived in the lower world . . . in the White World in the white water. She traveled all around it from north to west, south and east. Above this world was the Red World. Above it the Blue World and still further above the Yellow World" (Boas 1928, 222).

The lower earth-half of the world-sphere consists of four horizontal planes, with the fourth plane being this level of existence. There the sky and earth are held together by the vertical axis, which goes from the above to the below. The above and below are two directions of the six-directional system prevalent in the Pueblo world (fig. 3-4). The six directions (north, west, south, east, up, and down), define the outer perimeters of that world-sphere. North, west, south, and east are recognized on the horizontal planes and generally contain an anticlockwise direction, which moves from north to west to south to east. That anticlockwise motion is interpreted as the motion of the sun about the North Star, which defines the seasons. The daily east to south to west movement of the sun is a secondary motion and is recognized in a Keres story that tells about the sun who comes out of his east house in the morning and passes Spider's house before he goes into his west house every night (Boas 1928, 231).

Every direction also has an associated house, mountain, lake, color, and animal. The direction–house association is common. In a Keres myth, Nautsiti, who varies between being a man and being a woman, takes the anticlockwise journey from north to west, south to east, and returns to the north or to the place of emergence. He/she makes "four houses, north, west, south and east." His/her twin sister, Itcsiti, "travels around the world visiting the four houses" (Boas 1928, 230).

The direction–animal association is made in a Tewa story. "The bear |was| to guard the west region . . . |the| badger the south region, the white wolf the east region, the eagle the above . . . the shrew . . . the below, (and) the rattlesnakes and ants (were) to watch over the earth" (Harrington n.d.).

The direction–color associations, like the animal, mountain, and lake associations, vary among the different Pueblos. The following prayer illustrates the primacy of the six-direction system and gives the color associations for the Tewa world.

> *Here and now we bring you, O our old ones,*
> *Sun fire deity and Blue Cloud person of the north,*
> *Sun fire deity and Yellow Cloud person of the West,*
> *Sun fire deity and Red Cloud person of the South.*
> *Sun fire deity and White Cloud person of the East,*
> *Sun fire deity and Dark person of the below,*
> *Sun fire deity and All-colored person of the above,*
> *Here we bring you now our special prayer stick,*
> *We make for you an offering of sacred meal.*
> (Spinden 1933, 86).

The mountains of the four directions are located in the terraced part of the earth-bowl and hence describe the far perimeters of the four world levels and enclose each respective world space. For the Tewa people, these mountains were created by the *Kwi-sen* or women-men. "They took a little mud and they threw it this way |indicating the directions|, and there were the mountains and hills" (Parsons 1939, 145).

At each world level, there are four mountains, but six lakes. "The water for rains is secured from the lakes of the six regions" (Harrington n.d.). The six lakes, as well as other identified lakes, are connection points between the world levels. The people from below "frequent the lakes in the high mountains whence they look from the depths and observe the outer world" (Harrington n.d.). In a Tewa myth, the people, after their emergence to this world level, send a youth and maiden ahead to look for that connection place between this world and the underworld:

> He |the youth| ascended the mountain looking for game and he met the maiden who was hunting pinone . . . and the youth joined her in gathering the nuts. The youth asked the maiden (four times) "Do you care very much for me|?|" Then the youth said, "I will take you for my wife and he embraced the maiden, and in a little time she gave birth to nine children. The youth being alarmed cried out, "I must make a place for us, and it will be a place for our people to enter to the undermost world after death," and he descended the mountain and drawing his foot through the sand near the river he created a lake and houses in the depths of the lake (Harrington n.d.).

The central, vertical axis that connects the above and the below is not a fixed or static axis but rather a path of energy flow. It is along this path that the people traveled to the fourth world. They traveled sometimes through a bamboo plant or reed and at other times up a ladder. "Nautsiti ordered the Kurena shaman to make a prayer-stick of spruce with notches on each side . . . and the people climbed up to our world, as on a ladder" (Boas 1928, 222). In another Keres version, "Spider places a reed on top of the mesa and orders the people to escape through it to the world above" (Boas 1928, 231). In a Tewa story, the path or road from the innermost world to the outer world is made by the badger. The people travel up the path by climbing up different kinds of trees:

> The first step was from *Na'nune*, lowest world, to *Nan ki gi*, above. The ascent was by *Wan*, pine tree. From *Nan ki gi* they ascended by the *Ts'e*, spruce [tree], to *Opa kigi*. From this point they traveled by the *Wank ke*, silver spruce, to *Opa kigi*, more above. After a time they ascended by the *Nana pe*
> (aspen) to *Sipofena*, place of going out and thence to *No'owin*, outer world (Harrington n.d.).

Although upward emergence from the underworld is an important aspect of Pueblo thinking and myths, it cannot be seen as indicative of a general upward thrust or movement but rather must be viewed as part of a larger movement that turns back into the earth and to the place of beginning. Cyclic, not linear, movement is primary in that world. In addition to the path of movement that allows energy flow into and out of the emergence place and the four directional points connecting the above with the below and the four horizontal planes of human existence with each other, there is cyclic movement on the horizontal plane, movement that is spiral and leads inward to the center or to the place of emergence (fig. 3-5). Salt Woman of Acoma says "I shall travel anti-clockwise around the earth, circling inward to its center" (Nabokov 1986b, 1).

The center is where time and space meet. In the Okuwa-bringing ceremony of the Tewa, the beings of those other levels of existence are brought to the center. "Now . . . I see them coming over here to the very center . . . and now . . . they are reaching the *nan-sipu* (the center). . . . [They] have paused: they have laid down their fog rainbow and deposited the cloudflower" (Parsons 1939, 45). Further, elders of today's Tewa world refer to the *nansipu*, or center, which is usually no more than a pile of rocks or one inconspicuous stone, as "the water place" or as "the watery place of origin." It is where illusion and reality meet.

Each Pueblo form is located at the center of the cosmos, which, according to a Zuni story, the Water-Spider and rainbow determined:

> Water-Spider spread his legs to the north and to the south, to the west and to the east, and then he said, "Now indeed I have measured it. Here is the center of the earth and here you must build your city!" But the people said, "We have been hunting for the center of the earth a long time, and we wish to be sure." So, they asked Rainbow to measure it also. So the Rainbow stretched his bright arch to the north and to the south, to the west and to the east, measuring the distance. Then he too gave his decision: "Here at his place is the heart of the earth" (Carr 1979, 17).

In one Tewa story, finding the middle place proved to be more difficult:

> The Tewa built themselves a village . . . They had not been many years at this place when Poseyemu appeared to them and told them that they were not at the middle place; he said "You must cross the river," and he gave the people instructions as to where they would find the middle place. . . . Obeying . . . the people built a village. [The middle] point was found by the water bug stretching her legs to the north, west, south and east, the central point found directly under her heart (Harrington n.d.).

The spiritual, or ethereal, quality of the world is obvious. The physical world is alive, and the breath flows through it. It is filled with colors, dew, and clouds as in the Zuni myth that describes how the Corn Maidens "at the place of fog whiled away hours bathing in dew and dancing in a bower walled with cedar, fringed with spruce and

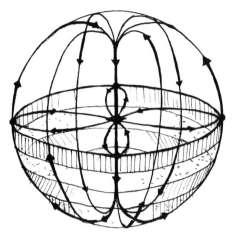

3-5 *Energy flow in the cosmos. (Drawing: Jeremiah Iowa.)*

roofed with cumulus clouds" (Alexander 1964, 199). Payatamu, in a Hopi story, has a house "of fog and cloud with a rainbow door" (Alexander 1964, 200). "Awonawilona, the supreme bisexual power of the Zuni who is the breath of life and life itself and called the All-container, creates the world with his/her breath" (Tyler 1964, 123). "In the beginning all was *shipolo* [fog], rising like steam with breath from his heart. Awonawilona created clouds and the great waters of the world" (Alexander 1964, 72).

The larger creation is reflected in the microcosm. The nonsubstantial elements are also given primacy in the town form. After the center-finding process, or determination of the void connecting this world with the underworlds, by Water-Spider (bug) and/or Rainbow, the void of the Pueblo form or the plaza is created (figs. 3-6 through 3-9). "Then there they stopped. First they made the plaza. After [that] they built the chief's house. Then they made four entrances to the plaza, and there they lived. They stay there a little while" (Boas 1928, 70). In Laguna, "the *kyimic* (of the Corn Clan) erects the rainbow with a sustaining pillar in the center of the plaza. Under the east entrance to the plaza the people bury four kinds of prayer-stick" (Boas 1928, 241).

The plaza, or empty place, of the Pueblo form contains the middle or center of the cosmos as the kiva also contains the center. The kiva existed in the world below, and in a Keres myth the people of Zuni tell about the time when Itcsiti and Nautsiti still lived in the world below. "They decided in the kiva that they ought to make light. Inspired by spider they make the sun of white shell, turquoise, red stone and abalone shell." They continue, creating the moon and stars. Later, they "reenter the kiva and make four houses—north, west, south and east" (Boas 1928, 230).

Even after the emergence to this realm, the kiva remains a connection to the world below. In some myths, there is a kiva at the place of emergence and there are kivas at the cardinal points or mountains as well. A Hopi maiden and youth travel on a rainbow to the San Francisco peaks and "land right close to a great kiva far up in the Peaks and they descend from the rainbow and walk up to it" (Nequatewa 1967, 107). The kiva is also the replication of the emergence place. It is the circular and subterranean cave from which issue the sustaining forces of life. Spider-Woman says to the people, "When you build your kivas place a small *sipapu* [symbolic emergence place in Hopi] there in the floor to remind you where you come from and what you are looking for" (Courlander 1971, 40). Through the kiva *sipapu*, the Hopi two-horned underworld god of fertility Miungwu sends "the germs of all living things." The kiva, as the *sipapu* or *nansipu*, is the "vital catalyst for bringing the fertile forces out of the underworld" (Taube 1986, 74). The kiva and *nansipu* are even talked about as being the same in a Tewa story:

3-6 *The cardinal landscape.*
(Drawing: Jeremiah Iowa.)

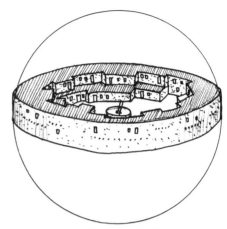

3-7 *Houses, plaza, and kiva.*
(Drawing: Jeremiah Iowa.)

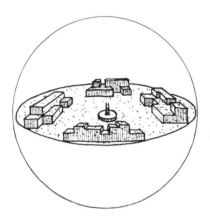

3-8 *The town: houses, plaza, and kiva. (Drawing: Jeremiah Iowa.)*

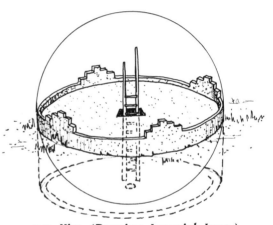

3-9 *Kiva. (Drawing: Jeremiah Iowa.)*

> At that time they would keep the boys . . . in the house [kiva] for twelve days. They kept them in for rain, to have good rains. And one of those boys, he was waiting until those who were taking care of them fell asleep. The guards saw a boy go going up, and they went after him, and they did not catch him; and he jumped in the water and he drank all he needed; and they brought him back and took him back to *Sipopene* (*nansipu*) (Parsons 1926, 16).

Not only is the kiva important as the connector with the underworld but it also serves as the connector with the sky forces. The sun, in a Hopi myth, descends and emerges into the west and east houses where two women live.

> Huruing Wuhti of the East and Huruing Wuhti of the West, lived in their east and west houses, and the sun made his journey from one to the other, descending through an opening in the kiva of the West at night and emerging from a similar aperture in the kiva of the East at dawn (Alexander 1964, 204).

Within the kiva the six-direction system also holds. An Acoma origin story states that "the four main beams are located directionally and color-coded turquoise deposits consecrate the cardinal points within its foundation" (Nabokov 1986a, 6). There are also the above and below directions represented by the entryway opening or "doorway into the sky" and the center or *nansipu* into the world below. Within both kiva and house form, the four walls symbolize the four directions, with the above and the below again represented by the opening out of the underworld and the opening (or *nansipu*) into the underworld.

The house and the kiva are microcosms and therefore breathe the world energy, or are alive. They must be fed, and they contain more than inert substances in their walls. In a Keres myth, a shaman "struck the north wall of the house, the middle of the wall. There south downward came out water. . . . Again to the west he came and next there in the west he struck it. Then there eastward a bear came out" (Boas 1928, 15). Often the entryway or opening into the kiva is referred to as being a lake, in the same manner as the emergence place or world center is a lake or water place. There are also, however, lakes within both kiva and house forms. In a Tewa story, "Spider-Woman took the cigarette and meal into her little room, where she had her medicine lake" (Parsons 1939, 288). In a Keres story, "a rainbow was pulled out of each of the northwest, southwest, southeast and northeast walls" (Boas 1928, 79). In another Keres story, when the people went eastward, "They saw a house. . . . Then in the north they went in. Inside there from all sides lightning was hanging down and there in the middle it was altogether with thunder" (Boas 1928, 54). Sometimes houses are built of white shell and Spider-Woman can mend cracks in the rock with ground sweet corn (Nequatewa 1967, 117). Even more, in the Tewa world, people were made when the first beings "rubbed cuticle from their bodies and mixed with it bits of turquoise, white shell, abalone shell and red stone" (Harrington n.d.).

In summary, the Pueblo myths, stories, songs, and prayers describe a world in which a house or structure is not an object—or a machine to live in—but is part of a cosmological world view that recognizes multiplicity, simultaneity, inclusiveness, and interconnectedness. It is an ordered, but flowing, whole that reflects a cosmos strongly biased toward the gentle and inclusive qualities of the universe. It is where cyclic rather than linear time is chosen; where movements are inward and spiral rather than outward and dispersed; where the ethereal and nonmaterial qualities of the cosmos are emphasized; where permanence of structure is not primary; where there is capacity to flow as well as sensuous concern with colors and shapes. It is a world in which, as Castaneda recorded in 1540, "The houses are built in common. The women mix the mortar and build the walls" (U.S. Department of the Interior 1890, 403).

REFERENCES

ALEXANDER, HARTLEY BURR. 1964. *The Mythology of All Races*. New York: Cooper Square Publication Inc.

BENEDICT, RUTH. 1930. "Eight Stories from Acoma." *Journal of American Folklore* 10:101.

———. 1935. *Zuni Mythology*. New York: Ams Press.

BOAS, FRANZ. 1928. *Keresan Texts*. New York: The American Ethnological Society.

CARR, PAT. 1979. *Mimbres Mythology*. El Paso: University of Texas Press.

COURLANDER, HAROLD. 1971. *The Fourth World of the Hopis*. Conn.: Fawcett Premier.

CUSHING, FRANK HAMILTON. 1974. *Zuni Breadstuff*. New York: Museum of the American Indian Heye Foundation.

HARRINGTON, JOHN. n.d. Untitled drafts. Washington, D.C.: Smithsonian Institution Collections.

NABOKOV, PETER. 1986a. "Continuity and Discontinuity of Circular Symbolism in Kiva Traditions." Unpublished paper.

———. 1986b. *Architecture of Acoma Pueblo*. Santa Fe: Ancient City Press.

NEQUATEWA, EDMUND. 1967. *Truth of a Hopi*. Flagstaff: Museum of Northern Arizona.

ORTIZ, ALFONSO. 1969. *The Tewa World*. Chicago: University of Chicago Press.

PARSONS, ELSIE CLEWS. 1926. *Tewa Tales*. New York: G.E. Stechert and Co.

————. 1939. *Pueblo Indian Religion*. Chicago: University of Chicago Press.

SPINDEN, HERBERT. 1933. *Songs of the Tewa*. New York: The Exposition of Indian Tribal Arts.

TAUBE, KARL A. 1986. "The Teotihuacan Cave of Origins. The Iconography and Architecture of Emergence Mythology in Mesoamerica and the American Southwest." *Res* 12. Peabody Museum of Archaeology & Ethnology, Cambridge: Harvard University.

TYLER, HAMILTON A. 1964. *Pueblo Gods and Myths*. Norman: University of Oklahoma Press.

U.S. DEPARTMENT OF THE INTERIOR. 1890. *Report of Indians Taxed and Not Taxed*. Washington D.C.: U.S. Government Printing Office.

Learning from the Pueblos 4

Tony Anella

On Christmas Day I went to a dance at Santa Ana Pueblo on the Jemez River. It is beautiful how the plaza where the dances are held opens up at the southeast corner to permit a view of the Sandia Mountains. The plaza not only frames the dances, it also frames (and defers to) the natural setting of which it is a part. How different an attitude this represents from that of nearby Albuquerque or Rio Rancho, which crisscross the desert with a bulldozed grid of roads anticipating decades of future development.

I think it is fair to say that the architecture of the Pueblos of New Mexico achieves a certain equipoise in relation to the surrounding natural setting. Whether this is inadvertently due to the limitations of their technology (they had no bulldozers, so they had to conform to the existing topography) or intentional is immaterial. They achieve a compelling balance in their architecture between the preconceived order of the ceremonies that their villages are planned to frame and the topographical circumstances and physical idiosyncrasies of the site. A tangible sense of place develops in their architecture because it is premised on such a powerful sense of belonging to a larger natural whole.

Vincent Scully (1975, 4), in his book *Pueblo: Mountain, Village, Dance,* points out the difference between "the vast majority of early civilizations—Mesopotamian, Egyptian, Meso-American and so on—[which] fairly obviously set out to imitate natural forms in their monumental buildings and to geometricize them at landscape scale, so creating conscious images of mountain, sun's rays, river, swamp and clouds" and the architecture of the ancient Greeks:

> The Greek revolts from this calculated symbiosis. Because the landscape is sacred, it embodies its own divinity separate from man, who completes it—completes the structure of things as they are—by placing in it a house, a *naos,* as a shelter for his own image of the god of that place. Then he surrounds it with columns, like images of standing men, and later in his history he describes them verbally in such terms. But for the exterior body of the peripheral temple as a whole, the Greek seems to have had only two special imagistic words: *aetos,* "eagle," for that broad triangle which the Romans were later to call the pediment; and *ptera,* "wings," for the peripheral colonnades. So, while the *aetos* may seem to echo mountain shapes a little, that is apparently not how the Greek primarily saw it. His temples embody not the natural, but the man conceived divinity. They are heroic; they confront and balance the earth shapes but are not of them. They are the eagles of Zeus, wingspreading, through whom mankind bursts free (Scully 1975, 4).

Western civilization has been premised on this concept of freedom from nature ever since (Scully 1975, 7). It is a concept that is intrinsic to our Western world view and a concept that is fundamentally different from the world view represented by the Pueblo architecture of New Mexico, which conforms to the land in which it is built and becomes a part of it. Pueblo architecture provides a glimpse at a different premise upon which to base the fundamental relationship between man and nature.

I do not intend to promote the myth that the Pueblos lived in complete harmony with nature. The story of the Pueblos and their ancestors' 700-year occupation of the Mesa Verde and its eventual abandonment testifies differently. According to Mesa Verde National Park archaeologist Dr. Jack Smith (1985), that story is "the story of a people trying to make a living in an arid land—at first as hunter-gatherers by dealing with the circumstances of the land and then as farmers by planting the circumstances of their livelihood as they simultaneously disrupted the balance of their own existence." Indeed, the sequence of development at Mesa Verde consists of four identifiable cultural periods in which an increase in food-producing capability led to an increase in the population and consequently the need for more food as the Anasazi struggled and eventually failed to maintain a balance and equilibrium with the land. The very act of cultivating corn is a human intervention in the landscape. But it is an intervention premised on a different reality. The farmer who carefully recycles last year's manure for next year's harvest is aware of the fact that by not doing so he jeopardizes his livelihood. It does not take long to deplete the soil in his fields. For him the logic intrinsic to such impartial considerations of long-term interests is self-evident. It may be less obvious for us who have lost even the Greek's constant awareness that nature indubitably exists (Scully, 1975, 7). For the Anasazi, man's relationship to nature was profound. For the Greek it was tragic. For us it is trivial: we buy our corn from the supermarket prepackaged in plastic wrap.

How can we begin to understand and truly integrate the architecture of the Pueblo Indians of New Mexico, who have such an entirely different view of man and nature from the one advanced by the modern European tradition of which we are a part? According to Alfonso Ortiz (1984, 136–7):

> A world view provides a people with a structure of reality; it defines, classifies and orders the "really real" in the universe, in their world and in their society. . . . But what would be some of the constituent parts or categories of a world view? Space and time are, of course, the obvious initial candidates, if only for the reason that phenomenologists—including anthropologists, philosophers, and historians of religion—have compiled an impressive record of evidence that space and time do provide man with his primary level of orientation to reality. This is true enough if we add the cavil that none of the Pueblos, to the best of my knowledge, has abstract terms for space and time; space is only meaningful as the distance between two points, and time cannot be understood apart from the forces and changes in nature which give it relevance and meaning. It is precisely when time becomes cut up into arbitrarily abstract units (weeks, hours, minutes, seconds) that tribal peoples lose all similarity in their time-reckoning customs with those of Western peoples. And these smaller units of time reckoning are precisely the ones which concern Western minds the most.

In the same way we reckon time by cutting it into arbitrarily abstract units, we organize our spatial world by subdividing it into square-mile sections. A bird's-eye view of the United States reveals a giant grid imposed on the natural landscape by the early surveyors carrying out the mandate of the Continental Congress. In 1785 a land ordinance was passed to survey the entire area of the United States into townships of six square miles. The townships were further subdivided into blocks of thirty-six sections of 1 square mile (640 acres) each (fig. 4-1). The relationship of this grid to the landscape is as arbitrary as it is egalitarian: the boundary requirements of cities, villages, farms, and open land were considered to be all the same. Nevertheless, it provided the matrix for a scientific order that has influenced our society ever since.

This matrix has its roots in ancient Greece during the time of Plato when Western man began conceptualizing what divine order should look like. Hippodamus of Milelutus (fig. 4-2) initiated the:

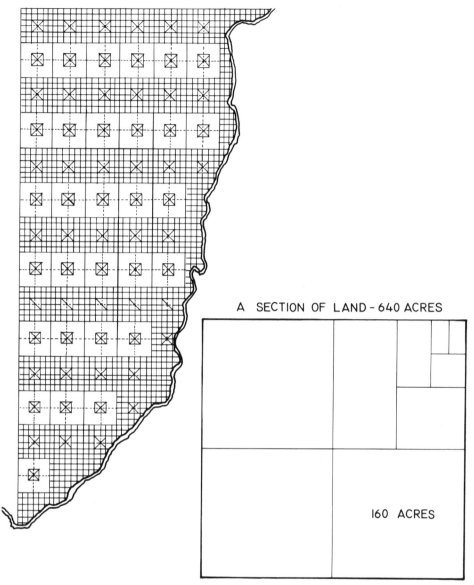

A SECTION OF LAND - 640 ACRES

160 ACRES

4-1 *Map of the first townships surveyed in Ohio according to the land ordinance passed by Congress in 1785. (Sibyl Moholy-Nagy, Matrix of Man, 1968, New York: Frederick A. Praeger. Reprinted with permission.)*

practice of the mathematical "plat" based not on a topographical reality but on numerical configurations, whether cosmological or demographic. The Milelutus plan is a Pythagorean theorem, based on ideal Pythagorean proportions of geometric relationships: $a : b = b : c$ (Moholy-Nagy 1968, 175).

Hence, when the founding fathers were considering how to settle our nation in ways that would be consistent with their vision of the world as advanced by their design for government, they chose to organize the landscape much differently than the Pueblos did.

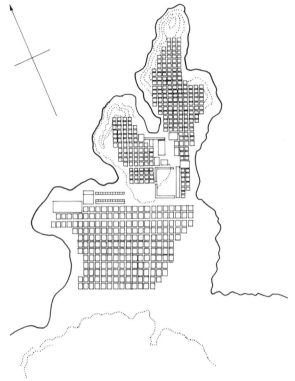

4-2 *The plan of Miletus in Ionia, ca. 470 b.c. as reconstructed by A. von Gerkan. (Sibyl Moholy-Nagy,* Matrix of Man, *1968, Reprinted with permission.)*

Thomas Jefferson's plan for Washington, D.C., appears as a checkerboard of square blocks, eleven blocks east and west and three blocks north and south (fig. 4-3) (Reps 1967, 10). Albuquerque is divided into quadrants by Central Avenue—old Route 66— and the tracks of the Santa Fe Railroad (fig. 4-4). Look at a map of the western United States, and you see a rectilinear grid superimposed on the landscape. The boundaries of states such as Colorado, New Mexico, Arizona, and Utah reflect this rectilinearity. So do the town plans for Albuquerque or Rio Rancho.

The Pueblos organize the same landscape and their place within it much differently:

> The first generalization that can be made about the Pueblos is that they all set careful limits to the boundaries of their world and order everything within it. These boundaries are not the same but, more important, the principles of setting boundaries are since all use phenomena in the four cardinal directions, either mountains or bodies of water, usually both, to set them. . . . All peoples try to bring their definitions of group space somehow in line with their cosmologies, but the Pueblos are unusually precise about it (Ortiz 1984, 142).

Just how precise the Pueblos are at organizing their architecture to reflect their cosmology is best exemplified by Taos Pueblo. There the great plaza is arranged around a view to Taos Mountain, from which flows the sacred creek that physically bisects the pueblo into northern and southern apartment blocks that correspond respectively to the winter and summer moieties that organize Taos society (fig. 4-5).

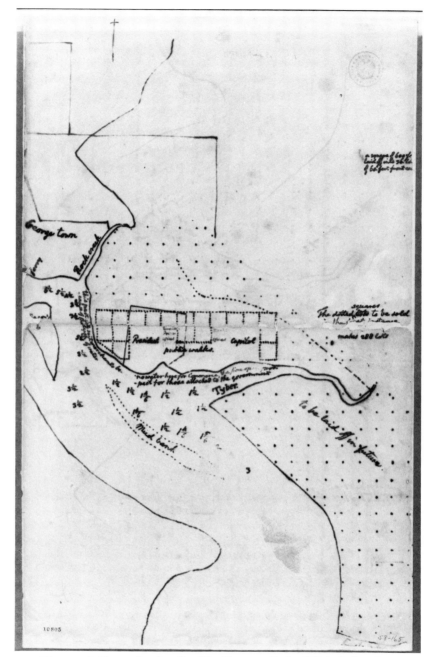

4-3 *Thomas Jefferson's plan for Washington, D.C.: 1791. (John W. Reps,*
The Making of Urban America, *1965, Princeton: Princeton University*
Press. Courtesy of the Library of Congress.)

Nestled within the peaks and ridges of the mountain is Blue Lake, which, according to
the Taos creation myth, is the great source through which all mankind emerged from
the underworld. All Pueblos share this creation myth and symbolize it in the floor of
their ceremonial kivas with a round, centrally located, earth navel notch called a *sipapu*
(Ortiz 1984).

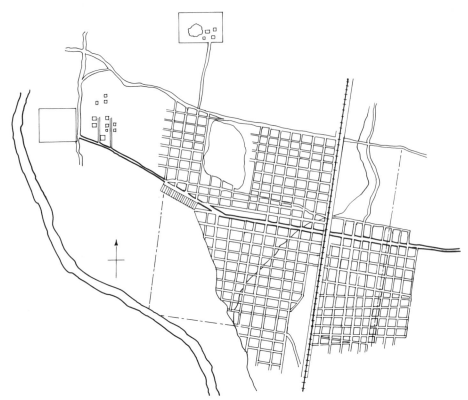

4-4 *Plan: Albuquerque 1898. (Kenneth C. Balcomb, A Boy's Albuquerque, 1898–1912, 1980, Albuquerque: University of New Mexico Press. Reprinted with permission.)*

At Sandia Pueblo, not far from Albuquerque, the plan of the town is inflected off the east–west axis to orient the plaza toward the dominant landscape focus on the horizon: the central horns of Sandia Mountain (fig. 4-6).

Santa Ana Pueblo maintains the principal east–west axis of the pueblo to maximize the southern exposure on the long dimension of the housing units. Here the significant landscape focus to Sandia Mountain is accommodated not in plan, as a. nearby Sandia Pueblo, but in section: at the southeast corner of the plaza the land slopes down, permitting a view to the mountain over the rooftops of the single-story houses that otherwise would be in the way (fig. 4-7).

At Tesuque, the main gap in the plaza leads the eye directly to Lake Peak, which is Tesuque's sacred mountain to the east (fig. 4-8) (Scully 1975, 157). At Taos, Sandia, Santa Ana, and Tesuque, the precise architectural representation of the Pueblo world view is completed by the natural mountain and the man-made building *together*. The perception of the natural setting engages the human construction: both are considered part of the same whole. Compare this sense of town planning with that of Albuquerque or Rio Rancho, which adhere to preconceived and arbitrary orthogonal grids for their infrastructure.

Another characteristic of Pueblo planning is to reserve the center of the town for a communal open space. This space is what receives the Pueblo's primary design attention; the domestic dwellings are arranged around this center so as to define the configuration of the plaza. Unlike European plazas, which read as complete forms with consistently defined edges, the Pueblo plazas read in plan as incomplete figures. What

4-5 *Plan: Taos 1950. (Adapted from* Bird's-Eye View of the Pueblos, *by Stanley A. Stubbs. Copyright 1950, University of Oklahoma Press.)*

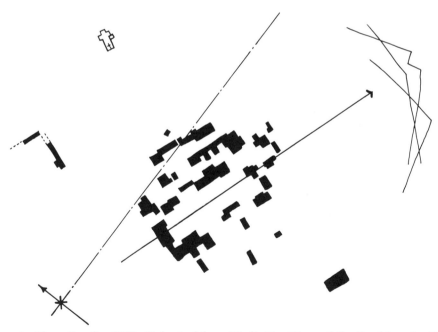

4-6 *Plan: Sandia 1950. (Adapted from* Bird's-Eye View of the Pueblos, *by Stanley A. Stubbs. Copyright 1950, University of Oklahoma Press.)*

37

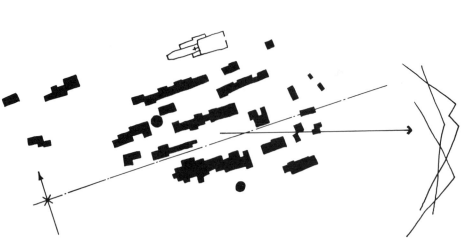

4-7 *Plan: Santa Ana 1950. (Adapted from* Bird's-Eye View of the Pueblos, *by Stanley A. Stubbs. Copyright 1950, University of Oklahoma Press.)*

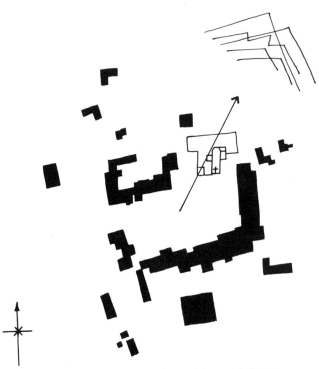

4-8 *Plan: Tesuque 1950. (Adapted from* Bird's-Eye View of the Pueblos, *by Stanley A. Stubbs. Copyright 1950, University of Oklahoma Press.)*

completes them are the views to the landscape their irregularities allow to become a part of the central space. The plaza at Taos Pueblo is completed by a view to Taos Mountain; the plaza at Tesuque is closed by a view to Lake Peak; both Sandia and Santa Ana incorporate Sandia Mountain as a fundamental part of their world view by bringing it into their plazas.

In contrast, the European plaza is a complete enclosure (fig. 4-9); it creates a social focus by protecting itself from what happens around it. Vitruvius (ca. 27 B.C.) identifies the forum—the prototypical European plaza—with a space that is defined by being closed all around by architecture:

> The Greeks lay out their forums in the form of a square surrounded by very spacious double colonnades, adorn them with columns set rather closely together, and with entablatures of stone or marble, and construct walks above in the upper story. But in the cities of Italy the same method cannot be followed, for the reason that it is a custom handed down from our ancestors that gladiatorial shows should be given in the forum. Therefore, let the intercolumnations round the show be pretty wide; round about in the colonnades put the bankers' offices; and have balconies on the upper floor properly arranged so as to be convenient; and bring in some public revenue (Vitruvius ca. 27 B.C.).

In *City Planning According to Artistic Principles*, a classic in city-planning literature, Camillo Sitte (1889, 32) discusses the close kinship between the ancient forum and the development of the European plaza:

> [T]he way in which churches and palaces used to form part of building complexes calls our attention once more to the nature of the ancient forum, which was so rigorously closed off from the outside. If one surveys Medieval

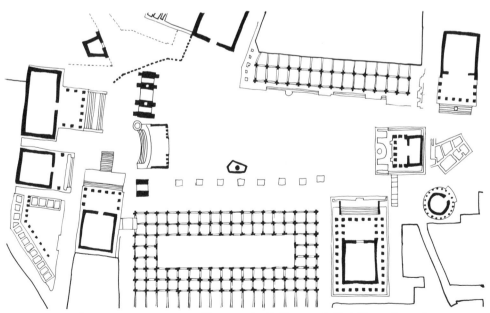

4-9 *Rome: The Forum Romanum. (George R. Collins and Christiane Crasehann Collins,* Camillo Sitte: The Birth of Modern City Planning, *1986, Rizzoli International Publications, Inc.)*

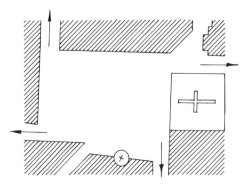

4-10 *Ravenna: Piazza del Duomo.*
(George R. Collins and Christiane
Crasehann Collins, Camillo Sitte: The
Birth of Modern City Planning, *1986,*
Rizzoli International Publications, Inc.)

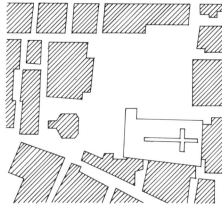

4-11 *Pistoia: Piazza del Duomo.*
(George R. Collins and Christiane
Crasehann Collins, Camillo Sitte: The
Birth of Modern City Planning, *1986,*
Rizzoli International Publications, Inc.)

and Renaissance plazas, especially those of Italy, with regard to this particular characteristic, one becomes aware that tradition persisted a long time in this respect and that it is largely this feature which makes for a harmonious total effect (Sitte 1889, 32).

The Piazza del Duomo in Ravenna (fig. 4-10) maintains this enclosure by becoming the hub of a pinwheel circulation system that rotates around the plaza. According to Sitte (1889, 32), "from any point within the plaza no more than one single view out of it is possible at a time, hence there is only a single interruption in the enclosure of the whole." This remarkable feature occurs so often, and with such a range of variations, that according to Sitte (1889, 32) "it must be considered to be one of the major conscious or subconscious principles of old city planning." Other examples include the Piazza del Duomo in Pistoia and the Piazza San Pietro in Mantua (figs. 4-11 and 4-12).

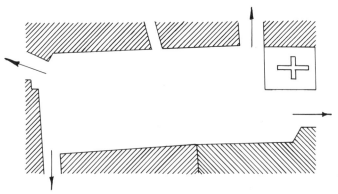

4-12 *Mantua: Piazza S. Pietro. (George R. Collins and*
Christiane Crasehann Collins, Camillo Sitte: The Birth of
Modern City Planning, *1986, Rizzoli International*
Publications, Inc.)

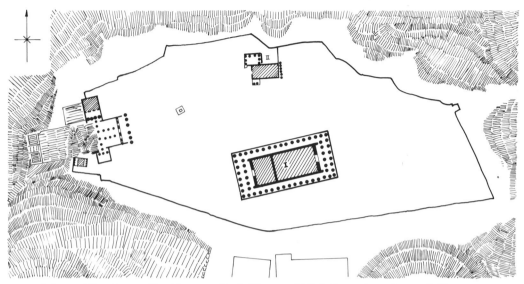

4-13 *Athens: The Acropolis. (George R. Collins and Christiane Crasehann Collins, Camillo Sitte: The Birth of Modern City Planning, 1986, Rizzoli International Publications, Inc.)*

The European notion of the plaza implies that the dominant spatial orientation as well as that of motion is centrifugal or outward. Man is conceived to be at the center of a pinwheel circulation system that rotates about him and the conceptualized universe of his religion. The Parthenon is an idealized architectural object-in-space placed in the center of the Acropolis (fig. 4-13). The forum at Pompeii (fig. 4-14) is completely enclosed by the temples of Jupiter, Vespasian, and Apollo as well as a basilica and various other public buildings. The plaza of St. Peter's in Rome (fig. 4-15) is calculated to frame the cathedral—the Catholic conception of ideal order.

The Pueblo plaza is much different: it is the point of intersection of views to sacred mountains. The landscape is intentionally brought into the plaza, not excluded from it. The Pueblos do not deny the principle of closure in the construction of their plazas; rather, they incorporate the natural landscape as part of the *perceptual* enclosure rather than excluding it, as the Greeks and Romans did, to preserve the man-made *conceptual* order. The Pueblo notion of the plaza reflects a completely different world view: man is not at the center of the Pueblo world view. The center is a void connoting the mystery of spirit. Only during the days of ritual is that void filled; only when they dance is the plaza transformed into a place of worship. Even then what is worshiped is not man himself—although he is perceived to be a part of it—but rather the sanctity of man's place within nature. The dances of the Pueblos ritualize the most important concern of Pueblo society: self-perpetuation. As agriculturists, they are preoccupied by fertility. The dances not only intend to bring about that fertility in specific ways (rain dance, corn dance, buffalo dance) but also more generally. In the act of making dances in the hollow spaces of their centralized plazas is symbolized, in a beautifully subtle way, the act of procreation. Man and Earth become one to the rhythmic drumbeat of deerskin stretched over cottonwood.

According to Karsten Harries (1983, 16),

|O|ne task of architecture is still that of interpreting the world as a meaningful order in which the individual can find his place in the midst of nature and in the midst of community. Time and space must be revealed in such a way that human beings are given their dwelling place, their *ethos*.

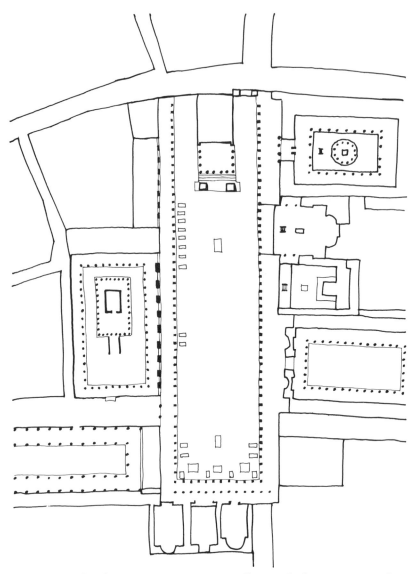

4-14 *Pompeii: The Forum. (George R. Collins and Christiane Crasehann Collins, Camillo Sitte: The Birth of Modern City Planning, 1986, Rizzoli International Publications, Inc.)*

Harries links the problem of arbitrariness in modern design to our greater freedom. "To this one may object that freedom has here been grasped inadequately, because only negatively: true freedom is not freedom from constraint, but rather to be constrained only by what one really is, by one's essence" (Harries 1983, 11). Modern man has emancipated himself from many of the natural constraints that confronted our "primitive" ancestors. In the process, modern man has also lost his sense of place in the larger whole to which he should belong. Both modern and post-modern architecture are really part of the same tradition in this regard. Both aestheticize architecture with their emphasis on the object-in-space without due regard for the relationship between the object and what surrounds it. Both elevate architecture to the status of hero by

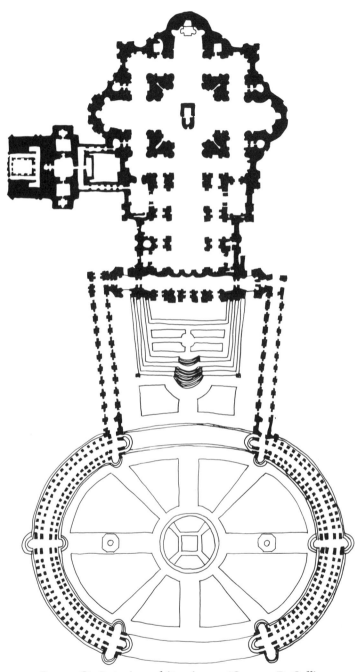

4-15 *Rome: St. Peter's and its piazza. (George R. Collins and Christiane Crasehann Collins,* Camillo Sitte: The Birth of Modern City Planning, *1986, Rizzoli International Publications, Inc.)*

looking almost exclusively to architecture for new directions rather than to the larger context. Both commit the sin of narcissism: the sin of regarding themselves perpetually in a mirror. And both inadvertently render architecture gutless because neither acknowledges that the problem of arbitrariness in architecture is not first of all an aesthetic one.[1]

Man's perception of his relationship to nature is the central issue of our time. We live in an age obsessed by its own inventiveness. The dilemma of such an obsession derives from the predicament such invention creates. Informed with experiences such as Three Mile Island; the Love Canal; Times Beach, Missouri; Bhopal, India; and now Chernobyl, we lose our faith in our inventiveness. We are forced to question the conceptual premise that leads to such destructive creation. It would be useless to try to ignore the dilemma posed by the modern world by retreating into simpler, agrarian existences. But we can learn to revere again the basic premise that sustains the Pueblo farmer: that man is a part of nature, not separate from it. We can learn again to build with the land and not merely on it. What makes the architecture of the Pueblos "a true, indigenous, American architecture whose beginnings predate imported European concepts" (Markovich preamble) so important is that it bridges the abyss that separates the two realities of human history: the one we used to organize *perceptually* and the one we now understand *conceptually*.

Lincoln Barnett has made the following observation:

In the evolution of scientific thought, one fact has become impressively clear: there is no mystery of the physical world which does not point to a mystery beyond itself. All highroads of the intellect, all byways of theory and conjecture lead ultimately to an abyss that human ingenuity can never span. For man is enchained by the very condition of his being, his finiteness and involvement in nature. The farther he extends his horizons, the more vividly he recognizes the fact that, as the physicist Niels Bohr puts it, "We are both spectators and actors in the great drama of existence." Man is thus his own greatest mystery. He does not understand the vast veiled universe into which he has been cast for the reason that he does not understand himself. He comprehends but little of his organic processes and even less of his unique capacity to perceive the world about him, to reason and to dream. Least of all does he understand his noblest and most mysterious faculty: the ability to transcend himself and perceive himself in the act of perception (Barnett 1948, 109).

The profound lesson we can learn from the Pueblos and their architecture is precisely the one suggested by the satellite image of earth against the backdrop of space: that man is part of nature, not separate from it. The architecture of the Pueblos should not be seen merely as the picturesque perception of a simpler world. It is an original pedagogue. If architecture is to intervene in the New Mexican landscape in a nonarbitrary way so that it helps man to dwell in and make sense out of this distinctively vast world, then it must begin with respectful attention to that which is truly indigenous. By learning from the Pueblos, architecture can begin to complement the land by helping man to live with the land, and not merely on or in spite of it. The sublime beauty of the New Mexican landscape is its ultimate indifference to man's presence. It is an indifference that should remind us of our place within nature and convince us that the continuity of dance that connects our pre-Columbian past with the future ought to be revered, not broken.

REFERENCES

Barnett, Lincoln. 1948. *The Universe and Dr. Einstein*. New York: Time Inc.

Harries, Karsten. 1983. "Thoughts on a Non-Arbitrary Architecture." In: *Perspecta 20*. Cambridge and London: MIT Press.

Moholy-Nagy, Sibyl. 1968. *Matrix of Man*. New York: Frederick A. Praeger.

Ortiz, Alfonso. 1984. "Ritual Drama and the Pueblo World View." In: *New Perspectives on the Pueblos*, ed. Alfonso Ortiz. Albuquerque: University of New Mexico Press, A School of American Research Book.

Reps, John W. 1967. *Monumental Washington*. Princeton, N.J.: Princeton University Press.

Scully, Vincent. 1975. *Pueblo: Mountain, Village, Dance*. New York: Viking Press.

Sitte, Camillo. 1889. (Republished 1965.) *City Planning According to Artistic Principles*. Columbia University Studies in Art History and Archaeology No. 2. New York: Random House.

Smith, Jack. 1985. In conversation: Mesa Verde National Park.

Vitruvius. ca. 27 b.c. Quoted in: *The Ten Books of Architecture* by Leon B. Alberti (1987). New York: Dover Publications.

NOTES

1. For a discussion of arbitrariness in architecture, read Harries (1983).

II

Historical Evolution

There is a widespread mistaken perception of Pueblo history and society as representing a stable and little-changing pattern extending over many centuries. The evidence contradicts this notion and reveals instead a dynamic history in which the various communities are continuously adapting structures and life-styles to ever-changing environmental circumstances. David Saile, in Chapter 5, provides an overview of Pueblo architectural history in which the change is evident while the continuity of the world view that sees buildings as both natural and spiritual entities is preserved. He calls for a more integrated approach to the study and interpretation of the development of Pueblo architecture. In Chapter 6, Stephen Lekson looks at the "Great Pueblo period" in the Four Corners region, which has often been hailed as the high point of Pueblo architecture and social organization. His research reveals an Anasazi world that was "almost perpetually out of balance," in which constant change and readjustment was the rule. He also stresses the historical distance separating that period from the modern Pueblo historical period. Theodore Jojola, in Chapter 7, takes the development of Isleta Pueblo as an example of the dynamic nature of the history of the Pueblos. As he points out, it is the constant adaptive behavior of the Pueblo Indians that gave rise to societies that are vital and progressive.

Understanding the Development of Pueblo Architecture   **5**

David G. Saile

Within the limits of a chapter, I cannot hope to provide a full description of the architectural and settlement forms of Pueblo culture as they developed through the past thirteen centuries. Neither can I offer a coherent framework through which to understand them, even though a richer, deeper, and more integrative understanding of Pueblo architecture has been my preoccupation for nearly twenty years (Saile 1981).

This brief sketch of the development of Pueblo architecture will outline two commonly known descriptions and interpretations:

1. The sequence of architectural forms (or remains of forms) in the Pueblo Southwest
2. A summary of different viewpoints that have been used in explaining or interpreting them.

It will conclude with a few questions about why architects need to understand this architecture. I urge others to enquire into the social, economic, or emotional ties with this architecture that have been sufficiently important for Euro-Americans to use and study its forms.

The builders and dwellers of Pueblo villages in northeastern Arizona and northern and western New Mexico are descendants of groups of people who have farmed, gathered produce, and hunted over a wide area of the southwestern United States for at least thirteen centuries. These villages, their residents, and their culture are termed "Pueblo" after the descriptions and early interpretations made of them by Spanish explorers.

During the years of Spanish exploration in the Southwest, from Francisco de Coronado's expedition in A.D. 1540–1542 until the first colonization expedition of Juan de Onate in 1598, more than 80 (and perhaps as many as 130) villages were counted in the region north from El Paso to Taos and west from Pecos to the Hopi mesas (Spicer 1962, 152–7; Schroeder 1979). More than thirty Pueblo villages remain today—twelve in Arizona and at least nineteen in New Mexico (more if modern settlements are included). Although substantially changed and including numbers of outlying modern single-family houses and government housing projects, a few are located on sites they have occupied for 800 years (fig. 5-1). Many have been where they are for three centuries.

The traditional forms of the existing villages have fascinated explorers, architects, scholars, and tourists for more than a century. So too have the ruins in the surrounding region, once inhabited by ancestors of the living Pueblos. Collections of southwestern photographs, tourist guides, and wide surveys of vernacular architecture constitute much of the architectural information, mostly visual, that is familiar to architects. Many of us can remember what the north building in the village of Taos looks like in the sunlight and how the familiar ruins of the Mesa Verde National Monument in southwestern Colorado are protected by their cave sites (fig. 5-2).

Familiarity with appearance, however, does not necessarily mean understanding. In fact, there are very few major architectural studies of the existing pueblos (Mindeleff 1891; Scully 1975; Saile 1981). The recent past has produced only a handful of shorter

5-1 *Taos Pueblo, north building, 1970. (All sketches and diagrams in this chapter are by David G. Saile.)*

5-2 *Part of the Cliff Palace ruin, Mesa Verde National Park.*

architectural studies and these either are examinations of very specific aspects of Pueblo architecture or are extremely general.

There are even fewer architectural studies of the pre-Hispanic periods, that is, of settlements prior to 1539. The majority of writings consist of supplementary or introductory chapters to other works or form a few pages within global cross-cultural surveys of indigenous architectural forms (Bunting 1976; Fraser 1968; Guidoni 1978, 115–30; Scully 1975, 1–45).

There are, however, literally thousands of studies in the disciplines of ethnology and archaeology that do examine many aspects of Pueblo culture. Although very few focus specifically on architectural and spatial topics, there are many that illuminate relationships between architecture and other aspects of society. Excellent studies have been published recently, including one by Steve Lekson on Chaco Canyon (1986) and others by Arthur Rohn (1971) and Alden Hayes and James Lancaster (1975) on Mesa Verde ruins and by Jeffrey Dean (1969) on Navajo National Monument ruins.

LANDSCAPE

Architecture and settlement organization are inextricably bound with the material, nutritional, and spiritual cycles and resources of the landscape. Most Pueblo settlements in pre-Hispanic and more recent periods have been situated in a band between 5000 and 7000 feet elevation and have been able to take advantage of the resources of different adjacent life zones of the valleys, tablelands, and mountains of the Colorado Plateau and its fringes.

Until at least the second quarter of the twentieth century, subsistence depended largely upon a mix of agriculture and hunting and gathering. Hunting and gathering was not a supplement to agriculture; it was an integral component of Pueblo life, both in terms of activities and in terms of diet. All pre-Hispanic Pueblo sites show evidence of this subsistence mix. In fact, all sedentary cultures in the Southwest show *some* mix, although the proportion of dependence upon these food sources has varied.

Agriculture has had to contend with vagaries of the climate. Periods of drought, flooding, arroyo cutting and stream-channel variations, late and early killing frost, wind and dust storms, and burning summer sun have all affected Pueblo farming in recorded history (Bryan 1954; McIntire 1968).

The crops grown by the Pueblos before the arrival of the Spaniards included corn, beans, squash, cotton, and tobacco. Crops introduced by the Spanish colonizers included wheat, alfalfa, chili and other vegetables in addition to some local cultivation of fruit trees. Although more and more Pueblos gain their livelihood by wage-earning, agriculture and agricultural cycles still play a large role in Pueblo life. The success of western Pueblo farming was and still is unpredictable.

The villages along the Rio Grande have also practiced the dry-farming techniques of the western groups but also irrigated their crops from the close permanent watercourses. Wheat, alfalfa, and chilies have become more important in the east because of the more dependable water supply. Many activities of the eastern Pueblos were concerned with canal and ditch maintenance and with maintaining level and larger fields.

Edible wild plants and herbs were gathered by both western and eastern Pueblos. During autumn and winter, diet included the dried and stored crops from the previous farming season and meat supplied by organized hunting expeditions. When survival depended upon the produce of these subsistence activities, the provision of adequate dry storage was an important component of each Pueblo dwelling. The main settlements were fully occupied during the winter, but during the summer, for example at Acoma and Santa Ana, there was a mass exodus to farming villages located near agricultural lands. Knowledge of environmental and climatic variables is critical to long-term survival in southwestern landscapes. Pueblo activities, beliefs, settlements, and architecture reflect this concern in numerous ways.

PREHISTORY

In this landscape, from the game hunters and the cyclical seasonal gatherers of 10,000 years ago, gradually emerged the cultures of the settled Pueblos. With influences and the knowledge of corn cultivation from southern basins and Mesoamerica, groups of people settled in more localized traditional areas, perhaps with winter and summer home bases.

Semisubterranean earth houses, often termed pit houses, usually accompanied by a few storage pits, were constructed as home bases in the Southwest at least 2500 years ago. Some may have been inhabited year-round, and others seasonally. The change from a more mobile hunting and gathering existence to a more sedentary and mixed subsistence living pattern was very gradual. Even in recent centuries, subsistence was still based on the triad of hunting, wild plant gathering, and horticulture.

It is, strictly speaking, not appropriate to discuss pit houses as Pueblo architecture, but they often possessed attributes of interest to the later themes of this chapter. Pueblo architecture developed from these earlier pit-house settlements, and it is important to examine briefly their temporal and formal relationships.

Most pit-house settlements were small, usually consisting of between three and twenty dwellings (Bullard 1962). There appears to have been no particular order to the arrangement of houses in a settlement. From approximately A.D. 600–700 in the Colorado Plateau area, storage structures and surface work spaces became more commonly grouped in an arc (regular and irregular) to the north or west of the pit house. As time passed, these surface structures at any one site possessed more features, indicating a fuller range of domestic activities. The pit houses sometimes lost domiciliary features and gained more formal, group activity and special features. They did not suddenly change from residences to group meeting halls, but it does appear that some "old" dwellings became associated with special group activities and eventually with religious and more symbolic functions. Prior to, and parallel with, this architectural specialization, when rituals or religious observances were required they were enacted in "special" pit houses or outside in the open air.

In the upper Little Colorado and Gila river areas, for example, pit houses remained irregularly arranged, with a sprinkling of some larger special pit houses, presumably for group activities, until the eleventh century. In many areas, pit houses were built near villages where surface-built dwellings had existed for many decades. Gradually, however, Pueblo-like villages, with surface house-blocks and at least partially specialized religious rooms on or below ground level, appeared all over the Pueblo region.

Pit houses have continued to be used for shelter until more permanent dwellings can be constructed. An example would be the pit houses built by the "hostiles" at Bacavi in 1909 after the factional split at the Hopi Pueblo of Oraibi in 1906 (Whiteley 1988, 91).

Certain features of pit houses and certain aspects of the changes from pit-house village to pueblo echo the themes of Pueblo architecture generally. Although their floor plans were usually variations from squares with rounded corners to circles, the orientation of pit houses has been judged from the direction of entrances and the alignment of these entrances with fireplaces, roof support posts, and other features (Bullard 1962, 111). In most areas entrance was gained to early pit houses through a sloping side passage or through an antechamber with a roof or side entrance. Some dwellings may also have been entered by a central roof hatchway that acted as a smoke hole above the fireplace (fig. 5-3) (Bullard 1962, 138–9).

As pit-house structures became less specifically domestic, the entrances became only of the roof hatchway type, and the side passages or antechambers became

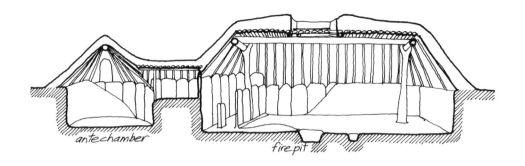

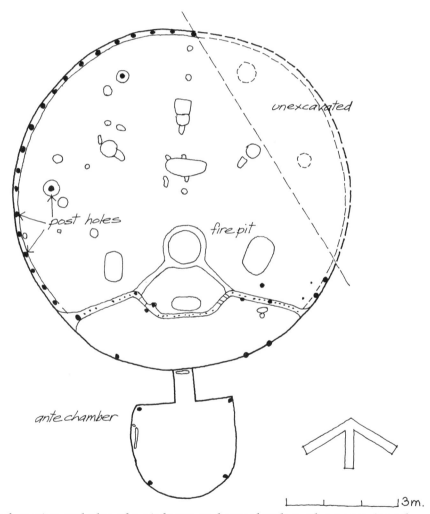

antechamber

fire pit

unexcavated

post holes

fire pit

antechamber

3m.

5-3 *Sketch section and plan of a pit house and antechamber, plan approximately*
A.D. *770.*

smaller tunnels. These tunnels, or ducts, are generally referred to by archaeologists as ventilators because they allowed fresh air to enter the lower chamber. They continued to be oriented in the predominant direction of their antecedent passages or entrance chambers.

Orientation of these features was remarkably consistent in most areas. It is more noticeably consistent when different areas are compared. In the northern San Juan region, orientation was mainly to the south; in Chaco Canyon, to the south and southeast. In the upper Little Colorado region, most faced southeast; in most other Mogollon areas they faced east or southeast. These predominant directions were repeated in the orientations of kivas and village house-blocks in later Pueblo settlements.

In looking for explanations for such orientations, convenience of access to pit houses varied from site to site. Other houses, fields, springs, and mountains were distributed in no discernible patterns around pit houses and did not appear to affect the choice of orientation. It also makes little sense to argue that the orientation of pit houses was due to microclimatic factors. Many were totally below ground level, local winds varied with the sites, pit-house plans were nearly square or circular, and there were few, if any, above-ground wall openings conforming to favorable solar orientations. It is most likely that the southern or eastern directions were considered important because of beliefs about them.

It is also interesting to speculate why it was that many special kivalike chambers did not also extend upward to the ground surface when the dwelling rooms were built there. Many later kivas remained partially or totally below ground, even when this meant excavating into bedrock. It is tempting to suggest that "below-groundness" or excavation was already important for some special communal activities (fig. 5-4).

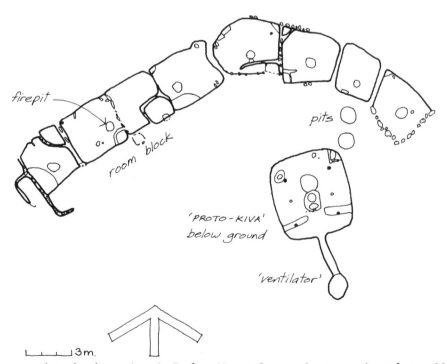

5-4 *Plan of a domestic unit, Badger House Community, approximately* A.D. *900 (from Hayes and Lancaster 1975).*

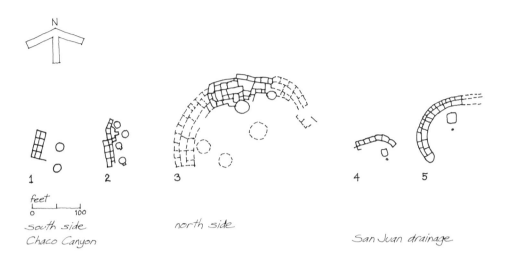

N

feet
0 ——— 100

south side
Chaco Canyon

north side

San Juan drainage

5-5 **Plans from Chaco Canyon and the San Juan drainage; early Pueblo Bonito is no. 3.**

An overall generic Pueblo settlement pattern emerged, with an exterior space to the "front" of a row of multipurpose habitation and storage rooms. The "front" direction varies regionally and locally between east and south. Generally, special ritual or communal chambers were placed in the front of the row or in the front space. The exterior settlement space was further defined by fire pits, work surfaces, and other rows of habitation and storage rooms. Storage rooms tended to be at the "back" of the rows. Such a pattern appears by A.D. 700 in many places.

In some areas, through the next centuries, a few settlements grew into larger arrangements with greater spatial complexity. These larger communities exhibit evidence of attempts at more cohesive spatial arrangements. This evidence includes larger communal spaces, both interior and exterior; more architectural planning and larger construction phases; more evidence of ritual structure and processes; networks of shrines on hills, in caves, near springs, and on mountaintops; increases in storage capacity; and an apparently increasing concern for both consistency of water supply for horticulture and water control (fig. 5-5).

Just as pit houses survived long into later Pueblo settlement periods, so too did smaller irregular villages survive, sometimes adjacent to the larger settlements. These larger ordered settlements occur earliest and in their most geometric forms in Chaco Canyon and surrounding areas A.D. 900–1150 (fig. 5-6). They also show evidence of a vast regional organization and what has been described as a community of unprecedented complexity in the Southwest (Lekson et al. 1988).

But larger settlements occurred in many areas and exhibit many variations on the Pueblo patterns on the Mesa Verde, in the Tsegi drainage, and along the upper Little Colorado, Salt, and Gila river drainages. In later periods (A.D. 1300–1550) these larger settlements were built in closer proximity to the more permanent watercourses of the Little Colorado, Zuni, Rio Grande, Chama, Galisteo, and the upper Pecos rivers.

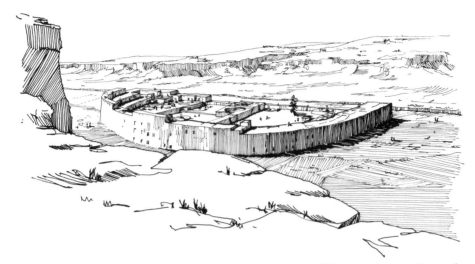

5-6 *Reconstruction of Pueblo Bonito from an original 1926 drawing by Kenneth J. Conant.*

VILLAGES IN HISTORY

Both smaller and larger settlements continued to be built until the major colonization expeditions of the Spanish in the late 1500s and early 1600s. Possibilities for large-scale social experiment and settlement building were stifled by Spanish domination, and although the century 1650–1750 saw great architectural experiment, many migrations of village communities, and a multitude of shifts in village site locations, there was, overall, a consistent decline in populations, in consolidation of settlements (i.e., fewer fringe villages), and in the size of villages. Zuni Pueblo, which was formed from six earlier villages, was an exception. Architectural changes included the building of new villages on defensive sites (for fear of Spanish retaliation for the widespread Pueblo revolt of 1680), joint Navajo–Pueblo architectural arrangements in northwest New Mexico, and joint Spanish–Pueblo towers, walls, and gates in some eastern villages in response to increasing raids by Navajo, Ute, Apache, and Comanche bands.

The consolidation of villages into areas along the northern Rio Grande, a few sites in western New Mexico and on the Hopi mesas, that had occurred by the later eighteenth century defines the extent of current Pueblo settlements. Considerable variability remains in existing settlements, although there are some common themes. At a general level, all the existing Pueblos live in or near permanent villages or small towns built, until the past quarter-century, predominantly of stone, adobe, and timber. Most have farmhouses or settlements in the surrounding area, and some villages are seasonally occupied. Most villages possess ceremonial and social chambers of some form (some termed kivas), but these vary in number and in the nature of the groups of people who are associated with them (fig. 5-7). All villages share some components of a common world view and broad generic ideas of their origins (Ortiz 1972).

Village siting and layout, however, vary considerably (fig. 5-8); ritual space and kiva forms, positions, and details also differ from group to group and within each group. Although construction methods are quite similar, different combinations of building materials occur. Six languages are spoken, and their linguistic roots may be traced to four widely separated origins (Hale and Harris 1979). Dialects may vary from village to village. Social organization differs markedly between the western and eastern villages, as do many aspects of ceremonies. The eastern Pueblos along the Rio Grande have experienced contacts with Spanish and American cultures widely different from those experienced by the Hopi and Zuni in the west. Each village has a largely unique history.

UNDERSTANDING PUEBLO ARCHITECTURE

Architecture is never context-free. It is built by someone for someone to occupy or to use in some other manner. It is built in places where resources enable its habitation or use. It is built from materials that have been removed from the natural environment. As a built work also, it modifies the natural environment in terms of microclimate, erosion, and deposition, and in terms of surrounding life forms.

Architecture also communicates. It intimates ideas about space, structure, appropriate behavior, and social responsibility. As part of experience it also modifies or reinforces these ideas. It affects and is affected by ideas about relative permanence, change, and time. Seen in this way, architecture is one of the media through which other aspects of a society act and have their substance. Conversely, these other aspects of society are media, along with aspects of the natural environment, through which architecture acts and has its substance.

Just describing Pueblo architecture and providing some selected illustrations does not necessarily help us understand it. We need to know how and why it changes and also to what other aspects of society or human events it is related and how. We need to understand the significance it possesses for the variety of residents and insiders to the cultural system of which it is a part and the significance for outsiders (like myself). How has Pueblo architecture been understood by scholars?

5-7 *Circular kiva near the south house at Taos Pueblo.*

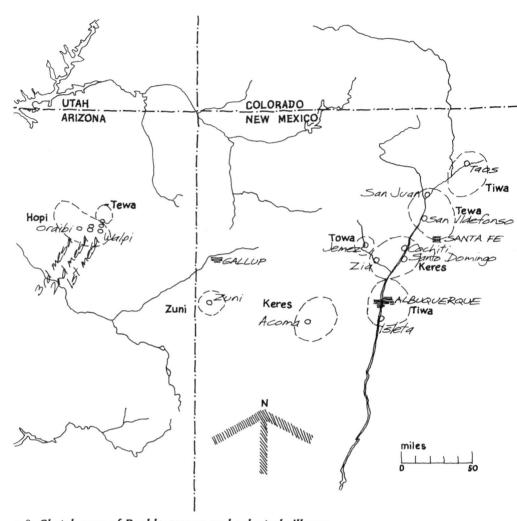

5-8 **Sketch map of Pueblo groups and selected villages.**

The word *architecture* is used frequently in southwestern archaeological literature. It is most commonly used as a substitute for the words *building* or *buildings*. It is also very often treated in the sense of a style or trademark of buildings produced in a particular area and time or by a particular group.

For more than a century, architecture as artifact (as distinct from the discipline or profession) has passed through a number of different interpretations in studies of the pre-Hispanic peoples of the Southwest. Differences in interpretations are very apparent in excavation reports and discussions of pre-Hispanic Pueblo architecture. Some common interpretations from an earlier study (Saile 1977a) are summarized in the following list. Architecture has been categorized and interpreted as:

- Evidence of cultural affiliation
- Evidence of cultural contact
- A reflection of cultural change
- A reflection of social organization
- Evidence of change in social organization
- A reflection of past behavioral sequences

- A reflection of specific political and religious organization
- Technical adaptation to environmental conditions
- A tool in analyzing artifact information

Although these interpretations imply that architecture and spatial order operate in cultural systems, there have been few attempts to clarify how this may work. Architecture is often seen as a *result* of other factors. Functional interpretations are often reinforced by terminology; "window," "door," "plaza," and "kiva" all have a host of interpretive predispositions attached to them. Much richer and more integrative interpretations have appeared recently that avoid this linguistic imperative (Wilcox 1975, 139–46; Lekson 1986; McGuire and Schiffer 1983). In most cases archaeologists have included detailed measurements in the documentation of spatial and environmental settings.

Such is not the case, however, in most ethnographic reporting of more recent situations in the Pueblo world. Ethnographic reports and anthropological analyses show as much about contemporaneous theories of social organization or the main aims and background of the researcher as they do about the activities and settings of the group studied.

In the 1940s there was considerable concern with the "personality" of Pueblo Indians (Goldfrank 1945; Thompson 1945), and in archaeology for many decades "defense" was used as an explanation for Pueblo village forms (Linton 1944).

Most ethnographers, while ostensibly examining the relationships among people, villages, and landscape in a Pueblo society, do not describe spatial and physical settings with any accuracy. Not only is there often very little description, but also there are few diagrams, sketches, or photographs. Much of this information is treated as supplemental rather than integral with the description of activities (but there are exceptions; see Ortiz 1969 and Stephen 1936).

In the architectural literature, things are worse for the opposite reason. Many architectural investigations of traditional architecture tend to examine one relationship, perhaps with climate, solar energy, available resources, or art forms (Fitch and Branch 1970; Anderson 1977; Knowles 1974), making little reference to a broader framework that includes environmental and sociocultural contexts.

The richest and deepest understandings of architectural form have come from rigorous explorations across disciplinary boundaries. Dennis Doxtater (1978), with his integration of architectural and cognitive anthropological approaches, is undertaking interesting work. Peter Nabokov is an applied anthropologist working toward interpretation of architecture (Nabokov 1986). My own work on world view and architecture and on the ritual making of home owes much to cultural anthropology and cultural geographers who have made interdisciplinary bridges (Saile 1981; 1985a; 1985b; Ortiz 1969; Tuan 1977).

Some themes that emerged from my earlier studies of Pueblo housebuilding may help tie together the foregoing descriptions of landscape, prehistoric architecture, and current villages. I examined records of rituals that were associated with stages in the construction and renovation of houses and other buildings, materials that had not been gathered together previously (Saile 1976).

Rituals accompanying house and kiva construction reiterated common ideas. There was a concern for cardinal directions and their "powers" and a recognition that built structure was "living" (Saile 1977b, 72–5) Persons directing the rituals or preparing ritual materials often held village positions connected with communication with spirits and supernatural beings. Prayers offered during house and kiva construction were for the strength of the building, for long life and health, for the fertility of people and their crops, and for rain.

Certain ideas were common to all villages (Dozier 1970, 203–9; Ortiz 1969; 1972). The world was constituted on three levels: upper and lower spiritual levels and the

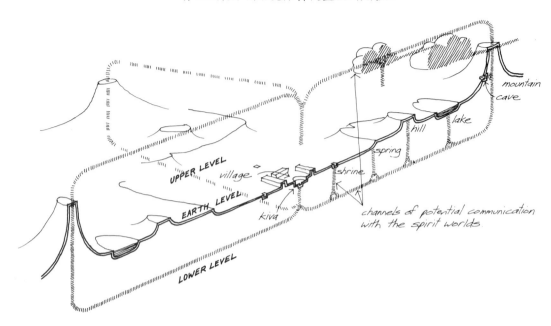

A SECTION THROUGH A PUEBLO WORLD

5-9 *A diagram of the network of communication with levels of the spirit world.*

earth lying between for the residence of people. Many irregularities in the earth's level provided places of possible contact with spirits. Mountains touched the sky and earth; springs and caves were potential passageways to the underworld. The origin myths of all Pueblos bore striking resemblances to each other and were related to this concept of world levels. The myths described the emergence from the lower world and the early travels of the first people and their guidance by supernatural beings. These myths gave significance not only to cardinal mountains, springs, colors, and animals but also to their sequence in ritual and prayer. Figure 5-9 shows a cross section through a generalized Pueblo world. Individual village schemes were more intricate and variable. The significance and power of the general model varied with specific landscapes, with the season, and with the constellation of supernaturals and first beings.

This background seemed to offer clues to the understanding of the places and purposes of construction rituals. Each building construction had to be "located" with respect to cardinal directions and their powers. Each house took its proper place in the world, becoming real and "endowed with a soul," a pattern that Mircea Eliade has shown to be common to many cultures (Eliade 1954, 20). Actions and material things possessed power and strength by following prescription, which was effective because it repeated the actions of the first beings and supernatural beings. Conversely, this prescription also embodied power and made it controllable and safer. It gave power a "house," which was more than a term for residence, kiva, or storehouse. Sun had his house in the sky during the day and in the earth at night. Spirits had their houses in clouds, rain, springs, mountains, and hills (Parsons 1939). Houses in this sense were not, then, mere places of habitation. They were also places of potential communication with the spiritual world, places where connections could be formed between the three cosmic levels. Although they might have been humble residences, village enclosures, or mountain peaks, these places have the character of "profound centres of human experience" (Ralph 1976, 43). They concentrated powers and meanings for the benefit of the humans who dwelt there.

A jump backward to the pit house may be instructive. In many pit houses a small floor hole existed near the axis of the house behind the fireplace. Few contained objects, although some were lined. Many were filled with clean sand or covered with clay. They are difficult to distinguish from post holes, pot-resting pits, or other holes. But their positions and care in their construction led many archaeologists to term them *sipapus* because of their similarity to counterparts in kivas. If they were *sipapus*, representations of the entrance to the underworld, if the below-ground position of special communal and ceremonial rooms was significant, then it is possible that the conceptual system of world levels and cardinal directions has existed in the Pueblo area for at least thirteen centuries.

Whatever their interpretive value, these studies of building rituals enriched by insiders' insights and tempered by struggles with materials and ideas in other disciplines made it possible to glimpse the intricacy and powerful significance of the structure of Pueblo spatial organization. It was possible to sense the ways in which Pueblo dwellings and ways of life were rooted in the places that have nurtured them.

Why these glimpses and sensings continue to move us is an important question. Architecture in the Pueblo world certainly has shown a resilience, at least for thirteen centuries, but it also has a resonance for *others* outside its original cultural contexts. One of the reasons for current reverberations may be a perceived need for a reappraisal of theory in the discipline of architecture. In times of theoretical reevaluation, architects seem to have looked more deeply for models in earlier building, demonstrating a desire to obtain significance and power through connection with first beings. In Joseph Rykwert's essay on the idea of the first hut in architectural history, he concludes: "The return to origins is a constant of human development and in this matter architecture conforms to all other human activities" (Rykwert 1972, 192). The resonance of Pueblo architecture and landscape may be due to the sharing of some fundamental and recurring patterns in human dwelling.

REFERENCES

ANDERSON, KAJ BLEGVAD. 1977. *African Traditional Architecture*. Nairobi: Oxford University.

BRYAN, KIRK. 1954. "The Geology of Chaco Canyon, New Mexico, in Relation to the Life and Remains of the Prehistoric Peoples of Pueblo Bonito." *Smithsonian Miscellaneous Collections* 122(7):1–65.

BULLARD, WILLIAM R., JR. 1962. "The Cerro Colorado Site and Pithouse Architecture in the Southwestern United States Prior to A.D. 900." *Papers of the Peabody Museum of Archaeology and Ethnology* 44(2).

BUNTING, BAINBRIDGE. 1976. *Early Architecture in New Mexico*. Albuquerque: University of New Mexico.

DEAN, JEFFREY S. 1969. "Chronological Analysis of Tsegi Phase Sites in Northeastern Arizona." *Papers of the Laboratory of Tree-Ring Research* 3.

DOXTATER, DENNIS. 1978. "The Hopi Ritual Landscape." Paper read at the 11th Annual Archaeological Conference, 1978, at the University of Calgary.

DOZIER, EDWARD P. 1970. *The Pueblo Indians of North America*. New York: Holt, Rinehart and Winston.

ELIADE, MIRCEA. 1954. *The Myth of the Eternal Return*. Transl. W. R. Trask. Princeton; N.J.: Princeton University Press.

FITCH, JAMES MARSTON, AND DANIEL P. BRANCH. 1970. "Primitive Architecture and Climate." *Scientific American* 203(6):134–44.

FRASER, DOUGLAS. 1968. *Village Planning in the Primitive World*. New York: Braziller.

GOLDFRANK, ESTHER S. 1945. "Socialization, Personality, and the Structure of Pueblo Society." *American Anthropologist* 47(4):516–39.

GUIDONI, ENRICO. 1978. *Primitive Architecture*. Transl. R. E. Wolf. New York: Harry N. Abrams.

HACK, JOHN T. 1942. "The Changing Physical Environment of the Hopi Indians of Arizona." *Papers of the Peabody Museum of American Archaeology and Ethnology* 35(1).

HALE, KENNETH, AND DAVID HARRIS. 1979. "Historical Linguistics and Archeology." In: *Handbook of North American Indians*, vol. 9, ed. Alfonso Ortiz, 170–7. Washington, D.C.: Smithsonian Institution Press.

HAYES, ALDEN C., AND JAMES A. LANCASTER. 1975. "Badger House Community, Mesa Verde National Park, Colorado." *Publications in Archaeology* 7-E. Washington D.C.: National Park Service.

JOHNSON, M., AND D. JOHNSON. 1971. "The Anasazi Great House." *Perspecta* 13/14:366–71.

KNOWLES, RALPH L. 1974. *Energy and Form*. Cambridge, Mass.: M.I.T. Press.

LEKSON, STEPHEN H. 1986. *Great Pueblo Architecture of Chaco Canyon, New Mexico*. Albuquerque: University of New Mexico Press.

_____, THOMAS C. WINDES, JOHN R. STEIN, AND W. JAMES JUDGE. 1988. "The Chaco Canyon Community." *Scientific American* July 1988:100–9.

LINTON, RALPH. 1944. "Nomad Raids and Fortified Pueblos." *American Antiquity* 10(1):28–32.

McGUIRE, RANDALL H., AND MICHAEL B. SCHIFFER. 1983. "A Theory of Architectural Design." *Journal of Anthropological Archaeology* 2:277–303.

McINTIRE, ELLIOT GREGOR. 1968. "The Impact of Cultural Change on the Land Use Patterns of the Hopi Indians." Unpublished Ph.D. Dissertation, Department of Geography, University of Oregon.

MINDELEFF, VICTOR. 1891. "A Study of Pueblo Architecture: Tusayan and Cibola." *Bureau of Ethnology 8th Annual Report 1886–87*:3–228. Washington, D.C.: Smithsonian Institution Press.

NABOKOV, PETER. 1986. *Architecture of Acoma Pueblo*. Santa Fe: Ancient City Press.

ORTIZ, ALFONSO. 1969. *The Tewa World. Space, Time, Being, and Becoming in a Pueblo Society*. Chicago: University of Chicago Press.

_____. 1972. "Ritual Drama and the Pueblo World View." In: *New Perspectives on the Pueblos*, ed. Alfonso Ortiz, 135–61. Albuquerque: School of American Research, University of New Mexico.

PARSONS, ELSIE CLEWS. 1939. *Pueblo Indian Religion*. 2 vols. Chicago: University of Chicago Press.

RALPH, E. 1976. *Place and Placeness*. London: Pion.

ROHN, ARTHUR H. 1971. "Mug House. Mesa Verde National Park, Colorado." *Publications in Archaeology* 7-D. Washington, D.C.: National Park Service.

RYKWERT, JOSEPH. 1972. *On Adam's House in Paradise*. New York: Museum of Modern Art.

SAILE, DAVID G. 1976. "Pueblo Building Rituals." Unpublished manuscript, Arizona State Museum Library.

_____. 1977a. "Architecture in Prehispanic Pueblo Archaeology; Examples from Chaco Canyon, New Mexico." *World Archaeology* 9(2):157–73.

_____. 1977b. "Making a House: Building Rituals and Spatial Concepts in the Pueblo Indian World." *Architectural Association Quarterly* 9(2/3):72–81.

————. 1981. "Architecture in the Pueblo World." Unpublished Ph.D. dissertation, School of Architecture, University of Newcastle upon Tyne, United Kingdom.

————. 1985a. "Many Dwellings: Views of a Pueblo World." In: *Dwelling, Place, and Environment*, ed. Robert Mugerauer and David Seamon, 159–81. The Hague: Martinus Nijhoff.

————. 1985b. "The Ritual Establishment of Home." In: *Home Environments. Human Behavior and Environment*, vol. 8, ed. Irwin Altman and Carol Werner, 87–111. New York: Plenum.

SCHROEDER, ALBERT H. 1979. "Pueblos Abandoned in Historic Times." In: *Handbook of North American Indians*, vol. 9, ed. Alfonso Ortiz, 236–54. Washington, D.C.: Smithsonian Institution Press.

SCULLY, VINCENT. 1975. *Pueblo. Mountain, Village, Dance*. New York: Viking.

SPICER, EDWARD H. 1962. *Cycles of Conquest*. Tucson: University of Arizona Press.

STEPHEN, ALEXANDER M. 1936. *Hopi Journal*, ed. E. C. Parsons, *Columbia University Contributions to Anthropology*, vol. 23, two parts.

THOMPSON, LAURA. 1945. "Logico—Aesthetic Integration in Hopi Culture." *American Anthropologist* 47(4):540–53.

TUAN, YI-FU. 1977. *Space and Place. The Perspective of Experience*. Minneapolis: University of Minnesota Press.

WHITELEY, PETER. 1988. *Bacavi. Journey to Reed Springs*. Flagstaff, Ariz.: Northland.

WILCOX, DAVID R. 1975. "A Strategy for Perceiving Social Groups in Puebloan Sites." *Fieldiana: Anthropology* 65:120–59.

6 The Great Pueblo Period in Southwestern Archaeology

Stephen H. Lekson

The Pueblo style derives much of its content from ruins. More money and effort have gone into the study of the ruins of the Southwest than into that of any other comparable region of the United States. It may seem that we know all we need to know about these ruins, and, indeed, we do know a lot about where and when; but questions of who, what, and why are still very open. Archaeology is still developing in both content and technique, and in this chapter I present some new ideas about the archaeology of the Great Pueblo period.

The Pueblos provide the living models, but the huge ruins of Chaco Canyon and Mesa Verde are the archetypes of the Pueblo style. Chaco and Mesa Verde, in the Four Corners area of the American Southwest, thrived during the three centuries A.D. 1000–1300; this is the era that archaeologists call the Great Pueblo period. When the term was first used in the 1920s, "great" seemed appropriate because Chaco and Mesa Verde appeared to be the peak of Pueblo building; the stage before Great Pueblo was termed Developmental Pueblo (A.D. 700–1000), and the stage following, when the Four Corners area was abandoned, was termed Regressive Pueblo (A.D. 1300–1600). With additional work in post-1300 Pueblo prehistory, we have come to see that the pejorative "regressive" is incorrect. Migration from the Four Corners heartland to the areas of the modern Pueblos did not entail any diminution of cultural or architectural vigor.

Still, we look back to Chaco and Mesa Verde as the places where it all began. Before the Great Pueblo period, the ancestors of the modern Pueblos, called by archaeologists the Anasazi, lived in semisubterranean pit houses and ephemeral part-masonry, part-wattle structures of no more than six or seven rooms. The first buildings that we would recognize as Pueblo style—with hundreds of rooms, terraced from five stories down to one and massed around a central plaza—were built at Chaco Canyon at the very beginning of the Great Pueblo period. Buildings in this style subsequently appeared over most of the Anasazi areas.

When writing about Anasazi ruins, we walk a thin line between the spectacular and the mundane. Movies and books about Chaco Canyon and Mesa Verde use words like "astonishing," "astounding," "monumental," and—my favorite—"staggering." Much of the popular literature treats the buildings of Chaco Canyon and Mesa Verde as though they were the Pyramids. But on a world scale of spectacle, where the Vatican, the Forbidden City, and Disneyland are near the top, Anasazi building is somewhere near the bottom. The engineering and labor that went into the Great Pueblo ruins are often described as "astonishing" and "staggering," respectively; but truly they are not. Anasazi building was sufficient to its purpose, and not much more. Even the most elaborate stone masonry, as at Chaco Canyon, was more a practice of patience than of skill (fig. 6-1). Claims of structural ingenuity and masterly craftsmanship have a condescending ring: what clever little Indians to be able to stack up all those rocks! Like every human society of which we have knowledge, the Anasazi were perfectly capable of effecting operations considerably more complex than those of daily subsistence. Their architectural achievements were real, and we respond to them with fascination and even awe; but they were not in any objective sense extraordinary (Lekson 1986).

64

6-1 *Pueblo Bonito, Chaco Canyon, N. Mex.*

It is important to keep Anasazi building in a realistic perspective. But the normalizing view, a reaction to southwestern hyperbole, carries its own dangers. We deromanticize inherently romantic ruins by making them boring. When you view ruins in the various parks in the Southwest, the story is nearly always the same: The Anasazi were conservative; they were grimly religious; they were self-sufficient farmers. The Anasazi had no government; they had no armies. They never changed. They were, in a catechism memorized by generations of tour guides and rangers, a happy, peaceful people who lived in harmony with their environment.

The idea of "happy, peaceful people" is a half-baked stereotype of the modern Pueblos. History tells us that this simple-minded characterization is untrue of the modern Pueblos (Ortiz 1979); prehistory shows it to be false for the Anasazi, too. We have an archaeological and historical record of 1500 years of dynamic *change* in the Southwest. The Anasazi world was almost perpetually out of balance; the need to be in careful harmony with the environment, in fact, may be fairly recent, the result of the modern world impinging upon the native Southwest and fixing its fluid elements in place.

The modern Pueblos are part of the modern world; indeed they are distal elements of the European colonial system (Wallerstein 1974; Wolf 1982). Centuries of remarkable mobility, attested to by both archaeology and the Pueblos' own migration stories, ended with Spanish conquest. The Pueblos were pinned down within formally defined land grants, like so many butterflies on a mounting board. Huge areas of wild resources that had been needed around each Pueblo settlement—for the Pueblos and their Anasazi ancestors were as much hunter-gatherers as they were farmers—was soon filled with Spanish settlers and non-Pueblo natives (Ferguson and Hart 1985). Terrible plagues of European diseases decimated the densely settled Pueblos, while neighboring nomadic groups, protected by their scattered life-styles, suffered far less (Ramenofsky 1987). Religious persecution forced Pueblo ceremony literally underground; it is likely that kivas, the remarkable subterranean ceremonial structures of modern Pueblos, acquired much of their ritual secrecy as a response to Spanish religious oppression.

Indeed, many Pueblo traditions may have achieved their remarkable tenacity precisely in response to the Spanish threat. This statement is not a contentious denial of Pueblo traditionalism. Remember that the Spanish arrived almost four centuries ago, so Pueblo responses to Spain would, today, represent traditions of greater antiquity than our Constitution or European settlement over most of the eastern seaboard. But traditions have to start somewhere, and traditionalism—the inherent conservatism of the modern Pueblos—may not have been the Anasazi way. Anasazi iconography shows a remarkable series of shifts (as well as continuities) in the archaeological record; the fixity of Pueblo symbolism and ceremony from the very latest prehistory through the Spanish period stands in contrast to the record of change over the preceding millennium (See, for example, Shaafsma 1980; Adams 1988).

That the Pueblos survived European conquest, which destroyed so many other Native American groups, is both remarkable and inspiring. But their preservation may be, to some extent, like that of flies in amber. The Spanish conquest devastated the Pueblos; for what was left, the evolution so evident in the Anasazi archaeological record was effectively halted.

Europe's impact on the Pueblos was profound, but it was matched by several other climactic events in prehistory. The Chacoan collapse of 1150 and the abandonment of the Four Corners area about 1300 probably had as significant an impact on Anasazi development as did the Spanish conquest on the Pueblos. Indeed, 1300 is a major chasm in southwestern prehistory, separating the Great Pueblo period's Anasazi ruins from their Pueblo descendants. The earliest archaeologists took it as their task to bridge that gap.

Archaeology, in one form or another, has been going on in the Southwest for well over a century. The pioneer archaeologists, in the 1870s and 1880s, were a brilliant, intuitive group, but they had no special set of methods that ensured that any of their conclusions were correct or accurate. And, indeed, many of the details (the dating of this ruin, the origin of that pottery type) were simply erroneous, as we should expect in the early stages of any field of study. Differences in detail are easy to recognize and correct; more fundamental errors can survive simply because they are buried so deeply in the structure of archaeological thinking. Some questionable but basic ideas of the early archaeologists survive, enshrined in textbooks and lecture notes. They are validated by infinite repetition but are unsupported by objective science.

In effect, archaeologists created their own myths about the Great Pueblo ruins and then communicated those myths to other interested fields—among them, architecture. This chapter will attempt to demythologize Anasazi building by tracing the motives of the early archaeologists and evaluating the basis of the Great Pueblo period.

POLITICS AND PREHISTORY

The archaeologists who first reached the Southwest in the late 1800s were part of an intellectual reaction—in fact, a revulsion—to the genocide that accompanied the westward expansion of the United States. Too late, we realized that we had eliminated hundreds of Native American groups as the frontier moved west. This reaction was by no means general; only a small group of anthropologists, historians, archaeologists, and concerned intellectuals realized the enormity of that loss and moved to salvage what they could from the wreck.

The Southwest beckoned. In the Southwest, native peoples had survived, in part because Spanish colonial policy was one of incorporation of native peoples within a class system and not the Jacksonian policy of removal. And too, in the turn-of-the-century Southwest, the Pueblos offered both an opportunity for study and a chance to actively help a beleaguered people survive. (The history that follows is more fully presented in Lekson 1988.)

By the late 1800s, the Pueblos had survived three centuries of Spanish colonization and Mexican administration. The United States acquired New Mexico in 1849. The Pueblos were something of an anomaly in our experience, in that they had written title to their lands (which included most of the prime arable land in northern New Mexico) through Spanish land grants—grants we had promised to honor in the Treaty of Guadelupe Hidalgo. Land grants worked both for and against the Pueblos. Initially, they prevented outright removal of the Pueblos from lands coveted by the new Anglo colonists; but later, when the U.S. Supreme Court ruled that Pueblo land grants were real estate and not reservations, a small army of land grabbers moved to acquire Pueblo lands through squatting, high-pressure purchase, and fraud. Eventually, over 3000 non-Pueblo claims on Pueblo lands were recorded—a situation that would not have been possible on the legally protected lands of a reservation. The Pueblos were in jeopardy.

Pueblo architecture played a major role in the ethical (and legal) defense of Pueblo lands. We had removed or eliminated tribe after tribe of thatched hut villagers and tent nomads, but the Pueblos built buildings that looked very much like our own. Indeed, Pueblos such as Taos were very much larger buildings than could be found in contemporary East Coast cities. The moral justifications for Anglo Manifest Destiny began to look pretty weak. How could we manipulate a people who built bigger buildings than we did?

The answer to that was simple: the Pueblos were not the originators of their own architecture but mere copyists of a vanished race, probably Aztecs, who had built the huge structures now in ruin at Chaco Canyon and Mesa Verde. Long after the Aztecs left, the Pueblo people stumbled upon these northern Aztec ruins and succeeded in building smaller and less sophisticated copies along the Rio Grande. In the mid- and late-1800s, the Aztecs were very much in vogue, thanks to Prescott's enormously popular *History of the Conquest of Mexico*. An Aztec origin for Mesa Verde and Chaco was quite acceptable; the Aztecs themselves said they came from the north. By making Pueblo architecture a second-hand copy of Aztec greatness, a major moral stumbling block for standard expanding frontier treatment was eliminated.

The first archaeologists in the Southwest had a very explicit political goal: Restore the Pueblo patrimony. They worked to prove that the Great Pueblo ruins at Chaco and Mesa Verde were in fact ancestral to the modern Pueblos and not the remains of long-departed Aztecs. In so doing, the early archaeologists not only corrected a major historical error but also helped to prevent the imminent loss of Pueblo lands.

After a long series of congressional and legal battles, which continued into the 1930s, Pueblo lands were granted reservation status, and non-Pueblo claims were disallowed. This happy conclusion was, to a very large degree, the result of intense lobbying by various friends of the Pueblos (women's clubs, business organizations, and the artistic community in Santa Fe and Taos). The main ammunition of this campaign was moral outrage over our despoliation of the Pueblo peoples, *who had lived in the Southwest forever*. The early archaeologists could take credit for the expert opinions upon which this moral argument was based.

They could also take the blame for starting Southwestern archaeology off, not on the wrong foot—for who could fault their motives?—but perhaps in the wrong direction. By advocating great antiquity for the Pueblo way of life, the early archaeologists inculcated a strategy in Southwestern archaeology of projecting the present back into the past. All prehistoric sites were interpreted, in a very straightforward way, as Pueblo; the modern Pueblos were the first and sufficient source for evaluating archaeological discoveries.

KIVAS OR PIT HOUSES?

A classic example of how this approach worked to the detriment of understanding the past is the kiva—the remarkable subterranean structure seen at almost all pueblos, housing male ceremonial societies that cross-cut kin and clan and keeping the loose Pueblo social fabric from unraveling (fig. 6-2). Kivas are the architectural expression of a particularly strong social glue that integrates inherently disparate village social structures.

Kivas were the star witness of the early archaeologists in proving the antiquity of the pueblos in the Southwest. Recall that formal similarity, alone, between the modern pueblos and the Great Pueblo period ruins would not be sufficient. The foes of the Pueblos could claim that superficial similarity was simply the result of Pueblo copying of earlier Aztec construction. What was needed was an architectural element so unique to Pueblo life that it could not be the result of imitation. That element was the kiva. Early archaeologists saw dozens of subterranean, masonry-walled, round rooms at Mesa Verde and Chaco Canyon; most of these had fire pits, benches, and other odd furniture that resembled the esoteric features of modern kivas. The round rooms of the Great Pueblo period were naturally assumed to be the same thing as the kivas of the modern Pueblos. Kivas were one of the most important links in the chain of argument proving that the Great Pueblo ruins were ancestral to modern pueblos, and they played an important part in the eventual defeat of the forces attempting to grab Pueblo lands.

The early archaeologists very consciously projected from the present back into the past. This kind of argument is teleological, in a retroactive way. When you search for the origins of something in the past, you are sure to find something you can call the original—particularly in archaeology, where the mute stones cannot speak in their own defense. There is another way of looking at the round rooms—the so-called kivas—of the Great Pueblo period that turns the search for origins more or less on its head: that is to see the round rooms not as the forerunners of kivas but as the continuation of the centuries-old Anasazi domestic structure the pit house.

We know that the Anasazi lived in pit houses—semisubterranean, single-room, earth-roofed, units—from at least A.D. 400 on (fig. 6-3). We know that over time pit structures became more formal and more elaborate; I am suggesting that this process continued until A.D. 1300 and that all the small "kivas" we see at Mesa Verde and Chaco Canyon are, in fact, simply the last stage in this history of formalization and elaboration of pit houses.

The received wisdom holds that a major transition from pit house to pueblo occurred about A.D. 700 or 800. Before that, everyone lived exclusively in pit houses; after that, everyone moved above ground into pueblos and the pit houses became kivas. This view does not make a whole lot of sense, except in the historical context of the search for kiva origins. Recall that archaeologists had already decided that pit structures after 800 or so were actually early kivas. And any above-ground living during pit-house times would make this transition unmanageably fuzzy. So to posit a radical shift from pit house to pueblo, we had to assume that when people lived in pit houses they lived *only* in pit houses.

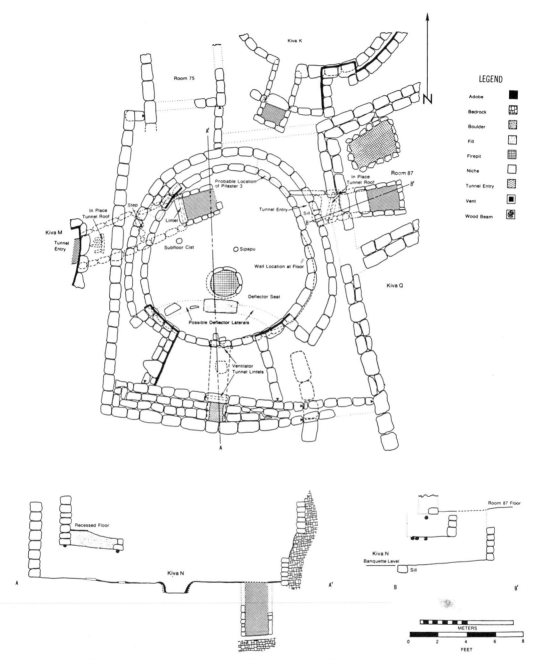

6-2 *Pueblo III kiva at Long House, Mesa Verde National Park, Colo. (From George S. Cattanach Jr., "Long House", National Park Service Publications in Archaeology 7H, Government Printing Office, Washington, D.C., figure 89.)*

We know this is not true. When we excavate behind and around pit houses, we find many hearths, work areas, plaza surfaces, and post holes that represent the remains of ramadas—open-walled post-and-beam structures. Pit-house dwellers probably did most of their chores (and spent most of their idle time) under ramadas—outside the pit houses but still in structures that we must regard as architecture. Instead of a radical

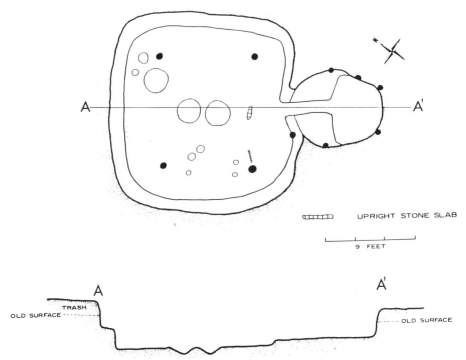

UPRIGHT STONE SLAB

9 FEET

6-3 *Pit houses at Badger House site, Mesa Verde National Park, Colo. (From Alden C. Hayes and James A. Lancaster,* "Badger House Community", National Park Service Publications in Archaeology 7E, *Government Printing Office, Washington, D.C., figure 13.)*

shift from a troglodyte existence in pit houses to above-ground living in pueblos, the record shows a gradual development of *both* pit-house and above-grade building, beginning with fairly crude pit houses and ramadas and ending, in the Great Pueblo period, with six- or seven-room masonry "pueblos" and a masonry-lined, fairly elaborate pit house that we are accustomed to calling a kiva. The largest Great Pueblo sites, like most of the Mesa Verde cliff dwellings (fig. 6-4), are simply aggregates of these little units, with fifteen or twenty seven-rooms-and-a-pit house units crammed into a huge sandstone alcove. Viewed from this perspective, the would-be kiva is just another room in the basic domestic unit, like a parlor in a Victorian home.

In my opinion, the many round rooms that are often called "kivas" in Great Pueblo period sites are nothing of the kind. Consider the room-to-kiva ratio at modern pueblos. This ratio varies, but generally there are scores or even hundreds of rooms for each modern Pueblo kiva. This ratio corresponds well to the function of modern kivas: the architectural embodiment of rituals that help integrate large Pueblo villages. Prior to 1300 (that is, during the Great Pueblo period), there were usually only seven to nine rooms per "kiva." Seven rooms is not a village, it's a house. What, precisely, is being integrated within the household?

There are some exceptionally large Great Pueblo sites at Chaco Canyon that do have hundreds of rooms per kiva. Rather than assuming the higher ratios at a few Great Pueblo period sites at Chaco as evidence of pit houses becoming kivas, I think it is more realistic to look at the pueblo rooms themselves. Are all those hundreds of rooms the same as the domestic rooms in the traditional Anasazi seven-room house? Were the big structures at Chaco early versions of pueblos? The evidence suggests, pretty convincingly, that they were not.

CHACO CANYON: ORIGINS OF THE PUEBLO STYLE?

Archaeologists at Chaco Canyon in the early 1900s—George Pepper, Neil Judd, and Edgar Hewett—all saw the huge ruins as early versions of modern pueblos. Intense professional rivalries within this small group led each archaeologist to limit his interpretive horizons to his own ruin. Judd wrote his reports about Pueblo Bonito, while Hewett confined himself to Chetro Ketl. While each was aware of the other huge ruins that crowded the central Chaco Canyon area, the density of architecture in "downtown" Chaco was obscured by the archaeologists' insistence that each ruin was an individual

6-4 *Cliff Palace, Mesa Verde National Park, Colorado. (From Jesse Walter Fewkes, "Antiquities of the Mesa Verde National Park, Cliff Palace", Bureau of American Ethnology Bulletin 51, Government Printing Office, Washington, D.C. plate 8.)*

Chaco Canyon

0   0,5   1,0
K M

6-5 *Schematic plan of central Chaco Canyon. Large squares represent great houses, small squares represent unit pueblos.*

pueblo, the same as the modern Zuni, Acoma, or Taos pueblos, and understandable as a separate unit (fig. 6-5).

For decades, this myopic perspective obscured one of the most complex archaeological puzzles in the Southwest. Rather than a series of autonomous Pueblo-like villages, the great ruins of Chaco Canyon are in fact parts of a much larger complex, a settlement of almost urban complexity. A rectangular precinct of over a square mile, outlined by a low wall, formed the center. Within this central area, half a dozen huge structures like Pueblo Bonito, Pueblo Alto, Pueblo del Arroyo, and Chetro Ketl were connected by wide, formal paths we call roadways. Platform mounds and other forms of public architecture were conspicuous; scores of smaller, more traditional Anasazi units clustered along the base of the canyon wall; much, perhaps most, of the central canyon area was architectural or artificial. From this center, more Chacoan roadways radiated out in all directions for hundreds of miles, connecting Chaco with numerous "outlier" communities—dozens of small Anasazi units clustered around miniature versions of Pueblo Bonito or Chetro Ketl. There are over 100 such outlier communities known, and more are being discovered every year (Lekson et al. 1988).

The largest buildings at Chaco Canyon are something of an enigma. Parts of these structures were certainly used as residences, but we believe that most of the many hundreds of rooms that make up a site like Pueblo Bonito were not domestic, at least in the same way the rooms of a small Anasazi seven-room house were domestic. Their true function is still a matter of debate; the likeliest explanation is that the hundreds of empty rooms represent an enormous amount of storage space—far in excess of the floor area required for the two-year food surplus Pueblo peoples always try to maintain—-for a regionwide food bank or a central trading center.

Archaeologists have developed many other arguments about Chaco, but they are too numerous and too complex to summarize here. The common characteristic of almost all discussions of Great Pueblo period building at Chaco is this: These structures are *not* simply early versions of modern pueblos, like Zuni or Taos, but something considerably more complex, in both architecture and function, than the autonomous, egalitarian pueblos we know today (Lekson 1987). Socially and politically, Chaco may have been the most complex achievement of the Anasazi—ultimately, a development that failed.

Sites like Pueblo Bonito and Chetro Ketl (fig. 6-6), which were almost certainly not "pueblos" in any useful sense, are the archetypes of the Pueblo style. We will return to

6-6 *Chetro Ketl, Chaco Canyon, N. Mex.*

the implications of this conundrum at the conclusion of the chapter. But archaeology at Chaco Canyon had another very significant effect on why we see the Great Pueblo period as the origin of the Pueblo style: this was the deep time-depth evidenced at the Chaco Canyon sites.

ROOTS REVISIONISM: PERMANENCE IN THE GREAT PUEBLO PERIOD

Recall that one of the defenses of the Pueblo lands was that the Pueblos had occupied those lands for a very long time—the Pueblos had been there forever. One of the most impressive things about Pueblo architecture is its time-depth. Oriabi and Acoma may have been occupied since prehistoric times; many of the other pueblos have histories of two or even three centuries. Archaeologists assumed that Great Pueblo period sites had similarly deep roots. The imputation of great time-depth for Great Pueblo period ruins follows the same logic as the more specific case of kivas. The ruins *looked* like pueblos; therefore the ruins should be expected to share all the qualities of pueblos, including great permanence. The ruins of Chaco Canyon suggested, very persuasively, that great time-depth was a tradition beginning in the Great Pueblo period. (The arguments in this section are presented at greater length in Lekson 1989.)

When archaeologists began excavating Southwestern ruins, they had no way to tell during what calendar years they were originally occupied. It was well established that the Great Pueblo period was pre-Hispanic, but by how many years was anybody's guess. All this changed in the 1930s when scientists discovered how to tell, to the year, when trees had been cut and used as roof beams. By determining the earliest and latest dates at a ruin, archaeologists could tell when, and for how long, that site had been occupied. Tree-ring dating revolutionized southwestern archaeology, and Chaco Canyon played a very important part in the early development of this technique.

Because the big ruins at Chaco were built so very massively, preservation of wooden roof beams was extraordinarily good. In fact, many roofs were still perfectly intact. Well-preserved wood was a magnet during the early days of tree-ring dating, and as a result Pueblo Bonito and Chetro Ketl were the first really well-dated sites in the Southwest. Indeed, Chetro Ketl still holds the distinction of having the most tree-ring dates of any Anasazi ruin (Lekson 1983).

The dates from Chaco showed that Pueblo Bonito and Chetro Ketl were built and remodeled over many decades—almost two and one half centuries in the case of Pueblo Bonito (Lekson 1986). This seemed to confirm the archaeologists' expectations for great time-depth of Great Pueblo period ruins. By reasonable inference, Great Pueblo sites outside of Chaco (which had not been dated) were also assumed to have similar time-depths. After all, all these Anasazi sites were simply early versions of the modern pueblos, were they not?

Unfortunately, the Chaco sites were not; I have discussed, above, the evidence that suggests that Chaco was unusual, even unique, in Anasazi prehistory. The very massive construction of Pueblo Bonito and Chetro Ketl, which preserved the wooden beams, was also responsible for their thorough dating at the very beginnings of the development of the tree-ring dating technique. But this first sample of Great Pueblo period tree-ring dates was an unfortunate one: the Chaco ruins were nearly unique among the Great Pueblo sites in their long construction histories.

The remarkable preservation at cliff dwellings, such as those at Mesa Verde, also results in good preservation of wood. Cliff dwellings are thus among the better-dated Great Pueblo period sites outside of Chaco Canyon. All the well-dated cliff dwelling sites appear to have been built, occupied, and abandoned in under 50 years. In most cases, this span was as short as 25 or 30 years, a single generation.

A single generation seems like a very short time for use and abandonment of large masonry structures. We associate masonry and large size with expense and permanence. But recall my earlier point that none of these sites were the Pyramids. Analysis of the labor required for the Chaco Canyon sites—by far the most "costly" Anasazi construction—demonstrated that no more complex organization of labor was required than the modern Pueblos employ for their annual irrigation ditch maintenance (Lekson 1986)—a significant amount of work, but not requiring gangs of slaves. Most Great Pueblo period sites are much less substantial than the Chaco Canyon sites.

Some of the largest Great Pueblo period sites are to be found near Zuni Pueblo. Some structures have up to 1000 rooms and appear to have been built to a plan; at least, they were begun with a massive enclosing wall and then completed by infilling room blocks. Yet even these huge sites appear to have been used for a comparatively short time. None are well dated, but our best estimate for even these huge sites is about a generation (Kintigh 1985).

With the exception of the remarkable buildings at Chaco, Great Pueblo period sites did not have the great time-depth that we associate with the modern Pueblos. Instead, there is an evident pattern of movement on a generational interval. Mobility is surprising if we carry expectations from the modern Pueblos back to the Great Pueblo period. But if we look at the earlier Anasazi world we see that mobility in the Great Pueblo period actually continued mobile settlement patterns of the preceding eight or nine centuries of the Anasazi. The useful life of a pit house was limited by physical constraints: the main structural members of the pit-house roof rotted after 10 or 15 years. During the early pit-house stage, movement (on some scale) was nearly constant. Mobility may have meant a short move to another building site in the same settlement or migration to another valley. We are only beginning to understand the scale and magnitude of Anasazi mobility, but we do know that movement was the rule, not the exception.

SPECULATIVE PREHISTORY

We are building a very different view of the Great Pueblo period than archaeologists held 10 or even 5 years ago. In place of early versions of pueblos, with all the architectural elements and the deep permanence of the modern pueblo, we now see Great Pueblo period structures that were, in the case of Chaco, far more complex conceptions and others that were far less permanent than the modern pueblos.

A speculative reconstruction of the Great Pueblo period (A.D. 1000–1300) incorporating these new views of its archaeology must actually begin in the early 900s. Over most of the Anasazi area, the ancestors of the modern Pueblos lived in pit-house villages or in pit-house-and-seven-room masonry units. In Chaco Canyon, a radical departure from this widespread Anasazi pattern signaled the beginnings of the Great Pueblo period and of the Pueblo style. At three sites in Chaco Canyon (Penasco Blanco, Pueblo Bonito, and Una Vida), the basic Anasazi ground plan was scaled up by a factor of 5 or 6, and second and third stories were added, terraced from the rear of these structures down to an enclosed plaza. The Pueblo style began in the early 900s, but for quite a while only these three sites shared the style. Thus the Great Pueblo period does not begin at A.D. 900 but considerably later when Great Pueblo construction appeared over much more of the Anasazi area.

A century passed. Internal developments in the canyon led to the creation of a huge regional network centered on Chaco. The first clear indications of this expansion appear, apparently suddenly, in the early part of the eleventh century A.D. (but evidence for continuous development from the 900s on may lie buried in the unexcavated ruins at Chaco). Gradual or sudden, once Chaco took off it developed with remarkable rapidity; by 1100, almost all of the Anasazi area was incorporated into its regional system (Lekson et al. 1988). We do not yet understand the nature of that system, but the geographic extent of roadways and "outliers" is compelling evidence that it was large and pervasive. A huge area, from Mesa Verde on the north to Zuni on the south and from the upper Rio Grande on the east to the Hopi mesas on the west, focused inward on the remarkable center at Chaco Canyon. The Chaco system dominated the first half of the Great Pueblo period, characterized by massive Chacoan buildings, "outlier" communities, great kivas, roadways, mounds, and what appear to be other forms of formal public buildings.

About 1150, Chaco collapsed. The energy from whatever had happened at Chaco radiated outwards toward what previously had been the peripheries of the regional system. Mesa Verde, the Zuni area, the upper Rio Grande, and the Kayenta area (around the Hopi mesas) all experienced remarkable development between 1150 and 1300. This was the second half of the Great Pueblo period, the era of cliff dwellings and the 1000-room Zuni sites. Gone, apparently, were the roadways (at least on a regional scale). Settlements were large but surprisingly impermanent. This period was marked by a great deal of mobility, but the geographic scale of movement was more restricted than in the Chaco era. Around the peripheries of the old Chaco system, each area began to take on its own regional cast, beginning ceramic and architectural traditions that we can trace to the Rio Grande, Zuni, and Hopi Pueblos; but one more major disjuncture was to come, which signaled the end of the Great Pueblo period in 1300.

For reasons that are not entirely understood (but which included a severe drought), most of the Four Corners area was abandoned about 1300. There was a major migration; the population of the Mesa Verde area was probably over 30,000 (Rohn 1986), and Mesa Verde was only one (although the most populous) of the districts that were abandoned at this time. These people went to the upper Rio Grande, the Zuni area, and the Hopi mesas. Displacement and immigration on this scale must have had a profound effect on social organization, economy, and almost every facet of Anasazi life. After the dust settled in the late 1300s and 1400s, we begin to see evidence of the kinds of social developments that culminated in the modern Pueblos; but the gap at 1300 is very real, and projecting modern Pueblo practices back across it is dangerous business.

SOME CAVEATS

Great Pueblo period structures were probably very different kinds of buildings than those of Taos or Zuni. Despite their formal and technological similarities to the later pueblos, the Great Pueblo structures had very different use-lives, different functions, and different histories. It is important to realize that the archetypes of the Pueblo style may not have been pueblos in any conceptually useful sense.

Of course, the ruins of the Great Pueblo period are arresting and interesting objects, but they can be only objects—empty forms—without the infusion of function. What were these buildings really used for? Anyone can speculate on the answer to that question; ruins invite speculation.

Archaeology is a set of methods for moving away from speculation and into increasingly rigorous strategies of proof. It tries to study what actually happened, not what *we want to think* happened. Some people want Pueblo Bonito to be a king's palace. Others want Pueblo Bonito to be like Taos or Zuni. There is a big difference between a royal palace and Zuni Pueblo; and, as it turns out, Pueblo Bonito was probably neither. We must let Pueblo Bonito have a say in all this and allow ourselves to be surprised by what it might tell us.

As archaeological methods are refined and new techniques are developed and our basic knowledge grows, we eliminate old theories and replace them with new ones that better fit the facts. Just as the old term Regressive Pueblo was discarded as our knowledge of the post-Great Pueblo era increased, so too the ideas I have presented will be eventually superseded. I suspect, however, that the developing picture of the Great Pueblo period will become even less like the old stereotype of "happy, peaceful people" and more like the dynamic record of change—vibrant change that seems so evident in the archaeological record but so absent in our current thinking about the Pueblos and their Anasazi ancestors.

REFERENCES

ADAMS, E. CHARLES. 1988. "The Appearance, Evolution and Meaning of the Katsina Cult to the Prehispanic World of the Southwestern United States." Manuscript on file, Arizona State Museum, Tucson.

FERGUSON, T. J., AND E. RICHARD HART. 1985. *A Zuni Atlas.* Norman: University of Oklahoma Press.

KINTIGH, KEITH W. 1985. *Settlement, Subsistence, and Society in Late Zuni Prehistory.* Anthropology Papers of the University of Arizona No. 44. Tucson: University of Arizona Press.

LEKSON, STEPHEN H., ed. 1983. *The Architecture and Dendrochronology of Chetro Ketl, Chaco Canyon, New Mexico.* Reports of the Chaco Center 6. Albuquerque: National Park Service.

———. 1986. *Great Pueblo Architecture of Chaco Canyon, New Mexico.* Albuquerque: University of New Mexico Press.

———. 1987. "Great House Architecture of Chaco Canyon, New Mexico." *Archaeology* 40(3):22–9.

———. 1988. "The Idea of the Kiva in Anasazi Archaeology." *The Kiva* 53(3):213–34.

———. 1989. "Sedentism and Aggregation in Anasazi Archaeology." In: *Proceedings of the Southwest Symposium*, ed. Paul Minnis and Charles Redman. Boulder, Col.: Westview Press.

———, THOMAS C. WINDES, JOHN R. STEIN, AND W. JAMES JUDGE. 1988. "The Chaco Canyon Community." *Scientific American* 256(7):100–9.

ORTIZ, ALFONSO, ed. 1979. *Handbook of North American Indians: Southwest*, Vol. 9. Washington, D.C.: Smithsonian Institution Press.

RAMENSOFSKY, ANN F. 1987. *Vectors of Death: The Archaeology of European Contact.* Albuquerque: University of New Mexico Press.

ROHN, ARTHUR H. 1986. "Prehistoric Developments in the Mesa Verde Region." In: *Understanding the Anasazi of Mesa Verde and Hovenweep*, ed. David G. Noble, pp. 3–10. Santa Fe, N.M.: School of American Research.

SCHAAFSMA, POLLY, 1980. *Indian Rock Art of the Southwest.* Santa Fe: School of American Research.

WALLERSTEIN, IMMANUEL. 1974. *The Modern World System.* New York: Academic Press.

WOLF, ERIC R. 1982. *Europe and the People Without History.* Berkeley: University of California Press.

7 Modernization and Pueblo Lifeways: Isleta Pueblo

Theodore S. Jojola

As scholars have sought to examine the process of community development, many examples have been drawn from the Pueblos of the southwestern United States. Perhaps this inquiry has been a consequence of the fact that the traditions of the Pueblos were considered to have remained essentially intact. Due to their isolation, few influences have been identified that are considered to have impacted significantly upon the "traditional" character of the Pueblo archetypes.

Contrary to scholarly opinion, however, I will attempt to demonstrate how the Pueblo community has undergone significant change over relatively short spans of time. In many instances, the village and community forms have undergone substantial modification. Such changes, in turn, have been the result of new lifeway patterns that have emerged within the Pueblo societies.

It has been the adaptive behavior of the Pueblos that has kept their communities vital and progressive. This dynamism has been in evidence ever since their earliest recollections. For purposes of illustration, examples will be drawn from one Pueblo community, Isleta Pueblo.

THE MODERN VILLAGE OF ISLETA PUEBLO
Demographics and Geography

The main village of Isleta is situated barely 12 miles (20 minutes by automobile on the freeway) from the center of downtown Albuquerque, New Mexico. The reservation straddles the common boundary line between the counties of Valencia and Bernalillo. The reservation encompasses a rectangle of land approximately 10 by 25 miles.

All residential and agricultural lands adjoin the fertile waterways of the Rio Grande between what are presently designated the Rio communities of Belen, the Peralta Bosque, and the South Valley of Albuquerque. These suburban bedroom communities have seen rapid increases in population over the past 10 years. These increases are tied into the general growth patterns of the Albuquerque metropolitan area. Indeed, if it were not for the reservation lands of Isleta, the urbanization of the fertile middle Rio Grande valley would be even more pronounced. Today, this is exemplified by the abrupt change between the suburban and the rural that occurs on the boundaries of the reservation.

The population of Isleta in 1980 was 2397 and encompassed some 702 households.[1] This gives the pueblo third ranking in size among the nineteen pueblos in New Mexico. Only Zuni Pueblo and Laguna Pueblo are larger. The population has remained essentially the same since 1960, although there has been a gradual upward shift in the proportion of non-Indian members within the Isleta households. This is the result of intermarriage. Non-Indians living within the community are estimated to comprise approximately 18 percent of the total population.

Social Community

Isleta Pueblo is a modern Pueblo community with a distinctive set of lifeways. At the heart of these lifeways is the Tiwa language. The language serves to bond and unify the

78

community, and it also serves to make the Isleta people distinctive as a society from the rest of the surrounding Hispanic and Anglo settlements.

Cultural maintenance is accomplished via the socioreligious institutions of the community. The institutions comprise the matriarchal ordered clans, the moieties, the special societies, and the Catholic Church. Communitywide functions are coordinated through a ceremonial activity cycle that contains time elements from both the solstice and Judeo-Christian calendars. Specialized buildings are maintained by the community to house such functions. In addition, open-space areas in the village proper are used for special activities and ceremonial dancing.

Most intravillage functions are regulated at the household level. The household is composed of the extended family and is among the most vital units in the community. Most key relationships among the extended family are maintained along matrilineal lines, and it is usually the eldest daughter who helps to coordinate the various activities of the household. Often it is the household that determines the reallocation of land and the division of property, especially when a widowed patriarch or matriarch dies.

The smallest operational unit in the village is the nuclear family. Most domestic, day-to-day activities are managed at this level. Unlike the household, however, the head of the nuclear family is the husband. This role has been gradually shifting toward the woman in recent years, however, due to the increased incidence of households headed by single women. In 1980 there were estimated to be 138 such households, or approximately 20 percent of all households. In spite of this, the male is still regarded as the basic household provider. Tribal policies still regard male membership on the federal/tribal rolls as determining the legal tribal status of his offspring.

PRECOLONIAL HISTORY

The earliest oral history recollections only hint at the evolution of what is now Isleta. History essentially begins with an event that recalls the separation of the communities at what is now Blue Lake, near Taos Pueblo. The name in Isleta for Taos Pueblo, Theu-whidh-nin,[2] is loosely interpreted as "those [people] that separated to live elsewhere." From this time onward, numerous other Tiwa culturally centered societies probably began their migration southward along the Rio Grande valley. Most settlements became concentrated around the present village of Sandia Pueblo. Tiwa villages like Chilili, Tajique, and Quarai were also settled on the eastern slopes of the Manzano mountain range. Such villages, though, were far fewer in number than the adjacent Tompiro villages that were found in what is now the geographic area of Salinas National Monument.

From Blue Lake, Isleta oral history recounts at least seven other village sites that were settled, occupied, and abandoned before the people finally settled upon their present site. One of these places was situated atop a mesa (Mesa de los Padillas) that adjoins the north boundary of the reservation. Commanding a strategic view of the whole of the valley, only the oblique sand mounds of an abandoned village remain today (fig. 7-1). This village was called Poo-reh-tú-ai, which is roughly translated as "the water basin village." A survey of pottery shards places the earliest occupation of this village from about A.D. 1515 to A.D. 1650 (Mera 1940, 18). The low-lying, L-shape arrangement of Poo-reh-tú-ai was characteristic of other prehistoric villages of the same period. These tended to be highly compact and geometric in plan. They were designed in such a manner as to become fortified in the event of intrusion.

This ancient site is still recollected in the popular Isleta folktale that recounts the exploits of two enchanted sisters whose treachery against an unresponsive suitor resulted in their being turned into rattlesnakes.[3] More symbolically, though, this tale is regarded as portending the abandonment of this mesa village.

Another ancient village site is recounted in another popular Isleta folktale. The tale recollects a contest between two rival villages. The Antelope-boy from Nam-bah-

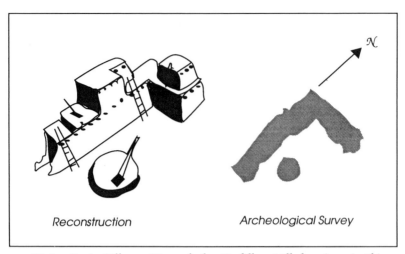

Reconstruction   Archeological Survey

7-1 *Water Basin Village: Mesa de los Padillas. (All drawings in this chapter are by Theodore S. Jojola.)*

tóo-too-ee (White Earth Village) is pitted against a runner named Deer-foot from the Nam-choo-rée-too-ee (Yellow Earth Village). The race is conducted around the four corners of the earth. The White Earth Village victory results in the destruction of the Yellow Earth Village and the slaying of its inhabitants, who are recollected as being mean and practicing witchcraft.[4]

Yellow Earth Village is known to have occupied an elevated site on the ridge overlooking the present village and east of the Rio Grande. This site has been neither surveyed nor excavated. The area is still considered to be a place where the spirits of witches are found. Today the site remains abandoned, and its adjacent lands have regularly been used as a trash dump. Its overall dimensions and site plan are unknown.

As for White Earth Village, its exact site is a matter of conjecture. One source has identified this site as what is presently called Ranchitos.[5] This is a small settlement that still exists today below the ruins of the Yellow Earth Village. There are no extensive archeological outcroppings that can serve to identify the exact site (fig. 7-2).

The site that is now the main village of Isleta has been abandoned and reconstructed a number of times. This area is bestowed the ceremonial name Shee-eh-whib-bak (the place of the whib stick). More commonly, though, the village itself is simply referred to as Tú-ai (village). On a windy day, the faint topwall outlines of an early village are uncovered near the northwest corner of the existing plaza. Most of this site has been obliterated by successive rebuilding around the central plaza. The site appears to comprise the outlines of a large complex that was constructed using a plan layout of successive, small square rooms. Its layout is similar to that excavated at the village of Puaray (Coronado National Monument). Puaray, in turn, was abandoned as a result of the siege conducted by the Spanish explorer Coronado in 1540.[6]

In sum, the oral history of Isleta serves to recollect the migratory nature of Pueblo lifeways. With each new site, new refinements were cast upon the settlements. Furthermore, Isleta was only one element of a larger cultural region. New migrations appear to be the result of the dividing of communities.

SPANISH EXPLORATION AND COLONIAL CONTACT (1539–1680)

The indigenous villages had already evolved a high degree of community organization by the time of first Spanish contact. Fray Marcos de Niza, who was the first Spaniard to venture as far as the Zuni village of Háwikuh, described it as having "the appearance of a pretty |Spanish| pueblo." A few years later, Coronado named it Granada, because "it resembles the Albanicín," one of sections of old Granada near the Alhambra (Bolton 1949, 118). However, the name *pueblo* stuck.

At the time of the first Spanish explorations into Pueblo country, Shee-eh-whib-bak was already settled atop a low outcropping of craggy volcanic knolls. Although the elevation above the floodplain was only 10 to 25 feet, it was more than adequate for keeping the habitations dry. Aside from the swampy areas (*bosque*) that lay next to the river bed, the flood plain of the old river bed of the Rio Grande provided a fertile and level bed that was ideal for irrigated agriculture. Yearly, with the spring runoff, the

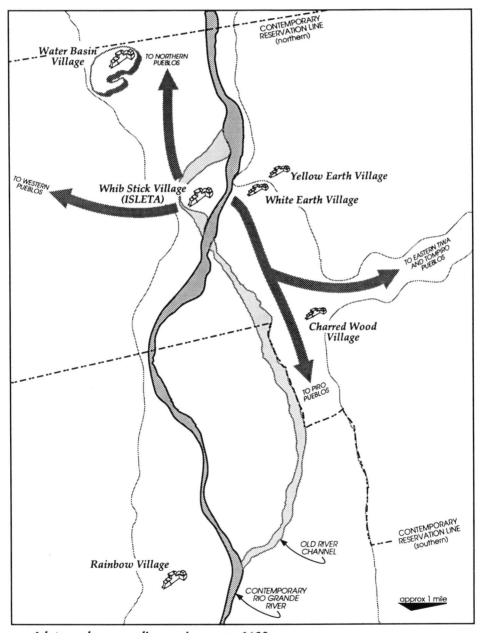

7-2 *Isleta and surrounding environs: ca. 1600.*

overflowing Rio Grande would completely encircle the village. This phenomenon was captured by the name Isleta (small island), which the Spanish regime, under the leadership of Juan de Oñate, gave to the village in 1598.

Prior to this, at the time of the first encounter with the Spanish expedition of Francisco Vásquez de Coronado in 1540, the area remained relatively nondescript. In his report to Coronado, Captain Alvarado narrated the first foreigner's description of the middle Rio Grande valley region with its "fields of maize [which lay] dotted with cottonwood groves (Bolton 1949, 184). He further went on to indicate that "there are twelve pueblos, whose houses are built of mud and are two stories high."

In the winter of 1540, the members of Coronado's expedition used this "province of Tiguex" (variant of Tiwa) as its base of operations. They described the villages, one of which they occupied, as being greatly fortified, enclosed by palisades, with small houses lacking entryways at the ground level.

During the Rodriguez expedition of 1581–1582, a more systematic survey was conducted of the southern Tiwa Pueblo villages. Unfortunately, the christening of these villages was rather esoteric (alternately employing Spanish and Nahuatl place-names), and, as a consequence contemporary scholars remain unsure about what descriptions match what known sites. Taxumulco, for example, which is thought to describe Shee-eh-whib-bak, was simply declared "another pueblo which had one hundred and twenty-three houses of two and three stories (Hammond 1966).[7]

Beginning with the first Spanish colonizing effort of Oñate in 1598, the Spanish occupiers quickly realized what a strategic place the village of Isleta occupied. The settlement was situated at an important junction of two heavily traversed pre-Columbian trails. To the south, the trail led directly toward the settlements of the Piro Pueblos (presently the abandoned sites are within or near the town of Socorro). Directly to the west were the Keresan, Zuni, and Hopi pueblos. To the east were the eastern Tiwas, the Tompiros, and the vast expanse of the Great American Plain. Finally, to the north lay the other Rio Grande pueblos.

Given such a strategic location, Isleta was one of the first pueblos to be missionized as part of the overall colonial effort. In September of 1598, Fray Juan Claros was dispatched to begin conversion among the villages in the proximity of, and including, Isleta. Due to the disastrous results of Spanish settlement efforts by Oñate in the northern frontier of New Mexico, a new colonial regime was installed in 1609. With the appointment of the first royal governor of New Mexico, Pedro de Peralta, the seat of colonial authority was moved to the newly founded villa of Santa Fe.

Once colonial rule was secured in New Mexico, the designation pueblo went far beyond mere description. Under a royal ordinance issued by King Philip II of Spain in 1573, new world towns were to be planned and laid out around an exacting set of specifications (Staníslawski 1947). The central organizing elements of a village were the church, the plaza, and the *cabildo* (council hall). Once the locations of these structures was determined, the streets were organized in a grid fashion. The streets followed the cardinal directions, and all measurements were originated from the threshold of the church's main doorway.

Under the ordinance, a village could not petition the crown for formal recognition until all township elements were in place. Lengthy descriptions that attested to the fulfillment of such requirements and a roster of Catholic converts served as documents for petitioning the *audencia* (head town), which was Mexico City. Upon review by the appropriate officials and clergy, the petition was forwarded to the court of the King of Spain for their concurrence.

The designation *pueblo*, therefore, was a legal title. A formal royal proclamation attesting to a township's authority was issued. More significantly, as part of this proclamation, the king alienated his title to the land encompassed by the town plaza and turned it over to the community (*fondo legal*). Canes of authority (*varas*) were issued to the town officials as a symbol of their acceptance into the Spanish governance. On a more functional level, the canes also became a standard unit of physical measurement, comparable to an American yardstick. The *fondo legal*, in fact, was often designated as the area bounded by measuring 1000 varas from the church door in each cardinal direction.

The Pueblo villages spared the natives from being devastated by the brunt of the relocation policies (*repartimientos*). The repartimiento was widely enforced among other natives who had neither *pueblos* (towns) nor *villas* (villages). It was the fact that the Pueblos had villages that were physically similar to Spanish townships that served to quickly incorporate them into colonial sovereign rule. It only remained that the Pueblo populations be converted to Catholicism and that churches be built, preferably next to the village plaza.

So it apparently happened that conversion efforts among the Isletans were very successful. By 1612, Fray Juan de Salas was assigned specifically to Isleta for the purpose of organizing the construction of a mission and convent.[8] About a year later, the church was completed with the labor of converts and dedicated as San Antonio de la Isleta. In meeting such criteria, Isleta formally became subsumed under Spanish governance, sometime in the 1620s [see discussion in Sando (1976), 203–5].

Playing a strategic and important colonial role, Isleta's church compound was doubtless transformed into a *presidio* (garrison). Within its walls were housed quarters for a Spanish militia, a missionary convent, and the offices of the colonial government and the Franciscan clergy. The compound occupied a prominent location and fronted on the north side of the pueblo's open plaza known as *pah-k' heuth* (a ground hollow where water collects). The pah-k' heuth was the largest open space in the village and the feature that became designated the *plaza mayor*.

The inroads of the Spaniards brought other changes to the community. New foodstocks harvested from fruit trees, wheat, and other plants were introduced. In addition, new livestocks such as sheep, cattle, horses, and pigs were readily adapted. This resulted in the transplanting of new archetypes like beehive ovens (*hornos*) and corrals (Schroeder 1972, 53). For a pueblo like Isleta, whose mainstay economy was derived from an extensive, irrigated agriculture to begin with, the impact of the introduction of new foodstocks and livestocks upon the trade and barter system must have been substantial.

The colonial government intensified its presence by establishing a centralized jurisdiction that radiated out of two principal regions. These two regions were designated the Rio Arriba (Upper River) and the Rio Abajo (Lower River), and their common boundary line was the dramatic escarpment of the Pajarito Plateau. Isleta Pueblo was designated the headquarters of the Rio Abajo for both the civil and ecclesiastical governments. From the pueblo, colonial jurisdiction radiated from Corrales (across the river from Sandia Pueblo) to Sabinal (12 miles south of Belen) (Espinosa and Chavez n.d., 91). In the 1670s, the residence of the lieutenant-governor was reported to have been established near Isleta (Simmons 1977, 66; Hackett 1942, Vol. I, lxvii).[9] His command was second only to that of the governor, who resided in the town of Santa Fe.

During this period of colonial settlement, Isleta was one of fifteen or sixteen pueblos that were considered to be in the province of Tiguex. Unlike other parts of this province, however, Isleta appeared to be one of the few places that continued to be prosperous, with a growing community. In 1634, the people were described as being "docile, all baptized and well instructed." (Hodge et al. 1945, 64). At its peak, the immediate community of Isleta encompassed seven Spanish ranchos and four lesser Pueblo villages, with an overall population of 2000 (Hackett 1942, Vol. I, xlix; Vol. 2, 213).

The largest Tiwa village other than Shee-eh-whib-bak was Beh-qhwee ú-ai (Rainbow Village).[10] In 1582 this village was described as having 100 two-story houses. It was situated 6 miles south of Isleta on the same side of the river. Under colonial rule, a visita (sub-mission) was established at this pueblo. The village was rechristened San Clemente, and its parish was established under the jurisdiction of San Antonio de la Isleta.

The smallest Tiwa settlement in the vicinity of Isleta was called Chical or Shee-lah ai (Charred Wood).[11] It was said to comprise a village of forty houses two stories in height. The village was sited approximately 3 miles south of Isleta on the opposite side of the river. Today this community consists mainly of a loose but distinct cluster of farmhouses. Nonetheless, its *acequias* (ditches) and fields remain separate from the main village of Isleta, and the community has certain ceremonial activities that are its own. In addition, another community, called Tai-kha'bédeh (Town Chief), is adjacent to Shee-lah ai. The origins of this area, however, are probably much more contemporary (Ellis 1979).

The third Tiwa settlement was the White Earth and Yellow Earth villages of early Isleta folklore. These villages were described as having "seventy houses two and three stories high [and] divided into two sections, one being an harquebus shot distant from the other." The settlements were directly across the river from Isleta in an area that is now known as Ranchitos.[12]

Elsewhere in the province of Tiguex, there was tremendous unrest. By the mid-1600s, political bickering between civil and ecclesiastical officials became public. In 1660, for example, reports emerged that the civil governor was inciting a rebellion among Isletans, the purpose of which was to depose the despotic rule of the mission priest. This type of action was accompanied by the widespread abuses of the *permicia* (tithes) (Jojola 1982, 83). The demands of the colonialists became especially unreasonable in the face of drought. In 1640 and again in 1670, severe droughts that lasted over several years resulted in widespread famine and death.

Additionally, incidents of nomadic raiding increased dramatically. Apache raiding and the kidnapping of women and children from Spanish colonial settlements prompted the government to establish border villages. These villages were populated with *genizaros* (Christianized nomadic Indians), and their settlements served as a first line of defense against intruders. One such village, Tomé, was established only 10 miles south of Isleta at the base of a volcanic knoll. This knoll, traditionally, also served as the southernmost boundary of the hunting lands of Isleta. Due to the exposure of Tomé to the frontier, the militia of Isleta was often deployed to provide added protection.

Epidemics of smallpox cost hundreds and even thousands of Pueblo lives. Beginning in the 1670s, the eastern Tiwa and Tompiro pueblos began to abandon their mountain villages. Their depleted populations migrated and joined the southern Tiwas and Piros. The eastern Tiwas, in particular, were permitted temporary refuge in an area directly across the river from the Pueblo of Isleta.

In summary, the community of Isleta had successfully commandeered a prominent role in the colonial government of New Mexico. A great part of its success was the strategic position it commanded with respect to other Pueblo outliers and with the surrounding Tiwa settlements. Another aspect of Isleta's success concerns its Pueblo vernacular style, which paralleled those of the new world Spanish settlements. The colonial record remains incomplete, but it appears that Isleta remained a vibrant and vital community throughout this period. This, however, was atypical of the general situation elsewhere in New Mexico.

THE PUEBLO REVOLT AND RESETTLEMENT (1680–1821)

It was the sum of the unrelenting Spanish conversion campaigns and administrative abuses, therefore, that led to the Pueblo Revolt of 1680. The revolt began on August 10, 1680, and was widespread throughout the territories of the Pueblo Indians. After the first foray, an estimated 1500 Spanish survivors sought refuge at the Isleta Pueblo. The survivors were immediately regrouped under the command of Alonso Garcia, lieutenant-governor and highest official of Rio Abajo, whose own hacienda near Isleta had been attacked. The village of Isleta provided an unexpected place of refuge, since its subjects purportedly did not take part in the rebellion (Hammond 1943, li). The survivors fled southward on August 14 along the Camino Real until they reached the junction where the Rio Grande shifted eastward. There they were to found the settlement of El Paso.

Reconnaissance of the Pueblo region was not attempted until the winter of 1681. On December 6, seventy soldiers under the command of the ousted governor of New Mexico, Antonio de Otermín, reentered the region. The Otermín expedition met no resistance at Isleta, which was the first village they encountered that was still inhabited. They were so well received that they managed to reconvert the 511 inhabitants almost immediately upon their arrival. In a village meeting, they admonished the natives for their past actions and particularly for allowing the monastery and church to be burned and for converting it into a pen for cows.

From a base camp in Isleta, Otermín coordinated a number of preliminary expeditions into the Tiwa regions. From these expeditions he quickly ascertained that all other pueblos, save Isleta, were still in a state of rebellion against the colonizers. After five days, Otermín's main group advanced to the northern pueblos in what would prove to be a futile attempt at reconquest.

After one month, on January 1, 1682, Otermín's beleaguered expedition launched its final foray within the rebellious Pueblo region. From a base camp on the opposite shore from Isleta, fifty soldiers were directed to round up the faithful converts. By this time the body of converts had diminished by one-third to 385 villagers (Hammond 1943, 358; Houser 1979, 336–42).[13] Otermín himself took the first action by setting fire to a large *estufa* (kiva) that was built in the middle of the main plaza. The rest of his contingent spent the remainder of that day destroying the rest of the village and any remaining foodstocks.[14] The remaining converts retreated with Otermín and were resettled in the village of Ysleta, near El Paso.

It took another 10 years before the colonizers attempted reentering the Isleta Pueblo environs. Under the command of Don Diego de Vargas, the reoccupation of Santa Fe in 1692 was accomplished with little opposition. This was due to the fact that many communities had been uprooted and displaced. Many villages were reported to be in ruins, and their fields lay fallow. Apparently the combination of continued nomadic raiding and internal factionalism among Pueblo leadership had caused widespread famine.

Upon Vargas's reentry into the province of Tiguex, all southern Tiwa villages were found to be abandoned. In fact, only a fleeting reference was made to the Pueblo of Isleta, which was described to be "in ruins, except for the nave of the church, the walls of which [were] in good condition" (Espinosa 1940). Most of the Tiwa-speaking populations had fled to the Hopi mesa lands. Those that fled from the vicinity of Sandia Pueblo reportedly established the Hopi village of Payupki on the Second Mesa. Those Isletans who had continued to defy the Spanish resettled in the Hopi region of Tusayan.[15]

When Vargas was able to demonstrate the peaceable reoccupation of the Pueblo territories to the audencia in Mexico City, the region would become realtered forever. The colonial reoccupation of the Tiwa lands was to be met according to the prescription of Vargas, who reported (Brandt 1979, 286–7):

> The [abandoned] lands are good, with their irrigation ditches. The said [Tiwa] pueblos are on the camino real, and it would be very desirable to settle the region with another one hundred colonists, who will be able to live very comfortably and prosperously . . .

For Isleta, however, he further went on to recommend:

> The natives of the said tribe now live in some miserable huts in the pueblo of Isleta, in this district of El Paso, and so it will be desirable to restore them to

their pueblo. . . . And they will be protected if the said intervening haciendas called "Las Huertas" are resettled (Brandt 1979, 286–7).

The reoccupation of the region by the colonists was swift and unrelenting. The original settlers were enticed to reoccupy their haciendas by some new land reforms that secured for them community land grants, homesites, and private grants. Large sections of Isleta's irrigated farmlands were usurped as favors to the colonialists who aided in the reconquest (see table 7-1). Ultimately, only the Pueblos of Sandia and Isleta would be repatriated.

The repatriation of Isleta was not immediate. It was not until 1709 that Fray Juan de la Peña obtained permission to resettle Isleta. Between 1709 and 1718, Fray Peña set about in earnest too "collect" and "assemble" families of the Tiwa nation who had resettled in Hopi and El Paso, as well as those who remained scattered in different pueblos and among the Apaches.[16] The majority of the converts from Ysleta in El Paso, however, never returned.[17] Moreover, it was never clear from the Spanish accounts whether it was the original Tiwa founders who returned.

By January 1710, Fray Peña had converted enough families to have the colonial governor rededicate the mission and church of Isleta to the patron saint, Saint Augustine. In 1742, another priest, Fray Carlos Delgado, who had "for years [been] minister at San Agustín de la Isleta," renewed missionary efforts among the Hopi and succeeded in replanting 441 "souls from Moqui" at Isleta (Thomas 1932, 102). Apparently conversion efforts were not confined to the Tiwas. The mission of San Agustín was used at different times to collect and relocate to Isleta converted Hopi families. Such resettlement actions may very well be the origin of the southernmost section of the Isleta community, which today is still named Orabi.[18]

Overall, colonial occupation during the 1700s remained tenuous at best. Reports concerning Isleta were sparse and inconclusive. An account of the visit of a bishop to New Mexico in 1760 gave a cursory description of the village. It had "107 families of Indians, with 304 persons, and 210 families of [Spanish] settlers . . . with 620 persons."[19] They were described as having good lands, with irrigation from the river. The church was described as being single-naved, with an adorned altar.

In 1776, the first complete detailed accounting of the village was given by Fray Francisco Atanasio Dominguez (Adams and Chavez 1956, 202–8). Isleta was reported to have 114 families with a total population of 454 persons. The pueblo itself was described as having

> . . . three beautiful blocks of dwellings, separated from one another at the corners, which are located in front of the church and convent, and form a very large plaza there to the south of them. Outside the plaza at various distances all around there are some twenty houses which would be as large as one block,

TABLE 7-1 *Spanish Land Grants to Spanish Colonialists in the Vicinity of the Isleta Pueblo After Pueblo Revolt*

YEAR	GRANT	ACRES
1716	Private grant, Mateo Sandoval y Manzanares (*San Clemente/Bosque*)	37,099
1718	Private grant, Diego de Padilla (*Peralta*)	51,940
1739	Private grant, Joaquin Sedillo and Antonio Guitiérrez (*Los Lunas*)	21,676
	Township grant (*Tomé*)	121,594
1746	Private grant (*Pajarito*)	28,724
1768	Township grant (*Atrisco*)	67,491

contemporary place names in parentheses.
Source: Williams and McAllister 1979, 36–7.

or tenement, of the plaza if they were all together. Everything is of adobe, very prettily designed and much in the Spanish manner (Adams and Chavez 1956, 207).

The next 50 years were filled with a continuous filing of petitions, primarily concerning encroachments by colonizers on the lands of Isleta. Some of these petitions involved the contested transfer of lands among Spanish heirs within Pueblo environs. Other petitions concerned the trespass of Spanish livestock to Pueblo lands.[20] The petitions were further complicated by the fact that under certain conditions the Pueblos were permitted to sell their lands to outsiders (Brayer 1979, 16).

The first Spanish grant consisted of a square "Isleta league," the perimeter of which was measured in each cardinal direction from the door of the church. It was granted under the laws of the Indies on May 24, 1597, and was originally estimated to have comprised approximately 17,000 acres.[21] At the turn of the seventeenth century, the boundaries proved to be extremely tenuous due to the shifting of natural markers such as the riverbank (fig. 7–3).

It was not until 1864 that the Isleta land grant was surveyed and patented to encompass approximately 110,000 acres. Moreover, it had been demonstrated that the 1700s was a period when land exchanges became commonplace. Segments of the Joaquin Sedillo and Antonio Guitiérrez grant and the Diego de Padilla grant were reacquired, and Isleta Pueblo was able to add onto their holdings, which now amounted to approximately 131,500 acres, or almost eight times the original Spanish grant.

Much of the impetus behind the shifts in land ownership came as a result of new trade networks that were established with the Mexican city of Chihuahua. Chihuahua, which was settled next to rich silver, gold, and copper deposits, became a trade town. The villa of Albuquerque, founded in 1706, became an intermediate port of call between Chihuahua and the surrounding missions and ranchos. The demands for finished goods from the Chihuahua fair spurred an entrepreneurial fervor among landed families who provided barter in the form of hides, blankets, and Indian captives (Coan 1925, 259).

As a consequence of trade, certain families became more landed than others. They accrued their wealth and mobilized their extended families within fortified haciendas. This particular regional house form was called the *casa-corral* (Conway 1951, 6–9). The hacienda was built in the shape of a square or rectangle. The living spaces opened inward to a large courtyard and the outermost walls were without entryways or windows so as to prevent intrusion. Only one gateway permitted access inside the compound. In time of defense, livestock were herded and confined within the hacienda's courtyard. The more affluent families built portals to embellish the courtyard. In general, the casa-corral lent itself to a diffuse settlement arrangement, and this appeared to provide the most acceptable life-style among the settlers.

In 1779, however, the settlement patterns of New Mexico were realtered with a pronouncement requiring the settlers to relocate in defensible plazas for the purpose of mutual defense (Simmons 1969). The settlers were relocated within the principal mission villages and were no longer permitted to locate on their isolated homesteads. They had to be reaccustomed to commuting daily to their farmsteads. The principal mission of San Agustín de Isleta served to refocus such relocations. The surrounding villas once again became dependent on Isleta for administration and security.[22]

The strategic relationship between Isleta and the small surrounding villages made for a peculiar interaction between the Isletan natives and the Spanish colonizers. Instead of becoming insulated, the Isletans apparently adapted many social and economic customs of the Spanish, particularly those of Christianity. Conversely, many Spaniards adopted Isleta customs and traditions as evidenced by the following excerpt from the lands court testimony of a New Mexican petitioner:

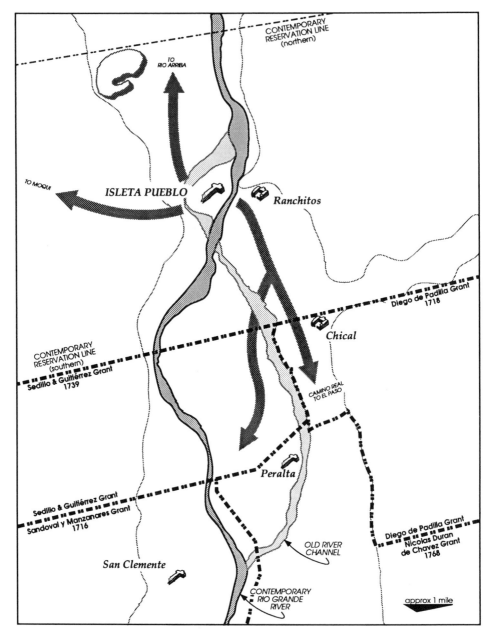

7-3 *Isleta and surrounding environs: post-Pueblo revolt, ca. 1700.*

> I have known the Indians |at Lentes| since I first knew Los Lentes, they were not more than half dressed, the women more mantas, and the men wore short breeches, and wore their hair just exactly like the |Isleta| Indians with a queue; this |Spanish| man's father that just testified here he wore knee breeches and wore a queue just exactly like an Indian; his wife was a half-breed Indian.[23]

In spite of this, the New Mexican authorities maintained a degree of social distance and reinforced this in the namesakes that they bestowed upon their converts. Hence, the surname Moquino was given to converts from Hopi, and Lente was given to the converts who persisted in farming lands belonging to their forefathers from the Rainbow Village of San Clemente or Los Lentes. There were other probable namesakes such as that of Zuni.[24]

In summary, the Pueblo Revolt and the consequent impacts of the reconquest had a profound impact on the settlement patterns of the Rio Grande valley. The short-term gains realized by the coordinated ouster of all colonial settlers by the Pueblos were quickly eroded upon the reentry of the Spaniards in 1692. The village of Isleta was repatriated on an initiative of the clergy. Perhaps this was done as a debt of gratitude for Isleta's continued allegiance to the crown. On the other hand, the whole of the province of Tiguex lay devastated as a consequence of Spanish intrusion and land reform. The community of Isleta would never attain the prominence and stature it once commanded. Nonetheless, the fact that it was able to reconstruct itself in light of the worst of colonialism is evidence of the tenacity of its society.

MEXICAN INDEPENDENCE AND AMERICAN TERRITORIALISM (1821–1912)

Matters among the New Mexico authorities would have probably continued uneventfully except for the worldwide dislocation of Spanish crown rule. In 1821, Mexico declared its independence from Spain. The Santa Fe trade and the fur trade became an alternative conduit from which merchandise flowed between St. Louis, Santa Fe, and Taos. Whereas the Mexican government continued to impose strict regulations and taxes on the trade with Chihuahua, the American traders subverted their authority through free enterprise. Soon New Mexicans became dependent on American goods and barter.

By 1823, Albuquerque was designated as the capital of one of four *partidos* (counties) into which the New Mexican jurisdiction had been divided. Isleta Pueblo was consequently subsumed within the representation of a town council although it regulated its own affairs through its own *alcalde* (mayor) (Coan 1925, 324). In 1844, the *partidos* were once again adjusted and the jurisdiction of Bernalillo was created of which Isleta became a part. Generally, however, few advances were made under Mexican rule, and this was attributed largely to the poverty and isolation of its colonial denizens.

The region, as such, would not be significantly transformed until the 1846 Mexican-American War. In September of that year, the American forces under the command of General Stephan Watts Kearny marched unopposed into Albuquerque. By 1850, the first provisional American territorial government was established.

One of the provisions established prior to the civil territorial government was the appointment of an Indian Agent, James S. Calhoun. It was under his advice that troops were mobilized to deter nomadic Indian raiding. By this period, even the nomadic Navajo had begun raiding settlements like Isleta. In response, from 1851 through 1855, the territorial government built six new military forts to control Indian unrest.[25] This proved to be an economical windfall for local herders.

In 1857, a petition was forwarded to the territorial governor asking for his assistance regarding the actions of the governor of Isleta, Ambrosio Abeita. It was alleged that he was using his position to grant lucrative concessions to his relatives as well as unjustly persecuting the parish priest.[26] Later in 1861, Abeita reportedly loaned 20,000 dollars in gold bullion to support the local Union troops against the invading Confederates. In 1863, Abeita was sent as a Pueblo representative to Washington, D.C., where he had a personal audience with President Abraham Lincoln.[27] Abeita was also for many years the chairman of the *principales* (headmen).[28]

In keeping with their status, the Abeita family had built a grand hacienda that was purportedly styled after the Palace of Governors in Santa Fe. Others who were also prominent from the community such as the Luceros from Isleta and the Padillas from

Chical also built comparable haciendas. They incorporated architectural elements directly from the Spanish *casa-corral*. Their homes became showcases within the confines of the older traditional village. The richest families constructed colonnaded portals that were finished with wooden floors made from milled timber. These colonnades were used regularly for community *bailes* and *fandangos* (dances and socials).[29]

This grand style of living became relatively commonplace in the village of Isleta toward the latter 1800s. A surveyor's observation gleaned from a U.S. government expedition in 1858 noted

> . . . Isleta [is] a town that in its style of building, as well as its situation, reminded us of Santo Domingo, except that some one-storied houses of Mexican settlers were interspersed among the two and three-storied dwellings of the Indians. As we approached the town, we saw numbers of the latter busily at work in their vineyards, and talking in loud cheerful voices as they cleared the ground of its seed-bearing weeds, whilst the *lazy Mexicans* were lounging before their doors smoking cigars (Möllhausen 1969, 34; italics mine).

In all probability, the "lazy Mexicans" were the *rico* Tiwa owners who, in addition to livestock, owned large vineyards, the grapes of which they used for producing wine and brandy for commercial trade. During critical periods of the planting and harvesting season they hired seasonal labor, and it was during this time that the U.S. Surveyor had made his observations. Their haciendas had been mistaken as belonging to those of the "Mexicans."

In the 1880s the life-style that the ricos had grown accustomed to would be challenged and, ultimately, changed forever. Whereas the community of Isleta had been renewed in relative isolation, the construction of a railhead there in 1879 would expose it to the outside thereafter. One vagabond, for example, who in 1884 walked the rail line into Isleta was Charles Fletcher Lummis. Lummis would continue his journey to Los Angeles, only to return 4 years later to New Mexico to regain his health. Through his association with a rico, Don Manuel Antonio Chavez of San Mateo, New Mexico, Lummis was introduced to the Abeita family. At their invitation he took up residence in a single room rented to him within the Abeita hacienda and stayed until 1892. During this period he authored many works and established his reputation as a southwestern writer. His writings supported the theme "see America first" and exemplified the quaint customs of the Pueblos, particularly Isleta.

Through such writings, and with the advent of improved transportation, the village of Isleta gained increased accessibility and visibility. The transcontinental railroad also fostered road improvements on what would become the transcontinental Pan American highway.[30] By 1910, the Rio Grande had been spanned by a two-lane bridge at Isleta. These improvements spurred a tourist trade that was conducted by both motor coach and railway.

The spur of the railway, which was the only junction of the major southern and western routes, separated at Isleta. As a consequence, trains waited at regular intervals at the Isleta depot to gain clearance to proceed. Entrepreneurial Isletans used this waiting time to peddle their items, which included vegetables, fruits, bread, handmade "Indian" trinkets, and poorly made pottery.[31] The exotic appearance of Isleta Pueblo dress as well as the hospitality of the native vendors added appreciably to the festival atmosphere of the stop. Railway officials encouraged this type of passenger interaction. Eventually, the Atchison, Topeka and Santa Fe Railroad Company commissioned distinguished artists, photographers, and writers to create the image of the "Santa Fe Indian" (McLuhan 1985, 19).

The main proponent of southwestern tourism was Fred Harvey. With the advent of the Model T touring car, the Fred Harvey chain of railroad hotels extended this interaction with half-day or full-day tours to the surrounding pueblos. Isleta was a major item on the itinerary, and several major structures were erected or modified to take advantage of this emerging trade. The Abeita family constructed an imposing two-story hotel and general store on the plaza, adjacent to the church.[32] The hotel was described as having a "peak roof," covered with corrugated iron with balconies extending along the front of the second story and constructed in a style "reminiscent of the south-German style of architecture—of the less admirable type (McGovern 1932, 131, 132).

The turn of the century was also a time when new developments ushered in a period of tremendous upheavals and conflicts in Isleta. In the early 1880s a faction comprising the traditional elements of Laguna Pueblo appeared before the village fathers and were granted refuge at Isleta. They fled Laguna on the grounds of religious persecution, which had been instigated by the American Protestant faction of the Laguna community. They moved many of their guarded clan and secret society objects of worship and were permitted to resettle within the subcommunity of Orabi. Their ceremonial center, however, was established south of the main plaza in an open area redesignated the Laguna Plaza (for a detailed discussion, see Parsons 1932).

In 1884, the Rio Grande flooded its banks and shifted its path considerably downstream of Isleta.[33] The river flooded once again in 1907, and improvements that significantly raised the embankment of the railroad ended up creating a natural dam (Keleher and Chant 1940, 62–6). Water that would have flowed harmlessly to the west of the village inundated a great number of fields instead. More significantly, natural boundaries were changed, and some communities like the Bosque de Peralta found their settlements now on the opposite banks of the river. Such changes further complicated the land tenure in the area.

Finally, in 1887, the last true *cacique* (traditional theocratic leader), Domingo Juipe of Isleta, died (French 1948, 13). He was never replaced, and the responsibilities of the position were divided among other tribal positions. But by this time the native Isletans were apparently resigned to a new life-style. No longer fearful of the Apaches and Navajos, Isletans adapted a seasonal migratory type of existence. An excerpt of a letter from a Presbyterian school teacher in May 1893 portrayed this life-style:

> . . . very few children [are] in attendance during the month of June, as by that time most of the families have left the pueblo and gone to their little farms where they remain during the Summer. Then as the days become hot, the air of the place from the accumulation of filth during the winter months becomes very impure making it quite necessary to leave the pueblo (Craig 1893).

In summary, this era witnessed a resurgence of Isleta Pueblo's role in the extended community setting. Economic changes brought about by political events and entrepreneurship established new socioeconomic classes among the villagers. The community, in great part, was a microcosm of the larger regional environment surrounding them. They were full participants in the mainstream economy as the result of inroads made by the transportation networks. Yet in spite of this they maintained the viability of their culture by cross-assimilation. This was nowhere more evident than in the new housing forms that had been adapted. Isleta had begun to evolve in a manner that reflected less a Pueblo vernacular tradition and more an adaptation of outside traditions.

NEW MEXICO STATEHOOD AND THE INDIAN REORGANIZATION ACT (1912–1934)

With the advent of New Mexico statehood in 1912, Isleta Pueblo was once again faced with social turmoil accompanied by change. The main determinant for such changes was the shift of the pueblo's legal status away from being an incorporated township, which had at least given it the semblance of being a full participant in American territorial government. The status of its inhabitants became that of the American Indian whose political status had evolved as a result of U.S. federal interrelationships with the British and French colonial governments.

These policy venues of the American Indian emplaced a wardship arrangement upon the Pueblo governments. Their Spanish land grants were translated into Indian reservations. Within the confines of the Indian reservation, the tribes were permitted to govern their people in accordance with "acceptable" principles. At the same time, however, the wardship of the federal government insulated the tribes from the state government.

As wards of the federal government, the Pueblos sought to use their new status to gain tax and legal protection of their land and natural resources away from the aggressive and corrupt elements of the regional and local nontribal governments.[34]

Unfortunately, wardship status also carried other restrictions and, most noticeably, many were embodied within the economic policies established by the Indian Trade and Intercourse acts. The 1892 Indian Prohibition Act was one of these, and with the change to Pueblo "Indianhood," the sale and introduction of liquor on Pueblo reservations was made illegal.

In a series of articles about Albuquerque in *Harper's* magazine in 1880, a journalist was moved to write

> The gardens and orchards along the Rio Grande strike unspeakably joyous
> notes of color . . . with the luxuriant and brilliant verdure of the orchard foliage
> that crowns them, [it] is exceedingly beautiful. The varieties of fruit that have
> been introduced from the East of late years attain a remarkably fine
> flavor. . . . Albuquerque is the centre of an important wine-growing district [with]
> some of the best vineyards in the valley . . . belonging to the industrious and
> frugal Indians at Isleta. . . . The late Madame Josephine Tondré, at Isleta, was
> famed for her wine, and was one of the most successful growers. (Wilson 1977,
> 32–3).

All of above, of course, was immediately curtailed under federal Indian laws. The grape vineyards were seized, and agents systematically uprooted all grape plants. Federal officers conducted covert house raids in an effort to locate, seize, and burn all wine-making apparatus. Isleta wine-makers who resisted were incarcerated in federal penitentiaries. Many of the native ricos became impoverished.

In response to the new community problems created by federal Indian laws, a social reform campaign under the auspices of the Department of Interior was initiated. There were three primary components to this campaign. These pertained to reforms in education, agriculture, and health.

The main goal of the education campaign was the redirection of the Pueblo youth "toward" American values. The community became inflamed by the competing educational philosophies of the Presbyterian and Catholic reformists. Many children were simply "kidnapped" and sent to Indian boarding schools as far away as Carlisle, Pennsylvania. In fact, such injustice became a personal campaign of Charles Fletcher Lummis, whose biting editorial "My Brother's Keeper" attacked the policies of the federal government (Lummis 1899).

Ultimately the matter was quieted with the construction of a village day school and housing quarters for teachers in 1915. Even then, village children, who in general were notorious for their truancy, were systematically rounded up by the Indian police and forced to attend the day school. By the 1920s, however, complaints were already issuing forth about the inadequacy of these facilities. This situation led one official to report that the teacher's quarters had become a "sublime joke" (U.S. National Archives 1921).

The second component entailed agricultural reform. Once again, schoolchildren became important vehicles for this aspect of the campaign. A significant part of their daily curriculum was dedicated to the agricultural and vocational arts. New potted fauna and seeds were sent home with the children. Under instructions from their teachers, they unconsciously assisted in transforming the ecological landscape with long-lived, nonindigenous species such as elm trees. Furthermore, extension agents were employed to reeducate the native farmers in their agricultural practices. Mechanization was gradually introduced into the farming practices of the community.

The third component entailed health reform. In 1916, the cemetery was moved away from the church courtyard to an area outside of the village and adjacent to the Laguna colony of Orabi. The move was justified on the basis of improving sanitation, particularly as the community continued to be plagued with significant numbers of deaths attributed to contagious diseases. The youth population continued to suffer from smallpox and measles epidemics. One innovation that did improve the quality of life was the construction of three windmills within the village. The wells served to provide clean and dependable sources of drinking, cooking, and laundry water.

Aside from the three reform campaigns, there were other federal interventions that had appreciable impacts. In 1925, the Middle Rio Grande Conservancy District (MRGCD) was formed to administer and manage water control projects designed to control flooding, to drain swampy land, and to provide for irrigation. Its jurisdiction was essentially the width of the valley riverbed and extended from Cochiti Pueblo to Socorro. With the cooperation of the U.S. Bureau of Reclamation, which maintained jurisdiction over the river itself, an extensive system of levees, drains, and irrigation ditches was constructed (Kelley 1974, 18).

Although these projects essentially doubled the number of irrigable acres on the Isleta reservation (U.S. Bur. of Reclamation 1947), the program was not altogether effective. The new laterals cut off and isolated large parcels of land from their traditional sources of irrigation, rendering them infertile. High laterals turned some farmlands into bosque (swampy land). In addition, reclaimed bosque, when planted, was found to be unproductive due to unanticipated high concentrations of alkali. Perhaps just as importantly, though, the aesthetic of the Isleta bosques, which overall had given Isleta its romantic name "the little island," was permanently obliterated. In its place, the image of the community became like that of any other desert "mexican" village.[35] Its tourist appeal became almost nonexistent.

With the landscape permanently changed, the Church of Saint Augustine became the most noteworthy tourist symbol of Isleta. In 1923, Isleta's French-born priest, Father Anton Docher, undertook a major remodeling, which, by and large, reflected his eccentricities. The flat roof the church was replaced by a pitched roof covered with corrugated iron. Two latticed wooden towers were erected, and each was liberally decorated by one central and four minor spires. To complete the composition, a portico, also constructed from the same corrugated iron, spanned the front of the church. The overall appearance of these elements gave the church one of the most distinctive and least appreciated facades of any church in the Southwest.[36]

Prior to this, however, tourism at Isleta had already declined greatly as the result of community pressure. The novelty of "outsiders" taking pictures had begun to wane. In 1897, a 50-second nickelodeon feature entitled *A Pueblo Day School* was produced at Isleta. By 1902, the village of Orabi in Hopi began prohibiting tourists from taking pictures at their ceremonies. In 1912, the first Hollywood feature was produced at Isleta with disastrous results. Exploiting Isleta's architecture and people as a backdrop, *A Pueblo Legend*, starring Mary Pickford, was produced by the legendary D.W. Griffith. After casting a Frenchman as a medicineman who "came dancing on the scene with bathing trunks underneath his short (very weird) skirt," Griffith was arrested and detained by village officials for mocking tribal customs.[37]

Similar repercussions had being felt among other creative works. The reprinting of the folktales retold by Charles Lummis renewed a tide of dissent in the community.[38] Consequently, in 1927, those individuals who were regarded to be the "most notoriously in touch with whites," Pablo Abeita and Candelaria Chavez, were called before the war captains in the village to account for their past actions in giving away secret information (Parsons 1932).

Law and order also became of increasing concern. So-called "unsavory" outsiders as well as trespassing incidents made their appearances with alarming regularity. In 1921 Isletan Louis Abeita, the chief of the Pueblo Indian police, was gunned down and killed aside the railroad embankment in Isleta by a black fugitive. Isleta maintained a one-room jailhouse, and this facility serviced the entire southern Pueblo region. The judge and notary public was none other than Pablo Abeita, who a few years earlier had admonished Chief of Police Louis Abeita for arresting two non-Indian county officials for their "interference in the discharge of |police| duty."[39]

In ending, it should be noted that all during the period an incredible amount of turmoil among leadership was occurring. The community divided itself between those elements that considered themselves ideological "conservatives or short-hairs" and those who considered themselves "traditionals or long-hairs." Although it could be concluded that education and federal receivership were the reasons for such factionalism, it should also be stressed that a new kind of change had been set. This change was insidious and came at the heels of federal experiments at community reform. Because community control had been inadvertently relinquished, vicious fights erupted among competing factions at Isleta. This established their notoriety among federal officials as "the most turbulent of the pueblos."[40] For the first time in its history, physical change in the community was largely the result of federal intervention.

POST-1934

The subject of change resulting after the Indian Reorganization Act of 1934 demands a separate treatise. Among some of the major trends, however, were the gradual decline of traditional building technologies. Traditions including the laying of terrones (sod blocks), the use of whitewash, and the harvesting of vigas (pine log beams) became outpaced by premilled lumber construction techniques.

Additionally, the tribal government itself became increasingly institutionalized. With the adoption of the tribal constitution, the tribal council and the officers of the tribal government became insulated from the rest of the community by protocol. Decision making and authority became highly stratified. The overall infrastructure of the village, which was traditionally governed by the *principales*, gradually became the purview of the tribal council. Their authority became more pronounced as a result of federal project activities designed to raise the standard of living in the village. Water and sewage systems, community and administrative centers, paved roadways, and even community parks were produced. Joint nonprofit ventures have resulted in the construction of playgrounds and community centers. Such construction was initiated in the 1950s.

With the inception of the federal Indian housing program in Isleta in the 1970s, the lifeways of the nuclear family and the extended families were significantly altered. Young families have migrated away from the central village, and frame houses have been constructed. For the most part, these were constructed within large housing tracts. Land tenure has been significantly realtered, and the housing tracts have resulted in the establishment of new community centers such as Pickle Heights and MouseTown.

The exodus of families onto their agricultural plots away from the village has further contributed to the decline of the village center. Certain "old" houses that remained vacant over extended periods of time gradually collapsed as a result of disuse. More commonly, though, a great number of village houses have become "second" homes and are generally occupied only during ceremonial occasions in the village.

The labor force has shifted from self-employed agriculture to employment in the federal, state, or tribal government sectors to the extent that only 4 percent continue to gain their livelihood from agriculture on the reservation, while 78 percent work for the three government sectors (U.S. Dept. of Commerce 1986). The profile substantiates a dependency relationship with the American Indian service providing the services of the three government sectors, the majority of their offices being located in Albuquerque. Daily job commuting using the private automobile, the eight-hour work day, and weekend farming as recreation have all become indelible facts of Isleta community life.

Few enterprises are located on the reservation. Most on-site facilities support the special program needs of the U.S. Indian Health Service, the U.S. Postal Service, BIA education, Head Start, and various other federal operations. These are also a number of tribal enterprises such as an Isleta bingo enterprise, a lake-recreation park, and an industrial shop. Private enterprises, on the other hand, are represented mainly by small cottage-type efforts. These are for the most part "ma and pa" operations, and they represent the gamut of enterprises from smoke shops to arts and crafts stores.

CONCLUSIONS

Modernization, it seems, is a process whereby elements of lifeways converge in a distinct time and place frame to cause new changes in the community. Successful change is characterized by the ability of the society to comprehend, accept, and control the changes that occur.

Isleta's community lifeways have been continually disrupted over the span of its known history. The most intense periods of disruption encompassed its prehistory, the Pueblo Revolt, and New Mexico statehood. With each challenge, its community could have disbanded and its settlements would then have been abandoned. Nonetheless, Isleta society remobilized and did so in a manner that was integral to the regional processes around it. The tenacity of its people to adjust by giving up "older" ways and adopting "newer" ones gave the community its ability to survive. In a fundamental way, therefore, Isletans were survivalists.

Modernization and cultural influx required that change be framed in terms of the common denominator. Spiritually, the common denominator of the community is its language and culture. Physically, the common denominator is the village main plaza, the mission church, and the basic centralized village settlement plan. These physical elements were inherited and transferred throughout the generations. These elements afforded validity (from the political standpoint) and continuity (from the settlement standpoint) over Isleta's rather incongruous history. Combined, the spiritual and physical denominators gave the community its sense of identity as well as its sense of place.

The processes of persistence, adaptation, and innovation have been the basic prescriptions of community settlement since Pueblo prehistory. The community settlement has not been a process of maintaining "tradition." What was regarded as traditional in one period would not have been considered traditional in another. The history of progress as reflected by changes in Isleta's settlement and building traditions was both intense and varied. Its community remained vital because of its ability to readjust to "new" traditions. Overall, Isleta is a dynamic community. To assume that its community traditions remain static is to underestimate the abilities of its culture to survive.

REFERENCES

ADAMS, ELEANOR B., ed. 1954. *Bishop Tamaron's Visitation of New Mexico, 1760*. Historical Society of New Mexico, Publications in History. Albuquerque: University of New Mexico Press.

_____ and FRAY ANGELICO CHAVEZ. 1956. *The Missions of New Mexico, 1776. A Description by Fray Francisco Atanasio Dominquez with Other Contemporary Documents.* Albuquerque: University of New Mexico Press.

BOLTON, HERBERT E. 1949. *Coronado: Knight of Pueblos and Plains.* Albuquerque: University of New Mexico Press.

BRANDT, ELIZABETH A. 1979. "Sandia Pueblo." In: *Handbook of North American Indians.* Vol. 9. *The Southwest,* ed. Alfonso Ortiz, 345. Washington, D.C.: Smithsonian Institution Press.

BRAYER, HERBERT O. 1979. *The Pueblo Indian Land Grants of the "Rio Abajo," New Mexico.* New York: Arno Press.

BUNTING, BAINBRIDGE. 1960. "San Augustin de la Isleta." *New Mexico Architect.*

COAN, CHARLES F. 1925. *A History of New Mexico.* Vol. 1. New York: American Historical Society.

CONWAY, A. W. 1951. "Southwestern Colonial Farms." In: *Landscape,* Vol. 1.

CRAIG, ELIZA V. 1893. Letter to the Presbyterian Board of Home Missions, May 6. Record Group 75, E-1759-1893, U.S. National Archives, Washington, D.C.

CRANE, LEO. 1928. *Desert Drums: The Pueblo Indians of New Mexico, 1540–1928.* Boston: Little, Brown.

ELLIS, FLORENCE. 1979. "Isleta Pueblo." In: *Handbook of North American Indians.* Vol. 9. *The Southwest,* ed. Alfonso Ortiz, 351. Washington, D.C.: Smithsonian Institution Press.

ESPINOSA, J. MANUEL, transl. 1940. "Vargas' Campaign Journal and Correspondence." In: *First Expedition of Vargas into New Mexico, 1692,* ed. George P. Hammond, 186. Coronado Cuarto Centennial Publications, 1540–1940, Vol. X. Albuquerque: University of New Mexico Press.

_____ and TIBO J. CHAVEZ. n.d. *El Rio Abajo.* Pampa, Texas: Pampa Print Shop.

FRENCH, DAVID H. 1948. *Factionalism in Isleta Pueblo.* Monographs of the American Ethnological Society, Vol. XIV. New York: J. J. Augustin.

FRIAR, RALPH, and NATASHA FRIAR. 1972. *The Only Good Indian: The Hollywood Gospel.* New York: Drama Book Specialists.

HACKETT, CHARLES WILSON. 1942. In: *Revolt of the Pueblo Indians of New Mexico and Otermin's Attempted Reconquest, 1680–1682,* ed. George P. Hammond. Albuquerque: University of New Mexico Press.

HAMMOND, GEORGE P., ed. 1943. *Revolt of the Pueblo Indians of New Mexico and Otermin's Attempted Reconquest, 1680–1682.* Albuquerque: University of New Mexico Press.

HAMMOND, GEORGE P. 1966. *The Rediscovery of New Mexico, 1580–1584: The Explorations of Chamuscado, Espejo, Castaño de Sosa, Morlete, and Leyva de Bonilla and Humaña.* Albuquerque: University of New Mexico Press.

HODGE, F. W., et al., transl. 1945. *Benvenides Memorial of 1634.* Coronado Historical Series, Vol. IV. Albuquerque: University of New Mexico Press.

HOUSER, NICHOLAS P. 1979. "Tigua Pueblo." In: *Handbook of North American Indians.* Vol. 9. *The Southwest,* ed. Alfonso Ortiz, 336–42. Albuquerque: University of New Mexico Press.

JOJOLA, THEODORE S. 1982. "Tribal Survival and Outside Contact: The Spanish Colonial and American Territorial Occupation of the Bontoc and Isleta Villages." Unpublished Ph.D. dissertation in political science, University of Hawaii.

KELEHER, JULIA, and ELSIE RUTH CHANT. 1940. "El Padre Sargento." *The Padre of Isleta,* 62–6. Santa Fe: Rydal Press.

KELLEY, VINCENT C. 1974. *Scenic Trips to the Geological Past,* No. 9. *Albuquerque: Its*

Mountains, Valley, Water, and Volcanoes. Albuquerque: New Mexico Bureau of Mines and Mineral Resources. University of New Mexico Printing Plant.

LANGE, CHARLES H., et al., eds. 1984. *The Southwestern Journals of Adolph Bandelier, 1889–1892.* Albuquerque: University of New Mexico Press.

LUMMIS, CHARLES F. 1894. *The Man Who Married the Moon and Other Pueblo Indian Folk-Stories.* New York: Century.

_____ 1899. "My Brother's Keeper." *Land of Sunshine: Magazine of California and the West,* XI(4):207.

McGOVERN, JANET B. 1932. "A General Survey of Isleta Pueblo with Especial Reference to Acute Transitional Conditions." Unpublished Master's Thesis, University of New Mexico.

McLUHAN, T. C. 1985. *Dream Tracks: The Railroad and the American Indian, 1890–1930.* New York: Harry N. Abrams.

MERA, H. P. 1940. "Population Changes in the Rio Grande Glaze-Paint Area." Laboratory of Anthropology Technical Series Bulletin No. 9.

MÖLLHAUSEN, BALDWIN. 1969. *Journey from the Mississippi to the Coast of the Pacific with a United States Government Expedition.* London: Johnson Reprint Co.

MONTOYA, JOE L. 1978. *Isleta Pueblo and the Church of Saint Augustine.* Isleta Pueblo: St. Augustine Press.

OPPENHEIMER, ALAN JAMES. 1957. "An Ethnological Study of Tortugas, New Mexico." Unpublished Master's thesis, Department of Anthropology, University of New Mexico.

PARSONS, ELSIE CLEWS. 1932. "Isleta, New Mexico." In: *47th Annual Report of the Bureau of American Ethnology.* Washington, D.C.: U.S. Govt. Printing Office.

SANDO, JOE S. 1976. "The Silver Headed Canes." *The Pueblo Indians.* San Francisco: Indian Historian Press.

SCHROEDER, ALBERT H. 1972. "Rio Grande Ethnohistory." In: *New Perspectives on the Pueblos,* ed. Alfonso Ortiz. Albuquerque: University of New Mexico Press.

_____. 1979. "Pueblos Abandoned in Ancient Times." In: *Handbook of North American Indians.* Vol. 9. *The Southwest,* ed. Alfonso Ortiz. Washington, D.C.: Smithsonian Institution Press.

SIMMONS, MARC. 1969. "Settlement Patterns and Village Plans in Colonial New Mexico." *Journal of the West,* 8:7–21.

_____. 1977. *New Mexico: A Bicentennial History.* New York: W. W. Norton.

STANISLAWSKI, STAN. 1947. "Early Spanish Town Planning in the New World." *Geographical Review,* XXXVII:95–105.

THOMAS, ALFRED BARNABY, transl. and ed. 1932. *Forgotten Frontiers: A Study of Spanish Indian Policy of Don Juan Bautista de Anza, Governor of New Mexico, 1777–1787.* Norman: University of Oklahoma Press.

U.S. BUREAU OF RECLAMATION. 1947. "Plan for the Development, Middle Rio Grande Project." November 21. Page 137.

U.S. DEPARTMENT OF COMMERCE. 1986. 1980 Census, Labor Force. Subject report: American Indians, Eskimos, and Aleuts on Identified Reservations and the Historic Areas of Oklahoma (Excluding Urbanized Areas).

U.S. NATIONAL ARCHIVES. 1921. 1921 Narrative Report, Southern Pueblo Schools. Record Group M1011, Roll 141, Southern Pueblo Schools.

WILLIAMS, JERRY L., and PAUL E. McALLISTER, eds. 1979. *New Mexico in Maps.* Albuquerque: Technology Applications Center/University of New Mexico.

WILSON, SKIP. 1977. *New Mexico 100 Years Ago: Assembled from Harper's 1880 and Harper's 1885.* The Sun Historical Series. Albuquerque: Sun Publishing Co.

NOTES

1. 1980 count as determined by the Special Supplementary Questionnaire on American Indians. Correspondingly, the usage of household in this context is based on the definition used by the U.S. Census Bureau.

2. No regularized orthography exists for the Tiwa language. Most Romanized spellings are taken from the books, unpublished manuscripts, and field notes of the writer Charles Fletcher Lummis (1859–1928). An early Anglo adventurer of the Southwest, Lummis lived in Isleta from 1888 to 1892. He spent a great deal of this time documenting the varied facets of Isleta village life and its language. It should be noted, however, that even these texts contained inconsistencies in the spellings of various Isleta words.

3. One version of the tale is given as "The Town of the Snake-Girl" in Lummis (1894, 130–6).

4. One version is given as "The Antelope Boy," (Lummis 1894, 12–21). Two other variants of the tale are to be found in Parsons (1932, 386–90).

5. The site is directly below the abandoned site of the Yellow Earth village (Parsons, 1932, 208).

6. It should be noted that scholars remain divided on whether this village really is the Pueblo of Puaray as chronicled throughout the colonial settlement period. Citations by Spanish administrators of the period describe this village as being on the same side of the river as the present village of Sandia. Puaray (Coronado National Monument), however, is on the opposite side of the river.

7. As an example of the continuing scholarly debate, the same site names vary significantly as correlated by Schroeder (1979).

8. Most chronological details can be referenced in Montoya (1978).

9. A fleeting site reference is also given in the testimony of Lt.Gov. Alonso García, who indicated that his hacienda was three and one-half leagues south of Sandia.

10. Assuming that *Taxumulco* was Isleta, Beh-qhwee ú-ai was also known as Piquinaguatengo, as referenced by the Rodriguez Expedition.

11. The village that once occupied this area would coincide with the one referred to by the Rodriguez Expedition as *Mexicalcingo*.

12. As chronicled by the Rodriguez Expedition these Tiwa settlements were called Tomatlan. See note 4.

13. Once taken to El Paso, the converts were made to settle a new pueblo, Sacramento de la Ysleta. See Houser (1979).

14. In the 1660s an underground kiva was reported to be near the convent, close to the west side of the church. See Schroeder (1979, 244).

15. It should be noted that the documentation on the resettlement of the Tiwa populations is inconclusive (Brandt 1979, 345).

16. Abridged from a report by Fray Vélez de Escalante (Adams and Chavez 1956, 203, fn. 2).

17. This is also true for the Tiwa converts who established another village called Tortugas (Oppenheimer 1957, 18–23).

18. Orabi is a Hopi village located on the third mesa. The origin of the Isleta's Orabi community is also referenced in Ellis (1979, 354).

19. This estimate is qualified by the reporting figures obtained from an earlier 1750 census. The 1750 census reported 79 Indian households with 421 persons (Adams 1954, 71).

20. A chronological listing of court petitions can be found in Coan (1925, 298–300).

21. A detailed reconstruction of the evolution of the Isleta reservation boundaries can be found in Brayer (1979, 56–76).

22. See, for example, the 1776 battle of Tomé in Espinosa, et al. (n.d., 93).

23. Land Court testimony by J. Francisco Chavez, plaintiff. From *J. Francisco Chavez versus the United States of America*, pertaining to the Ana de Sandoval y Manzanares San Clemente Grant, No. 64, Court of Private Land Claims, Santa Fe, August 1896. Transcript of trial, p. 17.

24. For origins of *Moquino*, see Lange (1894, 314, fn. 184). For discussion on the origin of *Lente*, see case dockets from *J. Francisco Chavez versus the United States of America* (see note 23). For origin of *Zuni*, see Parsons (1932, 237).

25. These were Fort Union (1851), Fort Fillmore (1851), Fort Defiance (1851), Fort Burgwin (1852), Fort Craig (1854), and Fort Stanton (1855).

26. New Mexico Territorial Papers, March 31, 1857.

27. The amount loaned to the Union forces varies from source to source. See the biography of Pablo Abeita in Crane (1928, 316, fn. 1).

28. See discussion of Isleta officials in French (1948, 11).

29. Collected from oral histories.

30. This was U.S. Highway 85, which was at one time considered to be one of the most important highways in the nation. In 1974, the final unfinished link of Interstate 25 was constructed between Albuquerque and Belen. This bypassed U.S. 85 altogether, and in 1987 it was downgraded to Highway 213.

31. Isleta's economy had always been based on agriculture, and its people have bartered for their wares. Most Isleta arts have been credited to families of the Laguna colony and to one woman in particular, Marie Chiwewe, whose parents were part of the original group that migrated to Isleta.

32. This structure belonged to Lupe Abeita, whose marriage produced no children.

33. From testimony presented in *J. Francisco Chavez versus the United States of America* (see note 23).

34. The core of the corrupt power elite in New Mexico fell into disrepute as a result of the infamous 1923 Teapot Dome scandal.

35. This observation seems to be the predominant comment by other Pueblo Indians!

36. Another major rennovation by German born Father Fred Stadtmueller would restore the church facade to a Pueblo motif in 1962. The renowned Southwest architectural historian Bainbridge Bunting was to remark, "One cannot fail to regret those perky little 1880 towers of wood which formerly crowned the ponderously buttressed facade. Incongruous as was that contrast, the combination was somehow indicative of a particular time and place. The new block towers [are] less distinctively and specifically Isleta—an interchangeable architecture for an interchangeable man in an interchangeable society." [Abridged from Bunting (1960)]

37. Recollections of Mary Pickford (Friar and Friar 1972, 119).

38. An apology, of sorts, by Charles Lummis is narrated in a chapter entitled "Charles Lummis Returns to Isleta." See Keleher and Chant (1940, 89–90).

39. A chapter entitled "The Indian Who Got Away," on the exploits of Louis Abeita, is to be found in Crane (1928, 377). It should be noted that Louis Abeita was no blood relation to Pablo Abeita.

40. This aspect of the community should not be taken lightly. Because this subject, however, is beyond the scope of this paper, I refer readers to French (1948).

III

Modern Tendencies

The Pueblo Indian architectural and settlement pattern scene reveals both change and continuity. The adaptive behavior discussed in Chapter 7 continues at the present, and yet a continuity of tradition still can be seen at work which links the earliest dwellings in the region, the pit houses, and the style and settlement patterns of today's Pueblos. Chapter 8 focuses on changes in building and planning at Zuni Pueblo over the course of this century. Once again the adaptive behavior pattern is highlighted, and the stress of function over form, a pragmatic approach to building and design is said to characterize the modern Zuni approach to building. Although the appearance of the pueblo changes, the functions remain the same. The authors warn about a threat from outside, however. The introduction of HUD housing brings stringent guidelines that ignore communal function and have a negative effect on the traditional Zuni way of life. In Chapter 9, Louis Hieb describes the more conservative building tradition at Hopi Pueblo, where building materials remain the same and strict attention is paid to old symbolic forms, and where function plays a secondary role to that of cultural meaning and values. In Chapter 10, Tsiporah Lipton analyzes the cosmology of the Tewa-speaking Pueblos and shows how the view of an intimate relationship between people and land is reflected in ceramic decoration, in dance, in architecture, and in village patterns. She emphasizes, however, that this does not mean a blending of the human into the environment, but an understanding of the human community as actively interacting with the natural environment.

Contemporary Zuni Architecture and Society   **8**

T.J. Ferguson • Barbara J. Mills • Calbert Seciwa

Zuni Pueblo, unlike Taos and Acoma pueblos, has undergone a dramatic architectural change in the twentieth century. The Zuni people have almost entirely reconstructed the old multistoried pueblo edifice (fig. 8-1) to create single-storied houses with more open space at ground level (fig. 8-2). New masonry styles and window forms have greatly changed the appearance of the pueblo. The historic room blocks in the core of the village have been surrounded by modern construction in a suburban settlement pattern. As the population of the tribe has grown from 1500 to 8000 in the last 80 years, the Zuni people have rebuilt their compact pueblo into a sprawling, modern town.

Architectural change at Zuni Pueblo has been swift and seemingly complete, but appearances are deceiving. Zuni Pueblo no longer *looks* like it did in the past, but in several important ways Zuni architecture continues to function as it always has. There is a strong vernacular architecture at Zuni, and many people continue the Pueblo tradition of building their own houses. At the same time, federally funded housing and construction programs have become increasingly important and have indelibly altered the architectural structure and character of the village. Contemporary Zuni architecture is thus a complex mixture of traditional and recently introduced elements.

In this chapter, we analyze the development of contemporary Zuni architecture and explain architectural change as a consequence of population growth, economic change, and federal policy. Traditionally, Zuni architecture was strongly integrated with Zuni society. Today, however, there is an increasing disarticulation of architecture and society. A critical analysis of Zuni architecture is needed to develop a better under-

8-1 *A major reconstruction of the multistoried edifice of Zuni Pueblo was initiated around the turn the century, when the Zuni people began to build larger houses with doors at ground level. (Photograph: A. C. Vroman, ca. 1899, courtesy of Los Angeles County Museum of Natural History, negative no. V-2362D.)*

8-2 *This photo, illustrating the same room block pictured in Figure 8-1, shows the tremendous architectural change that has occurred at Zuni Pueblo as a result of newly introduced masonry styles, building forms, and roof types. (Photograph: Barbara J. Mills, 1981, courtesy of T. J. Ferguson, Barbara J. Mills, and Calbert Seciwa.)*

standing of how and why Zuni Pueblo has developed as it has. We hope that this analysis can be used by the Zuni people, and the governmental agencies that serve them, to preserve the key features of traditional Zuni architecture while adding the new architectural elements desired by the contemporary residents of the village.

SOCIAL FUNCTIONS OF ZUNI ARCHITECTURE

At Zuni Pueblo, the formal and structural aspects of architecture cannot be divorced from their social and cultural functions. The Zuni architectural tradition is dynamic, with a genuine interest and well-demonstrated ability to incorporate new construction materials and designs. Since Zuni Pueblo was founded, about A.D. 1400, it has undergone continual reconstruction, and the facade of the core pueblo has evolved through several distinctly different styles. Underlying this constant change in the appearance of Zuni architecture, however, are the purposes for which Zuni buildings are constructed.

One of the main purposes is to house domestic activities. The basic domestic unit in Zuni society is an extended family that traces its lineage through a clan system comprising fourteen maternal clans. Traditionally, the mother's household is the social, residential, and economic base of the family (Ladd 1979, 482–48). Until married daughters establish economic independence, it is normal for them to reside in their mother's household, along with their husbands and children. This means that Zuni households are quite large; they typically occupy an interconnected suite of rooms in a pueblo building. Traditionally, the men of a Zuni household laid up the masonry walls of a house, while the women finished the structure by plastering it.

The social relations defined by kin and clan in Zuni society are cross-cut and tied together by Zuni religious organizations, including six kivas, twelve medicine societies, and two priesthoods. The activities of these religious groups require both private and public architectural space within the pueblo. The six kivas and the priesthoods maintain special rooms where religious activities are conducted in private. For public ceremonies, they use the plazas of Zuni Pueblo, which are connected by sacred pathways. During religious ceremonies the roofs of the houses surrounding the plazas are used as public galleries for viewing ceremonies. The open spaces of Zuni Pueblo, defined by the exterior boundaries of individual houses and kivas, play a very important role in the social integration of the tribe.

The clans and medicine societies conduct their ceremonies and other activities in the homes of their leaders, who have large rooms that are temporarily cleared of domestic activities for the occasion. In addition, during the winter Night Dances, the kiva groups dance in houses, moving between them through the sacred pathways of the village. The temporary conversion of domestic rooms to ceremonial use creates an intermediary category between domestic and ceremonial architecture within the pueblo (fig. 8-3).

The social connection between domestic and ceremonial architecture at Zuni Pueblo is culturally reinforced in the *Shalako* ceremony held every winter. Each year, six to eight houses are constructed or rehabilitated by clan groups, with a particular family within the clan serving as the sponsor. The sponsor's clan provides substantial assistance in the form of labor and materials. Shalako houses have a central room where the masked religious dancers perform their blessing ceremonies. Off this central room are wings of rooms where visitors are fed and sheltered during the ceremony; many people also gather about the outside windows to observe the ceremonies taking place inside. After the ceremony, the interiors of the houses are finished and the structures are used as a domestic residence by the sponsoring family. Shalako houses socially and symbolically integrate Zuni society through the religious activities that take place within them. In doing so, they are an important feature of Zuni vernacular architecture.

ZUNI ARCHITECTURE: A TRADITION OF INNOVATION

Zuni architecture comprises an indigenous Pueblo tradition freely elaborated by the adoption of new building technologies and materials over time. The Zunis adopted many architectural features from the Spaniards in the seventeenth and eighteenth centuries. Corner fireplaces with chimneys, adobe bricks made in wooden forms, stairs, and pintle doors became common. The size of individual rooms and houses increased, in part because the draft animals obtained from the Spaniards made it easier to

8-3 *This large Zuni living room, with its decorated interior, was also used for ceremonial activities. (Photograph: James D. Schuyler, 1904, courtesy of National Archives, record group 75.)*

procure longer beams and to collect the firewood needed to heat larger rooms. The Zunis used the new tools and technologies introduced by the Spaniards to create a domestic architecture with larger, better-heated spaces.

A major shift in the overall pattern of Zuni settlement occurred during the Pueblo Revolt of 1680, when the Zuni people consolidated themselves into a single settlement, defensively located on top of Dowa Yalanne, a sheer-sided mesa rising 800 feet above the surrounding valley. Prior to this, the Zuni people had occupied multiple villages. When the Spaniards first arrived in 1540, for instance, there were six or seven Zuni villages. Following the Pueblo Revolt, the entire tribe resettled at Halona:wa, one of the villages previously occupied, which became known as Zuni Pueblo.

Between 1540 and 1680, the size of the Zuni population had been substantially reduced by epidemics of European diseases, and consolidation into a single large community made it possible to maintain a rich social and ceremonial life and also facilitated defense from the Apache and Navajo raids that were common at the time. As the Zunis consolidated into a single permanent village, they developed a number of small farming villages that were primarily used during the spring and summer growing seasons. Most Zuni families maintained a permanent residence at Zuni Pueblo and a seasonal residence at one of the farming villages. The use of multiple residences enabled a family to pursue the wide range of farming and livestock activities that were the foundation of the historic Zuni economy.

The first accurate map of Zuni Pueblo (reduced to a block diagram in Fig. 8-4) was produced by Victor and Cosmos Mindeleff in 1881, as part of their classic comparative study of Hopi and Zuni architecture (Mindeleff 1891). At this time Zuni Pueblo consisted of seven large room blocks compactly arranged around a number of plazas and streets, covering a small hill on the north side of the Zuni River. The two small plazas formed by the room blocks at the crest of the hill had been occupied since prehistoric times. The historic growth of the pueblo had been agglomerative, and rooms had been added piecemeal as needed onto the existing architectural complex, either on top of existing rooms or at the edges of the village. After the Pueblo Revolt, when Zuni Pueblo was enlarged to accommodate the entire tribe, the limits to vertical growth were reached in the pueblo core, and new room blocks were constructed to the south, running downslope toward the Zuni River, and to the east, on flat ground (Kroeber 1917, 198–200; Mindeleff 1891, 97–8; Spier 1917, 229).

These three eastern room blocks were constructed almost entirely of adobe bricks made in wooden forms (Ferguson and Mills 1982, 139), evidence that they were definitely constructed during the historic period. They were lower and less dense than the original room blocks, and they enclosed the Catholic church. The church, with its graveyard, or campo santo, enclosed by a low wall, had been constructed in 1630 on a trash mound outside the pueblo (Spier 1917, 228). After the Pueblo Revolt, the church gradually came to occupy a central position in the middle of the village.

Until the twentieth century, the houses in each room block at Zuni Pueblo were constructed one upon another in a succession of terraces, so that the roof of one house formed a floor or yard for the house above. The terraces were used as public walkways, and many activities took place on them, including bread baking in domed ovens and food drying and processing. The largest of the room blocks had five terraces and encompassed several hundred rooms. The massive architectural structure of the pueblo, with few doors or windows at ground level, had been designed in part to provide protection from Apache and Navajo raids. When the ladders used to access the terraces were drawn up, the pueblo was converted into an impenetrable fortress, and the living rooms on the upper levels were protected.

The Zuni people constructed their pueblo in accordance with an implicit set of architectural principles. As Bainbridge Bunting describes,

> The old edifice possessed infinite variety tempered by a fine sense of order. The key to this order was the way in which all walls conformed to coordinate

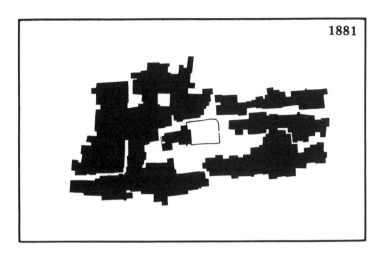

1881

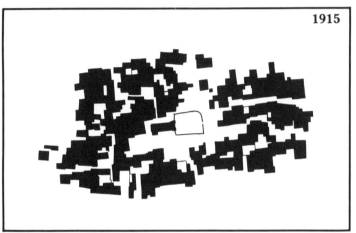

1915

1972

8-4 *This diagram of changes in the core architecture of Zuni Pueblo in 1881, 1915, and 1972 shows the increase in the amount of open space within the pueblo (After Mindeleff 1891: Pl. LXXVI; Kroeber 1917: map 6; Borchers 1972.)*

axes. Despite the extent of the complex, each house with its terrace was unique, and even though many persons lived in proximity, a sense of individuality and distinctiveness was preserved (Bunting 1976, 45).

The north–south and east–west coordinate axes used in the architectural plan of Zuni Pueblo reflect the symbolic directionalism important in the Zuni conceptualization of space, with its emphasis on the cardinal points. Use of these coordinate axes also enabled the Zunis to construct the rooftop terraces to take maximal advantage of the eastern and southern exposures optimal for passive solar heating. The largest room block in Zuni Pueblo was at the west end of the village at the crest of the hill. This room block had a high west wall with very few terraces or openings. On its north side it had only three terraces, while on the south and east sides, in keeping with solar design, were five terraces.

The location and form of this massive room block acted to shield the rest of the village from the prevailing westerly winds. These winds are especially strong in the spring during the Zuni months of *Li'dekwakkya Ts'ana* (Little Sandstorm) and *Li'dekwakkya lana* (Big Sandstorm), resulting in a significant amount of aeolian deposition at *So'biyahna:wa* ("where the sand drops off"), at the northwestern edge of the village. This hill slope was also used as a midden, where household trash was deposited (Kroeber 1917, 193). Several low terrace walls were constructed on this midden to help retain the slope (Collins 1983).

The stone and adobe masonry used to construct Zuni Pueblo was almost universally plastered with brown adobe in the nineteenth century (fig. 8-5). The wall plaster protected the structural stability of the masonry and provided a visual uniformity that aesthetically tied together the modular and individually varied houses and rooms comprising the room blocks. To preserve the wall plaster, and to shade the walls from the high sun of the summer months, terraces and roofs with southern exposures were often constructed with a slight overhang. Thin sandstone coping stones on the parapets of the roof overhangs, and carefully placed drains and splashstones, helped to further reduce the erosive force of rain and snow on the adobe plaster and walls. The roofs and terraces, constructed of dirt overlying willow thatch on two perpendicular sets of support beams, generally had a slight pitch to facilitate drainage (Mindeleff 1891, 148–56.).

In the nineteenth century, the architecture of the outlying farming villages was similar to that of Zuni Pueblo, but less massive. The farming villages were smaller than Zuni Pueblo, and the buildings in them were only one and two stories high, containing fewer rooms. As long as there was a need for defense, buildings at the farming villages were either tightly clustered or located on high ground. The farming villages lacked kivas or other specialized architecture, and this set them apart from Zuni Pueblo, the ceremonial heart of the tribe.

8-5 *Looking north at Zuni Pueblo, ca. 1899. (Photograph by A. C. Vroman, courtesy Pasadena Public Library, vol. 7, no. 710.)*

8-6 *Looking northeast at Zuni Pueblo and its adjacent waffle gardens, ca. 1911. (Photograph: Jesse L. Nusbaum, courtesy of Western History Department, Denver Public Library, negative no. N312.)*

The use of space in the community layout of Zuni Pueblo and the farming villages was very similar. Zuni Pueblo had more formal plazas, where religious dances were held, but all the villages had open areas where social dances were conducted. Houses in all the villages had yards where outdoor activities took place. Corrals for livestock and small kitchen gardens were located at the edges of the villages. The "waffle gardens," used to grow herbs and chiles, were divided by earthen borders into small compartments and were watered by hand (fig. 8-6). Beyond the corrals and gardens were larger corn and wheat fields and the rangeland used for grazing.

In 1881, the transcontinental railroad was constructed through the Puerco River valley, 40 miles to the north of Zuni Pueblo. Soon afterward, new building materials such as glass window panes and milled lumber became available. The Zunis quickly started to use these materials to construct doors and windows to let more light into domestic rooms. By the turn of the century, there was no longer a need for defense, and a more open pueblo was possible. Many Zuni families began to rebuild their houses with living rooms at ground level, with doors replacing roof hatchways and ladders.

ARCHITECTURAL CHANGE IN THE TWENTIETH CENTURY

The tradition of innovation that so strongly characterized the development of historic Zuni architecture has not stopped in the twentieth century. The Zuni people have continued to rebuild Zuni Pueblo to make modern improvements, and they have introduced new building materials and forms into Zuni vernacular architecture in the process. Virtually the entire pueblo has been reconstructed on a piecemeal basis, a house at a time, as each family made improvements to their domestic space. While each reconstruction event yielded a relatively small and discrete architectural change, in the aggregate these individual actions wrought a tremendous change in the overall structure and character of the pueblo.

Three basic structural trends are apparent in twentieth-century architectural change at Zuni Pueblo. These are:

1. Replacement of multistoried houses on terraces with single-storied houses at ground level
2. Development of more open space within the pueblo
3. Suburban expansion

Accompanying these structural trends have been marked changes in masonry styles, window forms, and roof designs. All of these changes have affected how the pueblo looks.

The trend toward ground-story living resulted in the eventual reduction in the number of the upper terraces of the room blocks. Houses on the upper terraces were allowed to fall into disrepair, and eventually they were dismantled, with the reusable roof beams and building stone recycled into new construction elsewhere in the pueblo. By 1915, when the anthropologist A. L. Kroeber produced a map of Zuni Pueblo at the same scale as Mindeleff's 1881 map, the room blocks in the core of the pueblo had been reduced to three terraces, with only a single small room remaining on the fourth level. This remaining room was the *Kyappachunna*, from which the town crier made public announcements (Kroeber 1917, 190).

Kroeber's 1915 plan of Zuni Pueblo is reduced to a block diagram in fig. 8-4. One of the most distinctive changes apparent in a comparison of Kroeber's 1915 plan of Zuni with Mindeleff's 1881 plan is the creation of more open space within the pueblo. While the 1881 plan shows massive, joined room blocks and restricted open space on the interior of the pueblo, Kroeber's 1915 plan shows that the eastern room blocks are no longer joined, the alley and room blocks in the southwestern part of the village have opened up considerably, and one of the two small plazas in the pueblo core has been greatly enlarged.

Much of the open space that was created in Zuni Pueblo was used for streets and alleys that allowed wheeled vehicles to be brought to the doors of ground floor houses. During Kroeber's time, these wheeled vehicles were horse-drawn wagons, conveyances that were soon replaced by automobiles and trucks.

The creation of open space was achieved in many ways. In some cases, such as with the eastern room blocks constructed of adobe, it was easier to raze whole houses or large sections of the room blocks and build them anew to the desired configuration. In other areas, such as the pueblo core around the plazas, there was a dense sandstone masonry construction that required other solutions. In this area, tearing down one room might lead to serious problems in the structural stability of the surrounding rooms. While the upper one or two stories were generally dismantled, the lower-story rooms were often filled instead. This was reported to be an old custom in the 1880s (Bandelier, in Lange and Riley 1970, 62). Roofs were cut around their edges and allowed to fall inside the room, and the room was then filled with trash, construction debris, ash, and charcoal, or clean sand from the riverbed (Ferguson and Mills 1982, 113).

As open ground was constructed in the room blocks, many interior rooms were totally buried. Other rooms were reconstructed to serve as low-walled open terraces in front of still-occupied houses. Since the founding of the pueblo, refuse, blowsand, and the wash from dirt roofs and adobe plaster have accumulated in the streets, raising their level (Kroeber 1917, 193–4). This deposition worked in conjunction with the filling of rooms in the interior of room blocks to sink the lower stories of the pueblo in a mound of cultural debris that is very similar to a Middle East tell.

Kroeber (1917, 194) thought that the rapidity with which Zuni Pueblo changed in detail, while preserving the same general outline and appearance over generations, was "really remarkable." He noted, however, that the general conservatism of plan was offset by a readiness to make changes of a few feet in the lines of any particular house. Kroeber estimated that the exterior walls of virtually every house in the pueblo were rebuilt along new lines every 30 to 40 years.

Much of the reconstruction of Zuni Pueblo took place in conjunction with the Shalako ceremony. In 1915, Kroeber noted that when houses were improved to host the Shalako they were invariably enlarged, and the roof was raised to admit the giant figures, substantially increasing the size of the rooms (Kroeber 1917, 195). Since the turn of the century, more than 500 houses in Zuni Pueblo have been constructed or rehabilitated for Shalako.

The trends toward larger, single-storied houses and more open space within Zuni Pueblo resulted in a lower residential density in the historic core of the pueblo. This, in conjunction with a rapidly growing population (Table 8-1), led to an increasing suburbanization of the pueblo (fig. 8-7). This expansion had begun in the late nineteenth century, when Zuni houses, missionary schools, government buildings, and trading posts were constructed outside the original core pueblo. By 1915, the suburban expansion had extended to encompass over fifty room blocks of various sizes in areas on both sides of the Zuni River (Kroeber 1917, maps 5 and 7). By this time, the building of individual family dwellings, or small room blocks for the houses of two or three closely related families, had become common.

One of the primary architectural principles applied during the early-twentieth-century expansion of the pueblo was that all the outlying houses were oriented to face inward, with their doors toward the village center. Kroeber (1917, 198) also noted that when a family moved their residence to the suburbs, they normally settled in that part of the outlying village that corresponded to the section of town they were moving from. For instance, people from the northeast room blocks of the old pueblo generally moved to the northeast suburbs. The basic orientation of the pueblo was retained, even as it was greatly expanded. The lateral expansion and suburbanization of Zuni Pueblo was thus closely correlated with the architectural reduction of the original room blocks.

A bold, ashlar masonry style rapidly gained popularity in the twentieth century, giving a new texture to the appearance of the pueblo in contrast to the smoothness of the earlier plastered walls. The square-cut, heavily dressed stones are closely fitted together, requiring no wall plaster to protect the structural stability of mortar-filled joints. Ashlar masonry required less maintenance than the earlier tabular masonry or adobe construction, which had to be continually replastered. The ashlar masonry style was introduced through a number of large-scale construction projects at Zuni employing Zuni masons, including the BIA construction of Black Rock Dam from 1904 to 1908, and the construction of St. Anthony's Mission in the early 1920s. In the 1920s and 1930s, ashlar masonry became the predominant style of stone masonry at Zuni Pueblo.

Since World War II, the architecture of Zuni Pueblo has continued to change rapidly. Electricity was introduced in 1950, and the numerous electrical wires, streetlamps, and television aerials visible in the pueblo today attest to the acceptance of modern conveniences. Water lines with services to individual households were installed in 1954 and improved in 1977, and sewer lines were installed in 1961. The ridged and gabled roofs common today at Zuni Pueblo were constructed on top of the

TABLE 8-1 *Twentieth-Century Zuni Population Growth*

Decade	Population
1900	1523
1910	1664
1920	1863
1930	1990
1940	2000
1950	2563
1960	4213
1970	6000
1980	7500

8-7 *Aerial view of Zuni Pueblo, 1948. (Photograph: Cutter-Carr Flying Service (for Stanley Stubbs), courtesy Museum of New Mexico, neg. no. 5049.)*

flat roofs of most buildings in the 1960s, to stop them from leaking. These new roofs provided the most cost-effective solution available at the time for weatherproofing the houses. The steeply pitched roofs obscure what remains of the rooftop terraces in the pueblo, but they have nonetheless become popular in Zuni vernacular architecture.

In the core historic room blocks, the tendency for architecture to change rapidly in detail, while preserving the same general plan, has continued in an attenuated form to the present day. This can be seen in fig. 8-4 (bottom), a block diagram based on a photogrammetric map of the core pueblo prepared by Perry Borchers in 1972. Many changes in the form and number of houses and in the amount of open space are evident, but there is still continuity to the past outlines of the room blocks. The linear orientation of the room blocks to the east is greatly reduced but still discernible, and the clustering of the western room blocks is still oriented around the small plazas, which are used as they have been for centuries.

The preservation of the general outline of the old pueblo at Zuni has been maintained, but otherwise this part of the village has undergone a complete architectural transformation. Fewer than fifty structures dating prior to 1937 still stand (Mimbres and Associates 1977, 81), and the pueblo core today is largely a cluster of recently constructed single-storied houses sitting on the mounded remains of the earlier multistoried village (fig. 8-8). The impact of the automobile has been immense, and virtually all exterior space, except for Ts:ya:a Dewidon:na, the smallest plaza used for sacred dances, has been modified so that it can be used as a roadway. New masonry styles, roof forms, and building materials have become popular, and new construction has obscured the old terraces that were once such a prominent aspect of Zuni architecture.

The trend toward suburban living has continued, accompanied by the rapid growth in the population of the Zuni tribe, which is now approaching 8000. The original pueblo is now surrounded on all sides by outlying houses, room blocks, public buildings, and government-subsidized subdivisions. There has been no zonation by historic character, and open areas between early-twentieth-century room blocks have been infilled with Zuni-built and HUD houses. New architectural forms and materials, such as wood-frame and cinderblock houses with sliding aluminum windows and ridged and gabled roofs, have greatly diversified the once-cohesive architectural character of the village.

8-8 *Contemporary architecture at Zuni Pueblo sits on top of earlier rooms that were filled to create open ground. (Photograph: Helga Teiwes, courtesy Arizona State Museum, University of Arizona, negative no. 46906.)*

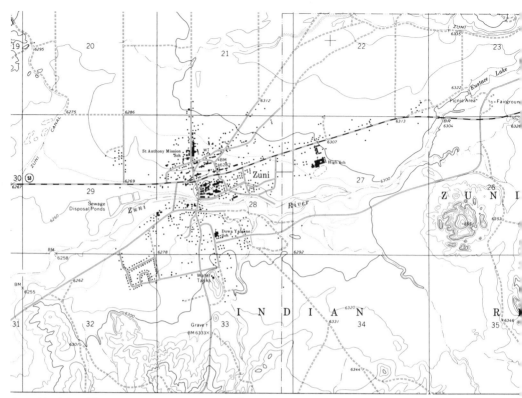

8-9 *Zuni Pueblo, 1972. (Map courtesy of USGS, Zuni Quadrangle, 7.5 Minute Series, [Topographic]).*

Zuni Pueblo has grown into a small town several square miles in size, with the layout of the larger settlement following patterns set by paved roads and utilities (fig. 8-9). A large tribal building housing the governmental complex, and five schools provide institutional foci in community orientation, but the old pueblo remains the central focus of the village, the "Middle Place." The area between Zuni Pueblo and Black Rock is gradually filling in, and more and more houses are being built on agricultural lands. Black Rock, located 4 miles to the east of Zuni Pueblo, was founded in 1904, when the first BIA Agency was established on the reservation. Today it is the site of many of the most recent subdivisions constructed at Zuni.

Since World War II, the seasonal occupation of the farming villages has been relinquished in favor of vehicle-supported commuting on a daily basis. The majority of the tribe now resides in Zuni Pueblo and its suburbs year-round. This change is due, in part, to the fact that farming has become less important than jewelry making, wage labor, and livestock as a source of family income and support. Until the seasonal occupation of the farming villages ceased, the architectural trends in them paralleled those of Zuni Pueblo. Today, it is more common to maintain old houses than to build new ones in the farming villages, and as a result many architectural styles no longer present at Zuni Pueblo can still be found there (fig. 8-10).

ENDURING FEATURES OF ZUNI ARCHITECTURE

Even though the architectural appearance of Zuni Pueblo has been dramatically transformed in the twentieth century, there are enduring features of Zuni architecture that still play an important role in Zuni society. The styles of Zuni vernacular architecture continue to change as they always have, and more open space is defined by fewer buildings, but there is a very strong continuity in the open-space structure of the pueblo. This continuity is due to the religious element of Zuni culture, which acts as a conservative force in architectural change.

This architectural conservatism is related to the key importance of certain areas in the pueblo core for ceremonial activity. Kiva locations, dance plazas, and religious pathways have maintained their locational integrity to a much greater extent than domestic structures, and it is around these points that the pueblo has been reconstructed. Thus, although religious areas have been enlarged, they have rarely been encroached upon. Those areas that have maintained the most integrity are the ones that are used by the most religious groups. The small sacred dance plaza in the core of the pueblo, used by virtually every group, is correspondingly the most stable architectural space.

The special rooms used by the kiva groups also represent a conservative architectural form. The kivas retain the oldest masonry styles in the village and are rebuilt only when structural reasons dictate reconstruction for safety reasons. Although the contemporary kivas now all have doors, they also retain the roof entryway and ladders, which are used for ceremonial purposes. The kivas are now the only buildings in Zuni with these features.

One enduring feature of Zuni architecture important in Zuni society is the use of rooftops as viewing galleries for spectators during ceremonial events, including both social and religious dances. The rooftops that ring the plazas have remained relatively level for this purpose, while almost all other roofs have marked pitches. The relatively flat roofs surrounding the plazas are also still used for access around the pueblo and are viewed as public areas.

Traditionally, most Zuni families acted as their own architect and builder, and many continue to do so today. Because of the contemporary wage-labor economy of Zuni, it is now easier for many people to purchase cinderblock and milled lumber than it is to take the time to quarry stone and cut roof beams. Thus, many houses built in the

8-10 *This house at the Zuni farming village of Upper Nutria was used as a storage facility in 1979. (Photograph: Barbara J. Mills, courtesy Zuni Archaeology Program, Pueblo of Zuni.)*

traditional way are now constructed out of nontraditional materials. While the gray cinderblock that has been popular since the 1960s has a different aesthetic than adobe or quarried sandstone, it is still a masonry element laid up into walls by local masons and thus is a form of Zuni vernacular architecture.

Only houses constructed by the Zuni people themselves are used in the Shalako ceremony, and since the late 1960s these generally have been newly constructed cinderblock houses built on stone foundations. In the last two decades the height of stone foundations on Shalako houses has steadily decreased, from approximately half the height of the wall to one or two courses. Sliding and picture pane aluminum windows have become the most common window closure. In recent years, most of the Shalako houses have been located in the suburbs of Zuni, although remodeling of houses in the pueblo core continues. Shalako houses today define Zuni vernacular style domestic architecture.

As the older architecture of Zuni Pueblo is gradually replaced with new construction, the cultural meaning of traditional Zuni architecture is being retained in art. Images of historic Zuni architecture featuring kivas with ladders or the old terraced room blocks symbolize important aspects of Zuni community life and have become a common depiction in Zuni art. The content for artistic inspiration is sometimes derived from historic photographs that show the pueblo at earlier times. The cultural meaning of Zuni architecture endures, even as its physical expression continues to change.

THE SOCIAL AND CULTURAL IMPACTS OF FEDERAL HOUSING PROGRAMS

Federally funded housing programs have had an increasing impact on the architecture of the Zuni village. In 1964, the Zuni Housing Authority was established to finance the construction of houses with federal funding. Since then, more than 680 federally financed homes have been constructed, many of them in newly developed subdivisions, others filling in open areas within the village (Ferguson, et al. 1988). The tremendous impact of federal housing is evident in the fact that the number of federally funded houses built in the last 25 years as exceeded the total number of Shalako houses that have been constructed since the turn of the century. HUD-financed houses now constitute more than 30 percent of the housing stock of the pueblo.

Federally funded programs provided a solution to a housing problem that became acute in the 1960s, when the Zuni population increased faster than the ability to provide housing using traditional means. In some respects, however, this solution has turned out to be a Trojan horse, with hidden social, cultural, and financial costs.

In applying national standards for single-family dwellings to housing within Zuni Pueblo, federal programs have reinforced the nuclear family at the expense of the extended Zuni family. The long-term impact this will have on Zuni society is only now being recognized. The small kitchens and living rooms of federally constructed houses are adequate for the needs of a single family, but they do not easily accommodate the large gatherings that typify Zuni social occasions. The lack of large rooms means that some social events, such as weddings or graduation parties, are fragmented into several different houses. Many Zuni people living in HUD houses still return to the house of their mother for ceremonial occasions, a house that is more often than not constructed in the vernacular style. Whether HUD houses, with their space limitations, can support a similar social arrangement when their occupants become the matriarchal leaders of their extended families remains to be seen.

The single-family dwelling orientation of federal housing has increased the social isolation of families. Related families cannot physically connect their households to form large room blocks with their relatives in federally funded housing projects. Housing in subdivisions is laid out by arbitrary, non-kinship-related criteria that decrease social interaction. People in subdivisions live in less proximity to one another than in other parts of Zuni Pueblo. The repetitive uniformity in the architectural plan of federal houses provides a less distinctive home environment than vernacular architecture. A spatial subdivision of the tribe by wealth is beginning as a consequence of low-income housing at Black Rock.

There has been very little Zuni involvement in the design of houses built through federal programs. Some of the first federal houses were built without fireplaces or wood stoves, an oversight that made them difficult to heat and also impeded the practice of Zuni culture. The Zuni people ceremoniously feed their ancestors by offering food in an open flame. Without the ability to burn wood, this cultural practice is difficult. In subsequent housing contracts, the Zuni Housing Authority provided a fireplace or stove appropriate for the needs of Zuni households.

HUD houses are often more expensive to own and maintain than the occupants anticipate. This is because the final cost of the house is not determined until project completion. The electric heating systems of HUD houses can cost several hundreds of dollars a month to operate during the winter, and for many people this is a substantial new expense that has to be budgeted. Finally, payment for a house is based at 30 percent of family income, none of which is tax deductible as it would be in the non-Reservation economy. For some tribal members this cost is prohibitive.

With Zuni people increasingly involved in wage labor, it has become difficult to assemble the communal work groups that traditionally assisted tribal members in house construction and maintained the public open spaces of the pueblo. As a result, the Zuni Tribe has found new ways to accomplish old tasks. Today it has become common for federally funded programs, such as the Home Improvement Program (HIP), to undertake rehabilitation and maintenance of historic architecture. In many respects, the HIP program is an extension of Zuni vernacular architecture. It employs small groups of Zuni workers who use the same materials and forms in construction that other Zuni people do. Zuni households that are rehabilitated by the HIP program can retain their internal permeability in larger room blocks, and this strengthens traditional Zuni social organization.

HISTORIC PRESERVATION

In the 1970s, Zuni Pueblo was listed on the National Register of Historic Places. Since then, virtually all federally funded projects in Zuni Pueblo have been reviewed by the State Historic Preservation Officer (SHPO) and the National Advisory Council on Historic Preservation. These agencies have offered many good recommendations for the retention of the historic character of the pueblo. However, adequate funding to implement historic preservation recommendations for rehabilitation of the pueblo is rarely provided by sponsoring agencies, and this tends to exacerbate the process. For instance, when historic preservation recommendations call for new sash windows to replace old ones, the project cost is increased, since sash windows are now available only by special order. When additional funds are not available to supplement the project, the overall scope must be cut back to implement the recommendations.

Since most Zuni people prefer aluminum windows in their own construction, there is an underlying tension between the tradition of dynamic innovation in Zuni vernacular architecture and the historic preservation orientation to preserve a particular architectural style. Zuni vernacular architecture and the strictures of historic preservation are guided by very different values. Zuni values are to provide adequate shelter at a cost the residents can afford. Historic preservation stresses appearance over cost and functional concerns.

Historic preservation at Zuni Pueblo presents a vexing problem in that decisions about what the pueblo should look like are removed from residents and concentrated in governmental agencies. Although the process is supposed to be a consultation

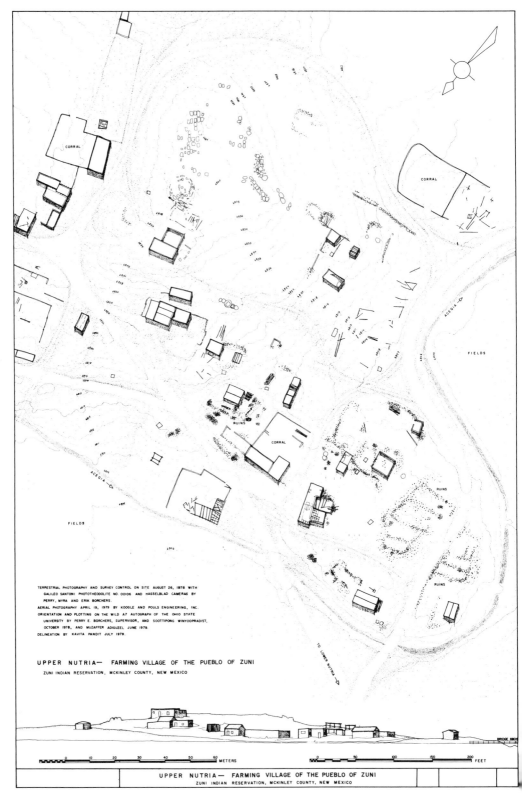

Within the map image:

CORRAL

CORRAL

ACEQUIA ►

FIELDS

ACEQUIA ►

RUINS

CORRAL

RUINS

FIELDS

RUINS

TO LOWER NUTRIA ►

TERRESTRIAL PHOTOGRAPHY AND SURVEY CONTROL ON SITE AUGUST 26, 1978 WITH
GALILEO SANTONI PHOTOTHEODOLITE NO. 00106 AND HASSELBLAD CAMERAS BY
PERRY, MYRA AND ERIK BORCHERS.
AERIAL PHOTOGRAPHY APRIL 19, 1979 BY KOOGLE AND POULS ENGINEERING, INC.
ORIENTATION AND PLOTTING ON THE WILD A7 AUTOGRAPH OF THE OHIO STATE
UNIVERSITY BY PERRY E. BORCHERS, SUPERVISOR, AND SOOTTIPONG WINYOOPRADIST,
OCTOBER 1978, AND MUZAFFER ADIGUZEL JUNE 1979.
DELINEATION BY KAVITA PANDIT JULY 1979.

UPPER NUTRIA— FARMING VILLAGE OF THE PUEBLO OF ZUNI
ZUNI INDIAN RESERVATION, MCKINLEY COUNTY, NEW MEXICO

0 10 20 30 40 50 60 METERS

0 50 100 150 200 FEET

UPPER NUTRIA— FARMING VILLAGE OF THE PUEBLO OF ZUNI
ZUNI INDIAN RESERVATION, MCKINLEY COUNTY, NEW MEXICO

8-11 *Map of Upper Nutria, a farming village of the Pueblo of Zuni. (Aerial and terrestrial photogrammetry by Perry Borchers, courtesy Zuni Archaeology Program, Pueblo of Zuni.)*

among equal parties, at Zuni Pueblo it is often perceived as a one-way interaction in which "Santa Fe" (the location of the SHPO) dictates what local residents can and cannot do. Often, the workers involved in projects do not understand the historic preservation values that dictate using higher cost materials or nonstandard forms, and this creates problems.

The New Mexico State Historic Preservation Program has taken positive steps to promote historic preservation at Zuni Pueblo. Among other things, it has sponsored programs that brought architects to the pueblo to talk to workers in federally funded rehabilitation projects about the importance of maintaining Pueblo architecture. And it has continued to consult on architectural problems in the core pueblo.

While the attitudes of Zuni people toward historic preservation are different from those of Anglos, the Zuni Tribe is not adverse to historic preservation. The Zuni Archaeology Program serves as a tribal cultural resources management agency, emphasizing historic preservation through documentation. Over the last decade, the tribal archaeology program has undertaken projects to record a substantial amount of the historic architecture in Zuni Pueblo and the farming villages (fig. 8-11). In one instance, a kiva group requested that its building be completely recorded prior to its reconstruction for documentary purposes. There was no federal involvement in this particular project, so this documentation was not required by law. The fact that the kiva leaders thought it was important to document their building for their own purposes is an indication of how the Zuni people are beginning to use their tribal archaeology program to fulfill self-defined needs for historic preservation. In addition to recording standing architecture, the Zuni Archaeology Program also investigates subsurface archaeological deposits when they are exposed by the construction of utilities or roads (Ferguson and Mills 1982; Collins 1983).

Another example of the Zuni interest in historic preservation was the restoration of the old Catholic church Nuestra Señora de Guadalupe. This church stood roofless in the big plaza of Zuni Pueblo for more than a century. It was restored in the 1960s in a cooperative project involving Zuni Pueblo, St. Anthony's Mission, and the National Park Service (Caywood 1972). Catholic mass is once again celebrated in the church, and Zuni artist Alex Seowtewa has painted beautiful murals on its interior walls, showing life-size kachinas enacting the annual ceremonial calendar.

ARCHITECTURE AND ARCHAEOLOGY

The past structures the present and future at Zuni Pueblo, in the very literal sense that the contemporary architecture of the pueblo conforms to the underlying rooms and cultural deposits that have become part of the archaeological matrix of the site. Today, the historic core of Zuni Pueblo is experiencing severe structural problems. Contemporary houses sit on top of many meters of soft cultural debris (fig. 8-12), and it is difficult to build a house there with solid foundations. Many houses in the core pueblo have settled, necessitating their reconstruction. Some rooms in the historic core were not filled with trash before they were sealed and buried and are now beginning to collapse, creating hazardous slumping.

In 1988, the Zuni Archaeology Program conducted an archaeological investigation of cultural deposits under rooms used by the head cacique as a religious retreat (Dr. Barbara E. Holmes, personal communication). This work, in the room block to the west of the small plaza, was designed to provide information needed to rehabilitate the deteriorated religious rooms, as well as contribute to Zuni history through an analysis of the artifactual material recovered during the excavations. During the project, severe structural problems were discovered affecting the entire room block. A broken sewer line that had been left unattended for years had saturated the entire area, undermining six houses as well as the religious rooms.

8-12 *A cut through the northern midden of Zuni Pueblo made during road construction in 1984 reveals that a recently constructed Shalako house sits on top of deep cultural deposits consisting of unconsolidated sand and trash. (Photograph: T. J. Ferguson, courtesy of T. J. Ferguson, Barbara J. Mills, and Calbert Seciwa.)*

How this most current architectural problem will be resolved is not entirely clear. The religious leaders want to preserve the historic fabric of their religious rooms. To some this suggests that the walls should be stabilized, much as the National Park Service does at its archaeological parks. Other people have suggested that the only structural answer is the complete reconstruction of the rooms, using a masonry style similar to the original construction to preserve a sense of the historic quality of architecture. The one thing that is clear is that the whole room block needs to be reconstructed at once as a structural unit. The need for such large construction projects, affecting many families at once, is a new phenomenon that will probably increase in the future at Zuni Pueblo.

CONCLUSIONS

The Zuni people have historically chosen function over form as they have rebuilt their village to keep pace with modern times. Innovation in Zuni architecture has been guided by a pragmatic approach that favors cost-effective solutions to basic problems of lighting and weatherproofing houses over the surface appearance of facades. The net result has been an increasingly diverse Zuni vernacular architecture, mixed with an increasingly standardized commercial architecture in federal housing projects.

What is the prognosis for the future? In the past, Zuni has not been able to afford the cost of Pueblo Revival architecture as it is defined in places such as Santa Fe. The low level of funding available for new housing projects and the rehabilitation of existing housing is adequate only for the provision of basic services. The extra expense entailed in providing historically inspired architectural details is hard to budget. This situation is not likely to change in the future.

To many Zunis, the facade or form of the house they live in is less important than the basic shelter it provides and how that house functions to support their social life. Zuni vernacular architecture often departs from the ideals of historic preservation, but it serves the contemporary needs of the Zuni people. Federal housing programs at Zuni Pueblo would be improved if they used standards drawn from Zuni vernacular architecture rather than national prototypes based on the single-family dwelling.

The Zuni HIP program provides a model for how federally funded construction programs can positively contribute to the architectural integrity of Zuni Pueblo. More such programs are needed, not only because they produce culturally appropriate housing but also because they keep the economic benefits of housing construction within the community. To date, the real economic benefit of the large federally funded commercial construction projects on the reservation have gone to the large off-reservation building companies that were awarded the construction contracts.

Zuni Pueblo will continue to grow. When paved roads and utilities are extended to all of the outlying farming villages, the Zuni people will probably once again take up residence in those communities. This process is already happening at Pescado, located along a highway with access to electrical lines. Even so, Zuni Pueblo will remain the ceremonial center of the tribe, and the Zuni tribal government will continue to play an increasing role in the never-ending construction and reconstruction of the pueblo.

REFERENCES

BORCHERS, PERRY E. 1972. Photogrammetric Map of Zuni Pueblo. Washington: Historic American Building Survey.

BUNTING, BAINBRIDGE. 1976. *Early Architecture in New Mexico.* Albuquerque: University of New Mexico Press.

CAYWOOD, LOUIS R. 1972. *The Restored Mission of Nuestra Señora de Guadalupe de Zuni.* St. Michaels, Arizona: St. Michaels Press.

COLLINS, SUSAN M. 1983. "Archaeological Testing of the Old Pueblo Refuse Mound, Zuni, New Mexico." Zuni Archaeology Program Report No. 198b, Pueblo of Zuni.

FERGUSON, T. J., and BARBARA J. MILLS. 1982. "Archaeological Investigations at Zuni Pueblo, New Mexico, 1977–1980." Zuni Archaeology Program Report No. 183, Pueblo of Zuni.

———. E. RICHARD HART, and CALBERT SECIWA. 1988. "Twentieth Century Zuni Political and Economic Development in Relation to Federal Indian Policy." In: *Public Policy Impacts on American Indian Economic Development,* ed. C. Matthew Snipp. Albuquerque: Institute of Native American Economic Development, University of New Mexico.

KROEBER, ALFRED L. 1917. "Zuni Kin and Clan." *Anthropological Papers of the American Museum of Natural History* 18(2):39–204.

LADD, EDMUND J., 1979. "Zuni Social and Political Organization." In: *Handbook of North American Indians,* Vol. 9, pp 482–91. Washington, D.C.: Smithsonian Institution Press.

LANGE, CHARLES H., and CARROLL L. RILEY. 1970. *The Southwestern Journals of Adolph F. Bandelier, 1883–1884.* Albuquerque: University of New Mexico Press.

MIMBRES AND ASSOCIATES. 1977. "Existing Land Use and Housing Plan." Unpublished report on file at the Pueblo of Zuni.

MINDELEFF, VICTOR. 1891. "A Study of Pueblo Architecture, Tusayan and Cibola." *Eighth Annual Report of the Bureau of Ethnology,* pp. 13–228. Washington, D.C.: V.S. GOVERNMENT PRINTING OFFICE.

SPIER, LESLIE. 1917. "An Outline for a Chronology of Zuni Ruins." *Anthropological Papers of the American Museum of Natural History* 18(3):211–331.

9   The Metaphors of Hopi Architectural Experience in Comparative Perspective

Louis A. Hieb

In the past twenty years, much of American, British, and French anthropology has undergone a shift in concern from "function" to "meaning" (Pocock 1961; Crick 1976; Schneider 1976; Geertz 1980). At the same time, a number of architects, urban planners, and cultural geographers have become increasingly concerned with "the human experience of time and space" (Buttimer and Seamon 1980; see also Rapoport 1969 and Tuan 1974). My interest is to examine the Hopi experience of architecture and other built environments from this distinctly anthropological stance and by so doing suggest some of the deeper realms of meaning that contribute to the mystique of Pueblo architecture and the later regional style it has influenced. As this interest in meaning entails a distinct analytic perspective, it will be helpful to briefly outline some of the assumptions involved.

The concern of "symbolic anthropology" is with "cultural systems" understood in a particular way. David M. Schneider's definition of culture is a useful starting point:

> A particular culture, American culture for instance, consists of a system of units (or parts) which are defined in certain ways and which are differentiated according to certain criteria. These units define the world or the universe, the ways things in it relate to each other, and what these things should be and do (Schneider 1968, 1).

It follows that these units—units of meaning and value—are expressed in symbolic form (Geertz 1975). These symbols include words, gestures, objects—anything on which meaning and value can be imposed.

Much recent attention in anthropology has moved to those complex symbolic forms known as metaphors. George Lakoff and Mark Johnson write (1980, 3), "Our ordinary conceptual system, in terms of which we both think and act, is fundamentally metaphorical in nature." "The essense of metaphor," they continue, "is understanding and experiencing one kind of thing in terms of another" (1980, 5). The focus of this chapter is on those metaphors in terms of which we and others understand and experience architecture.

Architecture is a physical form and a cultural construct, often of rich complexity, that differs from society to society and from time to time. The vicissitudes of time and space, of migration and adaptation to differing ecological conditions, have contributed to the differentiation and development of thousands of forms of vernacular architecture throughout the world. But "architecture" is also—so the symbolic anthropologists argue—a language or a number of languages in terms of which humans perceive, experience, and describe these physical forms.

This chapter is distinctly anthropological in several senses. It is concerned with the cultural, in this case the metaphorical, dimension of architecture. It will focus on the vernacular, which, aptly named, is like a language in being a "social fact." It will summarize several examples drawn from world ethnographic literature as series of "cases" (or "texts"). Finally, it will argue that the "meaning" of Pueblo architecture—its enchantment—is not inherent in it but has been attributed to it in the ancient past of myth.

THE OGLALA SIOUX AND THE CIRCLE

One of the most pervasive metaphors in architecture is the orientational metaphor. Whether it is a seemingly simple "front/back" as in many American homes or an elaborate multidimensional system as found in the African Atoni (Cunningham 1973), it is probably universal. Seemingly abstract or neutral, these categories provide the basis for complex systems of meaning and value.

The first example may be regarded as somewhat atypical because the dominant form is the circle. However, this classic case illustrates clearly how meaning and value are associated with architectural form. The following statement was made by an Oglala Dakota Sioux to James Walker near the turn of this century:

> The Oglala believe the circle to be sacred because the great spirit caused everything in nature to be round except stone. Stone is the implement of destruction. The sun and the sky, the earth and the moon, are round like a shield, though the sky is deep like a bowl. Everything that breaths is round like the body of man. Everything that grows from the ground is round like the stem of a plant. Since the great spirit has caused everything to be round, mankind should look upon the circle as sacred, for it is the symbol of all things in nature except stone. It is also the symbol of the circle that marks the edge of the world and therefore of the four winds that travel there. Consequently it is also the symbol of the year. The day, the night, and the moon go in a circle above the sky. Therefore the circle is the symbol of these divisions of time and hence the symbol of all time. For these reasons the Oglala make their tipis circular, their camp-circle circular, and sit in a circle in all ceremonies. The circle is also the symbol of the tipi and of shelter. If one makes a circle for an ornament and it is not divided in any way, it should be understood as the symbol of the world and of time (Walker 1917, 160).

Clifford Geertz finds in the Oglala symbol of the circle a symbol whose metaphorical dimensions are at once existential and normative:

> Here is the subtle formulation of the relation between good and evil, and of their grounding in the very nature of reality. Circle and eccentric form, sun and stone, shelter and war are segregated into pairs of disjunct classes whose significance is aesthetic, moral and ontological (Geertz 1957, 423).

The power of the symbol, he continues, "clearly rests on its comprehensiveness, on its fruitfulness in ordering experience." There follows one of the most evocative explications in anthropological literature:

> The common roundness of a human body and a plant stem, of a moon and a shield, of a *tipi* and a camp-circle give them a vaguely conceived but intensely felt significance. And this meaningful common element, once abstracted, can then be employed for ritual purposes—as when in a peace ceremony the pipe, the symbol of social solidarity, moves deliberately in a perfect circle from one smoker to the next, the purity of form evoking the beneficence of the spirits— or to construe mythologically the peculiar paradoxes and anomalies of moral experience, as when one sees in round stone the shaping power of good over evil (Geertz 1957, 424).

NAVAJO SPACE METAPHORS

The Navajo of the American Southwest are traditionally a pastoral, seasonally nomadic people. Their conceptual construction of space involves a system of four units or categories with direction as the primary denotation. Four sacred mountains provide convenient orientational guides, as one or more is visible from nearly any location in

Navajo land. These concepts of space are associated with others in time, as expressed in Navajo accounts of origin and migration. In the first world (black), second (blue), third (yellow), and fourth (white) various plants, animals and other objects came into being which are associated in this (fifth) world—in an elaborate system of correspondences—with the four directions. In this system, east (life) is the most auspicious direction and north (death) the least so. As with many other peoples, the traditional house of the Navajo, the hogan, is on certain occasions a microcosm reflecting this world view in elaborate detail. Berard Haile summarizes the chantway legends regarding the hogan, a conical structure built of wooden poles, laid over with sticks and a thick layer of earth:

> These prototype hogans mention either a four- or five-pole type of hogan, meaning the main poles upon which the structure leans. The four-pole skeleton was constructed of a white bead pole in the east, of a turquoise pole in the south, of an abalone pole in the west, of a jet pole in the north. The five-pole type adds a white, red-streaked stone pole in the northeast to complete the doorway structure. . . . The legends let the spaces between the poles be filled with shelves of white . . . turquoise . . . abalone . . . jet. The course here described introduces an important observance known in Navajo ritual as . . . 'guided by the sun' sunwise (our clockwise course). Sandpainting figures, lines of prayersticks, sewing of masks, winding of pouches, strewing of pollen or lotions, and numerous other prescriptions must be done sunwise and the reverse course . . . 'sunward' (our anti-clockwise), is taboo in ritual (Haile 1942, 42–B).

This then was the proper place for Navajo ritual as well as their dwelling. It is important to emphasize that this richly polysemantic metaphor has these meanings primarily in the ritual use of the *hogan*, especially during healing ceremonies, and that at other times other metaphors derived from kinship and the division of labor (by sex and/or by age) serve to define this space. It is not surprising to learn that Haile's article (entitled "Why the Navajo Hogan?") was written to explain why this architectural form has persisted next to other house forms derived from Anglo-American culture that began to appear on the Navajo reservation by the 1930s. While there was apparently no conflict between the meanings and values present in Navajo kinship, economic endeavors, and so on, the architectural form of the hogan was clearly coarticulated with a major system of meanings and values in Navajo life (see also Haile, n.d.).

KINSHIP METAPHORS AND THE PRINCIPLE OF OPPOSITION

In Enrico Guidoni's *Primitive Architecture* (1978), the dominant metaphors of vernacular architecture are derived from kinship: family, lineage, clan. But this generalization must not be limited to "primitive" architecture. The American "home" is the architectural expression of the basic unit of American kinship, the family. The metaphor of the family is extended architecturally to define quite clearly the existence and use of the "family room," the "bedrooms," and other spaces within the home. As Schneider (1968, 51) notes, "A system of a small number of symbols define and differentiate the kinds of relationships—that is, the codes of conduct—which members of the family should have with each other." The concept of family includes a number of oppositions based on sex and age and the unification of these oppositions to constitute the family. Schneider's observations in this regard are easily seen as being expressed in the differentiation of bedrooms in the American home. He writes:

> The members of the family are defined in terms of sexual intercourse as a reproductive act, stressing the sexual relationship between husband and wife and the biological identity between parent and child, and between siblings. . . .

The fundamental contrast is between the unification of opposites—the husband and wife in sexual intercourse—and maintenance of the unity of those who are differentiating—child from parents and sibling from sibling (Schneider 1968, 51–2).

There are, of course, many other forms of vernacular architecture in complex, functionally differentiated societies like that of the United States (e.g., "theatre," "filling station," "grocery store") whose organizational metaphors must be sought elsewhere. However, more fundamental to our interests here are the *oppositions* that are the basic conceptual units of metaphors like the "family" in American culture.

In an essay first published in 1909, Robert Hertz examined the opposition of right/left that is found in many human cultural institutions including architecture. What accounted for the "pre-eminence of the right hand?" Hertz rejected organic asymmetry as an explanation for the classification of ideas and values into right and left categories. He maintained that "the hands have become the symbols of polarities in thought and values because the duality of the universe must be centered in man who is the center of them" (E. E. Evans-Pritchard in Hertz 1960, 19). The source of the preeminence of the right hand is physiological. But "the slight physiological advantages possessed by the right hand," says Hertz, "are merely the *occasion* of a qualitative differentiation of which the cause lies beyond the individual, in the constitution of the collective consciousness" (1960, 111). Hertz's lasting contribution was his identification of the principle of opposition as a universal and essential relation in the constitution not only of symbolic classifications but of all forms of meaningful human institutions from social organization to architectural form. The notion of contrast or opposition is basic to the discrimination of meaning or value, whether this is explicit or tacit (cf. Trubetzkoy 1969, 31; Leach 1976, 59). Walls separate and oppose units of space, but sometimes meaning derives from much more subtle contrasts within vernacular architecture.

THE KABYLES AND THE PRINCIPLE OF OPPOSITION

In the mountainous coastal region of Algeria, near Algiers, lives a Berber tribe known as the Kabyles whose house form is a remarkable case in point. Pierre Bourdieu confronts us with a vivid portrayal of the Kabyle house:

> The dark and noctural, lower part of the house, place of objects that are moist, green or raw—jars of water placed on benches in various parts of the entrance to the stable or against the wall of darkness, wood and green fodder—natural place also of beings—oxen and cows, donkeys and mules—and place of natural activities—sleep, the sexual act, giving birth—and the place also of death, is opposed, as nature is to culture, to the light-filled, noble, upper part of the house: this is the place of human beings and, in particular, of the guest; it is the place of fire and objects created by fire—lamp, kitchen utensils, rifle—the symbol of the male point of honour (*ennif*) and the protector of female honour (*horma*)—and it is the place of the weaving-loom—the symbol of all protection; and it is also the place of the two specifically cultural activities that are carried out in the space of the house: cooking and weaving. These relationships of opposition are expressed through a whole set of convergent signs which establish the relationships at the same time as receiving their meaning from them (Bourdieu 1970, 53).

Stated more abstractly, the house is "organized according to a set of homologous oppositions: fire:water::cooked:raw::high:low::light:shadow::day:night::male:female:: *ennif*:*horma*::fertilizing:able to be fertilized::culture:nature" (Bourdieu 1970, 57). Moreover, the same oppositions exist between the house as a whole and the rest of the universe: in such a way that Bourdieu can state the logic of Kabyle space in a formula:

"*a:b::b1:b2*" (1970, 57, 60). The "most apparent opposition" is male/female but like right/left it seems to be a paradigm of a certain form of relation; the principle of opposition orders the set.

THAI SPATIAL ORDERING

In contrast to Bourdieu's French structuralist orientation, S. J. Tambiah provides a neo-Durkheimian portrait of house form in the village of Baan Phraan Muan in northeastern Thailand. Before Tambiah's study, other anthropologists (e.g., Douglas 1966; Levi-Strauss 1962; 1966) had noted a correlation between social and animal categories and rules regarding sexual availability and edibility. Edmund Leach (1964) described the English system as consisting of three correlated series: human beings categorized in terms of sex relationships, spatial or ecological categories (e.g., house, field, forest), and a scale of dietary rules relating to animals of certain kinds (e.g., domestic, farm, forest). A similar situation is found in the Thai case, and here "the spatial ordering of the house is a domain of conceptualization of sex and dietary rules" (Tambiah 1969, 425).

Village houses are raised from the ground on wooden stilts or pillars, with access provided by a ladder. The space on the ground under the house is used for keeping animals and storing household goods. The house is divided according to social categories (e.g., room for parents, room for son-in-law and married daughter). The floors of the named divisions are on different levels, and these levels are "symbols of the various values assigned to the divisions of the house" (Tambiah 1969, 430). Moreover, the four directions have values. Without going into detail, it is concluded that there is a "close correspondence between the marriage and sex rules pertaining to the human series and the house categories which *say the same thing in terms of* living space and spatial distance. The house and the kin categories are linked in turn to an animal series," which includes the division of space and animals under the house. The architecture of the house thus becomes a central grid to which are linked categories of the human and animal world in a "general, if not in a very precise manner" which is "homologous or isomorphic." Like Leach, Tambiah finds the metaphorical extension of these valued and concepts to derive from "man's need to express and order social relations, to forge a system of moral conduct, and to resolve the problem of man in nature" (Tambiah 1969, 457).

HOPI METAPHORS

In looking at Hopi architecture it is tempting to take the perspectives reviewed in the first part of this paper and to see if Hopi architecture is like that of the Oglala Dakota Sioux or the Kabyle or even the Navajo. Indeed, there are analogies. Like the circle in Oglala Dakota Sioux culture, the form of the Hopi kiva can be seen to be replicated in shrines, in dance, and even in the shape of the Hopi men's hair style. Like the Navajo, Hopi architectural form has layers of meaning rooted in the mythic past. Like the American home, much of the meaning of Hopi architecture—men's space and women's space—may be seen as closely tied to the categories and rules of Hopi kinship and social organization. Like the Kabyle, Hopi thought can be seen to consist of various oppositions with architecture (and various other symbolic devices) serving to mediate between the upper world of the living and the lower world of the spirits—between, ultimately, life and life after this life. And like the Thai, the Hopi may be seen to have a system of categories of space and a corresponding system of categories of persons who can occupy that space, from men's and women's and children's space within the village to shrines and other areas of sacred space that only religious specialists may visit. But this is to miss—if not distort—the Hopi's own perception, experience, and description of their architecture. It is here that the ethnologic innocence of an observer like A. M. Stephen is so valuable.

THE WESTERN PUEBLOS

The westernmost Puebloan people, the Hopi of northeastern Arizona, have long interested students of architecture. Victor Mindeleff's "A Study of Pueblo Architecture, Tusayan and Cibola" which appeared in the *Annual Report of the Bureau of American Ethnology for the Years 1886–1887* (Mindeleff 1891) is the first "classic" in Southwestern architectural literature. Mindeleff drew on two residents of the area, Dr. Jeremiah Sullivan, who lived on the Hopi First Mesa from 1881 to 1887, and A. M. Stephen, a prospector and explorer who lived in Keams Canyon from 1880 to 1894 and left over a thousand pages of descriptions of Hopi life, both social and ceremonial. Many later scholars—anthropologists, linguists, and human geographers—have examined Hopi architecture (see, especially, McIntire 1968), but Stephen alone was sensitive to the many layers of meaning and metaphor.

An evolutionary perspective on Hopi architecture (and, perhaps, Pueblo architecture in general) provides an understanding of the differentiation of architectural form (archaeological and ethnographic "fact") and, it may be suggested, of the differentiation of the metaphors of architecture as well. As fig. 9-1 illustrates, the two primary forms of Hopi architecture—kiva and ki'hu, ceremonial chamber and house, men's space and women's space—derive from the pit house of the Pueblo II period. Correspondingly, it might be expected that the metaphors of the kiva would derive from Hopi "religion" and those of the ki'hu from Hopi "kinship" or "social organization." However, it appears that the ancient metaphors of architecture have adhered to the kiva and only selectively have they been attributed to the ki'hu.

Edward Kennard has suggested that the fundamental idea underlying the Hopi world view is that everything is predetermined. He writes,

> What was determined in the beginning, at the time of the emergence, and by agreement with Masawu, the owner to the Earth when they arrived here, is still the basic fact around which life revolves. In Hopi speech, in songs, in formal address to the Kachinas, in announcements setting the date for the next ceremony, in advice given by ceremonial fathers to their sons at initiations, the same images are evoked and the same words and phrases are repeated. And

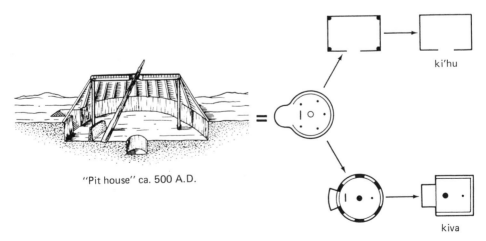

"Pit house" ca. 500 A.D.

ki'hu

kiva

9-1

often, the ritual acts, whose sequence in kivas is fixed, symbolize in acts what is otherwise symbolized in words (Kennard 1972, 469).

Kiva and ki'hu were also given their meaning during the emergence of the Hopi into this world.

Masawu is one of several persons (deities) who came into being at the time of creation. Masawu presides over the surface of the earth and is in charge of the dead and the afterworld. In his journal for November 4, 1893, Stephen recorded the following discussion with a Hopi elder:

> Masau'wu was the first house builder. His house was underground. . . . At si'papu he bestrode the orifice, and as the people appeared he took each person's right arm under his left arm and welcomed them to the surface. Wherever is man or woman, there also is Masau'wu.
>
> Masau'wu has a two story house underground. We must remember that Masau' is death. The graveyard is Masau''s kiva, Maski. The surface we see is the roof of the second story, we will not see the interior till we die. . . . The grave is the entrance to Maski, the dead go to the lower stage or story where the houses are as these we live in. The plan of the house was brought from the interior |underworld| and what is called dying is a return to the early house; men and women follow their usual avocations there. Graves are made very poorly now—people are lazy. Formerly graves were made with as much care as the dwelling house, with the same care and roof covering. Formerly when a girl

9-2 *The Third Mesa Hopi village of Oraibi as photographed by J. K. Hillers in 1879. Until the beginning of this century the Hopi ki'hu was entered at the second floor by a ladder. More recently doorways have been added at the ground level and the ladders and their meaning have been lost.* (**Courtesy of the Special Collections, University of Arizona Library.**)

9-3 *A. C. Vroman's 1901 photograph of Mishongnovi shows a* kiva *in the foreground and several houses with recently modified doorways along the street. Although the form of the Hopi* kiva *is usually described as a "rectangular key hole," this* kiva *appears remarkably like the geological feature in the bottom of the Grand Canyon which Hopis regard as their place of emergence. (Courtesy of the Special Collections, University of Arizona Library.)*

married, her uncles and brothers went out and selected timbers for her grave and put them away preserved till her death.

Kibvun'gkani, the house that is coming, the future house, the house they return to. When the people came up from underground they made the kiva to commemorate their early home; they could not use reed (*ba'kabi*) as ladder, but the mythic pine and spruce grew up through the reed opening, so people took pine or spruce and made a ladder of either. The hatchway is typical of the size and form of the first hole in the earth crust (Stephen 1936, 150–1).

The Hopi house, the ki'hu, is not simply architectural form or shelter. It is a microcosm of the Hopi world view whose principal tenet is the continuity of life in this world with life in the "interior" or underworld. Life and death, day and night, summer and winter are seen not simply as opposed but as involved in a system of alternation and continuity, indeed a fundamental consubstantiality. The ki'hu is a symbol of this continuity, and the tall ladder that Hopis climbed to the second level of their homes were a reminder of their emergence (see fig. 9-2).

Mindeleff charged Stephen with recording not only all the terms used to describe the various architectural features of the ki'hu and kiva, but to learn about the "significance of the structural plan" of the kiva as well (Mindeleff 1891, 135). Hopi cosmology includes the notion of the evolution of mankind in four worlds, with final emergence of the Hopi in the Grand Canyon, by way of the sipapu, or opening from the underworld below. The sipapu, an opening in the floor of the kiva, was readily identified as a symbol of "the place from which the people emerged," but the meaning of the overall plan was less obvious. Nevertheless, Stephen was led to "infer" that the various levels of the kiva typified "the four 'houses,' or stages, described in their creation myths" (see fig. 9-3 and 9-4).

9-4 *A Field Museum photograph (ca. 1900) of the interior of a Mishongnovi* kiva *showing the placement of the ladder on the "third level."* (Courtesy of the Special Collections, University of Arizona Library.*)*

In both kiva and ki'hu the ladder is much more than a functional device providing access from one level of space to another. In a area stripped bare of all trees for firewood and building materials, the extravagantly tall ladders leaning against the walls and protruding from roof tops richly symbolize both the emergence of the Hopi into this world and the continuity of this life with the life after this life. As Stephen made clear, the sipapu is a part of this same complex of ideas.

It should be clear that Hopis perceive, experience, and describe their architectural forms metaphorically in terms of their conception of the world and their place in it. It may be that part of the mystique of Pueblo-inspired architecture derives from the sense that Masauwu is lingering in the shadows, that these forms are enchanted even if our experience of them is not as fully "predetermined" as for the Hopi.

CONCLUSION

From a cross-cultural perspective, it is clear that vernacular architectural forms are not primarily a product of the human genetic make-up or of environmental adaptation—at least, not in any predictable, deterministic fashion (Von Frisch 1976; Levi-Strauss 1963; Rapoport 1969). Rather, any given instance is the product of the history and culture of a people. Its *shape* is a cultural construction. More important, the meanings and values of an architectural form are attributed to it; they are not inherent in it. The same physical form may have quite different meanings and values attributed to it by different peoples. As Mary Douglas has pointed out (1972, 321): "the organization of thought and of social relations is imprinted on the landscape. But, if only the physical aspect is susceptible to study, how to interpret this pattern would seem to pose an insoluble problem." If we are to understand fully the influence of Pueblo architecture on the mystique of New Mexico, we must have some appreciation of the metaphors of Pueblo architectural language.

In vernacular architecture a bond is formed between the physical form and the meaning and values imposed upon it, just as in language, sound and meaning form a unit that makes human communication possible (Benveniste 1971). There are, of course, differences. Architectural form must meet functional and adaptational requirements that are much more constraining than the physical requirements imposed on the sounds we make in communicating with each other. Nevertheless, the bond between the metaphors of architectural experience and the physical forms are sufficiently strong and "motivated" that they must be understood as having a significant role in the experience of all people.

REFERENCES

BENVENISTE, EMILE. 1971. "The Nature of the Linguistic Sign." In: *Problems in General Linguistics* (Miami Linguistic Series, No. 8), pp. 43–48. Coral Gables: University of Miami Press.

BOURDIEU, PIERRE. 1970. "The Berber House or the World Reversed." *Social Sciences Information* (UNESCO). 9:151–70.

BUTTIMER, ANNE, and DAVID SEAMON, eds. 1980. *The Human Experience of Space and Place.* London: Croom Helm.

CRICK, MALCOLM. 1976. *Explorations in Language and Meaning: Towards a Semantic Anthropology.* New York: John Wiley.

CUNNINGHAM, CLARK E. 1973. "Order in the Atoni House." In: *Right & Left: Essays on Dual Symbolic Classification,* ed. Rodney Needham, pp. 204–233. Chicago: University of Chicago Press.

DOUGLAS, MARY. 1966. *Purity and Danger.* New York: Praeger.

———. 1972. "Symbolic Orders in the Use of Domestic Space." In: *Man, Settlement and Urbanism,* eds. Peter J. Ucko, Ruth Tringham, and G. W. Dimbleby. Cambridge, Mass.: Schenkman.

GEERTZ, CLIFFORD. 1957. "Ethos, World-View and the Analysis of Sacred Symbols." *The Antioch Review* 17:421–37.

———. 1975. *The Interpretation of Cultures.* New York: Basic Books.

———. 1980. "Blurred Genres: The Reflections of Social Thought." *The American Scholar* 49:165–79.

GUIDONI, ENRICO. 1978. *Primitive Architecture.* New York: Abrams.

HAILE, BERARD. n.d. "Some Cultural Aspects of the Navajo Hogan." Unpublished paper. Berard Haile Papers. Special Collections, The University of Arizona Library.

———. 1942. "Why the Navajo Hogan?" *Primitive Man* 15:39–56.

HERTZ, ROBERT. 1960. *Death and the Right Hand.* Glencoe, Ill.: Free Press.

HIEB, LOUIS A. 1979. "Hopi World View." *Handbook of North American Indians.* Vol. 9. *The Southwest,* ed. A. Ortiz. pp. 577–80. Washington, D.C.: Smithsonian Institution Press.

———. 1981. "North American Tribal Religions." In: *Abingdon Dictionary of Living Religions,* eds. K. Crim et al., pp. 526–533. Nashville, Tenn.: Abingdon Press.

———. 1985. "The Language of Dance: Communicative Dimensions of Hopi Katsina Dances." *Phoebus: A Journal of Art History* 4:32–42.

KENNARD, EDWARD A. 1972. "Metaphor and Magic: Key Concepts in Hopi Culture and Their Linguistic Forms." In: *Studies in Linguistics in Honor of George L. Trager* (Janua Linguarum, Series Maior 52), ed. M. E. Smith. pp. 468–473. The Hague: Mouton.

LAKOFF, GEORGE, and MARK JOHNSON. 1980. *Metaphors We Live By.* Chicago: University of Chicago Press.

LEACH, EDMUND. 1964. "Anthropological Aspects of Language: Animal Categories and Verbal Abuse." In: *New Directions in the Study of Language,* ed. E. J. Lenneberg, pp. 23–63. Cambridge, Mass.: M.I.T. Press.

––––––. 1976. *Culture and Communication: The Logic By Which Symbols are Connected.* New York: Cambridge University Press.

LEVI-STRAUSS, CLAUDE. 1962. *Totemism.* Boston: Beacon Press.

––––––. 1963. *Structural Anthropology.* New York: Basic Books.

––––––. 1966. *The Savage Mind.* Chicago: University of Chicago Press.

McINTIRE, ELLIOT G. 1968. *The Impact of Culture Change on the Land Use Patterns of the Hopi Indians.* Unpublished Ph.D. dissertation. Eugene: University of Oregon Press.

MINDELEFF, VICTOR. 1891. "A Study of Pueblo Architecture, Tusayan and Cibola." In: *Annual Report of the Bureau of American Ethnology,* pp. 3–228.

POCOCK, DAVID. 1961. *Social Anthropology.* London: Sheed and Ward.

RAPOPORT, DAVID. 1969. *House Form and Culture.* Englewood Cliffs, N.J.: Prentice-Hall.

SCHNEIDER, DAVID M. 1968. *American Kinship: A Cultural Account.* Englewood Cliffs, N.J.: Prentice-Hall.

––––––. 1976. "Notes Towards a Theory of Culture." In: *Meaning in Anthropology,* eds. K. H. Basso and H. A. Selby, pp. 197–220. Albuquerque: University of New Mexico Press.

STEPHEN, ALEXANDER M. 1936. *Hopi Journal of Alexander M. Stephen* (Columbia University Contributions to Anthropology, Vol. 23), ed. E. C. Parsons. New York: Columbia University Press.

––––––. 1939–1940. "Hopi Indians of Arizona." *The Masterkey* 13:197–204; 14:20–7, 102–9, 143–9, 170–9, 207–15.

SULLIVAN, JEREMIAH. 1882. "Hopi Vocabulary." Unpublished manuscript. Smithsonian Institution. MS 792, NAA/SI.

TAMBIAH, S. J. 1969. "Animals are Good to Think and Good to Prohibit." *Ethnology* 8:423–59.

TRUBETZKOY, N.S. 1969. *Principles of Phonology.* Berkeley: University of California Press.

TUAN, Y.-F. 1974. *Topophilia: A Study of Environmental Perception, Attitudes, and Values.* Englewood Cliffs, N.J.: Prentice-Hall.

VON FRISCH, KARL. 1976. *Animal Architecture.* New York: Harcourt Brace Jovanovich.

WALKER, JAMES. 1917. "The Sun Dance and Other Ceremonies of the Oglala Division of the Dakota." *Anthropological Papers of the American Museum of Natural History* 16:51–221.

Tewa Visions of Space: A Study of Settlement Patterns, Architecture, Pottery, and Dance

10

Tsiporah Lipton

A culture sustains itself by providing the ways and means for the people to meet their basic needs. Orderly interaction among the people is facilitated by shared ideas and notions of organization. The organization of space is a fundamental adaptation of culture and society (Arnold 1983, 57). The definition of space is a study in contradiction. Space is the three-dimensional field of experience bounded by infinity (Morris 1973, 1237). It is the container and the contained. It denotes emptiness and encompasses the universe (Oxford Dictionary 1971, 2936). The perception of space is a basic component of the human cognitive process (Hall 1966; Kus 1983, 278).

We will explore the interrelationship between just some of the possible kinds of space. Boundary display, or the territorial division of space, is indicative of information flows in the social structure. Constructed space describes the manipulation of physical objects to create structures that shape people's actions. Cognitive perceptions of space find expression as symbolized space in visual representational forms. Actualized space concerns the way people inhabit, move through, and occupy space and describes the relationship between people as physical beings and other physical objects.

This chapter will focus on the Tewa Pueblo Indians of New Mexico and explore the relationship between boundary display (as manifest in settlement patterns), constructed space (as exemplified by architecture), symbolized space (as manifest in pottery decorations), and actualized space (as expressed through dance). That there is an affinity between the perception, symbolization, and actualization of space seems obvious, but to explore this affiliation in the context of the Tewa Pueblo Indians affords us the opportunity to attain a deeper understanding of the relationship and a clear example of how culture operates as a determining factor.

The Tewa cosmology, which is closely tied to the land, permeates Tewa life and the expression of space. The native religion is stratified between the extremities of secret rites and public ceremonies.

I will use the term *sacred* to refer to the more secret practices, and *secular* to denote public objects or actions intended for daily use, social purposes, or artistic expression. Both sacred and secular objects and actions have religious significance, but the former are the domain of initiated members of the society, and the latter belong to everyone.

BOUNDARY DISPLAY AND SETTLEMENT PATTERNS

Boundary display is one device for organizing interaction between people. It takes concrete shape in settlement patterns. Dolores Root stresses the processual aspect of settlement patterns by viewing them as indicative of information flows (Root 1983, 199–200). Margaret W. Conkey defines "social geography" as the way people use space, suggesting that the manner in which space is structured is connected to the formal and structural properties of society (Conkey 1984, 265–6). Amos Rapoport and Edward W. Soja stress the interactive nature of the relationship between people and space (Rapoport 1980, 289; Soja 1985, 98). In other words, spatial structures influence the actions of people, and people reinforce, readjust, or change the spaces they create and use.

According to Ortiz (1979, 284), the area within the village limits as marked by the shrines, the farms, and the lowlands are open to all the Pueblo Indians. Because of the association with subsistence and domestic activities, this sphere is considered to be the domain of the women. At the next level, the hills, the mesas, and the washes are accessible to everyone, but generally women and children would not go without adult male company. The mountains and sacred lakes are considered to be the domain of the men, as it is only they who do the hunting and gathering at this level.

A further layer of zoning emphasizes the hierarchical character of Tewa social structure. The village shrines are used by adult Tewa; they are accessible to adults of either sex. The sacred hills are associated with the Towa é, who are of the middle of the hierarchy. The mountain shrines are accessible only to the initiated male members of the various societies. Initiated female members are restricted to the shrines on the hills (Ortiz 1979, 284). Social boundaries are related to subsistence practices and institutionalized in a formal hierarchy. For the Tewa, space is organized in relation to the landscape, along the cardinal points (Scully 1975, 137), with boundaries marking the social limits according to age, sex, and social status.

CONSTRUCTED SPACE AND ARCHITECTURE

People need to mark place, to orient themselves and give shape to their world (Hall 1966, 105; Rapoport 1980, 283–4). Constructed space, or the "built environment" as Rapoport describes it, "encode[s], give[s] expression to and, in turn, influence[s] social, cognitive and other environments" (Rapoport 1980, 295).

All aspects of Tewa architecture reaffirm the relationship with the land. As Vincent Scully (1975) has demonstrated, buildings and their features echo the shape of the surrounding mesas and mountains. The rows of flat-roofed dwellings with single or double stories, which cluster around the plazas, visually reaffirm flat-topped mesas. As Ortiz states so succinctly, "this building pattern conveys a sense of being part of the earth itself, and, therefore, of fading into the landscape" (Ortiz 1979, 279).

Kivas are special buildings that mark sacred space. They are set apart from ordinary dwellings, sometimes in form and always in content. The entrance is often placed on the roof, so that people must enter with the aid of a ladder. The ladders are extra long, easily distinguished from other ladders in use around the village. Kivas are also differentiated through size or shape and architectural details (Scully 1975).

Both sacred and secular buildings are influenced by Tewa cosmology. Most dwellings are square, oriented along the cardinal points with objects meant for protection buried under the corners (Ortiz 1969, 54). Kivas are likened to the original home of the Pueblo under the lake (Ortiz 1969, 37). To enter a kiva is to enter the earth, to be closer to the spirits.

SYMBOLIZED SPACE/POTTERY

Symbolized space, as expressed through various visual representational forms, emphasizes some features of the cognitive landscape while de-emphasizing others. Anna O. Shepard (1956), Penny Van Esterik (1981), and Dorothy K. Washburn (1977; 1983) all make a case for using symmetry analysis as an objective means of studying visual representational forms. Since symmetry analysis describes technical operations, it can be used in cross-cultural comparisons or in comparisons of similar technical operations in other media.

For this study, I will use the most rudimentary form of symmetry analysis applied to Tewa ceramics. Following Shepard (1956, 269), regular band patterns are divided into seven classes:

1. *Translation* is the simple repetition of the fundamental part.
2. *Horizontal reflection* involves simple repetition and reflection over horizontal axis.
3. *Vertical reflection* repeats the fundamental part reflected over a vertical axis.
4. *Bifold rotation* repeats the fundamental part with a rotation of 180°.
5. The *combination of horizontal and vertical reflections* results in a four-part figure.
6. *Slide reflection* is when the fundamental part is moved along before being reflected over an axis.
7. The *alternation of bifold rotation and reflection* over an axis is the most complex of the seven basic design classes.

I will refer to the first four design classes, alone or in combination with each other, as *low-level symmetry* and to the last three design classes, alone or in combination with any of the seven basic designs, as *high-level symmetry*. I make the distinction in terms of complexity. By using the terms "low-level" and "high-level" we will be able to discuss designs in a broader sense, relating them to other expressions of space.

In his discussion of Tewa ceremonial pottery, Harlow tells us that the division between designs on sacred and secular vessels began in the sixteenth century, approximately 1550 (Harlow 1965, 22). Generally, the ceremonial pottery is decorated, using thus low-level symmetry, or in some cases, asymmetry.

Extrapolating cautiously from our small example, it appears that sacred vessels use asymmetrical designs or designs with low-level symmetry. Secular vessels are decorated in the full range of options: asymmetry or low- and high-level symmetry. Redundancy and variation in high-level symmetry integrates ambiguous interpretation, or multivocality (Van Esterik 1979, 504–5). Therefore it would seem that the intended range of interpretation for sacred pottery was deliberately limited. The designs on secular pottery span the range from low- to high-level symmetry. Further investigation will be required to discover the governing factors in the choice of designs for these vessels.

ACTUALIZED SPACE AND DANCE

Actualized space concerns the relationship between people as physical beings and other physical objects. In formalized situations such as dance, actualized or inhabited space is codified, emphasized, and portrayed. As Paul Spencer tells us, dance does this by "exaggerat[ing] and distort[ing] culturally significant features of everyday life" (Spencer 1985, 36). Joann Kealiinohomoku (1972) has demonstrated how dance acts as a microcosm of society with the Hopi Indians as an example. Jill D. Sweet explains that dance "reveals important notions about the Tewa world view" (Sweet 1981, 14). Perhaps more than any other form, actualized space highlights the various themes we have discussed so far.

For the Tewa, social structure is reflected in the dance event (Ortiz 1969, 127). Boundaries within the social structure are paralleled by boundaries within the structure of the dance event. The organization of the dance echoes the social structure, reaffirming its existence and legitimacy. The Made People are responsible for the progression of the ritual cycle. They plan and direct the dance events. In addition, at certain occasions the Made People, with the aid of masks, take the roles of the Dry Food Who Never Did Become. The Towa é see that the plans are implemented. At the public rituals, they are visible as they watch over the dancers, keeping the path clear. At winter solstice the Towa é impersonate the Tsave Yoh, who are supernatural whippers from the caves and labyrinths of the sacred hills. They serve to maintain social standards by whipping those who have been disobedient or lax in their attendance to ritual matters (Ortiz 1969, 74–7). The impersonal nature of the role of the

Tsave Yoh allows them to carry out their disciplinary task without recrimination. Their behavior is outside the realm of what is expected of the Dry Food People and also the realm of the Made People, or the personifications of the Dry Food Who Never Did Become. The Dry Food People perform the large public rituals. According to the season, the winter or summer moiety predominates in ceremonial activities, though both moieties participate in the overall event (Kurath 1958, 25).

All three levels of Tewa people share in the ritual events, but they maintain the social boundaries throughout. The dances are stratified with respect to who performs what role and the behavior appropriate to each. Generally, a dancer strives for moderation and conformity with the group (Kurath 1970, 35; Sweet 1985, 25–6). The type of dance dictates the solemnity or vigor of the style. Following social standards, the women dance with more restraint than the men. The men need to exaggerate the movements somewhat to sound effectively the bells and rattles that are part of their attire.

The Tewa define space in accordance with the cultural concepts expressed in their cosmology. The use of space within their dances follows these concepts. Ritual dances are performed most often four times, either once in each of the plazas in the village or three times in the plaza and once in a kiva (Kurath 1970, 49; Ortiz 1969, 142). The direction within each of the plazas is determined by the nature of the dance, the season, the time of day, or customs of the particular village (Kurath 1958; Ortiz 1969, 143).

Visually, the lines of dancers echo the horizontal lines of the rows of houses and mesas behind them. Kurath eloquently draws parallels between the performance and the landscape:

> The ever shifting patterns of the dances and the changing rhythms of the songs reflect the shifting lights and shadows cast by clouds and sunlight on the landscape, the restless course of the river, the motion of animals and birds, and the growth of plants (Kurath 1970, 21).

For the Tewa, music and dance intertwine, with the pulse of the movement following the pulse of the music and the melodies weaving "special tonal designs around the instrumental beats" (Kurath 1970, 86). Once again, there is a differentiation between sacred and secular. Kurath postulates that the most sacred line dances comprise simple choreography and complex melodies, while the reverse is true for social dances. Semisacred dances occupy the middle ground with "fairly simple music and simple to complex choreographies" (Kurath 1970, 112). Sweet implies that the emphasis on singing and dancing in unison in the performance of dances of religious significance, that is, sacred though not necessarily secret dances, is facilitated by repeating simple song and movement vocabularies (Sweet 1981, 170). Taking the point further still, Sweet emphasizes the high level of redundancy in religiously significant dances, suggesting that redundancy ensures transmission of the message (Sweet 1981, 169). In other words, when it is important to transmit meaning or message, the range of interpretation is narrowed and reinforced through repetition. Further studies are necessary to pursue the connection between rhythmic and choreographic complexity and "sacredness."

CONCLUSION

The examination of the various expressions of space in relation to Tewa cosmology illustrates the reinforcing character of idea and expression. The cosmology serves to shape consistent patterns. For instance, the boundaries that influence movement in and around the village are similar to boundaries that govern participation in the dances. Open access within the village is comparable to dances that require everyone's participation. Although some boundaries remain in either context, a sense of community is emphasized.

A division between sacred and secular is apparent in most of the expressions of space. Generally, the more sacred or secret the item or event, the more emphasis is placed upon specific interpretations of symbols. For instance, the multivocality of pottery designs is minimal on sacred vessels, being much more evident on secular pots and jars. Similarly, according to Kurath, the most sacred dances are choreographically the simplest, while social dances are more complex, allowing for a greater range of ambiguity.

Perhaps more emphatically than any of the other forms of expression, constructed space reaffirms the connection with the land. The villages carry out a visual dialogue with the landscape, not simply blending into the background but also being an active participant. On the same level, the dances, as shapes in space, interact with their physical surroundings. Rows of dancers, like rows of houses, like the row of a mesa top, draw attention to the vast expanse of sky. In another way, as the dancers focus inward and concentrate on their purpose, attention converges in the plaza as the center of the community.

Landscape is the vital force in the spatial awareness of the Tewa. Different expressions of space appear to be governed by consistent rules. For instance, symbolized and actualized space share comparable visual rhythms and musical rhythms. Boundary display and actualized space embody the hierarchical aspect of the cosmology, which can be seen as an abstraction of the surrounding terrain. The consanguinity of the land and the people permeates the interrelationships of the different expressions of space. The closeness of this connection is perhaps best represented in a few lines from a Tewa song: "Oh our Mother the Earth, oh our Father the Sky, Your children are we" (Spinden 1933, 94, quoted in Sweet 1985, 26). The Tewa have incorporated an awareness of this divine parentage into each type of spatial expression that we have examined. The various kinds of space are related like siblings, there are both similarities and differences—and like families they provide a rich source for further studies in an effort to learn more about ourselves.

ACKNOWLEDGMENTS

I thank Nina De Shane and Joann Kealiinohomoku for comments and suggestions on the ideas in this paper.

REFERENCES

Arnold, Dean E. 1983. "Design Structure and Community Organization in Quinua, Peru." In: *Structure and Cognition in Art,* ed. Dorothy K. Washburn, pp. 56–73. New York: Cambridge University Press.

Blacking, John. 1969. "The Value of Music in Human Experience." *1969 Yearbook of the International Folk Music Council,* 1:33–71.

Conkey, Margaret W. 1984. "To Find Ourselves: Art and Social Geography of Prehistoric Hunter Gatherers." In *Past and Present in Hunter Gatherer Studies,* ed. Carmel Schrire, pp. 253–76. Toronto: Academic Press.

Hall, Edward T. 1966. *The Hidden Dimension.* Garden City, N.Y.: Doubleday.

Harlow, Francis H. 1965. "Tewa Indian Ceremonial Pottery." *El Palacio,* 72(4): 13–23.

―――. 1977. *Modern Pueblo Pottery, 1880–1960.* Flagstaff, Arizona: Northland Press.

Kealiinohomoku, Joann. 1972. "Dance Culture as a Microcosm of Holistic Culture." *CORD Research Annual VI,* New Dimensions in Dance Research: Anthropology and Dance—The American Indian, pp. 99–106.

_____. 1980. "The Non-Art of the Dance: An Essay." *Journal for the Anthropological Study of Human Movement,* 1(2):38–44.

_____. 1986. "Wherefore Art Thou Art? Does 'The Art Of' Have To Be Affixed To The Word 'Dance'?" *CCDR Newsletter* 3:1.

KURATH, GERTRUDE PROKASCH. 1958. "Plaza Circuits of Tewa Indian Dancers." *El Palacio,* 65(1):16–26.

_____. 1970. *Music and Dance of the Tewa Pueblos.* With the aid of Antonio Garcia. Santa Fe: Museum of New Mexico Press.

KUS, SUSAN M. 1983. "The Social Representation of Space: Dimensioning the Cosmological and the Quotidian." In: *Archaeological Hammers and Theories,* ed. James A. Moore and Arthur S. Keene, pp. 277–98. Toronto: Academic Press.

MORRIS, WILLIAM, ed. 1973. *The Heritage Illustrated Dictionary of the English Language,* International edition. New York: American Heritage Publishing Co., Inc. and Houghton Mifflin Company.

ORTIZ, ALFONSO. 1969. *The Tewa World: Space, Time, Being, and Becoming in a Pueblo Society.* Chicago: University of Chicago Press.

_____. ed.1979. *Handbook of North American Indians, Southwest.* Vol. 9. William C. Sturtevant, general editor. Washington, D.C. Smithsonian Institution Press.

OXFORD DICTIONARY. 1971. *The Compact Edition of the Oxford English Dictionary.* Complete text reproduced micrographically. 8th printing June 1974. Toronto: Oxford University Press.

RAPOPORT, AMOS. 1980. "Vernacular Architecture and the Cultural Determinants of Form." In: *Buildings and Society: Essays on the Social Development of the Built Environment,* pp. 283–305. Boston: Routledge & Kegan Paul.

ROOT, DOLORES. 1983. "Information Exchange and the Spatial Configurations of Egalitarian Societies." In: *Archaeological Hammers and Theories,* ed. James A. Moore and Arthur S. Keene, pp. 193–219. Toronto: Academic Press.

SCULLY, VINCENT. 1975. *Pueblo/Mountain, Village, Dance.* New York: Viking Press.

SHEPARD, ANNA O. 1956. *Ceramics for the Archaeologist.* Washington, D.C.: Carnegie Institution of Washington, Publication 609.

SOJA, EDWARD W. 1985. "The Spatiality of Social Life: Towards a Transformative Re-theorisation." In: *Social Relations and Spatial Structures,* ed. Derek Gregory and John Urry, pp. 90–127. London: Macmillan.

SPENCER, PAUL, ed. 1985. *Society and the Dance. The Social Anthropology of Process and Performance.* New York: Cambridge University Press.

SWEET, JILL D. 1978. "Space, Time and Festival: An Analysis of a San Juan Event." *Dance Research Annual,* 9:169–81.

_____. 1981. "Tewa Ceremonial Performances: The Effects of Tourism on an Ancient Pueblo Indian Dance and Music Tradition." Unpublished Ph.D. thesis, The University of New Mexico.

_____. 1985. *Dances of the Tewa Pueblo Indians: Expressions of New Life.* Santa Fe: School of American Research Press.

VAN ESTERIK, PENNY. 1979. "Symmetry and Symbolism in Ban Chiang Painted Pottery." *Journal of Anthropological Research* 35(4):495–508.

_____. 1981. *Cognition and Design Production in Ban Chiang Painted Pottery.* Ohio: Ohio University Press.

WASHBURN, DOROTHY K. 1977. *A Symmetry Analysis of Upper Gila Area Ceramic Design.* Illustrations by Sarah Whitney Powell and Barbara Westman. Cambridge, Mass.: Harvard University Press.

_____. 1983. "Toward a Theory of Structural Style in Art" and "Symmetry Analysis of Ceramic Design: Two Tests of the Method on Neolithic Material from Greece and the Aegean." In: *Structure and Cognition in Art,* ed. Dorothy K. Washburn, pp. 1–7 and 138–64. New York: Cambridge University Press.

IV

Revival Architecture: The Romantic Tradition

The great technical advances and industrial developments of the nineteenth century caused questions to be asked as to the inherent meaning of building and dwelling. Technological societies there felt radical effects of such development on the society at large. The reevaluation of place, cultural myth, and a nostalgia for lost humanistic traditions induced a romantic revival of traditional architecture. In Chapter 11 David Gebhard discusses this romantic revival by showing the milieu of the Arts and Crafts movement in Europe and the United States. He then focuses on the California Mission and Pueblo styles as a substudy of that larger movement. In Chapter 12, George Kubler discusses two nineteenth-century explorers and students of the American Southwest, Holmes and Bandelier, whose work set the stage for the formal study of culture and archaeology in the Southwest. In Chapter 13 Carl Sheppard and Stephen Schreiber brings us to Minnesota and Florida in order to exemplify the extension of the romantic Pueblo style to other regions of the country. Finally, in Chapter 14, Chris Wilson focuses in on New Mexico's ongoing participation in the Arts and Crafts movement. He gives a rather encompassing overview and takes us through twentieth-century developments in New Mexico's Pueblo style up to the present day.

The Myth and Power of Place: Hispanic Revivalism in the American Southwest

11

David Gebhard

In 1910, the California architect-preservationist Arthur B. Benton spoke to a gathering of the First Southwest City Planning Conference in Los Angeles. His subject was "Shall We Plan for a Distinctive Architecture of the Southwest?" (Benton 1920, 18–9). In his usual penetrating manner, Benton explored the many complex and at times contradictory reasons underlying intense regional feelings that the Southwest and California should develop their own regional architectural mode. Taking what he considered to be the predilections of his audience, he proceeded from the pragmatic and practical to arguments that were more ethereal. "The railroads, the hotels, the commercial bodies," he remarked, "all use our old Missions [fig 11-1] to attract tourists and dollars to themselves. How disappointing for the traveler to stand on our business streets or before our civic buildings and see little to remind him that he is not in Chicago, New York or Kansas City? . . . Our Mission architecture teaches the adaptability of the ancient Roman architecture to the most primitive conditions of new countries (Benton 1920, 18). These primitive adaptations of the Hispanic tradition in the Southwest and California hold forth, he argued, two distinct possibilities: to let traditional forms "develop naturally" or to use them as a basis for a new "modern architecture." He concluded by emphasizing the essence of a regional architecture for the Southwest and California: the sense of romance and a deep-set desire to return to that which was natural, rural, and rustic.

Reinforcing the strong sense of the rural and rustic in the American Southwest were three added ingredients: the exoticism of its "strange desert" landscape; the presence of non-Anglo peoples, Native Americans and Hispanic; and the existence of something most of America lacked—real, honest-to-goodness ruins. At the California Academy of Science in San Francisco in 1916, the anthropologist George La Mont Cole concluded a discussion of the ancient pueblos of New Mexico with the statement, "Americans need not go abroad for here are ruins and monuments that rank well with any found in the old world" (Cok 1916, 107).

The urge to cultivate a Hispanic-Native American regional architectural mode has now existed for well over three-quarters of a century, and it is as potent today as it ever was. Perhaps at this stage of its existence it would be advantageous for us, using Arthur B. Benton's observations as guideposts, to see this affair in a broad context. What were its general as well as specific antecedents, how was the stage set for its development outside of the Southwest, and finally, how did these "new" forms of regionalism fit into both Traditionalism and Modernism during the first decades of this century.

THE CLASSICAL EUROPEAN BACKGROUND

The theme of the rustic, of rural life, of the vernacular farmhouse has been a recurring one within our Mediterranean/Western European tradition. During the first century B.C., Roman writer M. Terentius Varro made this a central thesis in his *De re Rustica*, and Pliny the Younger extolled the necessity of fleeing the urban world for the quietude of the country. Closely coupled with this retreat into nature was, to use Rose Macaulay's phrase, "the pleasure of ruins" (Macaulay 1966). When the Greek traveler Pausanius

11-1 *Arthur B. Benton, Title page, The Mission Inn. (Drawing: Wm. Alexander Sharp, Los Angeles Segnogram Publishing Co., 1907.)*

compiled his *Guide to Greece* in the second century A.D., the prominence of nature over the handiwork of man was a constantly recurring subject. The existence of ruins, the decay of the products of man's urban sophistication, made ever more vivid the ultimate desirability of returning to the simple rustic life.

A similar perception emerged centuries later in Baroque Europe during the seventeenth and eighteenth centuries. Rustic personages, rural abodes, and ruins set the atmosphere of many of the paintings of Nicholas Poussin and Claude Lorraine. Jean-Jacques Rousseau not only argued in the way he lived and in his writings for "le retour à la Nature," but also, in 1852, wrote an opera, *Le Devin du Village*, set appropriately in a rustic scene. No eighteenth-century picturesque garden was complete without its ruin or its primitive hut or dwelling. By the end of the eighteenth century the primitive dwelling had become the telling symbol of the rural vernacular (fig 11-2).

The evolution of the use of ruins or huts from this point on is fascinating—from their use as garden follies expressing "le retour a la Nature" to actual buildings to be lived in. The transformation from a garden folly to a livable rural retreat occurred in such episodes as Sir John Nash's village of worker's cottages at Blaise (1811). The writers of English pattern books, and above all such potent propagandists as Augustus Welby Pugin, added another twist: the return to nature via the rural cottage, which was

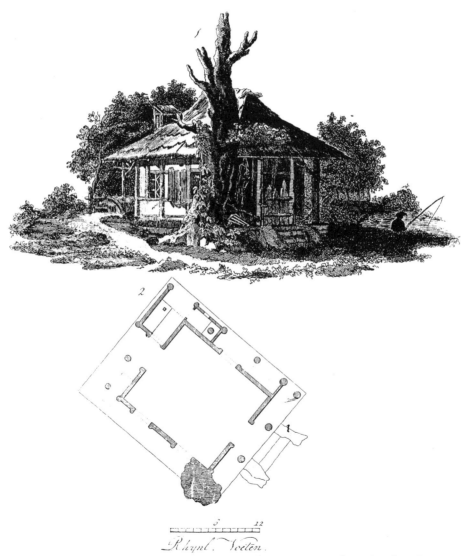

11-2 *G. Van Laar, Magazijn van tuin sieraaden. (Amersterdam: Jacobus Ruyter, n.d., c. 1902, plate CXXI.)*

in addition a symbol of resurgent moral rejuvenation, of regionalism, and, in some instances, of national identity.

By the mid-1850s, the rural or village cottage had in England become an essential ingredient of the English national architectural style. It was beginning to play the game of being the source for historical traditionalism on the one hand and for modernism on the other hand. As a case in point, Philip Webb could produce (together with William Morris) The Red House (Bexley Heath, 1859–61) as well as a full-scale version of the Queen Anne in his 1872 country house Joldrynds (Surrey).

The experience of travel and what was written about it also began to take a different tack, away from the urban scenes and the "great" monuments to the vernacular. When George Edmund Street recorded his experiences in Spain his interest was in the major monuments (Street 1869). In contrast, three years later when his colleague M. Digby Wyatt (1872) wrote on the "lesser" domestic architecture, small townhouses in Segovia or country houses on the outskirts of Toledo, he made plain that he did not mean to suggest that Spanish architecture be translated to England, but rather that since both English and Spanish vernacular architecture is European they have much in common, and that an examination and experiencing of one will enrich our ability to comprehend the other (fig. 11-3).

By the end of the nineteenth century the vernacular, as a symbol of anti-urbanism, anti-industrialism, and essentially anti-laissez faire capitalism, had seized hold of much of Europe. England continued to lead the way, and the vernacular image became not only the hallmark of a return to a rustic, simple, uncluttered life, but also a central element of the Arts and Crafts movement. Charles F. A. Voysey beautifully summed up the qualities that should emerge from an honest understanding response to the vernacular tradition:

> "Try the effect of a well proportioned room, with white washed walls, plain carpets, and simple oak furnitures, and nothing in it but necessary articles of use, and one pure ornament in the form of a simple vase of flowers (Gebhart 1975).[1]

This characterization sums up what the English and the continental Arts and Crafts exponents were attempting to achieve, and (needless to say) Voysey's description of an ideal Arts and Crafts room would fit perfectly as well the description of an interior of a New Mexico Pueblo Revival house of the 1920s or 1930s.

In Europe the return to the rustic entailed the same complexities of elements: the return to the aura of hand production (Arts and Crafts), the cultivation of a perceived "folk" democracy, the puritanism of the simple and unaffected, and nationalism. These continental episodes of romantic nationalism surfaced in Scandinavia, Germany, the Austro-Hungarian Empire, in the low countries and even far to the east in European Russia. Most of the early International style modernists had their beginnings in one version or another of the folk vernacular, generally coupled with the Arts and Crafts and the Art Nouveau. Charles Rennie McIntosh in Scotland, Hendrikus Berlage in Holland, Josef Hoffmann and Joseph Olbrich in Austria, Peter Behrens in Germany, and Eliel Saarinen in Finland absorbed and espoused the cause of the rustic, basing many of their major design contributions upon these folk vocabularies.

The Europeans' cultivation of their own rustic pasts (ideologically as well as expressed in artifacts) was reinforced and enriched by continual excursions into the exotic, especially the "primitive" cultures of Africa, the Pacific, and the New World.

The effect of this fascination with the primitive was threefold:

1. Ideologically it geographically expanded and made specific the universalism of the Voltairian "natural man."
2. It appeared to demonstrate the commonality of all primitive and folk art.
3. It provided physical artifacts: textiles, pottery, and wood carvings, which could express one's commitment to the rustic.

11-3 *M. Digby Wyatt, delineator, "Toledo View of the Remains of a Moorish Fortress on the River" (From M. Digby Wyatt,* An Architect's Note-Book in Spain, *London: Autotype Fine Art Co., Ltd., 1872, plate 35.)*

The allure of existing ethnological primitive cultures was given increased historical depth (and therefore increased intellectual justification) by the new disciplines of ethnology and archaeology. That which was rustic was not only worldwide but was, in fact, seen as underlying the classical civilizations of Greece and Rome and that of western Europe. The late-nineteenth-century, early-twentieth-century explorations and publications of Henry Schliemann on Troy, Mycenae, and Tiryns, and later those of Sir Arthur Evans on the Minoans of Knossos in Crete, were viewed as dramatically illustrating the folk bases of the Classical world. The discoveries and research in western Europe revealed a rich prehistory dating from the Paleolithic to the Bronze Age, a prehistory that also seemed to reinforce the commonality of folk art and architecture.

THE UNITED STATES

Americans, in the late decades of the nineteenth century, were keenly aware of and involved with the allure of the rural life and rural image. It could in fact be convincingly argued that the commitment to the rustic had been present on the American scene from the early 1800s on. Negatively, it was bound up with the classical Jeffersonian distrust of the city; positively, it was a theme that occupied the attention of a long line of American writers, from Ralph Waldo Emerson and Henry David Thoreau to Walt Whitman. As in Europe, the sentiment of folk nationalism sustained the democratic ideal of returning to the simple and puritanical rural life. The Centennial Exhibition of 1876 in Philadelphia was not simply a celebration of America's new industrialism and technology, it also set up as an ideal the Jeffersonian preeminence of the virtue of the rural life. The admiration for America's colonial past was expressed in the nostalgic reaction to Independence Hall, a building that was characterized at the time as entailing "dignity and repose" (McCabe 1876, 51), and the colonial country house

Lemon Hill in Fairmont Park, "a handsome old-time mansion" (McCabe 1876, 149). The Centennial Exposition took the nonurban, rural colonial theme back one step further by recreating "The New England log cabin" (McCabe 1876, 859), that artifact which was to emerge as the classic symbol of early settlement and the frontier.

The emergence of America's Colonial Revival architecture in the late 1870s provided a potent readable artifact to symbolize America's commitment to the rural, the vernacular, and the rustic. The Shingle style that emerged in the 1880s was an amalgamation of the imported English Queen Anne and the rural American Colonial. Henry Hobson Richardson and later McKim, Mead and White, William Ralph Emerson, and others initially looked not to the characteristic mid- to late-eighteenth-century New England or Philadelphia Colonial house, but to the earliest (i.e., the most medieval and primitive) colonial houses of New England, those dating from the late seventeenth to the early eighteenth century. This primitive basis for the early Colonial Revival made it easy for Americans to move over into the Medieval-based Arts and Crafts at the end of the century.

The urge of nationalism also encouraged Americans to rummage through their own prehistory so that they could equal or even possibly "one-up" Europe. Their own myth of an ancient past began to surface with the revelation of the pre-Columbian civilizations of Central America and Mexico, of the mysterious world of the Mound Builders of the Mississippi valley, and of the romantic prehistoric ruins of the American Southwest. Nineteenth-century Americans delighted in playing all sorts of games with these prehistoric "primitive" episodes. They could even outdo the supremacy of the classical world and Europe by arguing, as Ignatius Donnelly did in *Atlantis: The Antediluvian World*, that the ancient American civilizations of Central America, Mexico, and North America were the result of colonization by citizens of that ancient lost civilization (Donnelly 1882, 370–86).

It was the American Southwest, though, that became the most vivid exemplar of America's own ancient folk tradition. For this region, stretching from western Texas to California, possessed a number of additional elements not found elsewhere: the semiarid desert and mountain aspects of the place, the existence of settled native American folk within their own "pueblos," and the existence of a Hispanic overlay. Once the Anglo middle and upper middle classes had the means to travel—and the area had been made accessible in the years after the Civil War by the railroads—the Southwest became an internal mecca (for Anglo-Americans and Europeans) for experiencing the primitive and the rustic.

Considering its English Medieval folk source, it should not be a surprise to find that the American Arts and Crafts (the Craftsman) movement embraced the folk regionalism of the American Southwest and California. The first design for a house by Gustav Stickley's Craftsman Workshops (in 1904) was "a California House Founded on the California Mission Style" (Stickley 1909a, 9–11). The connection between the Craftsman movement and the regionalism of California and the Southwest was caught up in the style term "Mission," which quickly came to be applied to architecture as well as to the fumed oak furniture produced by Gustav Stickley, Elbert Hubbard, and many others. Stickley himself noted that the coining of the term "Mission" was "an interesting story" but one devoid of historical fact (Stickley 1909b). The association had to do, as he pointed out, with "commercial cleverness." "The mingling of novelty and romance instantly pleased the public and the vogue of 'mission' furniture was assured" (Stickley 1909b).

Initially the image adapted for the rustic regionalism of the Southwest were the mission churches of California. This image quickly came to be utilized by the Santa Fe and other railroads for passenger stations throughout New Mexico, Arizona, and California (as well as some other odd places). Though writers from the late nineteenth century on continually advanced the myth of semitropical southern California as a distinct place, the general approach, at least at first, was to look upon the whole of the

11-4 *El Ortiz Hotel, Lamy, N. Mex., 1909. Louis Curtiss, architect. (Photograph: Edward Kemp.)*

Southwest as a single wonderfully exotic Hispanic region. The employment of the singular Mission image throughout the entire area had several decided advantages. The Mission image tended to tie the whole together so that one could experience the Hispanic Southwest and California as a singular entity. For the railroads, with their interest in tourism, it meant that they could provide the traveler with a series of repeated images that strongly helped to establish their own corporate identity (figs. 11-4 and 11-5).

The possibility of experiencing the Southwest as something distinct from California was bound up in an added ingredient—the prehistoric ruins of the region and the very much alive Pueblo villages of the Rio Grande valley and elsewhere. By the 1890s, the distinct possibilities of this native American architecture began to appear in the pages of professional architectural journals. In 1897, the archaeologist Cosmos Mindeleff presented a long series of articles on Pueblo architecture in the Boston-based *American Architect and Building News* (Mindeleff 1897). Certainly the underlying purpose of such articles and their illustrations was to suggest to architects that here was a new image that could enter into their vocabulary.

As happened in the case of the Hispanic Mission image and the later Spanish Colonial Revival in California, the first examples of the Pueblo Revival occurred outside the Southwest. In 1894, San Francisco architect A.C. Schweinfurth designed a "country hotel" that looked to the pueblo rather than to the California mission as its precedent (Schweinfurth 1894). A few years later, in 1897–1898, the California brothers Samuel Newsom and Joseph Cather Newsom fashioned several designs that, while hardly the purest versions of the Pueblo, nonetheless exhibit the hallmarks of the style, such as stucco, parapeted adobe-looking walls, and rows of projecting vegas (Newsom 1897).[2]

11-5 *Hotel Alvarado, Albuquerque, N. Mex., The American Contractor. Charles F. Whittlesey, architect. (Architectural Drawing Collection. University Art Museum, Santa Barbara.)*

By the early 1900s, the Pueblo image was beginning to be perceived as a distinct style. Charles F. Whittlesey's grandiose 1903 project for a sanatorium at Alamagordo, New Mexico, played the images of the multistoried Pueblos within the context of the geometry of the Ecole des Beaux Arts (Whittlesey 1903; 1905). Mary Colter, with the need to catch the eye of the tourist, was more literal in her 1905 "Hopi House" on the south rim of the Grand Canyon, and in 1908–1909, Louis Curtis of Kansas City erected El Ortiz Hotel at Lamy, New Mexico, a romantic introduction to Santa Fe and the pueblos of the Rio Grande (Gratton 1980, 14–9; Gebhard 1962).

None of these early examples in New Mexico or elsewhere were, strictly speaking, archaeologically correct in all the details of their images. They were composed of varied Hispanic and Native American elements, though certainly the intent of their architects was to evoke a specific regional atmosphere of the rustic. In the case of the hotel at Lamy, for example, "The architect was commissioned to pattern this house from the early Spanish hacienda; and his image of the hacienda referred more to Mexico than to New Mexico" (Atler 1959). In California, when Charles F. Lummis and A. V. LaMotte wrote about adobes, they were thinking not simply of examples in coastal California but of those to be found throughout the greater southwestern region (Lummis 1895; LaMotte 1897).

By 1910, when the Adobe style was just beginning to establish itself in Albuquerque and Santa Fe, it was also being taken up elsewhere in the country. In New York in 1904, Clinton and Russell included a southwestern "Indian Room" in their mid-Manhattan Hotel Astor (Boston Architectural League 1908). In Los Angeles and San Francisco, Charles F. Whittlesey employed an "Indian Pueblo Style" in the design of a number of his houses (fig. 11-6), the most insistent being the hillside house for Mrs. Margaret Ward in San Francisco (1911–1912) (Whittlesey 1908; 1911; 1912).

It could well be argued that it was the 1915 Panama California International Exposition at San Diego that gave its impressive stamp of approval not only to the then-emerging Spanish Colonial Revival style, but also to the Pueblo Revival. The New Mexico building by Rapp and Rapp based in part on the church at the Pueblo of Acoma evoked, as Eugene Neuhaus commented at the time, "the primitive character of the life of the pioneers of the Southwest, the Franciscan monks" (Neuhaus 1915, 57–8; see also Sheppard 1988, 79–83). The primitive possibilities of the Native American pueblo tradition were, in addition, directly presented in another section of the exposition, the "Painted Desert." Here were erected reproductions of "picturesque Indian dwellings." "Skillfully and with fine regard for effect of genuineness, the habitations of the cliff dwellers and the 'Hogans' of the Navaho and other nomadic tribes are here set up" (Neuhaus 1915, 46).

In the four or five years preceding the opening of the San Diego Exposition, a sprinkling of archaeologically correct Pueblo-style dwellings were built in California. In Redlands, California in 1913, John H. Fisher, with his intense interest in recreating the life of the old west, built himself an adobe house authentic in design, construction, and

11-6 *Fisher Residence, San Francisco. Charles F. Whittlesey, architect. (From: "Concrete and Brick", The Architect and Engineer XIV:3, Oct. 1908, p. 59.)*

11-7 *Fisher "Adobe," Redlands, Calif., 1913. Fritz Fisher, architect. (Photograph: John C. Fisher, Pasadena.)*

materials (figs. 11-7 and 11-8) (Moore 1986, 14, 120). Within its walls Fisher provided rustic furniture, Navajo rugs, Pueblo pottery, and Mission baskets. In an architecturally more sophisticated vein, in 1913 the San Diego architects Mead and Requa created a beach cottage for another collector of Indian "artifacts," William J. Bailey. The Bailey Cottage (figs. 11-9 and 11-10), placed atop a cliff overlooking the Pacific at La Jolla, was referred to as an example of "Hopi Indian architecture." Its "interior decorations are of Hopi design and various knickknacks of the same tribe lend their picturesque aid to give local color" (Mead and Regna 1920).

As was occurring in Europe, the return to the primitive, the rustic, and the simple also helped set the stage for a decidedly different architectural direction, that of a refined geometric abstraction. In Europe, this process of abstracting the folk and primitive was seen as one of the basic sources of the new International Style Modern. A similar process should perhaps have come about in the United States, but it did not. Modernism, of both the High Art and popular varieties, entered the American scene not internally but via Europe. Two central European modernist transplants to the United States, R. M. Schindler and Richard J. Neutra, saw that the Hispanic/Native American Pueblo tradition of the Southwest was this country's equivalent of the folk traditions of Europe and the Mediterranean. Schindler not only visited New Mexico in 1915 and recorded his experience in a group of wonderful drawings, but also used the Pueblo image for one of his most impressive designs, the T. P. Martin House at Taos (1915) (fig. 11-11) (Gebhard 1965). Later he took the Pueblo theme two or three steps further in the abstracting process and produced his own patio-oriented Studio House on Kings Road in Hollywood (1922) and the Pueblo Ribera Court at La Jolla (1923).

11-8 *Fisher "Adobe," Redlands, Calif., 1913. Fritz Fisher, architect. (Photograph: John C. Fisher, Pasadena.)*

11-9 *Beach Cottage, La Jolla, Calif. Mead & Requa, architects. (From: W. J. Bailey, Western Architect, 29, June 1920, plate 4.)*

153

11-10 *Beach Cottage, La Jolla, Calif. Mead & Requa, architects. (From: W. J. Bailey,* Western Architect, *29, June 1920, plate 4.)*

Richard J. Neutra, who came to the Southwest and California much later (in 1925), was equally impressed. In a letter to his wife, Dione, while he was in New York in 1923, he spoke of his discovery of this primitive source. "I visited the Natural History Museum and came into the room of the Pueblo Indians. These are the people who influenced the modern California building activities" (in Neutra 1986, 101). When Neutra published *Wie Baut Amerika?* in 1927, he illustrated and discussed the pueblos of the Southwest and examples of twentieth-century architecture that he felt directly carried on this tradition (Neutra 1927). Among these designs were Lloyd Wright's 1923 Oasis Hotel at Palm Springs and one of Frank Lloyd Wright's precast concrete block houses in Los Angeles, the Storer House in Hollywood (1923) (Neutra 1927, 60–1, 75–6).

The Pueblo, along with California's Mission style, accompanied by frequent glances at the Christian and Moslem Mediterranean world, was recognized at the time as an inspirational source for America's own "new" architecture. Again, equating it with the contemporary European experience, this catholic interest in the rustic (both past and present) was coupled with modern technology—reinforced concrete and hollow terra cotta tile. In the east, as early as 1897, Grosvenor Atterbury had designed a group of seaside "Moorish" houses for Henry O. Havemeyer at Bayberry Point, Islip, Long Island (fig. 11-12). He maneuvered them into the rustic, and localized them by the use of stuccoed walls "made from the sand on the site so as to blend building and setting" (Dwyer 1980).[3] If Atterbury's 1897 Havermeyer houses were taken up and placed in the Southwest or California, they would be responded to as Mission or Pueblo. They are close in spirit to the work in southern California of Irving J. Gill, Mead and Requa, Charles F. Whittlesey, Arthur B. Benton, Leslie S. Moore, and others. Their equivalents occurred in the San Francisco region in some of the designs of Birgi Clark, Rousseau and Rousseau, and others.

11-11 *T. P. Martin House, Taos, N. Mex., 1915. R. M. Schindler, architect. (Photograph: Architectural Drawing Collection, University of California, Santa Barbara.)*

11-12 *Estate of H. O. Havemeyer. Houses at "Bayberry Point," Islip, Long Island, N. Y. Grosvenor Atterbury, architect. (From:* The American Architect, XCVL:1759, *Sept. 8, 1909.*

11-13 *House for the Maravilla Land Co., Oaji, 1921. "House A." George Washington Smith, architect.*

By the mid-1920s the Cubist overtones of the designs of Gill and others were (to one degree or another) absorbed within California's Colonial Revival. In the work of George Washington Smith (fig. 11-13) and others, Shelden Cheney observed that they were highly successful for, like their primitive sources, they concentrated on a "fine simplicity of the forms, and the sculptural massing of the house" (Cheney 1930, 270).

The Period Revival decades of the 1920s and 1930s were the heyday of the Southwest Adobe tradition as a distinct, recognizable style. Although centered in the Rio Grande valley, many of its most impressive examples were built in California: overlooking the Pacific in Santa Barbara or within an oak grove in the San Fernando valley north of Los Angeles. But where ever these Pueblo Revival dwellings were built, they pointedly argued for the rural, rustic, and primitive. These are the qualities that attracted architects, writers, and artists before and after the turn of the century and continue to seduce us to this day.

REFERENCES

ATLER, RALPH W. (Atchison, Topeka and Santa Fe Railroad System). 1959. Letter to David Gebhard, December 14.

BENTON, ARTHUR B. 1907. *The Mission Inn.* Los Angeles: Los Angeles Segnogram Publishing Co.

_____. 1920. "Shall We Plan for a Distinctive Architecture for the Southwest?" *Southwest Contractor and Manufacture* 6 (Nov. 19):18–9.

BOSTON ARCHITECTURAL LEAGUE. 1908. "Indian Room, Astor Hotel." *Yearbook of the Boston Architectural League,* p. 175. Boston.

CHENEY, SHELDON. 1930. *The New World Architecture.* London: Longmans, Green.

COLE, GEORGE LA MONT. 1916. "Primitive Architecture." *Architect and Engineer* 44 (March):107.

DONNELLY, IGNATIUS. 1882. *Atlantis: The Antediluvian World.* New York: Harper and Brothers.

DWYER, DONALD HARRIS. 1980. "Grosvenor Atterbuy." In: *The Dictionary of American Bibliography*, ed. John A. Garraty. Suppl. 6, 1956–1960, p. 26. New York: Scribner's.

GEBHARD, DAVID. 1962. "Architecture and the Fred Harvey Houses." *New Mexico Architect* 4 (July–Aug.):11–7.

_____. 1965. "R. M. Schindler in New Mexico." *New Mexico Architect* 7 (Jan.–Feb.):15–21.

_____. 1975. *Charles F. A. Voysey, Architect*. Los Angeles: Hennessey and Ingalls.

_____. 1979. *Samuel and Joseph Cather Newsom: Victorian Architectural Imagery in California, 1878–1908*. Santa Barbara, Calif.: University Art Musuem.

GRATTON, VIRGINIA L. 1980. *Mary Colter, Builder Upon the Red Earth*. Flagstaff, Ariz.: Northland Press.

LAMOTTE, A. V. 1897. "Adobe Houses." *Overland* 30 (Sept.):239–42.

LUMMIS, CHARLES F. 1895. "The Patio" and "The Grand Verandah." *Land of Sunshine* 3 (June–Nov.):12–6, 63–7.

MACAULAY, ROSE. 1966. *Pleasure of Ruins*. London: Thomas and Hudson.

MCCABE, JAMES D. 1876. *The Illustrated History of the Centennial Exhibition*. Philadelphia: National Publishing Company.

MEAD AND REQUA. 1920. "Beach Cottage in Hopi Indian Architecture for W. S. Bailey, La Jolla, California." *Western Architect* 29 (June): plate 4.

MINDELEFF, COSMOS. 1897. "Pueblo Architecture." *American Architect* 56:(April 17) 19–21, (May 22) 59–61, (July 24) 31–3, (Sept. 11) 87–8.

MOORE, WILLIAM J. 1986. *Fun With Fritz: Adventures in Early Redlands, Big Bear, and Hollywood with John H. "Fritz" Fisher*. Redlands, Calif.: A Moore Historical Foundation Book.

NEUHAUS, EUGENE. 1915. *The San Diego Fair*. San Francisco: Paul Elder.

NEUTRA, DIONE. 1986. *Richard Neutra: Promise and Fulfillment, 1919–1932*. Carbondale: Southern Illinois University Press.

NEUTRA, RICHARD J. 1927. *Wie Baut Amerika?* Stuttgart: Julius Hoffman.

PAUSANIUS. 1985. *Guide to Greece*, 2 vols., transl. Peter Levi. Harmondsworth: Penguin Books.

SHEPPARD, CARL D. 1988. *Creator of the Santa Fe Style: Isaac Hamilton Rapp, Architect*. Albuquerque: University of New Mexico Press.

STICKLEY, GUSTAV. 1909a. *Craftsman Homes*. New York: Craftsman Publishing.

_____. 1909b. "How Mission Furniture Was Named." *Craftsman* 16:225.

STREET, GEORGE EDMUND. 1869. *Some Accounts of Gothic Architecture in Spain*. London: John Murray.

SCHWEINFURTH. 1894. "Country Hotel Near Montalvo." *California Architect and Building News* 15 (April):39.

WHITTLESEY, CHARLES F. 1903. "Sanatorium Alamagordo, New Mexico." *The Builder and Contractor's* (June)25:1.

_____. 1905. "Sanatorium at Alamogordo, New Mexico." *The Architect and Engineer*, 2 (Sept.):25–26.

_____. 1908. "Residence of Mr. Fisher, San Francisco." *Architect and Engineer* 14 (Oct.):59.

_____. 1911. "Unique Design in the Indian Pueblo Style." *Architect and Engineer* 24 (March):58.

_____. 1912. "House for Margaret Ward, San Francisco, California." *Architect and Engineer* 29 (May):84–5.

Wyatt, M. Digby. 1872. *An Architect's Notebook in Spain.* London: Autotype Fine Art Co.

NOTES

1. From Charles F. A. Voysey, *The English Home*, as quoted in Gebhard (1975).

2. Samuel Newsom's article, "Parker House, San Rafael," originally appeared in the *California Architect and Building News*, Sept. 18, 1897. It is reprinted in Gebhard (1979).

3. The Bayberry Point houses were illustrated in *The American Architect* 26 (Sept. 8):n.p.(1909).

The Aesthetics of Holmes and Bandelier   **12**

George Kubler

The purpose here in bringing Holmes and Bandelier together is to show their differing relations to our theme—Pueblo style and regional architecture. They knew of each other, and they were nearly contemporaries studying the same area in different ways. But Holmes was an artist who became a geologist, while Bandelier was a sociologist who became an archaeologist. In retrospect, they were among the first students of the whole Southwest. But Holmes came from geology as an artist, and Bandelier, four years younger than Holmes, from sociology and archaeology.

WILLIAM HENRY HOLMES (1846–1933)

The geological panoramas by Holmes could still bridge the chasm that widens between science and art. I shall try to reconstruct the aesthetic foundations upon which Holmes was building as a geologist.[1]

William Henry Holmes began a long career as an artist, turned to geology and anthropological archaeology, and ended as curator and director of the National Gallery of Art. In 1879 he went to Europe for art studies in Munich and Italy, and continued in Washington during 1882–1885 in "museum work and the study of primitive art in its various branches."[2] In 1894 he was head curator in the Field Columbian Museum of Chicago, after having taken part in the installation of the exhibits of the Smithsonian Institution at the Field Columbian Exposition in Chicago. This was the most extended exhibition of ancient American art that had yet been assembled in the hemisphere, and its effects soon appeared in the architecture and arts of this country (Bancroft 1895, 629–63).[3] Full-size replicas of Maya buildings from Labna and Uxmal were shown as well as houses of cliff dwellers and other shelters of Amerindian peoples. All were arranged under the direction of F. W. Putnam for "comparative study" in the Anthropological Building as "Man and His Works" (Bancroft 1895, 631–5). Later on, in 1903, as chief of the Bureau of American Ethnology, Holmes opposed Putnam on the subject of Paleolithic remains in North America, saying that the stone tools from Trenton, New Jersey were not of glacial age but only "crude unfinished tools of later date." Stephen Williams (1977) says that both were right and wrong: "Holmes was correct in his analysis that many of these were not finished tools . . . but he was wrong in attacking the notion of glacial age man in America as many Carbon 14 dates now amply testify."

In 1920, after having been curator since 1906 (Fink 1983), Holmes was named first director of the National Gallery of Art in the National Museum building (now the Museum of Natural History) completed in 1910 on the Mall in Washington, D. C. He thereby returned to his first interest, the art of painting, and left the controversial field of Early Man in America (Willey and Sabloff 1973, 49–59).

Long before this, Holmes's published thoughts about aesthetics began with papers in 1883 on "art in shell" of Amerindian origin (Holmes 1883a). In 1883 his "ceramic art" in ancient America appeared together with articles on Pueblo and Mississippi pottery (Holmes 1883b), followed in 1888 by a similar general analysis of textiles (Holmes 1885). In 1890 he was ready to discuss the evolution of ornament in America (Holmes 1890). Two years later he released the first of two essays on aesthetic evolution (Holmes 1892), followed the next year by one on developmental order in aesthetics (Holmes 1893).

Holmes's views on aesthetics resemble the "technicism" of Gottfried Semper (1803–1879), and they prefigure those of André Leroi-Gourhan (after 1957) in proposing a biological metaphor for the developmental evolution of the forms of art (Semper 1878). He saw "the realm of the aesthetic" as the pleasures of seeing, hearing and thinking (Holmes 230) and as the "science of the beautiful" when the "simple, observable phenomena of the aesthetic" are "studied and classified, as the naturalist deals with the pheonomena of biology" (Holmes 240). Without "aesthetic sense," existence would be "ineffably stupid" (Holmes 242). He then states his biological metaphor: "the creations of art are growths as are the products of nature" which "are subject to the same inexorable laws of genesis and evolution" (Holmes 243). The physical and mental evolution of the individual appears on a graph, charted against growth from the prenatal period through infancy, youth, and maturity. The graphs[4] are like trumpets, physically expanding to a closed bell in old age and mentally opening steadily as to an "aesthetic field" until death. The graph is scaled in a ratio of 3:7 of all mental powers at old age (without the closing of the trumpet).

Holmes also alludes to the theory of child's play as aesthetic, citing Schiller and Spencer but rejecting their writings as inadequate accounts of adult aesthetics (Holmes 245), and passing on to an evolutionary diagram of national and total cultural evolution. He uses open "trumpet" graphs with aesthetic inner linings as before. They show "pre-human, savage, barbarous, civilized and enlightened" stages. Four "nations," their composite graph, and the graph for all biological history are with a ration about 6:5 between all experience and the inner lining of aesthetics, diagrammed in broken lines. Advanced peoples have wider aesthetic ranges; the less advanced, narrower. Finally, Holmes diagrams the various arts of space and time in their order of appearance. Painting came first, then sculpture, followed by architecture, all three with wide-mouthed trumpets. Then there appear in chronological sequence, as shortening graphs, music, poetry, drama, romance, and gardening, each diminishing as to the ratio between aesthetics and all experience. He concludes that the future is open to further stages beyond "enlightened," in a "magnificent sum total of the aesthetic that future generations will be privileged to enjoy" (Holmes 255).

Two years later (1895) Holmes returned to the evolutionary interpretation, on the smaller scale, of the shaping of stone tools. He refrained from any attempt to determine absolute chronology, insisting only on his ideas of the "order of development" and on the "phenomena of art" as giving "an insight into the initial stages of history" (Holmes, 288). He classified early manual arts (by materials, processes, functions, stages of culture, time periods, and peoples), concentrating on processes, especially manual, which he defined as fracturing, bruising, abrading, incising, modeling, and constructing, each in at least three modes (e.g., "splitting, breaking, flaking, etc." for "fracturing"). At times his terms prefigure those of André Leroi-Gourhan after 1971, as when Holmes writes of "the pre-anthropic stage" of the "auroral days" of humanity, (Holmes 1893, 291, 293), including fracture, bruise, abrasion, and incision. These four processes are diagrammed as "genetic columns" showing "relative progress" from "pre-art" to "enlightened" through savage, barbarian, and civilized periods. Although the four processes are assumed to coexist before "barbarianism" and after "pre-art," he allows for the "existence of flaked-stone period in Europe" only between points A and B in "savage" time (Holmes 1893, 299).

Holmes has been presented as "virtually self-taught in the use of pencil, pen and brush," in the face of "parental disapproval" (Nelson 1980). Drawn to art, he decided in 1871 to study at his studio in Washington with Theodor Kaufman (who had studied with Wilhelm von Kaulbach in Munich before emigrating to America in 1855). Holmes was encouraged by a fellow student, Mary Henry, the daughter of the Smithsonian Institution's first secretary, to draw the collections. He began drawing paleontological shells for F. B. Meek, and he met many of the illustrators with whom he would soon work on the U.S. Geological and Geographical Survey of the Territories. Meek tutored Holmes in lithography and employed him as a piecework illustrator among the young scientists living in the Smithsonian "castle" building (Nelson 1980, 263–4).

By May 1872 Holmes was considered ready to join the Yellowstone Division in Utah to do geological illustration in the national park. His panoramas and sections showed his "uncanny ability to portray accurately the details and depth of a geologic landscape" (Nelson 1980, 265–9).[5] His association with the photographer William Henry Jackson began with his investigations of archaeology and anthropology in Colorado and eastern Utah in 1875–1876. Holmes and Jackson then collaborated on the Pueblo cliff house country of Colorado, Utah, and New Mexico, in studies, models, and collections,[6] which were displayed at the Philadelphia Centennial in 1876 (Nelson 1980, 272).

Art became Holmes's main concern when the government discontinued the territorial surveys as of 1880. Holmes went to Europe to visit museums in Italy and to study painting in Munich among the Americans around Frank Duveneck in 1879–1880. He exhibited drawings and watercolors at the Corcoran Gallery and Cosmos Club on his return (Nelson 1980, 273). He was then reappointed as assistant geologist to the survey, to draw the Grand Canyon and assigned to help Clarence Dutton. The combination was of "an artist with geological training and a genius for the literal" with "a poetic and speculative geologist." Stegner wrote of Holmes's drawings here was "art without falsification" (Stegner 1954, 189, 191).

Returning to Washington in 1881, Holmes worked between tours to Mexico and the Yucatán on the publication of the survey's drawings. In 1889 he was drawn into the Bureau of Ethnology to prepare exhibits for the World Columbian Exposition in 1893. He resided in Chicago as curator of the Department of Ethnology at the Field Columbian Museum, but came home to Washington in 1897 to become chief of the Bureau from 1902 to 1909.

From the viewpoint of an art historian, a major work by Holmes came out of his travels in Mexico and specifically the Yucatán. In 1884 he and three professional photographers[7] traveled through Mexico on a private railroad car for two months, studying museums, cities, and people. In 1894 or 1895 he was invited to explore the Yucatán Peninsula from the yacht of Allison V. Armour of Chicago. The published results of these travels comprised two volumes, the first mainly about architecture and the second on sculpture (Holmes 1895, 1897).[8] Plans and drawings were by Holmes, including panoramas of Chichen Itzá, Uxmal, Palenque, Monte Albán, and Teotihuacán.

His descriptions of pre-Columbian architecture are still sound and his theories interesting, as when he offers a typology of roofing construction, from beam span to single, double, and circular leanto types. The "cuneiform arch" is his name for the corbel vault of Mayan building; he also calls it a "double lean-to" (Holmes 1895, 48–55). Anticipating Spinden's detailed analyses, he described Mayan ornament as owing most of its forms to "associated thought" in "geometric reductions" of animal shapes representing mythological figures. He estimated that "symbolism and aestheticism" take up three-fourths of the "labor and cost" of Mayan architecture, with "symbolism" determining the "location" of the work, and "aestheticism" determining the "spread" (Holmes 1895, 89). Maya drawing recalled Egypt, by its lack of perspective and mixing of sizes. As to the meaning of Mayan art, he believed, like Mayan scholars today, that "names, titles or devices of rulers" were the subjects in priestly accounts of rites and ceremonies. Like Stephens, Holmes rejected all analogies with arts elsewhere in the world than America (Holmes 1895, 53–5).

Holmes's opinion of the significance of Monte Albán in southern Mexico was of "an actual city . . . of an agricultural people who utilized the valleys" up to the "very crests of the mountains" (Holmes 1897, 226). Of Teotihuacán in the Valley of Mexico, he wrote that "the city was largely one of residence" by "a culture differing decidedly from that of Tenochtitlan." He saw an "absence of indications of a warlike spirit . . . though it is next to impossible to think of a great American nation not built up and kept together on a military basis" (Holmes 1897, 303).

Aztec sculpture was for Holmes dependent on "religious inspiration," marked by a portraiture more recessive than among the Maya. He saw its grace, symmetry, and refinement as being in tribute to "forces of nature," in feathered-serpent forms.

When Holmes became chief of the Bureau of American Ethnology in 1902 he was responsible for the *Handbook of American Indians* (Hodge 1907/1910). Holmes wrote on Amerindian craft practices and materials in 122 articles. His colleague N. M. Judd thought that Holmes wrote nothing of major importance at the Bureau (Judd 1967, 23–5), but for those needing information on specific crafts and materials, these *Handbook* articles by Holmes remain indispensable.

Paul Bartsch, writing for the *Dictionary of American Biography,* noted that Holmes's "special aversions" were to the "theory of pre-glacial man in America" and to "Neoism" and "futurism in art" (Bartsch 1944). As first director of the National Gallery of Art (1920–1933), Holmes wrote the catalogue of its collections in the north wing of the U.S. National Museum building (erected in 1910 to house the natural history collection of the country) (National Gallery of Art 1922).

From the point of view of people nearing the end of this century and preparing to face the 500th anniversary of Columbus's discovery of the New World, it is clear that when Holmes was a young artist in 1865 there were few if any museums of art in which he could display his now acknowledged ability with collections. But today, his appointment as director of a still unborn National Gallery of Art would be as unlikely as his being an anthropological archaeologist and curator.

In brief, Holmes's long life was devoted more to a search of Amerindian art than to anthropological science. It may be said to anticipate the present-day character of one school of American Studies: begun in the history of art, continued in anthropology and archaeology, finding support in ethnology, and returning to the art museum after appearance of the *Handbook.* Characteristic of this tradition is Holmes's "lesson": "that ideas associated with any . . . conventional decorative forms may be as diverse as are the arts, the peoples, and the original elements concerned in its evolution (Holmes 1890).

ADOLPH BANDELIER (1850–1914)

Adolph Bandelier, a self-taught disciple of Lewis Henry Morgan, found another means of expression in writing a novel, *The Delight Makers,* about Pueblo Indians. The letters by Bandelier to the anthropologist and archaeologist Lewis H. Morgan (1818–1881) reveal his debt to Morgan, whom he adopted as a scholarly father (White 1940, 8–10). When Bandelier converted to Catholicism in 1881 at Cholula, the Mexican historian Joaquin Garcia Icazbalceta (1825–1894) was his chosen godfather and they corresponded from 1875 to 1891 (White and Bernal 1960, 87–100). In 1888 he began, for Pope Leo XIII, the manuscript of *A History of the Southwest,* as if dedicated to the last of the surrogate fathers he needed to replace the bankrupt and fugitive father who had deserted the family in 1885 (Burrus 1969, 1:29).

Bandelier's principal motive when he began *The Delight Makers* in 1883 at Cochiti was to discredit the "romantic" fictions about Indians that were then current (Bandelier 1885), but at the same time, as he stated in his preface, he would "tell the truth about the Indian" by "clothing sober facts in the garb of romance."

The narrative of the love between Okoya and Mitsha occupies 21 chapters in which Bandelier tells what he knows as an ethnologist about his Indian friends and their Navajo enemies at Cochiti and Santa Clara pueblos. But following their traditions, he places his romance in the ruined towns of the cliff dwellers at Rito de los Frijoles and Puye, abandoned many centuries ago. He assumed that three centuries of Spanish government and Catholic missionary indoctrination had left no traces on the Keresan and Tewa peoples, whom he resettled in his imagination at Tyuonyi and Puye, with Navajo enemies nearby.

His underlying principles were stated in a lecture (Bandelier 1885, 10, 11). First, "religious creeds" and "social organization" were "molded on the same pattern" among all tribes *over the whole American continent.*" Second, "ruins in existence prove *not* a contemporaneous large population, *but the successive shiftings of that population over a vast area within a correspondingly long time.*"

Self-taught and turning to American ethnology and archaeology under the influence of L. H. Morgan, Bandelier had published papers in 1877–1879 on ancient Mexican warfare, land tenure, social organization, and government, all based on source material in many European and Native American languages, and making "fairly accurate guesses about [chronological] sequences" (Willey and Sabloff 1980, 51). Thus prepared, he began many years of field work, beginning in New Mexico at Pecos, Cochiti, and Santa Clara, pueblos, where he combined archaeology and ethnology.

He interrupted these studies to visit Charnay in Mexico. Disappointed by Charnay's return to France, Bandelier visited Cholula, Mitla, Tlacolula, and Monte Albán in 1881 and then returned to New Mexico to describe ruins until 1886. His frame of mind during these arduous years is described in his paper of 1885 as seeking to replace "romance" with historical criticism following the methods of Humboldt and Morgan (Bandelier 1885, 6–7, 13). At this time, however, he wrote *The Delight Makers* in order to discredit predecessors. In a letter to T. Janvier, September 2, 1888, he wrote:

> We have, Mr. Morgan and I under his directions, unsettled the Romantic School in Science, now the same thing must be in literature on the American aborigine. Prescott's Aztec is a myth, it remains to show the Fennimore [sic] Cooper's Indian is a fraud. THEY—I want to destroy first if possible (Radin 1942, xi).

Bendelier's private opinion of Indians appears in *The Delight Makers:* "The Indian views nature with the eyes of a materially interested spectator only." His main concerns had been with maternal descent: exogamous clans, government by clan representatives (he despised "democracy"); nuclear family separated by maternal and paternal clans. All these ethnological findings are applied by analogy to interpret the lost antiquity of Tyuonyi canyon (Frijoles canyon) and Puye. But his hermeneutic system requires an "Indian who speaks like a child," who "lacks abstract terms" and lives by "religious acts called forth by utterances . . . of higher powers" (Bandelier 1918).

In fact, Bandelier denied or ignored an aesthetic sense among his Cochiti Indians of 1884, although he was driven by their aesthetic absorption in ritual.[9] His criterion is to make Indians so similar to whites that they will understand Indians as he does: "Indian gossip . . . is as venomous . . . as among us" (286), and "children conceal their guilt, and so does the Indian" (303). Thus, in circular progression, Bandelier declared that Indians today [1890] "are at heart nearly the same Indians [as] we found them in this story" (485). Thus revealing that he was portraying them both, old and new, as identical in his private imagination (489).

Bandelier's meaning, when he rejected the "romantic school in American aboriginal history," was that lacking criticism of sources it "creates illusion, propagates fiction" (Bandelier 1885, 12–3). But Bandelier abandoned these principles when writing *The Delight Makers*[10] without historical criticism of any kind. His pronouncements about the nature of Indian thought are nevertheless frequent, in a text written to be read aloud, without interruption from footnotes, in a family gathering. Being such, they are commonplaces, as of that period.[11]

From 1892 to 1903 he was in Peru and Bolivia extending his research to sites and sources there, from Chan Chan to Lake Titicaca (Hodge 1914). His presence in La Paz in 1894 coincided with that of Max Uhle,[12] whose work and fame correspond to a later "horizon" of American archaeology, when it became possible to begin to correlate stratigraphic sequences with historical sources.

Bandelier's scientific work in New Mexico as recorded in his *History of the Southwest* (begun in 1888 and first published in its entirety in 1969) surveyed the field as he had seen it in New Mexico and Arizona. His novel about pre-Conquest peoples of the Rio Grande basin prefigures the ethnographic method of interpreting antiquity by modern practices (known as "upstreaming").

Paul Radin wrote in 1942 of Bandelier that "he did not like the Indian" and he wished "to reduce them all |Central America, Peru, Bolivia and the Southwest| . . . to simple, primitive democracies. For democracies he had the most profound contempt" (Radin 1942, x–xi).

Thus Holmes and Bandelier stood for opposite attitudes toward Amerindian life before 1900. Their opposition still persists between informed and uninformed persons in this country today. But in the lives of the uninformed today, Holmes is still nonexistent, while Bandelier's name is attached to the Bandelier National Monument, and to Pueblo life by *the Delight Makers*, as a name in the roster of sights while on vacation.

To turn to the central theme of this book: How are Holmes and Bandelier related to Pueblo Revival and architectural regionalism and their future continuation? For now, it can be said that before Holmes and Bandelier, there was no panoramic *vision* of the environment or of its history. Holmes saw New Mexico as a geologist and artist; Bandelier saw it as a sociologist and historian.

But until its architects and architectural historians appeared in this century, the "Pueblo style" could not come into being. And now that "Pueblo style" offers an alternative to "Los Angeles sprawl," which spreads as far as Tucson, the question arises as to Pueblo survival among other spreading regional styles from beyond the Rio Grande.

Indeed it seems that these chapters are about the survival of Pueblo Revival. In the present world of high-rise metropolitan expansions, regional styles are necessary to the survival of the ancient cultural codes from which they emerged. Thus architecture may be said to relate to society as seashells do to the various marine dwellers in them. Finally, the question of the Hispanic vernacular is hidden by the Pueblo Revival. Unraveling this still needs work.

REFERENCES

BANCROFT, H. H. 1895. *The Book of the Fair*, Vol. III, "Anthropology and Ethnology." Chicago: Bancroft Co.

BANDELIER, A. F. 1885. *The Romantic School in American Archaeology*. New York: Trow's Printing & Bookbinding Co.

_____. 1918. *The Delight Makers*, 2d ed.

BARTSCH, PAUL. 1944. In: *Dictionary of American Biography*, Suppl. I, pp. 427–8. New York: Charles Scribner Sons.

BURRUS, E. J., S. J. 1969. *A History of the Southwest*. St. Louis.

FINK, L. M. 1983. "Introduction." *Descriptive Catalogue of Painting and Sculpture in the National Museum of America Art*, ix–xii. Boston: National Museum of American Art.

HODGE, F. W., ed. 1907/1910. *Handbook of American Indians*. Bulletin 30, pt. 1, 1907; pt. 2, 1910. Bureau of American Ethnology.

_____. 1914. Obituary, A. E. Bandelier. *American Anthropologist*, Vol. 16: 114, 349–58; bibliography of 55 items.

HOLMES, W. H. 1883a. *Transactions of the Anthropological Society of Washington*

2:94–119 (1882–1883); *Annual Report of the Bureau of Ethnology*, 2:179–305 (1880–1881) |Washington, 1883|.

_____. 1883b. "Origin and Development of Form and Ornament in Ceramic Art." *Annual Report of the Bureau of Ethnology*, 4:437–65 (1882–1883); "Pottery of the Ancient Pueblos," ibid., 257–360 |Washington, 1886|.

_____. 1885. "A Study of the Textile Art In Its Relation to the Development of Form and Ornament." *Annual Report of the Bureau of Ethnology*, 6:13–187 (1884–1885) |Washington, 1888|.

_____. 1890. "On the Evolution of Ornament—An American Lesson." *American Anthropologist*, 3:137–46.

_____. 1892. "Evolution of the Aesthetic." *Proceedings AAAS,* 41:239–55.

_____. 1893. "Order of Development of the Primal Shaping Arts." *Proceeding AAAS*, 42:289–300.

_____. 1895/1897. *Archaeological Studies Among the Ancient Cities of Mexico.* Part 1: *Monuments of Yucatan.* Part 2: *Monuments of Chiapas, Oaxaca, and the Valley of Mexico.* Publications of the Field Columbian Museum, Anthropological Series. Chicago: Field Columbian Museum.

JUDD, N. M. 1967. *The Bureau of American Ethnology. A Partial History.* Norman, Okla.: University of Oklahoma Press.

National Gallery of Art. 1922. *Catalogue of Collections.* Washington, D.C.: Smithsonian Institution Press.

NELSON, C. M. 1980. "William Henry Holmes: Beginning a Career in Art and Science." *Records of the Columbia Historical Society,* 50:254.

RADIN, PAUL, ed. 1942. *The Unpublished Letters of Adolph Bandelier Concerning the Writing and Publication of The Delight Makers.* New York: Everitt.

ROWE, J. H. 1954. *Max Uhle, 1856–1944: A Memoir of the Father of Peruvian Archaeology.* University of California Publications in American Archaeology and Ethnology, 46:5.

SEMPER, G. 1878. *Der Stil in den technischen und tektonischen Kuensten oder praktische Aesthetik.* 2nd ed., two vols. Munich.

STEGNER, W. 1954. *Beyond the Hundredth Meridian.* Boston: Houghton Mifflen.

WHITE, L. A. 1940. *Pioneers in American Anthropology. The Bandelier-Morgan Letters 1873–1883.* Albuquerque:

_____, and I. BERNAL. 1960. *Correspondencia de Adolfo F. Bandelier.* Mexico.

WILLEY, G. R., and J. SABLOFF. 1980 (2d ed.), 1974 (1st ed.) *A History of American Archaeology.* San Francisco: W. H. Freeman.

WILLIAMS, STEPHEN. 1977. Introduction, *Holmes Anniversary Volume,* vii. Published 1916; reissued 1977.

NOTES

1. Written while Kress Professor (1985–1986) of the Center for Advanced Study in the Visual Arts (National Gallery of Art), at Washington D.C., as part of a volume on aesthetic recognitions of Amerindian material culture.

2. The "Brief Biography" with the subtitle "Artist, Geologist, Archaeologist and Art Gallery Director" (*Ohio Archaeological and Historical Quarterly,* 36, 1927, October, No. 4, 493–511) was probably written by the editor C. B. Galbreath in Columbus.

3. Louis Sullivan and Frank Lloyd Wright both knew the exhibition and used its forms in their own ways.

4. Such graphs are named "unimodal" by Willey and Sabloff (*1973*, 100) and described as representing "type frequencies."

5. F. V. Hayden, who led the eleven-man division, had Holmes appointed as assistant geologist in 1874.

6. A watercolor of a Mancos Valley cliff house by Holmes illustrates the exhibition catalogue *Art in New Mexico*, (Eldredge et al. 1986, 200, Fig. 9, dated 1875).

7. Mr. and Mrs. Chain, with W. H. Jackson, were the photographers (*"Brief Biography,"* 503). Mr. and Mrs. Chain provided the private car.

8. A third volume (not published) was to be on "Ceramic Art of Mexico." For part I he depended on books by J. L. Stephens, D. Charnay, A. Le Plongeon, A. Maudslay, A. Bandelier, and H. H. Bancroft. On ancient writings he also knew the works of E. Seler, E. H. Thompson, C. Thomas, D. G. Brinton, E. W. Förstemann, P. Schellhas, and P. Valentini.

9. A concern not fully shared by other scholars until the book by Vincent Scully (*Pueblo/Mountain, Village, Dance*. 1972. New York: The Viking Press) whose own emotional absorption matched that of the dancers themselves.

10. Only Pedro de Castañeda de Nacera, *Relación de la jornada de Cibola* . . . 1540 and Mota Padilla are mentioned without any identification on p. 347, but Bandelier's detailed knowledge of these sources was exceptional. The context is Indian creation at Rito de los Frijoles in Chapter 16 on the funeral of the *maseua* (war chief), Topanashka.

11. He asked Thomas Janvier, his friend assisting him in getting a publisher, to be allowed to write a "few short explanatory footnotes and supporting arguments" for his beliefs, but was presumably discouraged (Radin 1942, x, 2–3).

12. J. H. Rowe (1954) says that "each told the other as little as possible of his own research and each was critical of the other's results."

Escape from the Southwest: The Pueblo Style in Minnesota and Florida

13

Carl D. Sheppard • Stephen D. Schreiber

THE PUEBLO STYLE IN MINNESOTA

In addition to New Mexico and California, several other states have examples of Pueblo or Santa Fe style buildings. Among these are Florida and Minnesota. In fact, the Minneapolis suburb of Wayzata has the earliest school designed in the Pueblo style, and there still exists a private house in the style in immaculate preservation. Both buildings have all the characteristics associated with Pueblo style; they are not pueblo-ized fantasies as so often occurred in California. They were well designed as authentic interpretations of the style developing in Santa Fe at the time. These two structures and a gas station (now lost) were built in 1921, a remarkable date for the style to have escaped from the Southwest. Their only stylistic variance is the lack of the curvilinear roofline characteristic of the work designed by Isaac Hamilton Rapp for the Museum of Santa Fe, Sunmount Sanatorium, and the Gross Kelly Warehouse, all of 1914–1915.

A few other buildings were executed by the firm of Rapp and Rapp at Santa Fe before World War I absorbed the energies of the United States. The influential design of La Fonda, Santa Fe, was not accomplished on paper until 1920. The Minnesota buildings thus belong to the earliest period of Pueblo style. That they lack the "adobe" quality of the Santa Fe structures should not be surprising, but what is notable is the cubistic abstraction of surface and composition, very similar to the slightly later work in California of R.M. Schindler and Richard J. Neutra.

Widsten School (fig. 13-1) is located on a narrow plateau overlooking the downtown area of the village of Wayzata and the bays of Lake Minnetonka. The Wayzata

13-1 *Widsten School, Wayzata, Minn. (Photograph: Carl D. Sheppard.)*

School, as it was originally named, was dedicated on October 7, 1921. Sitting on a strongly contoured rise of two terraces, it dominates its site from the main approach from the north. Pictures of the building in the 1920s show that the street in front of it was already depressed, making a slope upwards toward the facade. The architects used a strictly formal symmetry for the design of each of the four sides of the block. The interior, where a court or patio could have been located, is devoted to the gymnasium, which rises above the surrounding one-story corridors and classrooms to give the effect of a second story.

There is no main entrance to the building; instead there are doorways at either side—openings to the corridor, which is wrapped around the sides and rear of the school. This conflicts gently with the strong axial symmetry of the facade and is reinforced by the layout of the sidewalks. The effect caused by the double entrances to the facade and by the elevation of the gymnasium roofline above that of the surrounding offices and classrooms is that of an interplay of cubes.

The coincidence of Pueblo and International styles in the Wayzata School probably accounts for the survival of the building in such excellent repair into the 1980s and certainly beyond. The only major change, an addition in 1939 by the firm of Haxby and Bissel, is so discretely in the same style and so fortunately placed to one side that it in no way distracts from the original design. The change of the window mullions from wood cross-pieces to clear sheets of glass in 1973 is unfortunate but does not seriously interfere with the original intentions of the architects, and the new roof of 1982 makes no difference at all.

The interior spaces are all amply proportioned with high ceilings. The detailing is utilitarian except for the doorways, whose framing has been carefully manipulated to give the effect of adobe surfaces. The classrooms are spare without embellishment. This is not true of what was once a community room at the northwest corner of the school. It was provided with its own entrance, within the porch of the west entry. The room is now used for instruction in music and has been in no way changed from its original appearance. The external viga ends, on the west outside wall, are carried into the interior as ceiling beams resting on brackets. Neither the beams nor their corbels are solid but are well enough done to encourage this impression. All the wood surfaces in this room, as throughout the building, have a deep oak finish. At the west end of the community room is a handsome fireplace. It is a perfect rendition of a Pueblo Revival fireplace and would not be out of place in a hall of the Museum of Fine Arts, Santa Fe. Over the thin narrow board of the mantle is an oil painting of the Pueblo of Taos, signed in 1921 by Edwin Hewitt, the designer-architect.

Edwin Hawley Hewitt was born in 1874 in Red Wing, Minnesota, and died in 1939 in Minneapolis. He received a degree from the University of Minnesota in 1896, studied at Massachusetts Institute of Technology; went on to the Ecole des Beaux Arts, Paris; worked for three-and-a-half years for the firm of Sheply, Ruben, and Coolidge of Boston; and in 1904 opened an office in Minneapolis. In 1911 he joined his brother-in-law in the firm of Hewitt and Brown. Both had the same first name. Hewitt should not be confused with Santa Fe's Edgar Lee Hewett. Edwin Hawley Hewitt had a very distinguished career in Minneapolis. He was an early board member of the Minneapolis Museum of Fine Arts. Perhaps some of his clients who had traveled to the Southwest directed Hewitt's interest in this direction. There is no other evidence of the Pueblo style in the area. Even the museum did not start its collection of Southwest artifacts at this time. Hewitt himself collected Japanese prints and sword guards.

The house at 5308 Russell Avenue South was erected by J. E. Lawton; its present owner, W. J. Quirk, takes immense and generous pride in the building (fig. 13-2). On the street side of the house an interesting composition of cubic solids is created through the changes in the rooflines. To the left, the garage starts the sequence of three similar shapes, which culminates to the right where the comb is raised over the entrance. The garage roof is correlated with the vigas across the rest of the front, making an easy

13-2 *Lawton-Quirk House, Russell Avenue, Minneapolis, Minn. (Photograph: Carl D. Sheppard.)*

integration. The Minnehaha Creek side of the house is two-storied. The play of levels of the rooflines of a porch, the vigas, and the double height at the top makes the water side of the house more complex than the street facade.

THE PUEBLOS OF THE EVERGLADES

The Florida land boom of the 1920s spawned a number of suburban developments in the newly drained savannahs and land-filled mangrove swamps surrounding Miami. The speculative villages, influenced by the rigid Beaux Arts planning of the City Beautiful movement, often linked public and private buildings with a common thematic architecture. George Merrick's Coral Gables featured a Mediterranean style in a heroic suburban network of plazas, boulevards, and gateways. Addison Mizner's Palm Beach mansions flaunted an architectural style "more Spanish than Spain." Perhaps the most unusual creation from this prosperous era of economic confidence and physical mobility was Country Club Estates, a Pueblo Revival village developed by the famous aviation pioneer Glenn Curtiss. The township was constructed on the flat grasslands owned by Curtiss's partner James Bright, a successful cattle rancher and aviation buff. Both men had become familiar with the austere adobe dwellings of the Native American pueblos through their frequent travels and substantial business interests in the southwestern United States. The first development of the two entrepreneurs had been Hialeah, based on the Spanish Mission style.

The partners became frustrated by Hialeah's rapid and uncontrolled growth and in 1922 decided to start a new village on the other side of the drainage ditch (the Miami Canal) (Rodriguez and Ammidown 1982). They named the subdivision Country Club Estates. Like other successful 1920s developments, Country Club Estates was oriented toward recreational activities (Arend 1964a, 1964b). Curtiss surveyed the site by plane in 1922, and two years later the infrastructure of streets, power lines, and water supply had been installed. Only necessary retail facilities were permitted in the clearly articulated commercial sector, as the town was specifically zoned against industry. Country Club Estates prospered, however, from the booming railroad yards, the factories, and the airport that hugged the fringes of the township on land donated by Bright and Curtiss.[1] Building codes were strict, requiring that houses be built in the Pueblo Revival style. No houses could be built without design approval from the Curtiss and Bright Company. A *Miami Herald* article (*Miami Herald* 1926) commended the developers for establishing an architectural style suitable to the region.

More than 150 adobe homes, apartments, and businesses were built in a 20-month boom period (1924–1926) before the September 1926 hurricane ripped through Florida

13-3 *Gate to Glenn Curtiss's house (now Miami Springs Villas), exterior view, 1989. (Photograph: Stephen D. Schreiber).*

13-4 *Glenn Curtiss's house (now Miami Springs Villas), exterior view. (Photograph from Curtiss-Bright brochure, ca. 1927. Courtesy of Miami Springs Historic Preservation Board.)*

real estate euphoria. Construction continued on only two more Pueblo Revival structures after the disaster. Country Club Estates was renamed Miami Springs after Curtiss's sudden death in 1930, a tribute to the development's contribution to the Miami water supply.

The picturesque "adobe" structures were actually constructed from popular local building materials, such as hollow clay tiles and termite-resistant Dade County pine. Exterior finishes were typically rough-textured stucco with blunted or rounded corners (to imitate the hand-molded, sun-dried mud of the Southwest). Flat roofs were hidden, Pueblo style, behind irregular parapets, with drainage allowed through exaggerated scuppers (*canales*). The austere ornamentation was restricted to stylized *bell cote* motifs or projecting wood beams (*vigas*).

Glenn Curtiss built the most magnificent Pueblo Revival home for himself and named it Dar-Err-Aha, Persian for "house of contentment" (Ash 1966). The rambling mansion, completed in 1925, is a one- and two-story multimassed structure wrapped around a central courtyard. The designer was Martin Luther Hampton.[2] See figs. 13-3 and 13-4.

The four original houses of Country Club Estates were built close together so they could share a common water pump. Martin Hampton designed "Alamo" (fig. 13-5), named for its resemblance to the Texas landmark, for Lua Curtiss, Glenn's mother. The 1924 house, at 85 Deer Run, is an eclectic mixture of Mission and Pueblo styles. Wooden vigas, among the few that have not rotted in the Miami humidity, still protude from the rough-textured exterior. Large glass windows face north through the thick walls, a requirement for Mrs. Curtiss, an artist.

Unhappy with "Alamo," Mrs. Curtiss asked her son to build her another house on the edge of the nearby golf course. The new home, 150 Hunting Lodge Drive, was also designed by Hampton. It is a two-story Pueblo/Mission style home that wraps around a walled front courtyard. Fenestration is recessed within the slightly tapered thick walls. Roughly textured stucco parapets and window openings give the illusion of adobe construction. Cosmetic roof-level vigas have been removed.

13-5 *"The Alamo," 85 Deer Run, Miami Springs, exterior view, 1989. (Photograph: Stephen D. Schreiber.)*

Another of the four original houses was the one-story dwelling at 22 Pinecrest Street. The house at 27 Hunting Lodge Drive was the last of the four.

The Hotel Country Club, completed a year after the devastating hurricane, was the cornerstone of the planned town (fig. 13-6). The terraced five-story structure, designed to resemble a Pueblo village, opened in the midst of the 1927 Florida recession. In 1929, Curtiss sold the hotel to Dr. John Kellogg, noted physician and cereal magnate, who transformed it into the Miami-Battle Creek Sanatorium. During World War II, the military used the hotel for the rest and relaxation of returning servicemen. Today, Fair Haven, a Lutheran retirement home, occupies the complex.

A number of the original 150 Pueblo style structures in Miami Springs have been lost to fire, floods, vandalism, and neglect. Private dwellings, a clubhouse, a bank (fig. 13-7), a bandstand, a fire station, and even the headquarters for the Curtiss and Bright Company have fallen victim to South Florida's wreckers. In 1985, seven structures—five houses, a store, and an apartment building—were listed on the National Register of Historic Places as thematic resources. The hotel and another house have been designated as local historic sites.

New buildings that respect the town's idiosyncratic yet powerful architectural origins have recently been completed. Additions to 851 Hunting Lodge Drive, finished in 1986, follow the thick austere modeling of the original home. Taxis Architects of South Miami have designed a new dwelling adjacent to the Pueblo style masterpiece at 424 Hunting Lodge Drive. The tightly controlled mass steps up to bold four-story terraces. The Pueblo style house is a tribute to Miami Springs. New Mexican craftsmen and artisans are completing the stucco work and the fireplaces of the house.

13-6 *Hotel Country Club (now Fairhaven Lutheran Center), exterior view. (Courtesy of Romer collection, Miami-Dade Public Library.)*

13-7 *First State Bank, Miami Springs (now demolished), exterior view. (Photograph from Curtiss-Bright brochure, ca. 1927. Courtesy of Miami Springs Historic Preservation Board.)*

REFERENCES

Arend, Geoffrey. 1964a. "Great Airports—Miami, New York." *Air Cargo News*, p. 56.

_____. 1964b. "How Miami Springs Started—Glenn Curtiss." *Home News*, April, p. 1.

Ash, Agnes. 1966. "In the House of Contentment, An Eagle Nested." *Miami News*, April 17, p. 16.

Miami Herald, 1926. "Section Progressing." August 8.

Rodriguez, Ivan, and Margot Ammidown. 1982. *From Wilderness to Metropolis: The History and Architecture of Dade County*. Miami: Metropolitan Dade Office of Community and Economic Development.

NOTES

1. Nomination form for Miami Springs Thematic Resource, National Register of Historic Places, 1985, pp. 4, 5.

2. For good general descriptions of Miami Springs buildings, see Mary Ann Taylor, "Self Guided Tour of Historic Sites, Miami Springs," available through Miami Springs Historic Preservation Board. See also nomination form cited in note 1.

New Mexico in the Tradition of Romantic Reaction

14

Chris Wilson

New Mexico regional architecture does not represent some backwater that refuses to join the modern age, but instead is a valuable example of the continuing romantic tradition, a tradition that stretches back more than two centuries. It is generally recognized as an artistic phenomenon, but it has political and economic components as well. In a sense, the romantic tradition can be viewed as a reaction against major forces favoring cultural standardization.

These forces began to emerge from the Renaissance over five centuries ago and were spread by the European colonization of the world. They intensified in the nineteenth century with the Industrial Revolution and in this century through mass communication. Resistance to cultural homogenization has taken two forms.[1] Traditional peoples such as the Pueblos and Hispanic Americans of New Mexico have defended their local, vernacular cultures from the pressures of the dominant, industrial culture. Resistance has also come from within Western Europe, beginning in the eighteenth century with the reaction of the Romantic movement against Classicism and broadening during the next century into a reaction against industrialism best typified by the Arts and Crafts movement. In the United States during this century the romantic tradition has peaked twice: once in the New Deal Regionalism of the 1930s and again in the counterculture/environmental movement beginning in the late 1960s.

At first, in the teens, New Mexico was an outpost of a widespread romantic attitude, although at times since then, especially during the 1950s, it has seemed more like an isolated enclave of romanticism. This chapter outlines the European and American background of the romantic tradition before considering how and why that tradition took root in New Mexico about 1910, and how romantic regionalism has evolved here since.

The rediscovery of classical antiquity and the discovery of new lands in the fifteenth century initiated a break from the Middle Ages and a devaluation of local cultures. Over the next three centuries the notion that ideal beauty and proportion could be derived from classical models gradually took hold in Europe and its colonies. By the late 1600s, the gentlemen-architect had become the arbiter of taste; anything Medieval or local in flavor was derided as uncultured, even barbarous (Mumford 1928; Illich 1980).

Starting in the mid-1700s, artists and architects of what is now known as the Romantic movement—people as various as Goethe, Horace Walpole, and the brothers Grimm—began to take an interest in local, traditional cultures, in their folklore and vernacular buildings. Rather than relying on Classical precedents for the immutable standards of art, the Romantics opened themselves to the world of experience and increasingly found inspiration in nature, in exotic lands, and in the past, especially the Middle Ages (Mumford 1928; Risebero 1982).

The influence of this Romantic movement on the visual arts came primarily through the notion of the Picturesque. Indeed, some late-eighteenth-century authors used the terms "romantic" and "picturesque" interchangeably. The word *romantic* developed from literature, while *picturesque* came from the visual arts. The term picturesque was first applied to landscape painting, then to romantic gardening, and finally to architecture. A house designed to complement a romantic English garden was seen as picturesque in two major senses: first, by its association with the dim past or exotic lands—be they Gothic or Islamic or Chinese—and second, by its irregular plan and asymmetrical facades (Hussey 1927; Collins 1965).

During the late eighteenth and early nineteenth centuries, the romantic, picturesque aesthetic was often confined to country houses and amounted to little more than a taste for the exotic. But by the 1830s it had emerged as a more fully articulated philosophy. During the first decades of the century, architectural theory was revolutionized through detailed studies of historic architecture, studies not only of Classical and Renaissance architecture but also of the Gothic and Egyptian traditions. Writers such as Vaudoyer and Viollet-le-Duc in France and Pugin and Ruskin in England asserted that architecture is shaped by climate, available materials, the state of structural engineering, and the nature of society. Classical architecture no longer stood as the repository of eternal, ideal forms but rather was viewed as one type of architecture among many, each valid and understandable as the result of its own time and place (Stanton 1971; Van Zanten 1988).

The English Romantics, who would have great influence on nineteenth-century American architecture, increasingly took a moralistic stance, lashing out at the evils of industrialization. Nowhere was the Industrial Revolution more advanced than in England, and nowhere was its assault on traditional, vernacular cultures more intense. English Romantic architects and critics such as Augustus Pugin, John Ruskin, and William Morris viewed industrialization as the logical continuation of the rationalizing and standardizing impulses of classicism. Repetitive industrial work, they argued, was destroying spiritual fulfillment and the simple but honest art of the medieval craftsmen. In response they proposed a return to the medieval spirit. This led, on the one hand, to the emergence of the Gothic Revival as the premier Romantic style and, on the other, to the formation of socialist, Utopian communities that promised a spiritual rebirth through a return to hand-craftsmanship and an end to capitalist exploitation. The romantic tradition in England after 1860 and in the United States after 1890 is generally known as the Arts and Crafts movement. The movement emphasized hand-craftsmanship and the honest use of local, often rustic materials, while beginning to look beyond Gothic cathedrals to the simpler, vernacular buildings of village and countryside in a search for locally appropriate forms (Stanton 1971; Lears 1981; Risebero 1982; Kostof 1985; R. Wilson 1987).

Two nineteenth-century applications of the romantic attitude were not as idealistic as the Utopian communities. When the benefits of industrialism—in particular, fast, safe travel—were combined with the romantic attitude, the result was tourism. Tourism offered, as it still offers, a temporary escape from the drudgery of industrial and bureaucratic work. Tourist attractions mirror romantic interests: nature, history, and exotic lands and peoples. A boundary drawn around a fragment of nature yields a national park. And this attitude finds history in those foreign lands and picturesque villages that are least touched by industrialization. Tourism has become an integral part of the modern, industrial world; it represents the infusion of the romantic attitude into mass culture (McCannell 1976; Hobsbawn and Ranger 1983).

At the same time, romantic rhetoric and architecture were also being appropriated for nationalistic purposes. Pugin argued that the decline of English architecture was the direct result of the introduction of Renaissance classicism; the revival of English Gothic architecture, as in his facade for the new Houses of Parliament, became an assertion of national identity. Likewise, the Finnish resistance to Russian domination at the turn of the century manifested itself as a resurgent interest in Finnish folklore and in the development of a National Romantic style as in the Finnish National Museum of 1910 by Gesellius, Lindgren, and Eliel Saarinen (Richards 1978; Risebero 1982). Indeed, the ideological use of architecture as a vehicle for local or national identity continues worldwide today, although it is clearest in the Far East and in vestigial city-states and ethnic regions that harbor anticentrist sentiments (Frampton 1983).

The romantic, picturesque aesthetic was first popularized in the United States in the 1840s through the American editions of John Ruskin's *The Seven Lamps of Architecture* and *The Stones of Venice* and through the writings of Andrew Jackson Downing. By the 1870s, American architectural journals were calling for the development of a distinctly American architecture, a desire stimulated by the nationalistic rhetoric of the 1876 centennial celebrations. Many architects sought inspiration in the study of colonial architecture, which included vernacular building traditions as well as classical Georgian architecture. One led to the informal plans and massing of the Shingle style, the other to the more formal Georgian Revival (Scully 1955).

In the 1890s, those architects who applied Romantic/Arts and Crafts principles in their search for an American architecture emphasized the significance of climate, local materials, history, and even the new, relaxed American life-style. The best-known regional developments at the turn of the century were Chicago's Prairie style and, on the West Coast, the Mission style and Green and Green's Craftsmen houses and their modest Bungalow cousins (Teall 1913; Gebhard 1967; Lears 1981; R. Wilson 1987).

The development of the Spanish Pueblo style was based on the romantic aesthetic in the arts but also on its primary economic corollary—tourism—and on its political manifestation—romantic nationalism or, in the United States, what might be termed romantic regionalism. The impetus of tourism came into play first. Pseudo-pueblos staffed by Indians were erected at every American world's fair from 1893 to 1915 and at key stops along the tourist's path through the Southwest (fig. 14-1). (Anon.

14-1 *Indian Room interior, Alvarado Hotel, Albuquerque, Mary Colter, 1901.*
(Photograph courtesy Museum of New Mexico, Neg. No. 14572.)

14-2 *Kawataka Dormitory, University of New Mexico, Albuquerque, E. B. Christy, 1906. (Photograph courtesy Museum of New Mexico, Neg. No. 30987.)*

1914; C. Wilson 1982, 25–6). The Santa Fe Railroad, which had been a leader in the use of the California Mission style to promote tourism, built the best of the pseudo-pueblos, the Hopi House (1905) at the Grand Canyon, and also the Harvey House hotel El Ortiz (1909) at Lamy, New Mexico. The designer of the Hopi House and Harvey House interiors was Mary Colter. Her exposure to the Arts and Crafts aesthetic through her art school education in San Francisco in the late 1880s is apparent in her emphasis on hand-crafted details and exposed natural materials (Grattan 1980).

The first civic application of the Pueblo idiom occurred in Albuquerque between 1905 and 1909 at the University of New Mexico (fig. 14-2). Under the leadership of university president William Tight, the administration building was remodeled, and four new structures were constructed in the Pueblo style. National magazine articles emphasized the suitability of the Pueblo style to New Mexico's climate and landscape and also to the "communal life of the University." Curiously, no one mentioned the Spanish component of these campus buildings—the open porches with corbel capitals fronting the dormitories, the balconied church facade entrance of the administration building, and the Spanish mission interior of the main auditorium. With Tight's dismissal in 1909, experimentation with the style ceased at the university, not to be officially revived until 1927 (Johnson 1907; Anon. 1908–9; Anon. 1911).

This early interest in the Pueblo style was diffuse and uncoordinated, fueled as it was either by tourism or by civic identity, or manifesting itself as what David Gebhard describes elsewhere in this volume as a sprinkling of archaeologically correct Pueblo style houses in California. It might well have remained a minor strain of southwestern regionalism such as the Moorish or Mayan Revival. But in 1912 at Santa Fe the promotion of tourism joined with the desire for an architectural image to represent New Mexico, which had just been granted statehood. Within a few years an art colony also began to emerge. This combination of tourism, civic identity, and romantic aesthetics brought New Mexico regionalism to a mature form that would have a broad and lasting impact.

Santa Fe had been stranded 18 miles off the main line of the railroad that passed through New Mexico in 1880 (fig. 14-3). The city lost its position as the mercantile center of the state, and its population declined by 10 percent each decade from 1880 until 1910, dropping from 6635 to 5072 residents. In 1912, the newly formed Santa Fe city planning board called for the development of tourism as the best way to stem the city's economic decline. Their report and the subsequent stream of publicity orchestrated by the Museum of New Mexico argued that Santa Fe was the natural jumping-off point for trips to northern New Mexico, an area rich in archaeological ruins and exotic cultures. But an ill-conceived Americanization had robbed the city of its attractiveness for tourists. The task of defining an architectural style with which to reconstruct the city's historic appearance fell first to archaeologist Sylvanus Morley and later to painter Carlos Vierra, both members of the museum staff (Morley 1915; W. Johnson 1916; Vierra 1918; C. Wilson 1982).

The new style was popularized in the teens and early 1920s through a series of government buildings: the renovation of the facade of the Palace of the Governors, a fine arts museum, a state school for the deaf, and a post office. The tourist hotel, La Fonda, was funded through public subscription. The rhetoric of the period emphasized the civic nature of the new architecture. The Palace of the Governors was spoken of as one of the "monuments to the Spanish founders of the civilization of the Southwest" (Acts of the Legislative Assembly 1909, 6–7). In 1917, at the dedication of the Fine Arts Museum, New Mexico lawyer Frank Springer explained that "we shall find at home the themes for boundless achievement, and our arts shall grow—as this temple has grown . . . —straight from our own soil" (Springer 1918, 5,7). A spate of national magazine articles likewise described this new Santa Fe Pueblo style as "so directly American," "a true product of America," and "a strictly American style of architecture" (Henderson 1920, 272; Sims 1922; Crawford 1923, 383; E. Johnson 1922).

New Mexico's architecture was distinctly American, these articles explained, because it derived from the indigenous Pueblos and from local Spanish architecture, the country's oldest colonial building tradition. This Pueblo and Spanish heritage had long raised doubts in the eastern states about the population's allegiance to the United States, doubts that had helped delay statehood for over 60 years. But this new line of argument, which appeared with the granting of statehood, turned that heritage into an

14-3 *South side of the Santa Fe Plaza, 1896. Photograph by Phillip E. Harroun. (Courtesy Museum of New Mexico, Neg. No. 14091.)*

14-4 *Fine Arts Museum, Santa Fe, Rapp, Rapp and Hendrickson, 1917.*
(Photograph courtesy Museum of New Mexico, Neg. No. 22968.)

advantage in the form of a distinctive image for the new state and for the fledgling tourist industry.

Perhaps the finest example of the new style, the Fine Arts Museum designed in 1916 by Rapp, Rapp and Hendrickson, is a classic application of picturesque eclecticism (fig. 14-4). (The museum is a slightly elaborated replication in more permanent materials of the Rapps' New Mexico Building at the San Diego exposition of 1915.) Its major components, drawn from at least four historic buildings, are combined into a pleasing picturesque composition. The organization of the building with the church form on the left, the one-story cloister in the middle, and the second-story open loggia to the right is derived from the mission at Acoma. But as Sylvanus Morley explained in true eclectic spirit (for the New Mexico Building, but equally applicable to the museum): "the introduction of the second story balcony between the two towers of the church considerably relieves the monotony of the facade and lightens an otherwise too massive effect [of the Acoma mission]," (Morley 1915, 298). The facade balcony was probably based on either the San Felipe or Santo Domingo mission. A side entrance was patterned on the Lagauna mission, and two sides were stepped back in imitation of the terraced residential blocks of the Pueblo villages. The open loggia at the corner forms the pivot point of the composition, balanced to either side by the church facades. As Carl Sheppard observed in his recent monograph on Isaac Rapp, the museum is designed to be viewed from various positions: from Lincoln Street, from the Santa Fe Plaza, and from Palace Avenue (Sheppard 1987).

The Rapps had shown little interest in the Arts and Crafts movement before their Pueblo style buildings in Santa Fe. They generally worked instead in the prevailing turn-of-the-century classic style. But the undulating forms of the museum, its handcrafted, historically accurate details, and its New Mexico Mission style furniture all suggest an Arts and Crafts connection. The most likely source of this influence appears to be museum staff members Sylvanus Morley, Carlos Vierra, artist Kenneth Chapman, and, in particular, archaeologist Jess Nusbaum, who designed the Museum furniture and was construction superintendent for the building (C. Wilson 1982; Taylor and Bokides 1987; Sheppard 1987).

Although the Taos art colony had formed during the first decade of the century, painters, poets, and writers only began to coalesce in Santa Fe after 1915. Members of the two art colonies saw the Pueblos, and to a lesser extent the Spanish culture, as offering to the loss of spiritual fulfillment in the modern world. Like the English Romantics' veneration of the medieval spirit, those in the New Mexico art colonies touted the Pueblos as an example of a simple, spontaneous life spent in harmony with nature and in touch with elemental forces.

Pueblo architecture offered perhaps the most tangible manifestation of this spirit. According to Carlos Vierra, the weathering of adobe by the elements was in large part responsible for this organic quality:

> That which was not essential did not endure, and that which did endure was marvellously enriched with the living, flowing quality of free outline and form. It is in reality a free-hand architecture, with the living quality of a sculptor's work, . . . (Vierra 1918, 42).

Irregular adobe buildings were viewed as the antithesis of precise, industrial age architecture; hand- and rain-shaped adobe emerged as a symbol of the creative spirit and the relaxed mores of the Sante Fe and Taos colonies (Henderson 1920).

Since about 1920, individual engagement with the Pueblo and Spanish cultures has varied in intensity, ranging from the collection of indigenous crafts to a life of art and hand-craftsmanship inspired by indigenous cultures, and even to life in a back-to-the-land commune. The communal socialism of Ruskin and Morris resurfaced in New Mexico in a tradition of alternative communities. The art colonies had a communal spirit most clearly manifested in Los Cinco Pintores, a group of Santa Fe painters who built their houses together in a compound during the 1920s. About the same time, Mable Dodge Lujan built a rambling house in Taos for the community of artists she would attract from New York (fig. 14-5). In the 1930s and 1940s, Seton Village flourished as an alternative community near Santa Fe. And during the late 1960s New Mexico became a magnet for counterculture communes (Butwin 1971; Veysey 1973; Lears 1981, 64–5, 95–6; Gibson 1983, 205; Williams 1986, 316–8; Gallegos 1987, 37–40).

A more frequent manifestation of the romantic spirit has been the artist's house. The finest examples of the type were built by Nicolai Fechin in Taos and Carlos Vierra in Santa Fe. Most artists, including Sheldon Parsons, preferred to start with a three- or

14-5 *Mabel Dodge Lujan House, Taos, 1920s. (Photograph courtesy Museum of New Mexico, Neg. No. 135246.)*

14-6 *Sheldon Parsons House, Santa Fe, 1920s. (Photograph courtesy Museum of New Mexico, Neg. No. 10540.)*

four-room historic adobe; if it stood partially in ruins, so much the better (fig. 14-6). The house would be refurbished to include modern utilities and conveniences, and frequently a large living room and studio addition was positioned to give the house an informal, picturesque massing. Historic doors, corbels, brackets, and vigas collected from Spanish mountain villages were incorporated into many houses, and most artists added their own carved wood details and painting decorations.

The fireplace and inglenook—that Arts and Crafts symbol of the elemental hearth of a pre-Industrial Age house—was translated in the Southwest into the Spanish corner fireplace with built-in adobe benches called *bancos* (fig. 14-7). Interior furnishings were a mixture of the antique and the newly hand-crafted; Navajo blankets, Pueblo pottery, and Spanish santos and tinwork alongside paintings and sculptures by the artists and their friends, and owner-built furniture in the New Mexico Mission style—what is now referred to as Taos furniture.

Porches and windows were positioned to capture picturesque views across the vast New Mexico landscape. An informal, outdoor life-style was also reflected in a courtyard or compound wall that enclosed patios, terraced gardens, and, if possible, a stream of water coming from the community irrigation *acequia*. Fruit trees, a vegetable garden, and above all the home studio symbolized the artist's self-sufficiency (Anon. 1927; E. Johnson 1927; Barker 1927; Bunting 1961; Lively 1985; R. Wilson 1987, 103; Gallegos 1987, 33–40).

If an artist's house attempted to integrate art with life as a means to spiritual fulfillment, then the houses of the wealthy tended more toward the display of the refined tastes of their owners (fig. 14-8). The two types of houses share many characteristics, so it is difficult to draw a firm line between them; some artists were wealthy, while many wealthy part-time residents had artistic aspirations. The homes and gardens of the wealthy, nevertheless, tend to be larger and more lavish, more in the tradition of the country estate than that of the craftsman house. Indeed, there is often less idiosyncratic hand-craftsmanship in the houses of the wealthy and more historical doors and porches. The presence of American colonial and European art and furnishings intimated the owner's family ties with the eastern elite. While the reduction in immigration from Europe was making servants less common in the East during the 1920s and 1930s, servants continued to be available in New Mexico, and servants' quarters were the norm in new houses. Sante Fe architect John Gaw Meem, himself a member of the transplanted elite, designed many of the best examples of this type, notably houses for Cyrus McCormick, Vilura Conkey, J. R. Cole, and Amelia Hollenbeck near Sante Fe and the Territorial Revival style Simms houses in Albuquerque (Saunders 1930, 635; Fincke 1937; Fisher 1939; Anon. 1951; Bunting 1961; 1983, 44–50, 106–10, 128–45).

While the Santa Fe and Taos art colonies were developing, New York was also emerging as the intellectual and artistic capital of the United Stated led by what has been referred to as the American liberal intelligentsia. This group has consisted over the years of writers such as Dwight Macdonald, Lionel Trilling, Norman Mailer, John Kenneth Galbraith, and Susan Sontag. They have dominated American intellectual life through journals such as the *New Republic* and the *Nation* and, in more recent years, the *New York Times Book Review* and the *New York Review of Books*.

During its formation in the 1920s, this intelligentsia was about equally divided between Anglo-Saxon Protestants and central and eastern European Jews, most of whose families had recently immigrated to the United States. Both factions reacted against the narrow provincialism of their upbringings, against the Anglo-Protestant values that had long dominated American intellectual life, or against conservative orthodox Judaism. Out of this shared reaction developed the notion of cosmopolitanism, a desire to transcend the limitations of any particular culture and to reach a higher, more comprehensive understanding of human experience.[2] This meant not the

14-7 *Studio, Sheldon Parsons House, Santa Fe, 1920s. (Photograph courtesy Museum of New Mexico, Neg. No. 135233.)*

14-8 *J. R. Cole House, Santa Fe, John Meem, ca. 1930. (Photograph courtesy Meem Archives, University of New Mexico Library.)*

melding of immigrant cultures into the Anglo-American mainstream, but the emergence of a new, ethnically diverse, politically liberal, hybrid culture.

While cosmopolitan intellectuals gave lip service to cultural pluralism in the name of tolerance, they placed little actual importance on the preservation of regional or ethnic traditions. In fact, whenever the intelligentsia were challenged by the dominant Anglo-Protestant culture, they assailed it as provincial, reactionary, and philistine. Sinclar Lewis's 1922 novel *Babbitt* was recognized at the time as the quintessential attack on narrow-minded Anglo-American boosterism (Hollinger 1975; Guilbaut 1983; Jacoby 1987).

Many sought to escape the hold of Anglo-American culture altogether. Some went to Paris, while others were drawn to northern New Mexico. New Mexico artists, like their counterparts in New York and Paris, disdained small town American values. And like artists and intellectuals the world over, they sought to broaden their understanding of human experience through the study of primitive cultures and to link avant garde art to the raw energy of preindustrial traditions. The role of Picasso's interest in African masks in the development of Cubism is perhaps the best known example of this phenomenon of primitivism. But few artists were as extreme in their rejection of the modern, industrial world as those in New Mexico. In a sense, these internal expatriates in Santa Fe and Taos formed the romantic wing of the New York intelligentsia. Indeed, many had lived in New York before relocating to New Mexico, and they were joined by a steady stream of summer visitors from New York (Gerould 1925, 202; Austin 1929; Saunders 1930; Rudnick 1984).

Although New Mexico primitivism coexisted with cosmopolitanism during the 1920s, the New York intelligentsia became openly antagonistic to the wave of regionalism that swept the country during the 1930s. In its most fully articulated form, represented by writers such as Lewis Mumford, 1930s regionalism supported decentralized, small-scale economic organization. In part, this was a reaction to the inadequacies of the modern industrial economy that became apparent in the Great Depression. For Mumford, an indispensable component in the defense of local, decentralized economies was an active cultural life based on the history and special conditions of each region. Regionalist artists, for their part, were openly critical of the elitism and abstraction of modern art, arguing instead for forms of art and discourse accessible to the common man. The New York intelligentsia, meanwhile, viewed regionalism as culturally reactionary: Southern writers were tainted by their association with segregation, while midwestern painters such as Thomas Hart Benton and Grant Wood personified Anglo-Saxon provincialism. As attention shifted to the international theater with the approach of World War II, regionalism was branded as isolationist and, almost overnight, ceased to be a vital nationwide movement (Mumford 1928; Anon. 1934; Baker and Beath 1936; Odem and Moore 1938; Benton 1951; Corn 1983).

But during the 1930s, with the climate of social and governmental support for regionalism, New Mexico arts and architecture flourished. The Spanish Pueblo style reached the height of popularity when it was used for public buildings across New Mexico and in neighboring Arizona, Colorado, and Texas. Santa Fe architect John Gaw Meem was most responsible for the massive, sculptural variety of the Pueblo Revival popular during the period (fig. 14-9).

Public buildings erected across the country during the 1930s were about evenly divided between ones in a regional, historical vein and those in what was then called the Modernistic style (Good 1938; Short and Brown 1939). At its most extreme, architectural modernism argued that a building should not only express its function and the nature of its materials and structure, but should also express the spirit of the modern era. For the strict modernist, this left no room for ornamentation or historical evocation, which could only contradict the industrial drive for precision and efficiency. Many architects of the period nevertheless felt that modernism was compatible with the evocation of an area's traditions. John Gaw Meem justified his approach in terms borrowed from Eliel Saarinen, who had been involved in the development of Finnish national romanticism before moving to the United States in the 1920s. Saarinen argued that great architecture is developed through an intuitive grasp of the fundamental form of the time. This form is affected by everything in a people's culture, by both their traditions and contemporary economic and material conditions. "Some old forms are so honest," Meem argued, "so completely logical and native to the environment that one finds—to one's delight and surprise—that modern problems can be solved, and are best solved by [the] use of forms based on tradition" (Meem 1934).

Although Meem's use of ornament and history were more overt than doctrinaire modernists could accept, he grasped two important aspects of modernism that were derived from the nineteenth-century romantic tradition: the emphasis on the honest use of materials and a feeling for the elemental simplicity of vernacular architectural

14-9 *Zimmerman Library, east facade, University of New Mexico, Albuquerque, John Meem, 1936. (Photograph courtesy Meem Archives, University of New Mexico Library.)*

forms. This interest in the vernacular, which had been a mainstay of the romantic tradition since William Morris, received its widest circulation in modernist circles through Siegfried Giedion's 1941 book *Space, Time and Architecture.*

Many American modernists who had no desire to employ historical styles, nevertheless were hesitant to completely adopt the pristine, idealized International style. By focusing on this romantic thread in modernism, they developed what contemporary journals termed regional modernism. This approach was strongest on the West Coast, where architects such as H. H. Harris, William Wurster, and Pietro Belluschi designed asymmetric houses that opened to the outdoors and were executed in local, rustic materials. Frequently, there was even a hint in their work of vernacular barns and cottages (Hamlin 1939; Morrison 1940; Belluschi 1955; Thompson 1959; Woodbridge 1974).

In New Mexico, regional modernism was centered in Albuquerque during the late 1950s and 1960s. It found its fullest expression in the early work of Antione Predock. In 1969, Predock wrote of his design for the La Luz housing complex,

> In many ways the cluster planning . . . and the buildings themselves are very traditional but not by assembling superficial trappings in the name of Pueblo architecture (i.e. fake vigas, elaborately contrived parapet erosion, etc.). In similar ways to the response of the indigenous builder, the buildings at La Luz respond to the climate and landscape of New Mexico (Predock 1969, 11).

Architectural Record wrote approvingly of La Luz that "where tradition is called on, it is called on for the way it works and not the way it looks" (Anon. 1970). Despite this modernist emphasis on functional determinants and aversion to ornament. La Luz evokes historic buildings through its use of adobe and its functional ornament—the cast concrete lintels and roof drains. For the general public, unconcerned with modern-ist theory, La Luz succeeds in large part because it touches local memory (Predock 1969; C. Wilson 1983).

During the 1950s and 1960s, through the heydey of New York cosmopolitanism and architectural modernism, Santa Fe and northern New Mexico remained an enclave of romantic regionalism that continued to attract sympathetic artists and architects. The Spanish Pueblo style in both its romantic and more severe modernist forms continued as one of the strongest regional idioms in the country. Even the emphasis on local economic self-sufficiency of New Deal regionalism was carried on by Peter van Dresser, who arrived in New Mexico in the late 1930s as a self-described dropout from the eastern establishment. In his major theoretical work, *Development on a Human Scale*, van Dresser argued for the revitalization of the small-scale, decentralized economy of the Pueblo and Hispanic villages. Economic and cultural factors figure equally in his detailed program.

Given his emphasis on economic self-sufficiency, it is understandable that van Dresser was also an early proponent of passive solar design, along with Santa Fe architect William Lumpkins. A house built by van Dresser in Santa Fe in 1958 combines tilted hot air collectors with adobe construction and Pueblo detailing (fig. 14-10). The combination of small-scale technology with traditional forms stemmed directly from the regionalist belief that decentralized economic development and local culture should be mutually reinforcing. In his writings and designs, van Dresser provided an important bridge between 1930s regionalism and the counterculture/ecology move-ment of the 1960s and 1970s (van Dresser 1961; 1972; Cook 1974; Lumpkins 1981).

Another exponent of passive solar design developed quite a different architec-tural vocabulary. Steve Baer's early-1970s house in Corrales near Albuquerque was viewed by some as the "prototype solar house of the future" (Cook 1974, 40). The modular building units, which Baer calls zomes, are a refinement of Buckminster

14-10 *Van Dresser House, Santa Fe, Peter van Dresser, 1958. (Photograph: Chris Wilson.)*

Fuller's geodesic dome. Although adobe is used for thermal mass inside the building, the house is sheathed in reflective aluminum panels. A variety of solar devices invented by Baer are integrated with older machines such as the windmill, evoking an earlier era of rural self-sufficiency. This mixture of old and new "low-tech" approaches in the Baer house characterizes the functionalist strain of the counterculture, which is perhaps best known through Fuller's writings and the pages of the *Whole Earth Catalogue* (Anon. 1972b; Cook 1974).

Given the strength of the romantic tradition in New Mexico, however, most communes and solar houses have employed local materials and forms. As in the 1920s and 1930s, the strength of American individualism has made the private solar adobe home, and not the commune, the primary, lasting architectural form of the counterculture. The quintessential solar adobe house, such as Balcomb House in Santa Fe (figs. 14-11 and 14-12), integrates passive solar technology with the artist's Craftsman house of the 1920s. The sculptural use of adobe and the rustic treatment of doors, cabinets, and ceilings remain essential. The addition of a solar greenhouse at the heart of the home provides a more direct connection to nature and a degree of self-reliance through the production of heat and (at least theoretically) vegetables (Anon. 1972a; 1977; 1979; Yee 1980; Lumpkins 1981; Schecter 1985).

The cultural ferment of the 1960s also initiated a critique of what Jane Jacobs and Robert Venturi characterized as the anti-urban results of urban renewal and the symbolically impoverished language of modern architecture. This led to a resurgence of historic preservation and the emergence of what has been variously called contextualism and postmodernism. Over the past 25 years, architects such as Venturi, Charles Moore, and Michael Graves have reintroduced ornament and the use of popular and historic forms in an attempt to make architecture richer and more accessible for the general public (Shane 1976; Jencks 1980; Frampton 1983).

14-11 *Balcomb House, Santa Fe, William Lumpkins and Sun Mountain Design, 1975. (Photograph: Chris Wilson.)*

14-12 *Balcomb House, Santa Fe, William Lumpkins and Sun Mountain Design, 1975. (Photograph: Chris Wilson.)*

Of course, many New Mexico architects never abandoned these concerns, but it was only in the early 1980s that overt signs of postmodernist thinking began to appear in New Mexico. Westwork Architects' Barelas senior housing project (Albuquerque, 1982) drew its forms from neighboring Hispanic vernacular houses of stucco and pitched metal roofs. This contextualism could have been taken even further if the white, lime green, and pastels common in the surrounding neighborhood had been used rather than the Spanish Pueblo Revival style palette of earth tones. In designing the Beach Apartments project (Albuquerque, 1984), Antoine Predock drew imagery from both the immediate context of the automobile strip that bounds the project and the wider, popular mythology of Route 66 and southwestern tourism. The building's stepped forms evoke both the terraced multistory pueblos and New Mexico mesas and mountains. The stratified stucco colors—desert browns below, mountain greens in the middle, and sky blues above—reinforce the landscape metaphor, while their geometric organization resembles Navajo blankets. The neon accents tie the building to the automobile strip (C. Wilson 1983; Predock 1984).

Since the romantic reaction took root in New Mexico early this century, it has remained the dominant force in the art and architecture of the state. Eighteenth-century romanticism contributed picturesque composition and an interest in exotic cultures to the state's architecture. The later Arts and Crafts movement infused the regional New Mexico aesthetic with a commitment to hand-craftsmanship and vernacular building forms. Nineteen-thirties regionalism more fully connected the desire to sustain local cultures with the need for regional economic self-sufficiency. All of these notions flourished in the counterculture/ecology movement that brought forth passive solar design. Today, the contextualist and historicist strands of postmodernism have provided renewed support for the importance of local traditions and identity.

Some have argued that industrialization and mass communication have so homogenized modern culture that regionalism is now superfluous. But a leading criticism of modern architecture, and I think a justifiable one, is that it too often overlooked the symbolic and psychological dimensions of architecture. The desire of the average person to live in a place with its own history and to belong to an identifiable, local community remains strong. Tourism is not some silly diversion at the fringe of our culture, but instead is an integral part of the modern industrial world. New Mexico is but one of the numerous examples throughout the world of the ongoing uses of the romantic tradition to define and sustain local identity.

NOTES

1. Although these two forms of resistance—from within traditional cultures and from the romantic reaction—often overlap and borrow from each other, they should not be confused. A Pueblo's struggle to maintain its language, religion, and way of life is substantially different from an Anglo-American's use of Pueblo forms as a symbolic alternative to the industrial world, just as a communal dwelling is different from a tourist hotel.

2. The reader should bear in mind that, particularly in Europe but also in the United States, the term "cosmopolitan" has sometimes been used as a code word by anti-Semites to attack Jewish intellectuals. My interpretation does not rest on supposed characteristics of Jews, any more that than it rests on inherent characteristics of WASPs. As David Hollinger has noted, such ethnic characterizations can lead to "the 'booster-bigot trap': the choice between the booster's uncritical celebration of 'Jewish contributions' and the bigot's malevolent complaint about 'Jewish influence.'" "One way to avoid this trap, and to overcome the historiographical inhibition attendant upon it," he continues, "is to recognize how historically specific and contingent were the concerns and preferences that Jewish and non-Jewish intellectuals brought to one another, and how dependent upon reciprocal, dialectical interchanges was the new cultural matrix created by these intellectuals for themselves and their successors" (Hollinger 1985, 56). Central to my discussion is the shared reaction of Anglo-Protestant and Jewish intellectuals against their own particular provincial backgrounds and their resulting intellectual, perhaps even emotional, antagonism to regionalism.

REFERENCES

Acts of the Legislative Assembly of the Territory of New Mexico. 1909. Santa Fe. n.p.

ANONYMOUS. 1908–9. "A Revival of Old Pueblo Architecture." *Architects and Builders Magazine* 10:282–5.

ANONYMOUS. 1911. "Pueblo Architecture Adapted to Modern Needs in New Mexico." *The Craftsman* 19(4):404–6.

ANONYMOUS. 1914. "The Grand Canyon of Arizona at Panama-Pacific Exposition." *Santa Fe Magazine* 8(8):49–50.

ANONYMOUS. 1927. "Arizona |actually Santa Fe| Adobe House With the Old Mesa Spirit." *Arts and Decoration* 27(3):72.

ANONYMOUS. 1934. "The Boom in Regionalism." *The Saturday Review* 10(38):600.

ANONYMOUS. 1951. "Rancho Las Acequias in Old Santa Fe." *House and Garden* 100 (Sept.):120–5.

ANONYMOUS. 1970. "La Luz." *Architectural Record* (mid-May 1970):92–3.

ANONYMOUS. 1972a. "A Genuine Response to the Region." *AIA Journal* 56(2):27–34.

ANONYMOUS. 1972b. "A Breakaway House That's Heated By the Sun." *House and Garden* 142 (August):46–9.

ANONYMOUS. 1977. Two-story greenhouse . . . for This Sante Fe Adobe." *Sunset* 158 (May):146–8.

ANONYMOUS. 1979. "A House Heated Solely by the Sun." *House and Garden* 151 (Oct.):176–9.

AUSTIN, MARY. 1929. "Indian Detour." *Bookman* 68 (Feb.):653–8.

BAKER, JOSEPH E., and PAUL ROBERT BEATH. 1936. "Regionalism: Pro and Con." *Saturday Review* 15 (Nov. 28):3–4.

BARKER, RUTH LAUGHLIN. 1927. "The Hearths of Santa Fe." *House and Garden* 51 (Feb.):86.

BELLUSCHI, PIETRO. 1955. "The Meaning of Regionalism in Architecture," *Architectural Record* 118 (Dec.):131–9.

BENTON, THOMAS HART. 1951. "What's Holding Back American Art?" *Saturday Review* 34 (Dec. 15):9–14.

BUNTING, BAINBRIDGE. 1961. "Residence of Mable Dodge Lujan." *New Mexico Architecture* 3(9–10):11–3.

_____. 1983. *John Gaw Meem: Southwest Architect*. Albuquerque: University of New Mexico Press.

BUTWIN, DAVID. 1971. "New Trail to Santa Fe." *Saturday Review of Literature* 54 (July 3, 1971):35–6.

COLLINS, PETER. 1965. *Changing Ideals in Modern Architecture*. Montreal: McGill-Queen's University Press.

COOK, JEFFREY. 1974. "The Varied and Early Solar Energy Application of Northern New Mexico." *AIA Journal* 62(2):37–42.

CORN, WANDA. 1983. *Grant Wood: The Regionalist Vision*. New Haven: Yale University Press.

CRAWFORD, R. P. 1923. "Discovering a Real American Art." *Scribners Magazine* 73 (March):380–4.

FINCKE, VIRGINIA. 1937. "I Wanted an Adobe House." *Arts and Decoration* 47(2):326–8.

FISHER, THEODORE. 1939. "American Home Pilgrimages, No. VIII—New Mexico." *American Home* 73(6):39–41.

FRAMPTON, KENNETH. 1983. "Critical Regionalism." In: *The American Dream: A Collection of Essays*. Atlanta: Georgia Institute of Technology, ASC/AIA.

GALLEGOS, MATTHEW E. 1987. "The Arts and Crafts Movement in New Mexico, 1900–1945." Thesis, University of Virginia.

GEBHARD, DAVID. 1967. "The Spanish Colonial Revival in Southern California (1895–1930)." *Journal of the Society of Architectural Historians* 26(2):131–47.

GEROULD, KATHARINE FULLERTON. 1925. "New Mexico and the Backwash of Spain." *Harpers Monthly* 151 (July):199–212.

GIBSON, ARRELL MORGAN. 1983. *The Santa Fe and Taos Colonies: Age of the Muses, 1900–1942*. Norman: University of Oklahoma Press.

GOOD, ALBERT H. 1938. *Park and Recreation Structures*. Washington, D.C.: National Park Service.

GRATTAN, VIRGINIA L. 1980. *Mary Colter: Builder Upon the Red Earth*. Flagstaff, Ariz.: Northland Press.

GUILBAUT, SERGE. 1983. *How New York Stole the Idea of Modern Art: Abstract Expressionism, Freedom, and the Cold War*. Chicago: University of Chicago Press.

HAMLIN, TALBOT F. 1939. "What Makes It America: Architecture in the Southwest and West." *Pencil Points* 20 (Dec.):762–76.

HENDERSON, ROSE. 1920. "Santa Fe's Art Museum." *Arts and Decoration* 12(4):272.

———. 1923. "A Primitive Basis for Modern Architecture." *Architectural Record* 54(2):189–96.

HOBSBAWM, ERIC, and TERENCE RANGER, eds. 1983. *The Invention of Tradition*. Cambridge: Cambridge University Press.

HOLLINGER, DAVID A. 1975. "Ethnic Diversity, Cosmopolitanism and the Emergence of the American Liberal Intelligentsia." *American Quarterly* 27:133–51. Reprinted in David Hollinger. 1985. *In the American Province: Studies in the History and Historiography of Ideas*. Bloomington: University of Indiana Press.

HUSSEY, CHRISTOPHER. 1927. *The Picturesque: Studies in a Point of View*. London: Frank Cass and Company, reprinted 1967.

ILLICH, IVAN. 1980. "Vernacular Values." *CoEvolution Quarterly* 26:22–49.

JACOBY, RUSSELL. 1987. *The Last Intellectuals: American Culture in the Age of Academe*. New York: Basic Books.

JENCKS, CHARLES. 1980. *Late Modern Architecture*. New York: Rizzoli.

JOHNSON, E. DANA. 1907. "A University Pueblo." *World's Work* 14 (Oct.):9468–74.

———. 1922. "The Architecture of Santa Fe." *House Beautiful* 51(1):76–8.

———. 1927. "Building Old Houses in New Spain." *House Beautiful* 61(1):68.

JOHNSON, WILLIAM TEMPLETON. 1916. "The Santa Fe of the Future." *El Palacio* 3(3):12–27.

KOSTOF, SPIRO. 1985. *A History of Architecture: Settings and Rituals*. New York: Oxford University Press.

LEARS, T. J. JACKSON. 1981. *No Place of Grace: Anti-modernism and the Transformation of American Culture, 1880–1920*. New York: Pantheon Books.

LIVELY, JOHN. 1985. "The Nicolai Fechin House." *Fine Housebuilding* 25 (Feb./March).

LUMPKINS, WILLIAM. 1981. *Casa del Sol: Your Guide to Passive Solar House Design*. Santa Fe: Santa Fe Publishing Co.

McCANNELL, DEAN. 1976. *The Tourist: A New Theory of the Leisure Class*. New York: Schocken Books.

MEEM, JOHN GAW. 1934. "Old Forms for New Buildings." *American Architect* 145(2627):10–21.

MORLEY, SYLVANUS GRISWOLD. 1915. "Santa Fe Architecture." *Old Santa Fe* 2(3):278–302.

MORRISON, HUGH. 1940. "After the International Style—What?" *Architectural Forum* 72(4):345–7.

MUMFORD, LEWIS. 1928. "The Theory and Practice of Regionalism." *Sociological Review* 20(1):18–33, 20(2):131–41.

ODEM, HOWARD W., and HARVEY ESTILL MOORE. 1938. *American Regionalism: A Cultural-Historical Approach to National Integration.* New York: Henry Holt.

PREDOCK, ANTOINE. 1969. "La Luz." *New Mexico Architecture* 11(7–8):7–12.

_____. 1984. "Housing—Five Different Stories." *Mass* (Journal of the School of Architecture and Planning, University of New Mexico) 2:6–13.

RICHARDS, J. M. 1978. *800 Years of Finnish Architecture.* London: David and Charles.

RISEBERO, BILL. 1982. *Modern Architecture and Design: An Alternative History.* Cambridge, Mass.: MIT Press.

RUDNICK, LOIS PALKEN. 1984. *Mabel Dodge Lujan: New Woman, New Worlds.* Albuquerque: University of New Mexico Press.

SAUNDERS, SALLY. 1930. "Santa Fe's New Conquistadores." *Outlook and Independent* 155 (Aug.):607–9.

SCHECTER, DOVEEN. 1985. "The Coziest Adobe." *Diversion* (Dec.): 179–82.

SCULLY, VINCENT. 1955. *The Shingle Style and the Stick Style: Architectural Theory and Design from Downing to the Origins of Wright.* New Haven, Conn.: Yale University Press.

SHANE, GRAHAME. 1976. "Contextualism." *Architectural Design* 46 (11 Nov.):676–79.

SHEPPARD, CARL D. 1988. *Creator of the Santa Fe Style: Isaac Hamilton Rapp, Architect.* Albuquerque: University of New Mexico Press.

SHORT, C. W., and R. STANLEY BROWN. 1939. *Public Buildings . . . Constructed . . . with the Assistance of the Public Works Administration.* Washington, D.C.: U.S. Government Printing Office (?).

SIMS, ALIDA F. 1922. "Pueblo—A Native American Architecture." *House and Garden* 41 (April):50–2.

SPRINGER, FRANK. 1918. "Dedicatory Words." *Art and Archeology* 7(1, 2):5–7.

STANTON, PHEOBE. 1971. *Pugin.* New York: Viking Press.

TAYLOR, LON, and DESSA BOKIDES. 1987. *New Mexican Furniture, 1600–1940.* Santa Fe: Museum of New Mexico Press.

TEALL, GARDNER. 1913. "The Modern Colonial House: . . . in the Development of an American Architecture." *The Craftsman* 24(1):61–8.

THOMPSON, V. K. 1959. "The West in Architecture." *Western Architect and Engineer* 218(3):17–21.

VAN DRESSER, PETER. 1961. "Rootstock for a New Regionalism." *Landscape* 10 (Fall):11–4.

_____. 1972. *Development on a Human Scale: Potentials for Ecologically Guided Growth in Northern New Mexico.* New York: Praeger.

VAN ZANTEN, DAVID. 1988. *Designing Paris: The Architecture of Duban, Labrouste, Duc, and Vaudoyer.* Cambridge, Mass.: MIT Press.

VEYSEY, LAURENCE. 1973. *The Communal Experience: Anarchist and Mystical Communities in Twentieth Century America.* Chicago: University of Chicago Press.

VIERRA, CARLOS. 1918. "New Mexico Architecture." *Art and Archeology* 7(1, 2):37–47.

WILLIAMS, JERRY, ed. 1986. *New Mexico in Maps.* Albuquerque: University of New Mexico Press.

WILSON, CHRISTOPHER. 1982. "The Spanish Pueblo Revival Defined, 1904–1921." *New Mexico Studies in the Fine Arts* 7:24–30.

———. 1983. "Regionalism Redefined: The Impact of Modernism in New Mexico." *Mass* 1:16–21.

WILSON, RICHARD GUY. 1987. "American Arts and Crafts Architecture: Radical though Dedicated to the Cause Conservative." In: *The Art That Is Life: The Arts and Crafts Movement in America, 1875–1920*, ed. Wendy Kaplan. Boston: Little, Brown/New York Graphic Society.

WOODBRIDGE, SALLY. 1974. "The Great Northwest Revival." *Progressive Architecture* 55(8):46–63.

YEE, TOM. 1980. "A Modern Adobe." *House and Garden* 152 (May):194–7.

V

Revival Architecture:
Anglo Initiatives

The revival of the indigenous Pueblo and early Spanish architecture of New Mexico was due to a combination of political, social, economic, and aesthetic forces. A primary thrust of this revival was a directed move away from the more popular Eastern architectural styles of the late 1800s toward the regional dialectic of architectural form and image. New settlers in the area found value in the ancient regional architecture and joined hands with natives to promote regional traditions. Chapter 15 by Nicholas C. Markovich focuses on Santa Fe's first year as a state capital and the concerted effort made by academicians, politicians, and businessmen to promote the traditional, regional style in new Santa Fe developments and to preserve the old important structures. The initiative brought forth the first city planning commission and the reestablishment of Santa Fe as a place of Spanish origin and culture. Michael Welsh, in Chapter 16, tells the story of the Pueblo style—its inception and its incorporation into building design and planning at the University of New Mexico. Ethel Goodstein, in Chapter 17, discusses Georgia O'Keeffe's fascination with the landscape and indigenous built form of New Mexico. Goodstein shows us the inseparable connection of that individual to the land and the history of New Mexico by explaining why the mystique of the region and its architecture lives on.

Santa Fe Renaissance: City Planning and Stylistic Preservation, 1912

15

Nicholas C. Markovich

In 1912, the first year of New Mexico statehood, Santa Fe civic debate often centered on the issue of the culturally destructive acts of newcomer developers. The "modern conquistadors," as they were called, had been rapidly extending the boundaries of the ancient city during New Mexico's Territorial period (1848–1912).[1] Their concept of culture and architecture dismissed traditional regional built forms with a blatant lack of interest in the unique Southwestern architectural context that had developed in the region over centuries. The new architecture reflected eastern models of architectural substance, the neoclassical and late Victorian styles of the period. The conflict of values between traditional architecture and the new became a major focus of attention for Santa Fe citizens during this critical formative period.

An agreeable compromise was reached in the debate between conservative factions of the city interested in protecting Santa Fe's heritage and progressive individuals looking primarily at development prospects. Civic leaders decided that new growth should proceed with rigor but remain within the construct of Santa Fe's indigenous architectural heritage. That tradition reflected the regional Native American adobe architecture that the Spanish had closely adapted since the 1600s. The mayor, the Chamber of Commerce, and academic and community leaders concurred, establishing boards and policies that ensured strong preservationist sensibilities and actions. Their interest initiated the education of the Santa Fe community in the richness of its established culture and the impending environmental doom of unchecked growth. It was efforts such as these that secured a traditional concept of city—a southwestern, Hispanic, and Indian city—and ensured the preservation of traditional cultural meaning. The directives sent forth at this time influenced the form of all architecture to be built in Santa Fe during the twentieth century and established farsighted precedents in historic preservation comparable and ahead of other major preservation movements in the country.

THE SANTA FE PLANNING BOARD

Mayor Arthur Seligman responded to civic leaders' demands for contextually sensitive development by creating the Civic Center and City Planning Board on March 9, 1912. The new board chose Harry Howard Dorman (fig. 15-1) as their director.[2] He was described by the *Albuquerque Morning Journal* as a "happy man who loves Santa Fe and loves to advertise it. . . . quiet and business-like with the eye of an architect, the hand of a master builder and the soul of an artist."[3] As a real estate developer, he had successfully mixed new methods of construction with tradition and craft; he was a man who "believed in electric lights and piped water but also in putting a dash of pebble into his architecture."[4] Dorman's good-natured diligence and tenacity engendered the support of businessmen and business organizations as well as that of the public at large.[5]

The duties of the new planning board centered on overseeing development as well as helping to preserve and promote the architectural heritage of the city. Dorman, in accepting his post as board chair, asked Santa Fe citizens to cling to the charm of

15-1 *Harry Howard Dorman, 1912, Santa Fe's First City Planner. (Photograph courtesy Museum of New Mexico, Santa Fe, Neg. No. 7173.)*

architecture as seen in the old Palace of the Governors, the Governor Prince home, and the delightful patios of the old Spanish haciendas. He felt that in this way the uniqueness of their city's heritage would be preserved.[6]

This first planning board under Dorman included Santa Fe citizens Bronson M. Cutting, Miguel A. Otero, James L. Seligman, and Marcelino Garcia. They were charged to take whatever actions they deemed proper to achieve appropriate planning goals.[7] To ensure successful city planning actions on the part of the board, and to design an environmental plan of action for the city, Dorman enlisted the assistance of many city planners across the country, writing to the American Civic Association and the cities of San Francisco, Seattle, Boston, New York, Chicago, Washington, D.C., and as far away as Berlin, Germany.[8] Dorman also contacted the famous American landscape architect Frederick Law Olmstead of Brookline, Massachusetts. Mr. Olmstead offered planning studies to the city of Santa Fe that he had made of Pittsburgh, New Haven, Utica, and Rochester as well as plans and perspective drawings of the towns of Boulder, Colorado and La Siguanea, Cuba, which his firm had designed. Olmstead also suggested that Dorman make use of the ideas delineated in the German publication *Der Stadtebau* by J. Stubben and in Raymond Unwin's *Town Planning in Practice*. He offered Dorman his services as a consultant at a fee of $150 per day. These studies would be useful in establishing a preservationist planning approach and policies in Santa Fe. Not having the financial means to retain Olmstead, Santa Feans kept written contract with him on city planning progress and made a symbolic turn westward toward San Diego for advice.[9]

The Board invited Colonel D. C. Collier to speak to the citizens of Santa Fe on March 26, 1912. Collier, a prominent San Diego citizen and future president of the California-Panama Exposition, had made a lifelong study of western towns and their patterns of development. He maintained that intangible, indefinite rules were determining the growth of most cities in the Southwest, but that the city of Santa Fe was different and should handle affairs differently. His message to Santa Feans centered on the importance of the city's antiquities and environment, the tangibility of ancient architecture and human history there and finally the necessity to promote these factors nationally.[10]

His regional development studies proved that human settlement and city growth in the American West was greatest along lines of tourist travel. He pointed out that despite rather unfavorable conditions for growth, San Antonio was the largest city in Texas. This was not because it had great harbor facilities, great transport, proximity to markets, or fertile soil, but because it had capitalized on the tourist industry in promoting the Alamo, other old mission churches, and its climate. This was also true of Los Angeles. Despite the natural and historic appeal of those cities, Collier went on public record with the claim that the state of New Mexico and the ancient city of Santa Fe had more to offer the tourist, the investor and the colonist than any other state in the Union.[11]

According to Collier, Santa Fe needed to promote the qualities it possessed as a city and a region, advertising those things that attract tourists and healthseekers. For example, he proposed promoting the area by taking Pueblo Indians to California, building a pueblo, and leaving it there to promote New Mexico. Physical displays such as this would encourage tourism, which in Colonel Collier's eyes was more important than colonization "because of the inevitable law that the colonist and investor follow the tourist" (Walter 1912). In fact, this promotional pueblo was erected at the Panama-California Exposition of 1915 in San Diego (fig. 15-2). This international exposition was devoted to progress and opportunity, presenting the "history of man housed in buildings of Spanish Colonial architecture."[13] Collier was to be president of this exposition, and Edgar Hewett, director of Santa Fe's School of American Archaeology, was invited to San Diego as director of the exposition (fig. 15-3). New Mexico's buildings at the Panama-California Exposition emulated New Mexican Spanish Colonial and Pueblo design.

In part it was through Collier's encouragement that the Santa Fe Planning Board gained credibility for its initiatives in promoting quality growth, tourism, and economic prosperity in the city. With the subsequent increase in public support, preservation and development plans for the city moved rapidly forward. Some five months later, on August 19, 1912, A. B. Renehan, president of the Chamber of Commerce, convened a

15-2 *New Mexico Pavilion, Panama-California Exposition, 1915, front view, photograph by Jesse Nusbaum. (Courtesy Museum of New Mexico, Santa Fe, Neg. No. 60256.)*

15-3 *Dr. Edgar Hewett, director of the School of American Archaeology, Santa Fe, 1912. (Photograph courtesy Museum of New Mexico, Santa Fe, Neg. No. 7365.)*

meeting to receive new city plan recommendations that Dorman and his planning board had developed, and one week later this first city planning initiative was presented to the public and approved for acceptance.[14]

The initiative suggested that the preservation of the old streets was of the first order of importance, so that they might be "safe from modernization and destruction," because the winding, narrow streets "lend a charm and distinction to Santa Fe"[15] (fig. 15-4). In keeping with this concept, Hewett renamed city streets to their original Spanish titles from their historically recent titling in English or chose new Spanish names.[16] The board further recommended that

> no building permits be issued to any person intending to build on any street listed and indicated on the map as ancient until proper assurance is given that the architecture will conform exteriorly with the Santa Fe style.[17]

The plan proposed that the riverbed be altered with a series of low dams and pools and bordered with streets on both sides of the river to transform it into a "beauty spot." A third proposal of the plan was to link the north and south sides of the Santa Fe River, running east to west through the city and dividing it. The sides were to be joined by a series of bridges that would connect with some of the established streets and form a series of drives or boulevards encircling the city. A fourth proposal was to establish city playgrounds and parks and open approaches to the plaza.[18] These developments exhibit qualities parallel to the City Beautiful movement at the turn of the century.

It was the unanimous opinion of the board that the preservation of the ancient streets, roads, and structures in and about the city was of primary importance and that "the monuments of the first Americans should be preserved intact at almost any cost."[19] In the board's determination, there was nothing, including climate or scenery, that compared in value as an asset to Santa Fe with those relics of romantic history. Members of the board felt that city officials should guard against any change that would affect the appearance of historic architecture. They suggested tax rebates as an incentive to build in the Santa Fe style and to preserve ancient buildings.[20]

The planning board also recommended that the various wards of the city be called barrios. This would be done in conformity with the policy of maintaining the character of Santa Fe as a town of Spanish origin. For example, Ward One would now be called Barrio Analco, which was its original name.[21]

Measures such as those mentioned here were the first to stem the unplanned progress of Santa Fe and stopped California style bungalow development in new sectors of the city. More important, they set the framework for development to be followed throughout the twentieth century (fig. 15-5). The approval of such an initiative was a far-reaching step for the city of Santa Fe has continued to be of great meaning today. A city planning ordinance of May 25, 1988, still reconfirms the tenets of the original, extending the directive of style to areas of the city now well beyond the historic center. That directive finds that first

> It is in the best interest of Santa Fe's social and economic welfare to preserve and promote the city's unique cultural heritage, distinct visual character and regional architectural traditions.[22]

15-4 *Santa Fe streets, residential neighborhood, 1912; de Vargas Street looking east, photograph by Jesse Nusbaum. (Courtesy Museum of New Mexico, Santa Fe, Neg. No. 11054.)*

15-5 *New Santa Fe development, ca. 1960; Casa Solana subdivision, photograph by Tyler Dingee. (Courtesy Museum of New Mexico, Santa Fe, Neg. No. 7417.)*

Other important issues detailed in the new ordinance include the following.

1. Creation of an aesthetically cohesive and harmonious urban townscape is essential to future development in Santa Fe.
2. Architecture outside the historic district must be compatible with architecture inside the district.
3. Designs must be reviewed with respect to building massing, form, color, proportion, texture, and materials and approved before issuance of a permit.
4. Contextual issues of scale, landscaping and street relationships must also be considered.[23]

It is still important to Santa Fe's survival as a southwestern center to promote and preserve the city's image and cultural traditions.

THE NEW/OLD SANTA FE EXHIBITION

The August 27, 1912 Chamber of Commerce meeting was attended by the academic leaders headed by Dr. Hewett and other professors from the School of American

Archaeology whose western branch was headquartered in Santa Fe. They expressed their concern with the quality and aesthetic direction of new city growth, which they insisted must retain the unique traditional architectural image. The school's faculty comprised archaeologists interested in the study of indigenous American cultures in both North and South America.[24] The extension of their academic interests to the preservation of native cultural and architectural issues in the Southwest was a simple and natural action for them, due to their already established interest with the topic of indigenous American cultures.

Professor Sylvanus Morley, noted Mayan scholar (fig. 15-6), was the School's representative in the city planning initiative and a leader of the Old Santa Fe citizens' group, which included artists, writers, historians, archaeologists, conservative business leaders, and citizens interested in "preserving and perpetuating the cultural and architectural traditions of the past."[25] He proposed two important preservation con-

15-6 *Professor Sylvanus Morley (1883–1948), director of the Old/New Santa Fe exhibition. (Courtesy Museum of New Mexico, Santa Fe, Neg. No. 10316.)*

cepts at this meeting that were unanimously approved. The first was the establishment of a State Landmarks Association, whose charge would be to look after the preservation and restoration of the historic landmarks of New Mexico. The Women's Board of Trade, the Daughters of the American Revolution, and the Mothers Club were asked to attend an organizational meeting, and it was hoped the Landmarks Association would be launched with the help of the women of the state.[26]

Morley's second proposal was that a Civic Improvement Exhibition be held to focus on the ancient city and its architecture. That exhibition was conceived with the following interests and hopes in mind:

1. To further the movement of civic improvement in Santa Fe along the lines laid down by the *founders* of the city.
2. To educate public taste to the proper appreciation of our [Santa Fe's] wonderfully charming *native architecture* and to demonstrate its practicality and possibilities in home building.
3. To urge upon our citizens the vital necessity of *preserving* our historic landmarks and picturesque adobes.
4. Using these buildings as the *dominating note* in all plans for civic improvement.
5. To hasten the realization of an inevitable fact—Santa Fe, the *TOURIST CENTER* of the Southwest.[27]

The following week, Sylvanus Morley again delivered a passionate plea for the preservation of the traditional local culture and architectural character. In this speech, he asked all, despite sentimental attachments to other places in their past, to decide on the type of architecture best to follow in Santa Fe. In so doing, he appealed to the economic and social conscience of citizens, entreating them to turn from the brick cottage, which was, as he said, as much in place in Santa Fe as "a flea on the back of a well-groomed dog.[28]

Morley verbally painted a picture of thousands of little American towns faithfully following the trail of the common red brick and pleaded that Santa Fe need not fall into this large, uninteresting class of cities. He urged that Santa Fe should preserve its most priceless possession, an individuality that had invested the city with a distinction and reknown unequalled in the United States. Santa Fe should not try to compete with larger cities and their Classical architecture but compete on her own level and in her own regional architecture dialectic. In Morley's opinion, Classical architecture such as

15-7 *The El Ortiz Hotel/Train Depot, Lamy New Mexico, photograph by Jesse L. Nusbaum. (Courtesy Museum of New Mexico, Neg. No. 61669.)*

15-8 *The Colorado Supply Company, rendering by Rapp and Rapp architects, photograph by Jesse L. Nusbaum. (Courtesy Museum of New Mexico, Santa Fe, Neg. No. 61210.)*

that found in the city halls, Carnegie libraries, churches, etc., of the nation, does not impress travelers because of the universality of the Classical image. Even the cost of Classical architecture, he felt, was prohibitive for Santa Fe. The fine, inexpensive indigenous style that already existed there was the most appropriate for this environment as a "Native Institution.[29] According to Morley, it was the indigenous style that would advertise Santa Fe and increase property values more than miles of red brick cottages or squares of Greek and Roman public buildings. The style would make Santa Fe the most unusual tourist city in the United States and be the most economical architecture to build in the region.

Two examples of early twentieth century construction were chosen by Morley as proof of the new/old Santa Fe style's relevance to the needs of modern construction; the El Ortiz hotel/train depot in Lamy, New Mexico (fig. 15-7), and the Colorado Supply Company building in Morley, Colorado (fig. 15-8). The first designed by architect Louis Curtis of St. Louis, working with the Fred Harvey Company of Kansas City, Missouri, in 1910 and the second developed by the architects Rapp and Rapp of Trinidad, Colorado, and Santa Fe in 1911,[30] these buildings were proof that the old style was adaptable and fit the demands of twentieth century business houses. Morley said that the principal features of the Santa Fe style that confirmed the need of its use in Santa Fe were its individuality and distinctive character for tourism, the economy of construction, the style's adaptability to many types of buildings, and, finally, its propriety as "the style originated by the first Santa Feans for Santa Fe."[31]

He concluded that evening with the following prophetic statement:

None of us may live to see the day, but sometime in the future there will surely come a generation of Santa Feans who will not be eternally sleeping at the switch; but who will realize the possibilities of a Glorified Adobe City, and reap the golden harvest therefrom. Then, and not until then, will Santa Fe enter upon the epoch of increased and ever increasing prosperity, which is hers by right of every association, historic, geographic and climatic.[32]

Morley's proposal was accepted enthusiastically by local citizens. Mayor Seligman then appointed him as director of the exhibit to be held in Santa Fe in the fall of that year. This exhibit was a graphic representation of traditional architecture. It also presented the new city plan and ideas for future growth and development in the form of photographs, maps, sketches, and architectural models.

15-9 *La Parroquia San Francisco, ca. 1867, photograph by Nicholas Brown. (Courtesy Museum of New Mexico, Santa Fe, Neg. No. 10059.)*

Photography was the primary vehicle of the exhibition and was to depict choice bits of old Santa Fe city fabric that still remained as well as historic buildings in their original condition. Included in that agenda were De Vargas Street, Canyon Road, Agua Fria, Acequia Madre, and the old buildings as they were when photographed prior to 1912. Included in the photographs were the old church of San Francisco, the old San Miguel chapel, Rosario and Guadalupe churches, as well as all that remained of the native architecture (fig. 15-9). Photographic prints were in sepia tones to approximate the original color of adobe. The overall purpose of the photographs was to create an inventory of the essence of Santa Fe architecture from which one could extrapolate new architectural ideals.

Another important aspect of the exhibit were the maps prepared by the City Planning Board. They showed planned improvements and the method in which the City Planning Board would bridge the gap between the Santa Fe that is and the Santa Fe that was to be.

The third type of presentation was sketches of proposed improvements showing how different parts of the city would look when the plan of the Santa Fe Planning board was carried out.

Plaster of Paris models of the most historic buildings were also to be included in the exhibit. Historic buildings were modeled "as they were originally" (fig. 15-10). It was hoped that these models would elevate the architectural aesthetic of the community,

> . . . by showing the original charm of these public buildings, now unfortunately obscured or destroyed by vandalistic renovations. Having seen this exhibit, the future home builder may have been influenced to build along the right lines and, thus, in time, the right kind of civic improvements will be permanently assured.[33]

In September of 1912, Mr. Morley contacted the regional architect I. M. Rapp and requested original drawings, maps, elevations, etc. of the Colorado Supply Company's

15-10 *Model of the San Miguel Chapel, by Jack Adams, on exhibit in Palace of the Governors, 1912, photo by Jesse L. Nusbaum. (Courtesy Museum of New Mexico, Santa Fe, Neg. No. 61356.)*

store at Morley, Colorado, for the exhibit. They desired this building for the exhibit because, "the thing was absolutely in the spirit of the 'Santa Fe Style'". Morley further wrote that the "extension of the Native architecture to all kinds of buildings, I believe possible, and your success in adapting an old church to the highly specialized needs of a commercial house, confirms me in my belief."[34] Rapp's Colorado office sent a watercolor of the store to Santa Fe from the Rapp's Colorado office, and it was received on November 12 in time for the exhibit (fig. 15-11).[35]

15-11 *I. M. and W. M. Rapp, architects, 1903, (Photograph courtesy Museum of New Mexico, Santa Fe, Neg. No. 122883.)*

15-12 *La Fonda Hotel, 1920, photograph by the Cross Studio. (Courtesy Museum of New Mexico, Neg. No. 23103.)*

City planner Dorman requested architectural services of the Rapps, asking them to submit proposal sketches for a new Santa Fe hotel, which was to be designed in the traditional local style and built near the Santa Fe river. These proposal drawings would then be used in the exhibit. Mr. Dorman sent the Rapp architects a number of photographs of old adobe buildings that showed interesting details and might be used for "hotel design."[36] The Rapps did not submit hotel proposal drawings for the November exhibit, but it was this request of October 1, 1912, that initiated the eventual conception of the La Fonda Hotel (fig. 15-12). In a few short years, the first phase of that famous hotel's construction began with the Rapps as project architects.

Louis Curtis, architect of the El Ortiz—considered the best building of the historic Santa Fe style applied to "modern" construction—was also asked to participate.[37] Morley encouraged Curtis also to submit prospective designs for the new Santa Fe hotel for the exhibit, as he did earlier of Mr. Rapp. Both were sent a description of the proposed new hotel, the name of which then was to be "The Onate." It was to be first class, with 75 to 100 guest rooms and a grill, and, most important, it was to be designed for expansion in units of 50 rooms without marring the harmony of the architectural scheme, which was to be in the Santa Fe style.[38] Due to prolonged poor health, Mr. Curtis did not respond to the proposal request but sent two drawings of the El Ortiz, and we now know that the Rapps eventually were hired as the La Fonda hotel architects.

The work of the Rapps and Curtis was to be the highlight of the exhibit. Other architects and notables invited to participate included V. O. Wallingbird of Los Angeles; Charles F. Whittlesley of Topeka, Kansas; MacLaren and Thomas of Colorado Springs; Summer P Hunt of Los Angeles; members of the American Institute of Architects, the Octagon, Washington, D.C.; and Hector Alliot, founder of the Southwest Museum, Los Angeles.[39]

Edgar Hewett, Director of the School of American Archaeology, then housed in the Palace of the Governors, promised that the school would do everything possible to aid this public work. To achieve this he offered the use of the Palace building for the exhibition as well as all the facilities at its disposal, such as rooms for the preparation of exhibits and photographic equipment. He also gave 200 dollars toward the success of the exhibit, which in total cost 1225 dollars.[40]

Jesse Nusbaum of the school offered his time to explore and photograph the finest examples of early Santa Fe architecture and architectural details. He also directed installation of the exhibit. Percy Adams made measured drawings and scale models of the historical buildings. T. A. Hayden provided maps of Santa Fe showing improvements, and Carlos Vierra made a series of wash drawings showing the new city improvements (fig. 15-13).[41]

The New/Old Santa Fe exhibition opening was timed to coincide with the dedication of Santa Fe's new Scottish Rite Cathedral, a Masonic temple. That inauguration occurred during the weekend of November 16/17 with the main ceremoney on Sunday evening. The cathedral itself was intended to be sympathetic in design to the Spanish heritage of Santa Fe by evoking a Moorish design in its image, following the style of the Alhambra (fig. 15-14).[42]

The New/Old Santa Fe exhibition opened the following evening with a gala reception honoring the Masons at the Palace of the Governors.[43] The exhibit was immediately acclaimed a success. *The Santa Fe New Mexican* pointed out the next day,

> No one could look at the painted pictures which presented to our view what is hoped that Santa Fe may be in the future without growing enthusiastic and having aroused the feeling of intense desire to push the good movement along.[44]

The unexpectedly singular hit of the exhibition was the Joseph Uruttia map of Santa Fe, created sometime between the years 1715 and 1735 and discovered by a Miss Friere-Marecco in the British Museum in London a short time before the exhibit. The map had been used by the faculty of the School of American Archaeology in modeling the old structures of Santa Fe for the exhibit. It showed the positioning of building plans as they originally were.[45]

15-13 *Wash drawing by Carlos Vierra for the new proposed plaza bandstand, 1912, photo by Jesse L. Nusbaum. (Courtesy Museum of New Mexico, Neg. No. 61464.)*

15-14 *Scottish Rite Temple, Santa Fe, opening day, November 17, 1912, photo by Jesse L. Nusbaum. (Courtesy Museum of New Mexico, Santa Fe, Neg. No. 61379.)*

CONCLUSION

The actions of these early-twentieth-century Santa Feans who joined together to save a traditional concept of city and cultural heritage are unparalleled in New Mexico history and rival efforts elsewhere in the nation. This courageous effort required the coopera-tion of all citizen factions, setting aside academic and political conflicts for one year to achieve higher-reaching goals affecting the city's future.

At stake was the loss of the traditional architectural and cultural meaning that had developed over many centuries. That vision was founded in the earth, the pueblo, and the substance of adobe. The Spanish who settled in the region extrapolated that meaning to an image more comfortable to their conception of built form but did not negate or destroy the original concept. The continuity of this tradition, lasting over 1000 years, is the true spirit, the mystique that these wise individuals set out to save.

The vision of Edgar Hewett, Sylvanus Morley, Arthur Seligman, Henry Dorman, Jesse Nusbaum, and others gave to us the preservation of a city concept that still retains the city of Santa Fe as unique in the country. If these men and women of vision had not seized the opportunity of the year, the first of New Mexico's statehood, the traditions of Santa Fe architecture might have been lost forever.

NOTES

1. "The Ancient City and the New Santa Fe." *Albuquerque Morning Journal*, editorial, Monday, March 4, 1912.

2. Letter from the office of the Mayor, Arthur Seligman, Santa Fe, New Mexico to Mr. H. H. Dorman. Weiss-Loomis Papers, Museum of New Mexico, History Library, Santa Fe.

3. See note 1.

4. See note 1.

5. Nusbaum, Jesse; "Van Morley and the Santa Fe Style," in *Morleyana*, published by *El Palacio*, 1950, p.165.

6. See note 1.

7. See note 2.

8. Letter to H. H. Dorman from Richard B. Watrous, secretary and Horace B. McFarland, president of the American Civic Association, Washington, D.C., April 10, 1912. Also letters from H. H. Dorman to many city planners and associations asking assistance in Santa Fe city planning endeavors, March 18 and April 15, 1912. All included in the Weiss-Loomis papers, Museum of New Mexico, History Library, Santa Fe.

9. Letters from Frederick Law Olmstead to H. H. Dorman, May 17 and June 1, 1912. Weiss-Loomis Papers, Museum of New Mexico, History Library, Santa Fe.

10. Paul F. Walter, editor. "An Expert's Advice," editorial, *The Santa Fe New Mexican*; March 27, 1912.

11. See note 10.

12. See note 10.

13. Letter to Mr. P. A. F. Walter from Dr. Edgar Hewett, as director of the Panama-California Exposition of 1915, San Diego, California; November 26, 1914; Weiss-Loomis Papers, Museum of New Mexico History Library, Santa Fe.

14. Letter of Public Notice from John S. Harris, Santa Fe Chamber of Commerce secretary. Museum of New Mexico History Library, Santa Fe; Weiss-Loomis Papers.

15. "Civic Improvements the Topic Last Night," editorial, *The Santa Fe New Mexican*; August 28, 1912.

16. List of street name changes executed by Edgar Hewett. Weiss-Loomis Papers, Museum of New Mexico History Library; Santa Fe.

17. City Planning recommendations; City Planning Board, Santa Fe; presented to the Chamber of Commerce on August 19, 1912; Museum of New Mexico History Library; Santa Fe; Weiss-Loomis papers.

18. See note 15.

19. See note 17.

20. See note 17.

21. See note 17.

22. Planning Department Santa Fe; Planning Ordinance 1988; enacted May 25, 1988; Harry Moul, Planning Department Director; Santa Fe, New Mexico.

23. See note 22.

24. Hewett, Edgar. 1907–1917. *Archaeological Institute of America. Organic Acts and Administrative Reports of the School of American Archaeology 1907–1917*. Santa Fe: School of American Archaeology, Division of Anthropology, Museum of New Mexico.

25. Springer, Frank; Address by Mr. Frank Springer; *El Palacio*; January, 1917; Paul F. Walter, editor; Vol. IV, no.1, p.99. See also note 5, pp. 167–169.

26. See note 15.

27. See note 15.

28. Morley, Sylvanus G. "A Most Selfish Thing For Santa Fe." Speech September 4, 1912. Weiss-Loomis Papers, Museum of New Mexico History Library, Santa Fe.

29. See note 28.

30. Letter to H. H. Dorman, Santa Fe from Harvey Corp., Kansas City Mo., October 24, 1912. Also letter to H. H. Dorman, Santa Fe from the Rapp's Trinidad, Co. office, October

16, 1912. Both included in the Weiss-Loomis papers, Museum of New Mexico History Library, Santa Fe.

31. See note 28.

32. See note 28.

33. See note 28.

34. Letter from S. G. Morley, as director of the exhibit, to Mr. I. H. Rapp, September 20, 1912. Weiss-Loomis Papers, Museum of New Mexico History Library, Santa Fe.

35. Letter from W. M. Rapp, Trinidad, Co., to S. G. Morley, Santa Fe, October 15, 1912. Weiss-Loomis Papers, Museum of New Mexico History Library, Santa Fe.

36. Letter from H. H. Dorman to Mr. I. H. Rapp, Trinidad, Co., October 1, 1912. Weiss-Loomis Papers, Museum of New Mexico History Library, Santa Fe.

37. Letter from S. G. Morley to Mr. Curtis, Kansas City, Mo., September 14, 1912. Weiss-Loomis Papers, Museum of New Mexico, History Library, Santa Fe.

38. See note 37.

39. Letters from S. G. Morley, September 13, 1912 to Louis Curtis of Kansas City, Mo., to Mr. V. O. Wallingbird, Los Angeles, Charles F. Whittlesley, Topeka, Kan.; MacLaren and Thomas, Colorado Springs, Co.; Summer P. Hunt c/o The Southwest Museum in Los Angeles, Ca.; the American Institute of Architects, the Octagon, Washington, D.C.; and Hector Alliot, founder of the Southwest Museum. All included in the Weiss-Loomis Papers, Museum of New Mexico, History Library, Santa Fe.

40. Letter from Edgar L. Hewett to H. H. Dorman and A. B. Renehan, November 1, 1912. Also statement of expenses, the New Old Santa Fe Exhibition, 1912. Both included in the Weiss-Loomis papers, Museum of New Mexico, History Library, Santa Fe.

41. See note 40 (statement of expenses).

42. "Masonic Order is Powerful Influence, says A. C. Stewart," *Santa Fe New Mexican*, Monday, November 18, 1912.

43. "Great Exhibition Almost Ready," *Santa Fe New Mexican*, Friday, November 15, 1912.

44. "It Was A Great Success," *Santa Fe New Mexican*, Tuesday, November 19, 1912.

45. "Did You See The Old Map Of Santa Fe?" *Santa Fe New Mexican*, November 26, 1912.

Author's Note: The recently published book *Creator of the Santa Fe Style: Isaac Hamilton Rapp, Architect*, by Carl D. Sheppard (Albuquerque: University of New Mexico Press, 1988), also gives an account of the events in Santa Fe surrounding the year 1912, particularly in Chapter 6, "Santa Fe Style."

Symbol and Reality: The Cultural Challenge of Regional Architecture at the University of New Mexico, 1889–1939

16

Michael E. Welsh

On June 5, 1939, Harold L. Ickes, U.S. Secretary of the Interior, spoke at the commemoration ceremonies for the fiftieth anniversary of the founding of the University of New Mexico. Ickes had been invited by the UNM president, James Fulton Zimmerman, because of his generosity as purveyor of federal public works projects to the nation in the depths of the Great Depression. Through a series of grants and low- interest loans, the largest of which was for 700,000 dollars, the university had built several imposing structures in the now popular architectural southwestern Pueblo style.

The journey that the university, and the style itself, had taken to that moment reflected several important themes. Most institutions of higher learning, especially in the American West, cultivated an atmosphere of instant respectability and tradition through mimicry of architectural forms from the east and midwest, which in turn were often derivative of European styles. The founders of the University of New Mexico had wished the same, as they resided in a territory that in 1889 was nearly 80 percent non-Anglo. Yet over the succeeding five decades the school wrestled with its mission to serve the public of New Mexico, whoever they were, while seeking to emulate the high academic standards of midwestern state universities.

From this came a circuitous logic that culminated in the statements that campus architecture made to residents of the state of New Mexico and to the newcomers so desperately sought by economic boosters. Creating a style of buildings was indeed easier than restructuring the cultural life of the state, but the debate on the national scene over modernism versus regionalism made even this effort problematic. An assessment of the dual track of architecture and society might help students of the university's past to decipher the mixed signals that the facilities presented to the native peoples, whose indigenous folkways inspired the work of many architects of the region, the most famous of whom was John Gaw Meem.

Secretary Ickes, considered one of the most powerful figures in the Roosevelt administration, took pride in the accomplishments of the university as evidenced by its physical appearance. "Here, in an environment reflecting the beautiful architectural style of the Indian pueblo," said Ickes, "which is so characteristic of this region and so unique, students and professors meet and work and think and play." The university spoke, through its buildings as well as its curriculum, to "a region where no less than three great ethnic strains and cultural streams have converged." Inside the massive walls of the new library, the administration building, or the adobe classrooms, Ickes hoped that the university could live out the dream of James Zimmerman, as expressed in the 1934 university *Bulletin*: "Our environment, our history, and above all, our diversified racial and cultural elements, provide us first hand a laboratory in the humanistic and social sciences upon which we may well concentrate our best efforts."[1]

Golden anniversaries, no less than centennials, allow public officials the opportunity to engage in hyperbole and aggrandizement on the accomplishments of the past. Ickes had a different perspective on UNM and its architecture that he kept to himself and recorded in his "secret diaries" upon his return to Washington. "I had never seen UNM before," he noted, "and I liked its appearance, even though there is little green on the campus." The university had "wisely adopted a pueblo style of architecture" that Ickes considered "indigenous to that region and which distinguishes it from other universities." As for the celebration of UNM's fiftieth birthday, Ickes remembered that "the crowd at Commencement was about what one would expect for a small college (1400 students) in a small town (30,000 people) in a state like New Mexico."[2]

The divided thinking of Secretary Ickes revealed the basic problem facing the university, whether externally (via architecture), or internally (with students, faculty, or citizens of New Mexico). What was adobe construction? What did it say about the uniqueness and complexity of New Mexican life? Did acceptance of Southwestern building styles by the recently arrived Anglo population also indicate a willingness to accommodate other aspects of Indian and Hispanic culture, such as language, art, music, cuisine, government, or religion?

A clue to the challenge still awaiting UNM came later that summer in an article by Ronald Hilton in the national magazine *The Fortnightly*. Offering his "impressions of American universities," Hilton chided the state universities of New Mexico, Louisiana, and Washington for "attracting attention by their material growth," which they had acquired with generous "federal backing" from Ickes' Public Works Administration (PWA). "Until the Depression almost unknown," said Hilton, these schools' rapid, and perhaps artificial, expansion lacked good taste or wisdom. Hilton singled out UNM as "the most remarkable" of the "freaks" of higher education in the 1930s, arguing that the sentiments behind the "Indian pueblo style" were to blame (Hilton 1939).

Speaking in the acerbic tones of social critics like H. L. Mencken, Hilton called the UNM style "a fruit of the Americans' love of local colour, which, finding their ordinary cities monotonous, they are prepared to discover in New Orleans or San Francisco." Hilton conceded that "the pseudo-adobe buildings of the University of New Mexico are striking and not too unconvincing." But he especially disliked "the massive Coronado Library, which tries to disguise its steel and concrete as an Indian pueblo (Hilton 1939).

The quest to balance the future with the past, the East with the Southwest, or the Anglo with the Native American, did not concern the founders of UNM. Echoing their midwestern entrepreneurial backgrounds, the first board of regents in 1889 knew clearly the meaning and purpose of the territorial institution entrusted to their care. In architectural style, curriculum, and student body, the university would speak to outsiders of the commitment New Mexico had to the future, and would speak to natives of the futility of resisting the inevitability of change (fig. 16-1). To that end the regents considered the Victorian style of red brick and stone only for the first (and only) campus building, placing it on the far northeast mesa to avoid valley flooding and to encourage migrants to move eastward from the railroad yards to the campus neighborhoods.

The University of New Mexico was not alone in its disregard for regional tastes in designing its physical plant. Throughout the West of the 1890s, only Stanford University sought to make an original statement through the contours of its buildings. Even this was as much a function of the personality of its first president, David Starr Jordan, as it was regional sensitivity. The Stanford family, using the great wealth earned by Leland Stanford in the California railroad business, lured Jordan away from the presidency of Indiana University to develop their school into a uniquely western phenomenon. Kevin Starr (1973, 307–10) wrote of Jordan, "As a natural scientist and as a social thinker, he was fascinated by what (California novelist) Jack London called the Strength of the Strong." Jordan worked feverishly to sculpt a campus that reflected California's fantasies about itself as "a vigorous folk, on the spearhead of history." From architecture to curriculum to student life, Jordan hoped that by sheer exertion Stanford would "translate opportunity, mobility, and pioneer values into modern action."

The UNM regents, whether consciously or otherwise, had the "Jordan syndrome" in mind when they cast about in 1901 for a new president. The tall, muscular, virile

16-1 *The first structure on the University of New Mexico campus, the administration building, constructed in 1889–1890. (000-293-0008, Special Collections, General Library–University of New Mexico, Neg. no. 000-293-0008.)*

William G. Tight, a geologist from Denison University in Ohio, swept onto the UNM campus that fall determined to carry the institution to greatness (fig. 16-2). Among his first gestures was a beautification project conducted by student volunteers. As the budget contained little or no money for such extraneous items as trees or shrubs, Tight joined the students in planting vegetation that gave the university a more classical collegiate appearance. Arbor Day became a campus-wide celebration, with students traveling in wagons to the nearby Sandia and Manzano mountains to collect saplings and plants to be distributed about the 30-acre grounds (Mitchell 1941, 70–1).

From beautification Tight moved to expansion of the campus physical plant. In 1903 he decided that the architectural plan of the university had no unifying theme. His travels throughout New Mexico and other parts of the Southwest had enamored him of the simplicity and other-worldliness of Pueblo adobe construction. Such buildings could be erected at a fraction of the cost of frame or stone, with all the materials and skilled labor readily available. Adobe would also be pleasing aesthetically, Tight believed, since the early residents of the Santa Fe and Taos art colonies promoted native design as New Mexico's most endearing architectural quality. Tight informed the Albuquerque *Journal Democrat* that his plans remained vague but that the concept would "attract world attention" to the small and undistinguished-looking campus (Mitchell 1941 and see note 2).

This architectural style at first appealed to the regents and faculty for its uniqueness and economy. Charles Hodgin, for whom the old administration building would be named, defined it as a "new-old style which would make the University absolutely distinctive," and he depicted Tight as "absorbed with this prospect of breaking away from the common place." The president visited several Pueblo communities, taking photographs of their structures and utilization. Tight and Edward Cristy, designer of the administration building and also a former UNM instructor, fashioned a hybrid of Pueblo forms into a master plan for the new facilities (Mitchell 1941, 73–4).

Tight's first foray into native architecture came with the electric powerhouse. Then architects designed the meeting room of the Pi Kappa Alpha fraternity, named the

16-2 *University of New Mexico President William G. Tight (1901–1909), the "father" of the campus architectural style. (Special Collections, General Library–University of New Mexico, Neg. no. 988-019-0032.)*

"estufa" after the secret religious chambers of the native societies in New Mexico. Finally two dormitories received funding from the legislature, and Tight wanted to give them New Mexican Indian names. He asked Ethel Hickey, associate professor of English, to help draft names for the buildings. Their choices were Kwataka, which they translated as "man-eagle," for the men's dormitory, and Hokona, which they said meant virgin butterfly," for the women's hall. These figures were then painted on the side of each building. No explanation survives about the origins of these words or about which native communities have these terms in their lexicons (Mitchell 1941, 74).

The last building affected by the Pueblo style during Tight's tenure was the large brick administration building known today as Hodgin Hall (fig. 16-3). Tight had it remodeled along Southwestern lines, and attached to it an assembly hall that imitated the famous Catholic chapel at Ranchos de Taos, New Mexico. The Victorian style of the original building included a very high pitched roof that suffered wind damage every year. Between 1893 and 1903 it had had to be repaired twice, and the president suggested a flat roof for safety and economy. The rectangular style would also allow remodeling along Pueblo lines. The administration dedicated the addition to Judge Bernard S. Rodey, author of the enabling legislation of 1889 that created the university. The first Rodey Hall became the site of many social and cultural activities on campus and is remembered today with Rodey Theatre in the Fine Arts complex (Mitchell 1941).[3]

By 1908 William Tight had served seven years as president of the university. He had boosted enrollment, expanded the curriculum, hired more faculty, and set UNM's campus master plan into action. Yet these successes also led Tight to contemplate the serious obstacles still facing the university before it became well respected nationwide. The strain began to tell on Tight when some members of the community criticized the adobe style of architecture as "un-American" or as reflecting a regression to more primitive conditions. Folk wisdom holds that this provincial rejection of New Mexican design led to Tight's departure in the spring of 1909. But the underlying pressures he faced in building UNM, as well as personal conflicts with some faculty and staff, contributed greatly to his demise (Mitchell 1941).[4]

Whatever Tight's troubles at the end of his tenure, his campus development had made both technical and aesthetic contributions to New Mexican life. The PKA estufa, said Tight in his last report to the New Mexican governor, gave "another touch in harmony with the Pueblo ideal which the Regents adopted for the University." Publicity on Tight's architectural efforts had reached far and wide, with the future editor of the *Santa Fe New Mexican*, E. Dana Johnson, writing a favorable story for *World's Work* in October 1907. The London *News* and "a large Paris Magazine," in Tight's words, picked up Johnson's article and commented on the campus, leading Tight to assume that "the wisdom of the Regents in adopting this Pueblo style for the future University of New Mexico is in my mind beyond all question" (Mitchell 1941, 74).[5]

The regents never acknowledged this praise from Tight, as they turned their attention to selection of his replacement in the spring of 1909. The likeliest candidate for president, Edward Dundas McQueen Gray, certainly met the standards of scholarship, experience, and urbanity that Tight's architectural critics craved. Steeped in the ancient humanities traditions of European universities, Gray often appeared amused at the pragmatism and present-mindedness of American higher education. He promised the regents to work diligently to overlay UNM with the sophistication and culture he felt that it needed, yet within three years he too would be dismissed from his post because his ideas did not resonate with the community at large.

Uplifting the unassuming territorial university, Gray believed, required bold and at times ruthless strokes to overcome opposition. Whether because it had been his predecessor's idea, or because it struck his British sensibilities as primitive, Gray soon informed the regents that no new facilities would be designed in the Pueblo style. This position irked the UNM Alumni Association, which mailed a circular letter seeking public opinion on the matter. "Do you believe," asked alumni secretary William B. Wroth, "that the Pueblo Architecture as modified by the late Dr. William G. Tight is advantageous to the development of the greater university and most characteristic of our Great Southwest?" If respondents decided in the negative, Wroth wanted them to suggest alternative designs and explain their logic.[6]

16-3 *The renovation of the administration building, ca. 1909. (Special Collections, General Library–University of New Mexico, Neg. no. 000-003-0093.)*

This issue stimulated debate on campus and in town that fed upon the acrimony generated by Tight's dismissal. R. W. D. Bryan, a regent when the adobe design had received authorization, contacted Edgar Lee Hewett, the director of the School of American Archaeology in Santa Fe and a future UNM faculty member in anthropology. Bryan hoped that Hewett, a proponent of the revival of native cultural practices and a renowned archaeologist, could energize the art colony in Santa Fe to oppose Gray's actions, since that community had undertaken efforts to restore the Pueblo-Spanish touch in architecture temporarily lost to the quasi-Victorian "Territorial" style.

Bryan informed Hewett that Gray, "a talented and cultured gentleman," found it "difficult . . . to see anything meritorious in any strictly American production." The president wanted the regents to consider Mission architecture, which had become popular in southern California after the arrival of the railroad and tourism in the late nineteenth century. Gray preferred the more ornate, sweeping lines of this style, as well as its mythical connection to Spanish nobility and grandeur. He believed that it could coexist with the buildings already on campus and that Easterners would be more inclined to attend UNM if it reminded them of Moorish or Iberian origins rather than of aboriginal societies for whom Gray himself showed little respect or admiration.[7]

Although Bryan, like many Albuquerqueans, was not native to the territory, he realized the deeper cultural and historical significance of the Pueblo architecture initiated by William Tight. Bryan thus informed Hewett that the UNM regents remained divided over the issue but that Governor William Mills favored the campus design. Bryan hoped that Hewett could prevail upon the governor to voice his support publicly, thus rallying opinion to the cause of adobe. The stakes were high, Bryan contended, and a successful defense of UNM might inspire a young architect to "produce an entirely new and distinctive architectural type which would be notable, truly American . . . and absolutely beautiful." Perhaps anticipating the rise of John Gaw Meem two decades later, Bryan saw such buildings as "peculiarly adapted to University life" and as giving UNM an indigenous style that not even the Ivy League schools, with their echoes of Cambridge and Oxford, could claim. At that point UNM would silence local detractors, like its own president, who saw "such architecture [turning] for inspiration to barbarism" and who claimed that the "whole idea [was] belittling for the head of the educational system of the Territory."[8]

The publicity campaign orchestrated by the UNM alumni association failed to dissuade President Gray on the issue of campus architecture. Gray prepared for the 1910–1911 academic year by ordering that all future construction have a generic style that could be modified to suit the tastes of later generations. Gray had little chance to carry out his directive; when statehood was granted to New Mexico the following year, all prominent territorial officials, like the president of the university, lost their jobs. Accepting the appointment as Gray's successor was David Ross Boyd, who had been the president of the University of Oklahoma from its inception in 1892 until his own firing with statehood 16 years later.[9]

When David Boyd accepted the presidency of UNM, he was living in New York City as the superintendent of the Indian schools of the Presbyterian Board of Home Missions. Making use of his proximity to East Coast artisans, Boyd asked several architectural firms for advice on the design of university campuses. William Orr Ludlow, of the firm of Ludlow and Peabody, offered his services. Ludlow cited his company's experience with the Stevens Institute of Technology in New Jersey, Hampton Institute, the Universities of Georgia and Virginia, and the George Peabody Teachers College in Nashville. Ludlow spoke to Boyd's concern about the disjointed campus scheme he inherited from Gray, noting that officials at Hampton had regretted their earlier "hit or miss arrangement" when they saw the merits of a campus master plan.[10]

Once on the ground in Albuquerque, the new president declared as one of his first priorities "a landscape architecture scheme." He corresponded with his closest associate from their days in Norman, Oklahoma, Vernon Louis Parrington, about a strategy for UNM. Parrington, a future Pulitzer prize-winning author who had been fired along with Boyd in the Oklahoma statehood purge, knew of his friend's interest in architecture as a means of stating a campus's relationship to its region. While in Norman Boyd had asked Parrington to help design a master plan that utilized the Plains environment most effectively. Parrington despised western universities that cloned themselves after elite eastern colleges, and he railed against shortsighted administrators who saw no value in linking their physical plant to its surroundings. At Boyd's behest he had visited several midwestern universities, and wanted Oklahoma to take advantage of its open space and limitless horizons. "To prefer the utilitarian and assume that . . . it must necessarily be ugly," said Parrington, "or [to think that] the beautiful is useless and therefore effeminate, is one of our national heresies."[11]

Knowing that he addressed a kindred spirit, Boyd told Parrington about William Tight's passion for Pueblo architecture. "The idea is an excellent one," said the UNM chief executive, in effect reversing the policies of Edward Gray. Boyd found fault only with the poor quality of construction and "a lack of adaptation," which he defined as "too much imitation in the plan." Boyd wanted Pueblo dormitories, dining halls, and "social halls," based around a quadrangle "with an effective addition of old Mission style of architecture."[12]

No stranger to academic controversy, Boyd moved slowly in his efforts to draft a new plan of architecture. He asked another New York designer, Beverly King, to comment on the merits of native techniques. King, at the moment constructing a "Spanish mission" science hall for the University of Denver, called Boyd's decision "a bold step in the right direction." Because America had "so few traditions," King felt that the nation "should not only carefully preserve those we have but seek to amplify and encourage them whenever possible." King wanted campuses to reflect regional characteristics, and to harmonize with such environmental factors as sun, wind, aridity, and temperature.[13]

King then engaged Boyd with his interpretation of the "southwestern" style currently being exploited in different ways in New Mexico's art colonies of Taos and Santa Fe. "Many of the early Pueblo and Spanish Mission examples," he noted, "are particularly coarse and uninteresting." King disliked the excessive Victorian ornamentation of college architecture preferred by southwestern schools, calling instead for the "noble and dignified sentiment" that adobe offered because of its "mass and proportion." The architect felt excited about UNM's potential, and praised Boyd's awareness of the "more spiritual and personal side of architecture.[14]

Armed with testimony such as that offered by Ludlow and King, David Boyd in 1913 declared that the campus must "represent, as much as possible the historic background of the State." He advertised for an "up-to-date landscape architect and town planner," with the most famous respondent being Louis H. Sullivan of Chicago, designer of some of America's first skyscrapers. Sullivan, who had coined the phrase "Form Follows Function," revolutionized urban planning by rejecting the overstated exteriors of Victorian design. UNM's attempt to revive and modify William Tight's Pueblo scheme interested him greatly, Sullivan told R. W. D. Bryan. Sullivan knew that UNM lacked the funds for a grand design but felt that the indigenous cultural milieu of New Mexico offered any architect an opportunity for experimentation found nowhere else in America. He asked to be informed when UNM's architectural master plan went out for bid.[15]

If Boyd could attract the services of a prominent figure like Louis Sullivan, he might defuse whatever criticism Tight had received about the primitive and backward statement that adobe made to transplanted New Mexicans. In 1915 he engaged in preliminary negotiations with Walter Burley Griffin of Chicago, whom he described as the "prize winner of the plan for the Federal City and District of Australia." Griffin would make UNM "as distinctive as Leland Stanford |University| is," said the president, differing only "in that it would be based |on| the lines of the Indian pueblo style combined with the features of the so-called 'Mission Architecture.'"[16]

Events late in his presidency—World War I and his own resignation soon there-after—kept Boyd from carrying out plans for UNM's architectural scheme. In his stead came David Spence Hill, president of UNM from 1919 to 1927. A distant, aloof, cultured individual, not unlike Edward Gray, Hill tried to incorporate some of Boyd's ideas into his own campus master plan. The collapse of the artificial wartime prosperity of New Mexico made Hill dependent upon private donations, which in turn restricted his use of the newer architectural forms developing in Santa Fe and Taos.

In 1920 President Hill managed to raise the sum of $12,000 to construct and equip a new home economics building, named Sara Raynolds Hall for its major sponsors, the Raynolds family of Albuquerque. Eager to adopt some type of regional architecture, Hill solicited proposals from design firms for the project. Frederick Trent Thomas, an associate of the renowned Santa Fe artist Carlos Vierra, offered his services at dras-tically reduced rates. Thomas hoped to apply Vierra's techniques in adobe to the campus, but serious financial restrictions, and political favoritism, prevailed. The UNM regents employed instead a graduate of the university, Arno K. Leupold, to design Sara Raynolds Hall—a circumstance that David Hill considered uneconomical, if not unwise.[17]

Two factors emerged late in the 1920s to change forever the course of UNM campus architecture. James Zimmerman, a graduate in history and government of Columbia University, assumed the presidency in 1927. Committed to the causes of regionalism and government-sponsored economic and social change, Zimmerman at once fell in love with the many historical traditions of his new home. He also held deeply the Progressive era faith in the expert and the manager as custodians of a more cooperative world.

Joining Zimmerman on campus, ironically enough, were the hard times of the nation's Great Depression. In 1927 the board of regents agreed with the new president that adobe architecture should be the controlling emphasis on campus. This would fit with Zimmerman's call for a regional focus in the curriculum and research for his faculty. With the ascendance of Zimmerman's Columbia colleagues to high positions in Frank-lin D. Roosevelt's New Deal, UNM stood to gain from the generosity of government officials in search of examples of "grassroots" activism and the celebration of America's cultural diversity.

Zimmerman came to learn of these forces, and especially of the prominence of Santa Fe architect John Gaw Meem, when UNM bid in the late 1920s for the Laboratory of Anthropology. John D. Rockefeller, Junior, son of the wealthy industrialist, offered money to establish this research center and a small museum on southwestern Indians, not unlike his efforts to revive colonial American history at Williamsburg, Virginia. The university wanted the prestige, and the funds, that the laboratory would bring to a struggling campus of 600 students that would not be accredited for graduate programs until 1933. The university lost the competition to the art colony of Santa Fe, but Zimmerman's presence on the laboratory's board of directors brought him into contact with Meem, the winner of the national search for the laboratory's headquarters.

Other architects attempted to solicit work from Zimmerman prior to the hiring of Meem in 1933. Hunter Scott of Albuquerque had first sought the design for the Santa Fe research center, based upon his work in New Mexico and California and his writing of a manuscript comparing the indigenous architectural styles of each locale. Scott asked Zimmerman to use his influence to have him considered for the Lab, and then sent the UNM president his chapter on the university's adoption of Pueblo-Mission buildings. Scott also claimed to have discussed this matter with William Tight as early as 1905, telling Zimmerman that he had "encouraged |Tight| in his plans to the fullest extent." He lamented the suspension of the Pueblo technique on campus, even as it

16-4 *John Gaw Meem, University of New Mexico's consulting architect from 1933–1960. (Meem Collection, Special Collections, General Library–University of New Mexico.)*

had adherents elsewhere, specifically the Franciscan Hotel and Wright's Trading Post, both in downtown Albuquerque. It seemed to be a good time for UNM to experiment with the designs developed by Scott, and the architect emphasized Zimmerman's call for regionalism by quoting George C. Nimmons of the American Institute of Architects that the tiered system of Pueblo design "has gradually brought about the creation of the most interesting shapes and sky lines that American architecture has ever produced."[18]

John Gaw Meem (fig. 16-4) and his focus on Indian and Hispanic traditions could not have come to UNM at a better time. The severity of the depression cried out for bold gestures to break the grip of austerity and the threat of intellectual decline. In addition, Zimmerman's vaunted programs in cultural and historical pluralism had encountered opposition from the Anglo elite, whose children excluded Hispanics from university fraternities and sororities. Calls for legislative punishment for UNM triggered a disastrous campaign by psychology professor Richard Page and demographer George I. Sanchez to utilize the "objective" measurements of social science questionnaires to defuse racial tensions on campus. At the close of the 1933 spring semester, Page had resigned in haste, Sanchez had sought refuge in the vast recesses of the New Mexico State Department of Education, and Zimmerman faced yet another biennium of budget cuts and rancorous dispute.

Bainbridge Bunting has called John Gaw Meem the finest practitioner of regional design in the Southwest. "More than any other worker in the art of building," said Paul Horgan in his foreword to Bunting's biography of Meem, the architect brought "a comprehensive image to civilized life in the Rocky Mountain Southwest." This quality was desperately needed by Zimmerman, as he beseeched federal officials to finance a unique strategy of regional curricula and facilities. Meem, who had come to Santa Fe in 1920 for the tuberculosis cure, sympathized with the struggles of Zimmerman and quickly embraced the preservationist movement in his new home. Receipt of the Laboratory of Anthropology contract made him the only figure Zimmerman considered for his experiment in cultural awareness (Bunting 1983).

The place of John Gaw Meem in the history of UNM is secure, well-documented, and richly deserved. From 1933 to 1958, the firm of Meem and his associates designed and supervised construction of all University of New Mexico buildings, a total of eighteen separate facilities. Bunting spoke for many when he identified the library and administration buildings as "among Meem's finest." Bunting also noted Meem's commitment to Zimmerman's dream, to the extent that Meem wrote several proposals to federal agencies for no advance fee, contingent upon acceptance. Without this help the university would have failed in its scheme for development. The library (fig. 16-5), student union, health laboratory, and heating plant were funded jointly in 1936, on the basis of Meem's free drawings. The Public Works Administration granted UNM a total of nearly $700,000, toward which the university could contribute a mere $8000, or slightly more than 1 percent, of matching funds. The university's poverty and Meem's design had come together to provide the university with the central core of a new campus and solidify UNM's architectural reputation as among the most original in the United States (Bunting 1983, 33, 50, 60, 89–91).

Because of Zimmerman's vision and Meem's artistic sense, Harold Ickes had the inspiration before him in 1939 of the "merging and meeting" of cultures (fig. 16-6). The Interior secretary was not aware of the deeper currents of tension that had preceded Meem's arrival of campus, nor could he have realized that adjusting the curriculum and student life would not be as simple as drafting plans for buildings to house those

16-5 *Zimmerman Library, completed in 1938, is considered among the finest examples of New Mexican architectural design. (Special Collections, General Library–University of New Mexico, Neg. no. 000-003-0079.)*

16-6 *The vast expanse of the University of New Mexico campus in 1906, with the pueblo design in the foreground. (Special Collections, General Library–University of New Mexico, Neg. no. 988-027-0005.)*

professors and pupils. But he knew of the permanence of Meem's structures, and the rightness of Zimmerman's cause, when he bid farewell to his audience at the school's golden anniversary:

> May the University of New Mexico, conscious of the distinctive niche that it is creating for itself in our ascendant American civilization, always stand firm for the truth, even though the truth be unpalatable to some, and for the right of all to have free access to the truth.[19]

REFERENCES

BUNTING, BAINBRIDGE. 1983. *John Gaw Meem: Southwestern Architect.* Albuquerque: Univ. New Mexico Press.

HILTON, RONALD. 1939. "Impressions of American Universities, II." *The Fortnightly*, August: 206, 216.

HOFSTADTER, RICHARD. 1968. *The Progressive Historians: Turner, Beard, Parrington.* Chicago: Univ. Chicago Press.

HORGAN, PAUL. 1983. Foreword to *John Gaw Meem: Southwestern Architect* by Bainbridge Bunting. Albuquerque: Univ. New Mexico Press.

MITCHELL, LYNN B., ed. 1941. *Remembrance Wakes: Memorial Day Exercises of the University of New Mexico, 1928–1941.* Albuquerque: University of New Mexico Press.

MORRISSEY, ROBERT STEPHEN. 1973. "David Ross Boyd and the University of Oklahoma: Analysis of the Educational Contributions of the First President." Ph.D. dissertation, University of Oklahoma.

STARR, KEVIN. 1973. *Americans and the California Dream, 1850–1910.* New York: Oxford University Press.

WIEBE, ROBERT H. 1967. *The Search for Order: 1877–1920.* New York: Hill and Wang.

NOTES

1. Harold L. Ickes, "Where Cultures Meet and Merge," Commencement Address, University of New Mexico, June 5, 1939, Harold L. Ickes Secretary of the Interior File, Speeches #226, UNM 6-5-39, Box 317, Harold L. Ickes Papers, Manuscript Division, Library of Congress (hereafter cited as MD, LC).

2. Albuquerque (NM) *Journal Democrat*, May 11, 1903.

3. James Wroth, University of New Mexico Board of Regents, to Herbert J. Hagerman, Governor of New Mexico, December 24, 1906, Governor of New Mexico Corres-

pondence to UNM (1894–1912) File, Board of Regents, Box 2 of 2, University of New Mexico Archives (hereafter cited as UNMA).

4. Charles Hodgin told of a comment made to him by an Albuquerque resident critical of adobe architecture: "How foolish to go back 300 years for a type of building—not much evidence of progress in that." Hodgin's response was, "What about going back two or three thousand years to copy Greek architecture?" The critic replied: "Well, if you are going to be consistent, the President and faculty should wear Indian blankets and feathered coverings on their heads."

5. Territorial Archives of New Mexico (cited as TANM), Roll 165, Frames 993–1008.

6. William B. Wroth, Secretary, University of New Mexico Alumni Association, to "Alumni and Friends of the University," June 11, 1910. Edgar L. Hewett Collection, Box 22, File 3, Part 2, 1910 Correspondence. Museum of New Mexico History Library, Santa Fe, NM (cited as MNMHL).

7. R. W. D. Bryan, University of New Mexico Board of Regents, to Edgar Lee Hewett, Director, School of American Archeology, Santa Fe, June 22, 1910, Hewett Collection, Box 22, File 3, Part 2, 1910 Correspondence, MNMHL.

8. See note 7.

9. Albuquerque *Morning Journal*, August 10 and October 8, 1910; Minutes of the Board of Regents' Meeting, UNM, August 1 and October 24, 1910, pp. 510, 513, 518.

10. William O. Ludlow, New York City, to David Ross Boyd, President, University of New Mexico, May 6, 1912, David Ross Boyd Correspondence, January–May 1913 File, Presidents' Boxes, No. 2 of 4, UNMA.

11. Boyd to Vernon L. Parrington, University of Washington, July 22, 1912, Boyd Correspondence, 1911–1912 File, UNMA. Hofstadter (1968, 371–3); (1973, 181–2).

12. See note 11.

13. Beverly S. King, New York City, to Boyd, July 17, 1912, Boyd Correspondence, 1911–1912 File, Presidents' Box No. 2, UNMA.

14. See note 13.

15. Boyd to Ralph Campbell, Editor, Kansas City *Star*, July 12, 1913; Louis H. Sullivan, Chicago, Illinois, to R.W.D. Bryan, June 4, 1913 Boyd Correspondence, January–May 1913 File, Presidents' Box No. 2, UNMA, Wiebe (1967, 42).

16. Boyd to J. O. Notestein, Professor, "University of Wooster (Ohio)," May 19, 1915; Boyd to James T. Brown, Beta Theta Pi Club, New York City, August 9, 1915, Boyd Correspondence, January–September 1915 File, Presidents' Box No. 3 of 4, UNMA.

17. Regents' Minutes, January 6, 1920, Volume 4, p. 42; March 3, 1920, p. 48; Frederic Trent Thomas, Santa Fe, to David Spence Hill, President, UNM, January 19, 1920; Hill to Thomas, January 1920; Press Release on Dedication of Sara Raynolds Hall, n.d., Buildings, Grounds, Offices, Home Economics Building Specifications File, Box A1, Group 1927–Prior, UNMA; Elizabeth Simpson interview, Albuquerque, NM, February 12, 1988.

18. Hunter D. Scott to James F. Zimmerman, President, UNM. January 1, 1929; Scott, "Albuquerque's Contribution to a New Architecture," Chapter X. "Pueblo-Mission Architecture," unpublished manuscript, Laboratory of Anthropology Folder B, Box 27, Record Group (RG) 1928–1948, UNMA.

19. See note 1.

Georgia O'Keeffe's New Mexico: The Artist's Vision of the Land and Its Architecture

17

Ethel S. Goodstein

Few individuals' influence have been as pervasive in the history of American art as Georgia O'Keeffe. The images she painted, from sensuously detailed and richly colored billowy flowers to stark and structural bleached bones, have become icons. Her aesthetic independence as she gained acceptance as a female American artist has become legendary. Together, her unique deportment and her provocative style, which explored an undefined territory bridging the abstract and the representational, filled a void in twentieth-century American art. It is difficult to isolate a singular aspect of O'Keeffe's oeuvre, but it is her instinctive appreciation of the larger American landscape that is a key to understanding the spirit and significance of her work. This special sensitivity to the land, and the architecture and plant and animal life that punctuate it, is manifested in her long-lived passion for the Southwest, especially the New Mexico countryside.

From the last years of the 1920s until her death in 1986, Georgia O'Keeffe delighted in and drew inspiration from the New Mexico valley where she lived and worked. The influence of New Mexico's indigenous architecture and natural landscape provides a thread of continuity through more than half a century of painting. O'Keeffe's discovery of and strong rapport with this environment, and her transformation of it into a very personal, but equally painterly, language speak clearly to the emergence of a uniquely American style in the art of the first half of the twentieth century and crystallize one woman's romance with the "mystique of New Mexico." Moreover, the artist's perceptions and depictions of New Mexico's built and natural environments suggest experiential connections between architecture and the visual arts that begin to establish a broad and meaningful context for the role of regionalism in American cultural history.

AN AMERICAN FOUNDATION FOR AN AMERICAN ART

Regionalism in American art and architecture has always been connected, to some degree, to the North American quest for an indigenous expression that could rival the long-established traditions, principles, and techniques of western Europe. Nineteenth-century American aesthetic theory is imbued with the belief that cultural parity with the human-made wonders of European art and architecture could be challenged only by Americans turning to the land for inspiration, as a source of the intrinsic meaning and visually exciting character that were deemed so admirable in the works of artists of other parts of the world. A fine balance of romantic idealization and scientific realism stimulated concern for the land among such individuals as Henry David Thoreau, Frederick Law Olmstead, and George Perkins Marsh. "The continued culture of the land, and the culture of the mind through the land, was considered the mark of a highly developed civilization" (Mumford 1931, 27). This legacy is important in establishing a historical context for O'Keeffe's peculiarly American outlook concerning art and environment.

Born in Sun Prairie, Wisconsin, in 1887, O'Keeffe was a product of the promise of the American West that was inherent in the nineteenth-century's reverent attitude toward the land. Descriptions of her childhood confirm an early fascination with nature and a demonstrated interest in art. She delighted in the vastness of the plains and the intricacies of wild flowers that grew in the woods near her childhood home (Castro 1985,6). In 1902, the O'Keeffe family moved to Williamsburg, Virginia, and enrolled Georgia in a boarding school between Danville and Lynchburg; in this rural setting, the imagery of the Blue Ridge Mountains provided a backdrop for her maturing artistic endeavors. O'Keeffe had developed a unique sensitivity to detail in nature since her youth, and through an impressive breadth of training this awareness evolved into the foundation of a personal style and vision.

O'Keeffe's studies with John Vanderpoel at the Art Institute of Chicago (1904–1905), with American Impressionist William Merritt Chase at the Art Students League of New York (1907–1908), and with Arthur Dow and Alon Bement at Columbia University Teacher's College (1916) placed her in the mainstream of American art. Although Bement's teaching stressed oriental modes of composition and a Kantian viewpoint, the traditions she learned were generally conservative, grounded in the Impressionism and Post-Impressionism of the late nineteenth century. Through her professional and personal relationship with photographer Alfred Stieglitz, a leader among New York avant garde artists, O'Keeffe's exposure to the state of the art of contemporary painting and the burgeoning role of abstraction in art was completed. With Stieglitz, she came in contact with European-trained American painters, including John Marin, Arthur Dove, Charles Demuth, and Marsden Hartley, all of whom were influenced by trends in nonobjectivity yet, like O'Keeffe, also inspired by nature.

Although the circle of artists that revolved around Stieglitz first at the "291" Gallery and later at American Place, flirted with abstraction and the still commanding influence of the European sphere, neither Stieglitz nor O'Keeffe followed the paths of the many American artists who fled to Europe in the 1920s. Stieglitz promoted the idea that an indigenous American aesthetic could evolve from the nonobjectivity of twentieth-century modernism, and O'Keeffe's "pure American spirit" was one of the qualities that had drawn him to her (Lisle 1981, 162). O'Keeffe was aesthetically committed to portraying the power of the American landscape, and she was frank in her contempt for those artists who theorized about being American in their art but had little experience with the America that existed west of the Hudson River. In this connection she emphatically stated, "One cannot be an American by going about saying that one is an American. It is necessary to feel America, live America, love America, then work" (Matthias 1926).

O'Keeffe's belief that an American art should be vested in uniquely American subject matter was shared by critics who, by the 1920s, were demanding an expression that would reflect the realities of twentieth-century technology, politics, and socioeconomics. Prominent among them was Lewis Mumford, an early proponent of O'Keeffe's work and a foresighted observer of architecture, who asserted that American culture should be responsive to the elemental necessities of life (Mumford 1928). This idea embodied regional specificity; each area of the country was encouraged to develop its particular culture to the fullest extent, and in the years between World Wars I and II the styles of American Scene painting and Regionalism celebrated the diversity of the American landscape and its people. Although O'Keeffe is not generally considered a Regionalist among American painters, her affinity with the open spaces of rural America, the effects and forces of nature, and the peculiarities of local customs are in the spirit of this movement.[1] These qualities characterize her images of New Mexico, but they emerged gradually through earlier explorations of environments she knew well.

CONFRONTING THE CITY, THE COUNTRY, AND THE PLAINS

O'Keeffe's attraction to the southwestern landscape was firmly established over ten years before she began to paint the land and architecture of New Mexico. From 1916 to

1918 she taught at West Texas State Normal College. There, O'Keeffe was profoundly influenced by the region's canyons and plains, and her casual appreciation of nature began its transformation into a conceptual vehicle for her art. She later wrote of this experience, "I couldn't believe Texas was real. When I arrived out there, there wasn't a blade of green grass or a leaf to be seen, but I was absolutely crazy about it" (quoted in Heller and Williams 1979). The breadth of O'Keeffe's sensibilities about character of place begin to reveal themselves in reminiscences that not only describe awesome physical features, such as the Palo Duro Canyon—to her eyes a "slit in the plains"— but also respond to such diverse stimuli as sunset skies and cattle wailing in their pens (O'Keeffe 1976). Her 1916 portrait of Palo Duro Canyon, *Painting No. 21*, conveys the spectacle of experiencing the canyon and traversing its narrow winding cowpaths. Boldly outlined but flat-shaped slopes painted in warm colors suggest the intensity of the sunset sky against the frightening depth of the canyon. Memory of place kept the Texas landscape alive in O'Keeffe's work after her return to New York in 1918, as evidenced by *From the Plains I* (1919). This work is also suggestive of a holistic sense of place. The haunting, repetitious rhythms of the sights and sounds of the plains generated a nonobjective composition in which O'Keeffe sought to express emotion rather than to imitate nature.

Nature was dominant in O'Keeffe's recording of the West Texas landscape, but architectural subjects began to appear sporadically in her work during the 1920s, establishing striking precedents for her depiction of New Mexico's indigenous architecture. During this era of the construction of such dramatic high-rise structures as the Chrysler Building and the Empire State Building, the aesthetic of the steel frame fascinated O'Keeffe, but she focused on those aspects of the emergent New York cityscape that paralleled the qualities that appealed to her in the western landscape. In the great height of the skyscrapers and the shadows they cast on city sidewalks she sensed the creation of an infinite space not unlike that of the West Texas canyons. Her efforts to document the architectural scale and complexity of the city were initially rejected by Stieglitz and other men who argued that such subject matter was essentially alien to her Middle American background. They contended that nature was the feminine sphere, not buildings requiring structural draftsmanship (Castro 1985, 66).[2] O'Keeffe persisted and interpreted the city on her own terms, underscoring that "one cannot paint New York as it is, but rather as it felt" (quoted in Looney 1965).

O'Keeffe's mid-1920s observations of city and country alike in paintings executed from her suite in the Shelton Hotel and from the Stieglitz family summer home in Lake George are environmental portraits. More than a record of an interested observer, they were the artist's means of coming to terms with unfamiliar places or new dwellings. Paintings of urban scenes ranged from direct, pictorial depiction of specific buildings or views, such as *New York Night* (1929), to more abstract communication of the vast, vertical space of the city in *City Night* (1926). In both instances, it is the planar qualities of the buildings that attract O'Keeffe, and their essential geometry is apparent in the composition of the picture plane. Her forms are stark, rhythmic, and monumental, the height of the high-rise somewhat exaggerated; people are notably absent, and a flickering night light establishes an atmospheric quality. In a series of sweeping perspectives of the East River, including *East River from the Shelton* (1927/28), a broadly cast horizon line establishes the ranging parameters of the river's length and breadth; buildings on either side of the river are diminished into shadows. Again, O'Keeffe's suggestion of spatial infinity, ever present in her vision of the west, is implicit.

In Lake George, vernacular architecture similar to that of the Wisconsin landscape of her childhood inspired works that further document O'Keeffe's evolving expression of the built environment. *Lake George Barn* (1926) is characterized by the articulation of the building's broad, horizontal planes. Subtle modulation of tone in the weathered gray walls conveys the presence of light rather than the development of massing. Fenestration is indicated with blunt, square penetrations in the wall, absent of detail. O'Keeffe's keen observation of architectural facts is further evidenced in *Lake George Window* (1929), which, in contrast to the typological character of her barns, is painstakingly precise in its detailed rendering of clapboarding, shutters, wooden door panels, and the jigsawed door lintel. In contrast to the cityscapes, the Lake George paintings seek an essence of environmental meaning rather than a quality of space through architecture. Together, these works begin to reveal the artist's unique ability to convey a true sense of place through architectural facts and spatial references.

DISCOVERING THE ESSENCE OF NEW MEXICO

A sense of emptiness and claustrophobia pervades O'Keeffe's cityscapes of the late 1920s, reflecting both her growing uneasiness with the city and its community of artists and critics and the developing strains in her relationship with Stieglitz. Desirous of more time and greater freedom to paint, O'Keeffe accepted the invitation of art patron Mabel Dodge Lujan to visit Taos. New Mexico had attracted artists since the late nineteenth century, but the quest for regionalism brought this area to the forefront of the arts in the 1920s. D. H. Lawrence came to Taos with the intention of establishing a community of artists in 1924; New York painters John Sloan, Marsden Hartley, and John Marin, and photographer Paul Strand were also attracted to the region's seemingly untouched natural landscape and distinctive quality of light. Of his experience in New Mexico, Lawrence had written, "In the magnificent fierce morning of New Mexico one sprang awake, a new part of the soul woke up suddenly" (Lawrence 1931). His observation well describes the profound influence New Mexico had upon O'Keeffe, who proclaimed, "You know, I never feel at home in the East like I do out here—and finally feeling in the right place again—I feel like myself and like it."[3]

The vastness of the New Mexico landscape, the contours of its hills, and the profiles of its remote mountains invigorated the artist. In its vistas were the infinite spaces that had captivated O'Keeffe in Canyon, Texas. In geological formations and the relics of plant and animal life of the desert she found the essential forms that had dominated her earlier still life paintings. New Mexico's intense light, subtle colors, and expansive space not only inspired O'Keeffe, but psychologically bound her with the west.[4] In response to the land, O'Keeffe's painting matured through a merger of the Post-Impressionist, colorist, and compositional techniques of her early training with the insightful observations of the built environment that characterized her cityscapes and country scenes. The paintings produced in this period have been considered unprecedented in the history of art.[5]

O'Keeffe's assimilation of her new environment may well have figured in the development of her *Ranchos de Taos Church* (1929–1930) series. With Mabel Lujan's husband Tony, a Taos Pueblo native, as her guide, O'Keeffe explored the architecture of the pueblos and the customs of Native Americans. At once a participant and a voyeur, the artist seems to have had an acute appreciation of the historical consequences of the Spanish Conquest and the imposition of Catholicism on the native people and cultural circumstances of New Mexico. Such insight brought depth to her interpretation of the traditional form of the adobe church.

The Church of St. Francis of Assisi at Ranchos de Taos dates to the eighteenth century, typifying the parish church of this period of Spanish settlement of the American southwest. By its very nature, the building is an abstraction of the traditional pilgrimage or monastical church of the Middle Ages. Its traditionally derived two-towered facade, transepts, pronounced apsidal end, and protruding buttresses are starkly sculptural in massing, absent of decorative detail, and formally defined by the planar smoothness of hand-finished adobe walls. O'Keeffe described the church as "one of the most beautiful buildings left in the United States by the early Spaniards" (O'Keeffe 1976). The profound massing and implicit geometry of the rear (west) elevation are understood and exploited in O'Keeffe's paintings. Portrayed in a variety

17-1 *Ranchos Church, 1930, oil on canvas, 24" x 36." (Phillips Collection, Washington, D.C.)*

of light conditions that capture the local optical quality, this protuberant element is the focal point of each composition; the transepts recede in shadow. It is the building's continually changing relationship with the landscape through the imposition of sunlight that is the primary variable among the works of this series. Although the relationship of the church to its site is pictorially compressed, the parallel horizontal planes of sand and sky allude to the expansiveness of the larger environment, recalling the spatial suggestiveness of her *East River* series.

The paintings of the *Ranchos de Taos Church* series are relatively small—most are approximately 24 by 36 inches—but O'Keeffe's compositional organization vests the architectural statement with monumentality. Depicted in isolation against barren, bleached sands and an expansive, sometimes cloud-filled sky, the church becomes more than a fact of the built environment; it is transformed into an icon of the desert (fig. 17-1). Comparison of the O'Keeffe paintings with photographs of the building evidences the pictorial accuracy of the artist's impressions, but she believed that

> . . . even if I could put down accurately the thing that I saw and enjoyed, it would not give the observer the kind of feeling it gave me. I had to create an equivalent for what I felt about what I was looking at, not copy it (O'Keeffe 1976).

Clearly, getting to the essence of place was the painter's key objective. O'Keeffe also painted isolated fragments of the church. Out of the context of the building–ground relationship, the adobe wall is inherently abstract, conceived in planar geometry and light. Later, the artist reflected that such vignettes of the building said "all I needed to say about the church" (O'Keeffe 1976). This analytical exploration of detail in the built environment seems a logical extension of her observation of detail in nature; the microscopic depiction of the wall is reminiscent of her similarly intensive studies of flowers, shells, and bones.

A later painting, *Cebolla Church* (1942), portrays quite a different vision of New Mexico's ecclesiastical architecture (fig. 17-2). The Taos church was rendered as a gem

17-2 *Cebolla Church, 1945, oil on canvas, 20" x 36." (North Carolina Museum of Art, Raleigh, N.C.)*

in the desert; the Cebolla church is its humble counterpoint in which O'Keeffe wished to portray the hardship she perceived in this small village in northern New Mexico, then one of the poorest areas in the United States (O'Keeffe 1976). The rudiments of building design are precisely, if starkly, delineated. The profile of the church's steeply pitched roof is distinctive; its adobe walls are distilled to flat planes defined by hard shadows cast by the overhanging roof. Classically inspired details of window surrounds seem wholly incongruous. Contrary to the painter's characteristic interest in the dynamics of space, there is little depth in the picture plane. The church is thrust into the foreground of the canvas, the relationship of building to the ground and sky is compressed, and the absence of signs of life or suggestion of distance are haunting. That O'Keeffe wished to enrich her work with sociocultural as well as environmental content is certain, for she thought of this painting as "one of my very good paintings, though its message is not as pleasant as many of the others" (O'Keeffe 1976).

A similar sensitivity to regional customs related to the character of the land is evident in O'Keeffe's reaction to the Penitente crosses she saw in the New Mexico hills. For her, painting the crosses was yet another way of painting the country. In *Black Cross, New Mexico* (1929), an ancient, pegged Penitente cross dominates the composition with a startling power, fully evoking the dark connotations of the religiosity the artist perceived and attaining a scale considerably larger than life, against a background of rolling hills meeting a brilliant yellow horizon. In effect, the cross becomes strongly architectonic, presented with the same combination of clinical observation of detail and subtle simplification of form and space that inform O'Keeffe's paintings of regional buildings.

Together, O'Keeffe's first New Mexico paintings of churches, pueblos, and crosses involved intense and direct observation of the physical facts of her immediate environment. Her architectural subjects were defined through radical simplification of shape and detail, yet a pictorial representation of regional specificity, which can be considered neither strictly realistic nor abstract, resulted. As the artist's familiarity with a particular place increased, she produced "less representation, more interpretive works, exploring various aspects of the environment and her emotional reaction to them" (Messinger 1984). It is in O'Keeffe's landscape paintings of the canyons and mesas in the vicinity of Taos, Santa Fe, and Ghost Ranch, executed in the 1930s and 1940s, that this becomes apparent.

O'Keeffe's New Mexico landscapes were vehicles for further evolution of her paradoxically realistic and abstract style through an intimate study of nature. Art historical analysis has focused on the painterly and stylistic features of these works, with regard to their composition, viewpoint, color, and form.[6] In the context of a discussion of regionalism and the built environment, however, the landscape paintings are also instructive, for they establish acutely that sense of the character of the land that informs the design and enhances the imagery of its architecture. Composition such as *Hills—Lavender, Ghost Ranch New Mexico II* (1935), *Near Abiquiu, New Mexico* (1941), and *Gray Hills* (1942) express the underlying geometry and expansiveness of the landscape (fig. 17-3). Her emphasis on the massing of the land, juxtaposed against a high horizon line results in the emergence of landscape features with a strongly architectonic character, as suggestive of the built as of the natural environment. It is not surprising that the horizontal organization, unyielding frontality, exclusion of a middle ground, and absence of extraneous subject matter, from people to plants, in the landscapes is strongly analogous to the artist's treatment of architectural subjects. Both share O'Keeffe's evocation of the timeless qualities of place set in an infinitely ranging frame of space.

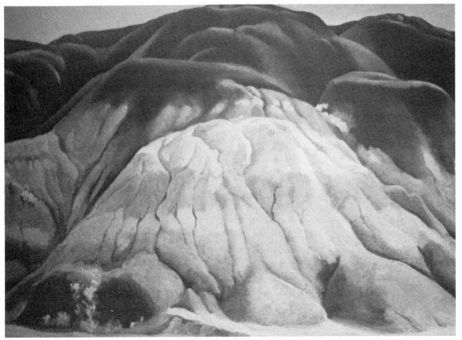

17-3 *Gray Hills, 1942, oil on canvas 20" x 30," Copyright © 1989, (Indianapolis Museum of Art, Gift of Mr. and Mrs. James W. Fesler.)*

ESTABLISHING A PERSONAL SPACE—
GHOST RANCH AND ABIQUIU

The influences of New Mexico upon the artist are further revealed by her passion for her own houses, both examples of indigenous building types intrinsically related to the sites they occupy. In her dwellings, the painter sought the same simplicity and the elimination of all but that which was truly necessary that she strived for in her paintings. "A house should be just a shelter," and it is, perhaps, the vistas of the landscape that her houses command that held the greatest appeal and meaning for the artist (Lisle 1981, 313).

In 1934, O'Keeffe moved into an adobe house at Ghost Ranch, a large complex owned by conservationist Arthur Newton Pack and operated as a dude ranch. O'Keeffe's house was situated on a flat stretch of desert, obscured from the main ranch. A U-shaped structure built around a large patio, it is typical of regional construction featuring planar walls, whitewashed rooms, and wooden-beamed viga ceilings. Its siting, however, was remarkable, for it afforded the artist two imposing yet contrasting views of the landscape. The Pedernal Mountains rose to the east, and a canyon surrounded by cliffs of striated rock layered with reds, ochres, golds, and the grayish white of limestone dominated the opposing view. O'Keeffe lavished attention on a garden she created in the patio, but her front yard was, in fact, the vista she often observed and painted from the roof of the house. This unique merger of building and site that so distinguished Ghost Ranch is communicated in *The House Where I Live* (1937). Like her earlier paintings of New Mexico architecture, this work reveals the long, narrow house in a frontal, horizontal view, but the painting is distinguished by her personal rendering of the Pedernal as a blue, truncated peak rising behind the house. "The blue color was an illusion created by the bright desert sun, the distortions of distance, and O'Keeffe's imagination" (Castro 1985, 110). It would seem that the search for an ideal of universal truth and beauty that generations of artists sought in academic traditions, Parisian salons, and American cities had been satisfied for O'Keeffe in the solitude of New Mexico's hills.

O'Keeffe also became interested in an abandoned Catholic mission located in the village of Abiquiu, then a remote and impoverished community populated by fewer than one hundred people of mixed Spanish and Indian heritage (Castro 1985, 119). The compound, surrounded by a deteriorating adobe wall, was something of a "ruin," but the area was rich in history and tradition. Set in a high plateau overlooking the Chama River valley, Abiquiu was originally a Tewa pueblo; its settlement can be traced to a fifteenth-century Indian migration from Mesa Verde. During the nineteenth century, the area was colonized by the Spanish. In the midst of the mission was a house believed to date to the pre-Civil War period. It had passed from its original owner, General Jose Maria del Socorro Chavez, an Indian fighter and Brigadier General in the U.S. Army, to his son, who finally sold the property to the Santa Fe Archdiocese of the Roman Catholic Church.

In 1945, after nearly ten years of persistent negotiations, O'Keeffe convinced the Church to sell her the Abiquiu mission. She thus acquired a property that was an uninhabitable array of rooms, patios, courtyards, and passageways. Its viga roof had collapsed in places, but its hand-hewn doors were intact. The interplay of space between the interior and exterior throughout the rambling structure greatly pleased O'Keeffe. She never considered the house an architectural masterpiece, but something that grew, like her paintings, in her own style (*Architectural Digest* 1981). In keeping with her respect for regional traditions, rehabilitation of the structure, whose original abode brick walls were two feet thick, was undertaken in the spirit of its indigenous character. No new walls were built, and traditional adobe construction was employed in repairing the existing house and garden walls. Some license was taken with the original character so that greater advantage could be taken with the original character so that greater advantage could be taken of the panoramic view of the Chalma Valley; this involved breaking through the adobe walls to install glass. Additionally, fireplaces were built in every room, an ancient Pueblo ceremonial cooking room was restored, and adobe benches were built along the walls of the living room. A structure that had once housed cattle became O'Keeffe's studio; a building that once sheltered wagons became her bedroom.

For O'Keeffe, there was no inherent conflict in maintaining two houses; each had a unique character, determined by its respective natural environs, the green river valley of Abiquiu richly contrasted with the rocky landscape of Ghost Ranch. The architectural relationship of the two properties suggests that the smooth adobe planes and clearly massed forms of Pueblo-influenced architecture appealed to O'Keeffe's conviction that simplicity derived not from elimination, but from getting to the essence, an idea not unlike the architectural truism "less is more."

O'Keeffe long maintained that the significance of her painting was not symbolic; it simply depicted her environment in terms of objects whose pleasing shape, color, or texture attracted her attention. Her fascination with one element in the Abiquiu house, its patio door, generated a series of paintings executed from the time of the Abiquiu renovations of the mid-1940s through the mid-1950s.[7] Like so many ordinary objects she had painted in the past, this door became another icon in O'Keeffe's vocabulary and a symbol of her most personal connection to New Mexico's built environment.

In its initial appearance in *In the Patio* (1946), the door, indicated as a mere rectangular hole in a thick adobe wall, frames a vista suggestive of the complex spatial relationships of the house. Architectural facts have been distilled to a series of flat, overlapping planes, but the penetration of sky into these bold geometric forms, their hard shadows, and their layered planes create an uncomfortable but unmistakable sense of depth. By the mid-1950s, "her relative isolation, both physical and psychological led to more self-derivative works" (Castro 1985, 27), and her patio door remained a preferred yet increasingly abstracted subject. The series grew to include *Patio with Black Door* (1955), *Patio With Cloud* (1956), and *Black Door with Snow* (1956), all of which examine the door–wall relationship at sharp angles. The consistent depiction of long diagonal shadows and a limited palette of colors also distinguish these works as a conclusion to O'Keeffe's definition of place and space with utter simplicity, reminiscent of the power of the Ranchos de Taos Church *Fragments*. The culminating work of this series, *White Patio With Red Door* (1960), is a minimalist treatment of the architectural scenario painted at an unusually large scale and size (48 by 84 inches). Wall, door, and flagstones are reduced to a series of pale red squares on the flat enveloping white wall. The painting is far more representational than literal; only light and planes remain truly recognizable. The allusions to adobe wall and desert sun are O'Keeffe's visually concise metaphor for a spirit of place indigenous to New Mexico.

MEANING IN O'KEEFFE'S NEW MEXICO—AN ASSESSMENT

By the time O'Keeffe had completed the Patio series, abstract expressionism had finally established for American painting the premier role on the cutting edge of the visual arts that the nation's arbiters of culture had long demanded. The search for an indigenous American aesthetic that had brought several generations of painters to New Mexico had fundamentally changed; regionalism was not a great concern of the 1950s and 1960s. In this period of new formal interest and fast-changing definitions of "painterly," critics readily reassessed the simplicity and inherent abstraction of O'Keeffe's oeuvre in the context of contemporary works and theories.[8] It is very unlikely that O'Keeffe's late works were derivative of outside influences; her expression continued to be the outcome of long-standing aesthetic principles and her own idiosyncratic way of visually evaluating the world around her as she experienced it

(Castro 1985, 134). Esoteric theories that made hard distinctions between realism, representation, and abstraction were never of any interest to her. "Objective painting is not good painting unless it is good in the abstract sense." she stated.

> A hill or tree cannot make a good painting just because it is a hill or a tree. It is lines and colors put together so that they say something. . . . The abstraction is often the most definite form for the intangible thing in myself that I can only clarify in paint (O'Keeffe 1976).

It would seem that since her earliest explorations of Taos, that "intangible thing" was inherent in the mystique of the built and natural New Mexico environment.

From the New Mexico landscape, O'Keeffe's paintings attained an iconographic quality and a mythical tone. With an expansive vision of space and her unique manipulation of light and color, she brought animation to an environment that to others seemed stark, static, and intimidating. Even the notably progressive painter Stuart Davis, who traveled to New Mexico in 1923, noted, "I don't think you could do much work there except in a literal way, because the place . . . is always there in such a dominating way."[9] O'Keeffe was never overwhelmed by the landscape. Nature, environment, and experience provided both points of departure and points of reference for her paintings. The artist, in effect, became one with the land to a degree that was unequalled by the many other eastern painters who attempted to commit the aura of New Mexico to canvas. For example, Stuart Davis' *Pajarito* (1923), Marsden Hartley's *New Mexico Landscape*, and John Sloan's *Southwest Art* (1920) all explore styles previously well established by each artist and are colored by the emotional detachment of the casual observer, a tourist's memorandum. Their works stand in strong contrast to O'Keeffe's imagistic combination of naturalism, piety, and respectful regard for the merger of physical facts, historical circumstances, and cultural traditions. From the land, O'Keeffe derived a spiritual presence of both the present and the past that was an intrinsic part of her experience. A consciousness of religiosity and the symbols of life and death inherent in the desert also set her images of New Mexico apart from those of her contemporaries.

O'Keeffe's paintings indicate that she was not only at home with the environs of New Mexico but also conversant with its history and culture. This was typical of O'Keeffe's confrontation with the built environment, and her observations of a wide range of historic architecture are thus revealing.

O'Keeffe made her first journey to Europe in 1953, but she found little inspiration in western, high-style architecture. She was repelled by the scale of Christian art in the Vatican, and, generally, she described "everything in Rome" as

> extraordinarily vulgar. The baths, the coliseum, the palaces—as if being huge makes them good . . . Coming as I did from the Middle East . . . where everything is made to man's measure, one is particularly aware of this. There, though the palaces were large, they were made up of small units where you felt you belong (quoted in Willard 1963).

The spatial quality O'Keeffe described in the middle eastern palaces recalls the rambling and varied spaces of her own Abiquiu house. She was similarly attracted to the artifacts of eastern cultures in which she saw analogies between the views surrounding Abiquiu and oriental vistas; even the knarled branches of stunted sagebrush seemed to her reminiscent of bonsai (Lisle 1981, 375).

The artist's commentaries on American architecture are also meaningful in establishing a context for her appreciation of New Mexico's indigenous architecture. As she aged, New York's tempo and violence frightened her, but a 1976 visit to Washington, D.C., delighted her. In the Washington Monument she saw the same gradations of light and formal simplicity that intrigued her in her own patio door; in the Mall, she sensed a wideness of space, revealing the open sky that had always appealed to her in eastern and western American landscapes alike (Cowart et al. 1987, 11). In view of her own affinity with the land, it is not surprising that O'Keeffe admired Frank Lloyd Wright, one of the greatest proponents of the idea that an American architecture could emerge only from the intrinsic relationship between a building and the land upon which it is situated (Cowart et al. 1987, 232).

It has been said of contemporary architecture that "regionalism reveres the making of place. It views architecture as a means to the end of cultural vitality and expression" (Speck and Attoe 1987). Character of place and creation of place are interwoven; vernacular traditions of expression and space have the potential to be conceptual points of departure rather than preconceived aesthetic ends. Georgia O'Keeffe's paintings of New Mexico and its architecture were conceived in this spirit of place. For nearly 60 years, she translated the amplitude of nature, the sanctity of cultural traditions, and the imagery of indigenous architectural forms that she observed in New Mexico into a personal, painterly vision. Her works speak to that special blending of place, time, and space that architects often strive to create. Her words describe that essence of experience that creates memory of the extraordinary in the environment, the very meaning of regionalism in art or architecture. "A place is a fusion of human and natural order, a peculiar window on the whole (Nelson 1984). The artist's vision of New Mexico's land and architecture give tangible expression to her words, a statement that might well be construed as an allegory for design and an argument for the continued role of regionalism in the work of the painter and the architect alike.

REFERENCES

ANONYMOUS. 1981. "Architectural Digest Visits Georgia O'Keeffe," *Architectural Digest*, 38 (July):81.

CASTRO, JAN GARDEN. 1985. *The Art and Life of Georgia O'Keeffe*. New York: Crown.

COLLINS, JAN DOWNER. 1980. "Georgia O'Keeffe and the New Mexico Landscape." Master's thesis. George Washington University.

COWART, JACK, JUAN HAMILTON, AND SARAH GREENOUGH. 1987. *Georgia O'Keeffe: Arts and Letters*. New York: New York Graphic Society Books/Little Brown.

HELLER, NANCY, AND JULIA WILLIAMS. 1976. *The Regionalists*. New York: Watson-Guptill.

_____ AND _____. 1979. "Georgia O'Keeffe: The American Southwest." *American Artist*, 40 (January):81.

LAWRENCE, D. H. 1931. "New Mexico." *Survey*, May 1.

LISLE, LAURIE. 1981. *Portrait of an Artist: A Biography of Georgia O'Keeffe*. New York: Washington Square Press.

LOONEY, RALPH. 1965. "Georgia O'Keeffe." *Atlantic Monthly*, April.

MATTHIAS, BLANCHE. 1926. "Stieglitz Showing Seven Americans." *Magazine of the Art World, Chicago Evening Post*, March 2.

MESSINGER, L. M. 1984. "Georgia O'Keeffe." *Metropolitan Museum of Art Bulletin*, 42 (Fall):29.

MUMFORD, LEWIS. 1931. *The Brown Decades: A Study of the Arts in America 1865–1895*. Reprint 1971, p. 27. New York: Dover. (Originally published by Harcourt, Brace & Co.)

_____. 1928. "The Theory and Practice of Regionalism." *Sociological Review*, 20 (April): 133.

NELSON, M. C. 1984. "Landscape of the Mind." *American Artist*, 48 (February):76.

O'KEEFFE, GEORGIA. 1976. *Georgia O'Keeffe*. Unpaginated. New York: Viking Press.

SCHWARTZ, S. 1976. "When New York Went to Mexico." *Art in America*, 64 (July):95.

SPECK, LAWRENCE W., AND ATTOE, WAYNE (eds.). 1987. "New Regionalism." *Center: A Journal for Architecture in America*, 3:5.

WILLARD, CHARLOTTE. 1963. "Portrait: Georgia O'Keeffe." *Art in America*, 51 (October):84.

NOTES

1. Heller and Williams (1976, 22) argue that O'Keeffe's work "is only related to regional art. Although she is closely identified with a specific region (namely, the American Southwest), O'Keeffe's paintings of natural forms . . . have nothing to do with the relation of people to their everyday environment."

2. It has been suggested that the paintings of city scenes were O'Keeffe's response to unspoken challenges from male artists, especially Charles Sheeler and John Marin, whose interpretations of architectural forms were well known. Stieglitz declined to exhibit any of her New York buildings until 1928. The impact of the architectonic compositions upon critics who had hailed the inherent femininity and eroticism of O'Keeffe's earlier paintings of flowers, sea shells, and country landscapes was considerable and controversial.

3. Georgia O'Keeffe to Henry McBride, letter of Summer 1929, Taos, New Mexico, cited in Cowart et al. (1987).

4. Beaumont Neuhall, interview, June 1981, Santa Fe, New Mexico, cited in Castro, 1985, 83.

5. Ibid.

6. The stylistic qualities of the landscape paintings and identifies specific sites documented in O'Keeffe's paintings are codified in Collins (1980).

7. Of this architectural element, she wrote, "that wall with a door was something I had to have" (O'Keeffe 1976).

8. Such attempts include Hilton Kramer's "The American Precisionists," *Arts*, March 1961, and Barbara Rose's "O'Keeffe's Trail," *New York Review of Books*, March 31, 1977.

9. Stuart Davis to James Sweeney, cited Schwartz (1976).

VI

Regionalism

The inherent polemic of the concept of regionalism is diversity, dependent upon culture, climate, and available building materials. In Chapter 18, Buford Pickens covers the topic of regional architecture throughout North America. He shows us the developments of Spanish, French, Indian, and English cultures in various regions, from the American Southwest to Canada and the Caribbean. Folke Nyberg and Farouk Seif concentrate on the growing alienation of personal identity and place in Chapter 19. They discuss Pueblo architecture's ability to create an authenticity of place through human ritual. Hopi ritual and religion are compared to the ritual and mythological base of the Egyptians. The chapter further presents regional architecture as an extension of culture and concludes that regionalism is not a style. In Chapter 20, Amos Rapaport engages in a full discourse on regionalism and what it means geographically, environmentally, socially, and aesthetically, drawing on many cultures and places to explain his thesis. Glade Sperry, in Chapter 21, gives a very personal display of his design philosophy as a regional architect. He presents a rationale for the creation of a regional dialectic in contemporary architecture with examples from his personal work.

Regionalism in American Architecture: A Comparative Review of Roots

18

Buford L. Pickens

My interest in architectural regionalism began in Chicago during the late 1920s and early 1930s. I lived in Oak Park, working through the summers as an apprentice in the old-time "Prairie School" office of George W. Maher. After graduation from the University of Illinois, I transferred to the office of a close friend, George Fred Keck. At the time, he was the only architect in the city who, at some risk, limited his commissions to noneclectic practice. His interest was technological (anti-stylist), but not regional. Today he may be remembered as the developer of the early "solar house." He was architect of the experimental "House of Tomorrow" (1933) and the "Crystal House" (1934) at the Chicago World's Fair. Later he served as first head of the architecture department at the new (Bauhaus) School of Design.

In the early 1930s, Frank Lloyd Wright was at his nadir; the Beaux Arts hegemony, having dismembered the Prairie School, was itself fast waning; New York's Museum of Modern Art began riding high; and Hitchcock and Johnson had just invented the International Style for their prolonged "Pied Piper" march. The regional approach to architecture seemed to be a better way to go, but there were no established leaders to pick up the tradition of Sullivan and Wright. We found inspiration in the writings of Lewis Mumford, George Kubler, et al. and our own study of history. It was not an easy time in the Midwest for regionalist architects to make a living; academia offered an alternative. My seven years in New Orleans (at Tulane University) became a regionalist's dream come true. Santa Fe held a similar attraction for many others.

Many architects, especially those returning from work in third world countries, have now recognized—as did Wright and Le Corbusier earlier—the potentials for an "authentic regionalism" in vernacular architecture. Today, for the first time it seems possible to study regionalism in America (a) aided by sympathetic cross disciplines, and (b) in a place that retains a strong affinity to the creative prehistoric peoples who once lived here.

CAVEAT TO U.S. REGIONALISTS

Writing in London during World War I, the late Sir Nicholas Pevsner, eminent international scholar—later responsible for a monumental survey, the *Buildings of England* series—produced the pocket-sized, "GI" edition (1942) of his one-volume architectural history *An Outline of European Architecture*. When it was first published for laymen across the Atlantic in 1948, Pevsner appended "An American Postscript" explaining his contention that an outline of Western architecture can "do without any mention of buildings in America prior to the 18th, or indeed the 19th century."

Perhaps as amends for this sobering putdown, he deftly sketched the highlights of American architecture in five or six pages, closing with a jolly pat on the back for the "seriousness" of architectural researchers in the United States. But also, Pevsner warned against unevenness of judgment:

> There is in the American concentration on local, regional, and national
> architecture the danger of parochialism. Things are regarded as peculiarly

American because all their antecedents, phases, and particulars are by now better known in America than in Europe. Thus English, or Continental precedent is often disregarded because not familiar (Pevsner 1960, 709, 722).

After more than a generation of intensive research, Americans can easily reject Pevsner's yardstick for evaluating our architecture. At the same time we should be grateful to have his implied encouragement to focus on the differences and variations from European prototypes.

Even though we may be transient citizens, Americans can regain a rootedness of spirit as we try to understand our pluralistic inheritances.

> It is not *imitation* that justifies an intense study of the past. It is *inspiration* that is urgently needed . . . [deriving] from the eminent prototype an understanding of that which is timeless as against that which is timebound (Moholy-Nagy 1957, 42).

ARCHITECTURE AND HUMAN ECOLOGY

As a "nation of immigrants," Americans need to remind themselves that Asian and European architecture developed gradually, within discrete geographical peoples related by social customs and common technological means and conditioned by the nature of the land—seacoast, rivers, mountains, plains, deserts, and so on. Century by century they developed a way of life and a way of building. Innovations germinated slowly, spread by chance, conquest, and commerce. The quality of architecture, then as now, was an index to the creativity within a society. But modifications of style—by which we mean those aspects of form that express a society's aims and attitudes— were measured by epochs and eras rather than by decades, years, or the monthly publication of design journals. Tradition, not computers, tested results.

Greek culture as seen in its regional architecture, for example, the Doric order, unfolds like a flower from century to century. Even the vast building program of the Roman Empire retained certain insular features of old Latin traditions together with an inheritance from earlier Etruscans and Greeks. Later, peoples of well-defined environmental regions—the Italian and Iberian peninsulas, British Islands, France, and Germany, among many other countries—produced their own distinctive architectural variants within the international spread of Medieval and Renaissance building styles.

American architecture, on the other hand, presents a different kind of historical growth. It evolved more like an ecological experiment, testing the effects of many new environments and the adaptability of traditional building forms that had matured in some distant motherland (Zavala 1962, 25). Colonists from diverse European settings and with dissimilar purposes suddenly transplanted to a new world their social and technical ideals embodied in their native architecture. Certain factors remained constant, while others had to be adjusted as in a biological laboratory. The seeds from Old World species of architecture and town plans were sown at different places on virgin soil, under conditions capable of producing vital new characteristics.

But unlike the controlled laboratory, even before a new strain could be clearly identified, transplants were crossed and recrossed with inbred descendants of the original species. Occasionally, promising young mutants struggled to express adaptations to the new life in America. But Americanisms were usually mistaken for hinterland hybrids (weeds) and quickly repollenized at the architectural fashion centers to eliminate the "raw" organic regional characteristics acquired during their encounter with a new environment.

The New Significance of Vernacular Architecture

During such periods of continuously interrupted mitosis, the New World has produced few entirely new building types. Recent state and local inventories, however, reveal a rich variety of unique and expressive form-styles, more or less vernacular, conditioned by place and time. At the same time, scholars have been trying to discover why so few American cities in their growth process have retained the viability and visual attraction of their older European prototypes. This search has led to a new interest in vernacular building types, here and in developing nations.

Henry Glassie's writing and drawings have aided in understanding the discipline of folklore and pattern of the material culture regions in the eastern United States. Glassie has been a pioneer in the careful study of work by early builders. It may be helpful here for us to quote a few of Glassie's definitions that distinguish between regional space and time:

> In general, folk material exhibits major variation over *space* and minor variation through *time*, while the products of popular or academic culture exhibit minor variation over space and major variation through time . . . that is, a search for patterns in folk material yields regions, where a search for patterns in popular material yields periods (Glassie 1968, 33–4).

While Glassie's studies are concerned primarily with rural areas, the history of cities suggests that the permanent, desirable qualities of urban spaces may be more dependent upon the composite, living forms of vernacular architecture than upon single architectural gems. Innumerable urban neighborhoods with modest but authentic regional variations of eighteenth- or nineteenth-century styles along their streets and squares have preserved values as significant as those around isolated masterpieces.

Strength of character in buildings has a cumulative kind of sensory effect. For example, the Vieux Carré, the Bayou St. John, or the Garden Districts in New Orleans—built up over many generations, accepting the changing vernacular types consistent with the spirit of the place—are irreplaceable units that defy mechanistic replication. Few major cities lack some similar renewable areas, but they are not always recognized by the general public before vested interests of "progress" first slander and then demolish them. Hundreds of smaller towns and villages still have similar architectural treasures that await evaluation. It is possible that in their haste, those who judge may not heed Sir Nicholas's words of caution.

COLONIAL EXPERIENCE: THE SPANISH

The conquistadores and missionary urbanists who sailed from sixteenth-century Spain brought architectural and planning concepts bearing little resemblance to the northern Puritan traditions of rural English settlers who crossed the Atlantic a century later. Fur traders and business-minded colonists coming from France during the eighteenth century were accompanied by professional military architects trained during the great building period of Louis XIV. European homelands were generations apart in the assimilation of Renaissance ideas. Social conditions, affecting the way buildings were built in each of the motherlands, changed rapidly during the colonizing periods. This time lag helps to explain the evidence of originality, or lack of it, in the New World's architectural offspring.

By the time Columbus completed his final round trip, architectural ideas, printed and graphic, could cross national boundaries, thanks to Gutenberg's printing press. By means of books the Italian demonstrations of architectural theory were destined to affect the form of buildings and urban spaces of western civilization for centuries to come.

In New England and New France the Renaissance influence arrived in America much later, considerably altered by the climate, by northern traditions in building, and by religious and social changes. But in New Spain it came vigorous and full-bodied, propelled by missionary fervor and guided by intellects who understood the expressive power of building as an art. The originality, grand scale, and general competence of their building designs may come as a surprise to many who are unfamiliar with them and who have been accustomed to interpret the term "colonial" as necessarily provincial, inferior, and *retardataire*. But the continuity of architectural traditions from Italy to the Spanish colonies affected the essentials of environmental design: conditions of site, ordered refinements of building design based upon preplanned function, and the utilization of structural means, especially the vault and dome, to achieve dramatic spatial results.

The Spanish West Indies

By the year 1550, the Cathedral at Santo Domingo, capital of Hispaniola, was finished. The urbanization of Mexico was well under way; sixty-eight churches are known to have been started, several of cathedral importance and scale. In England, Henry VIII added to Hampton Court Palace, the Great Hall (1536) with its hammer-beam roof in the still viable Gothic tradition; indeed, for nearly a century the term "Renaissance" in English architecture referred to a new kind of ornament, not a way of designing buildings.

Changes in vernacular building in the northern countries followed normally, well behind the avant garde "court style," but in New Spain building design and town planning kept abreast and in some cases surged ahead of the work being done in the motherland. There are many explanations for this progressive colonial architecture, based upon such obvious economic factors as the newly discovered mineral wealth of New Spain, but the prime motivating force was a Renaissance compulsion to use this new wealth to build. In Mexico, urbanism, architecture, and the arts were all employed as a means of conquest, frequently among native Indians who already had creative town-building traditions of their own.

The linkage between humanist building concepts and New Spain at its inception was positive and direct. Pope Alexander VI (1492–1503) was a Spaniard. At his suggestion, Ferdinand and Isabella, the Catholic monarchs who financed Columbus's promising explorations, also commissioned the foremost Italian architect, Donato Bramante, in 1502 to design and build the famous Tempietto in Rome; it was a small but exemplary monument to St. Peter's martyrdom. Gold from America helped to pay for this building, called the first example of the High Renaissance. 1502 was also the year Columbus began his fourth and last voyage westward.

New Spain and the Architectural Continuum of the Renaissance

The most authentic and influential source for the underlying humanistic principles (which are surprisingly modern) can be found in the ten books on architecture written in the first century A.D. by the Roman Vitruvius, architect for the emperor Augustus, but they were radically revised by the great Italian architect Leone Battista Alberti (ca. 1404–1472) during the last twenty years of his life. This "ideal man of the *quattrocento*" wrote voluminously on many subjects including such twentieth-century themes as peace of mind, the family, and morals, as well as sculpture and painting.

First, Alberti considers the placement of the ideal town with regard to its region and natural setting—analysis of hills, plains, and coast; its functional orientation to sun, sea, and wind; the advantages and disadvantages for defense, health, water supply, and drainage. In the designing of buildings, Alberti is primarily concerned with the organization of space through the arrangement of architectural forms. Social and functional implications are woven into his detailed recommendations. He encourages originality rather than blind imitation of the ancients and delights in making exceptions.

Classical principles of design were carried in print to the New World, where they were reinforced by different agents, modified by local environments, and blended with native customs and craftsmanship. The zealous avant garde mendicants who founded

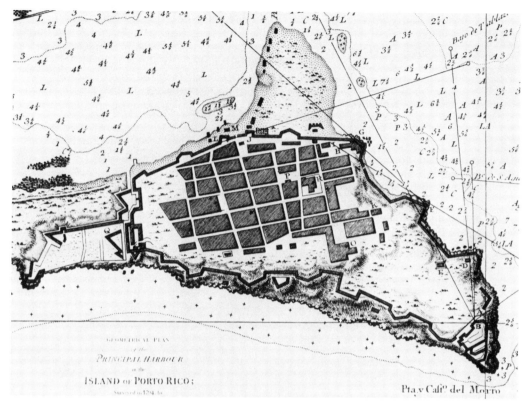

18-1 *Town Plan of San Juan, Puerto Rico, by Churruca, 1794. (Photograph: British Library. Reprinted with permission.)*

innumerable towns, established hundreds of missions, and built countless numbers of churches were often intellectually radical humanists; they received their inspiration not only from the church fathers, but also from the social concepts and ideals of the Dutch Erasmus and the English Sir Thomas More, as well as from architectural theories of ancient Rome and later Italians who followed Alberti. The preeminent architectural historian George Kubler presented convincing evidence that in Europe

> . . . the possibilities of realizing a theoretical program were limited by the abundance of inherited urban material. Hence it would appear that the Spaniards in Mexico, working with an extremely plastic human material and under no obligation to preserve the monuments of an old culture, were able to implement Italian theory with extensive practice (Kubler 1948, 99).

San Juan, Puerto Rico (fig. 18-1) is the oldest city now under the American flag. Columbus landed on Puerto Rico in 1493 and named it San Juan Bautista. (The names of the islet city and the larger island were reversed by Ponce de Leon, their first governor.) For more than 400 years the subtropical island remained a Spanish colony until 1898 when it was ceded to the United States.

The most authentic and helpful description of sixteenth-century San Juan comes directly in English from the Reverend John Layfield, D. D., Cambridge scholar and coauthor of the King James version of the Bible, who as chaplain accompanied the English sea captain Lord Cumberland when he captured San Juan in 1598. The chaplain's report includes discerning comments on the effects of climate on architecture:

The Towne consisteth of many large streets, the houses are built after the Spanish manner, of two stories height onely, but very strongly, and the roomes are goodly and large, with great doores in stead of windowes for receit of aire, which for the most part of the day wanteth never. For about eight in the morning there riseth ordinarily a fresh breeze (as they call it) and bloweth till foure or five in the afternoone, so that their houses all that while are very coole, of all the artificiall day the space from three in the morning till sixe, is the most temperate (Layfield 1906, 70–1).

Life in the American Spanish colonies centered around two architecturally planned spaces: The ubiquitous open plaza generated the civic and social activity in the town; the patio in the house served a similar but more intimate purpose for the family. As symbol and function, both were vital. The Spanish colonial house that Reverend Layfield described in San Juan of 1598 had not changed in principle from the recommendations outlined by Alberti, the humanist, and published more than a hundred years before:

For indeed, in my opinion, a wise man should build rather for summer than for winter. We may easily warm ourselves in Italy and the Mediterranean area against the cold by making all close, and keeping good fires; but many more things are requisite against heat, and even all will sometimes be no great relief. Let winter rooms therefore be small, [with] low and little windows, and summer ones, on the contrary, large, spacious, and open to cool breezes but not to sun or to hot air that comes from it (Alberti 1955, 110).

Alberti's analysis no doubt comes from his own personal experience, not simply as taste or fashion, but as the rational basis for a regional form-style: the collective wisdom tested by many ages of Mediterranean peoples. What may seem within a narrow context to be merely one man's opinion concerning orientation, if taken in a broader view suggests the common abstract basis for much in Classical architecture, especially for vernacular houses of southern Europe, North Africa, and the Middle East. There is recognition of the primacy of the sun, and thus of the importance of natural light and shade in the design of a socially pleasant environment for humans.

From this basic premise comes the search for open forms wherever possible: shade-creating (i.e., horizontal) elements dominate, implying the use of flat or low-sloping roof forms, colonnades, porticos, balconies and loggias, and other architectural devices that relate man-made space to the natural shade of trees, plants, and garden, to water and fountains. This premise accounts for the sheltered, inside–outside quality of space that is traditional in Greece and Italy; also it explains the purpose of the intricate screen walls common to North Africa and to the Mudéjar buildings of Spain— to provide well-ventilated privacy. In San Juan, hurricanes also affected the structure of houses.

The Spanish Borderlands: New Mexico and Santa Fe

From Mexico City, which from ca. 1550 was the largest city in the Spanish world, settlements spread centrifugally; by 1574, there were nearly 9000 Indian towns. Secularization beginning in 1572 added impetus to the search for more remote Pueblos to evangelize. (Fig. 18-2). The greater the distance from the colonial capital, the more the mission builders were dependent upon local conditions; with a blend of empiricism, wisdom, and humanist sociological theory, they respected many practices of pre-Conquest Indians. The result is a fusion of primitive and regional influence, with transplanted, universal elements in their new architecture. Even in frontier settlements the buildings themselves have a kind of integrity that today commands attention for its direct visual impact and deserves study as evocative functional form.

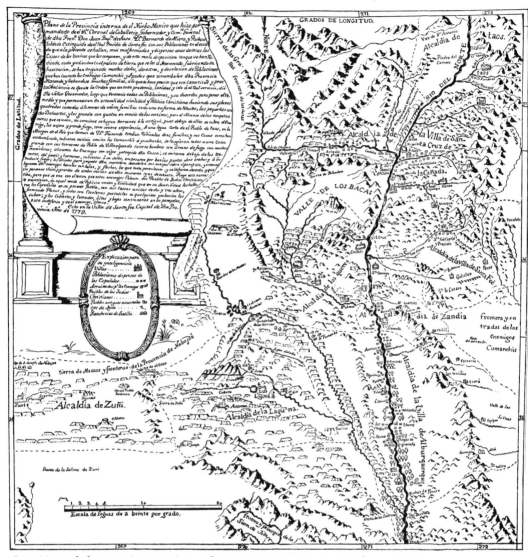

18-2 *Map of the Interior Province of New Mexico, Miera y Pacheca, 1779. (Photograph: British Library. Reprinted with permission.)*

Although Mexico functioned as the major architectural center of New Spain in the northern hemisphere, several widely separated areas within the present borders of the United States have preserved significant examples and building types: Puerto Rico, Florida, New Mexico, Texas, Arizona, and California. In none of these places do the intrinsic architectural values depend upon metropolitan grandeur and sophistication or upon the ultimate political consequences of the colonization.

Pre-Spanish Towns and Buildings

The stone-and-adobe pueblos of the American Southwest evolved from a 2000-year-old Anasazi culture whose highly organized social life and ritual we are still trying to understand after more than 100 years of study. Creative imagination, apparent in their

18-3 *View of Tyúonyi site, Bandelier National Monument. (Photograph: Buford Pickins.)*

crafts and painting, also played a role in their selection and use of natural building sites, alternating from cliffs to valley to mesa top. Design originality is demonstrated in the endless combinations of architectural elements fixed by tradition: the kiva as clan sanctuary, the plaza, the single chamber, the matrilineal family home, and finally the ensemble as unified town resembling the pyramidal mountain background in its irregular abstract geometry.

Pueblo builders sought a reconciliation of conflicting aims, to achieve man's universal need for shelter, physical security, and privacy within an open-ended structural form—one that would permit the utmost expansion potential by adding house units with new chambers on top, front, back, and sides (fig. 18-3). Even today, with space-age construction techniques, this kind of ideal group-form continues to haunt planners of housing and towns.

Data about human behavior patterns, drawn from aboriginal and historical vernacular buildings, may have a salutary effect on architecture if and when these considerations replace the primary concern in America with what one anthropologist has termed "the rather limited inventory of architectural styles based on the European intellectual tradition."

> Domination by European culture caused the indigenous cultures to lose many of their characteristic features and native vigor. Yet the genius of the Indian |in the arts| did not die out. . . . The missionaries cultivated these talents and skills and converted the Indian artisan into a collaborator in the production of the colonial culture (Zavala 1962, 273).

Another factor was the degree to which transculturation may have affected the Europeans. How can the differences between the vernacular architecture of New and

Old Mexico be explained? The form-style of the upper Rio Grande valley is unlike later Spanish colonial building in Texas, Arizona, and California (Kubler 1943, 39–48). Something in the spirit of the Pueblo *place* seems to have been communicated to the newcomers through the traditions of a *people* who had been living and building there for centuries.

The Mission as Frontier Institution

Their distance from the metropolitan centers of New Spain contributed to the distinctive blending of pre-Conquest Pueblo technology and decoration with European architectural ideas in the mission buildings of New Mexico (fig. 18-4). The situation was unique. According to the visitation memorial of Fray Beñavides (Kubler 1940, 7), a group of twenty-six friars dispersed among the Indian villages and by 1628 had built about fifty churches; vaguely they might be compared to an overly ambitious "peace corps" for although not professional architects, some were specially trained in the field laboratory methods established nearly a century before in Mexico City (Barth 1950, 46, 59).

The building program continued until 1680 with not more than one or two Europeans, usually to supervise the construction of each mission. As an essential part of their primary calling to convert heathen souls, the friars' combination of talents

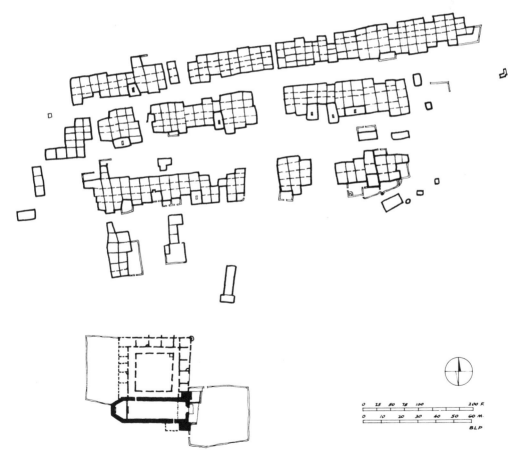

18-4 *Plan of Acoma pueblo and mission. (Historic American Building Survey. Drawings: U.S. Dept. of the Interior.)*

included the ability to teach a wide variety of the industrial arts with a minimum of equipment and to inspire Indian artisans to an intensive, constructive effort. Later, and in certain mission areas, the friars were able to obtain the service of *maestro mayores* to supervise design and construction (Schuetz 1983, 17–71).

COLONIAL EXPERIENCE: THE FRENCH

In the history of vernacular building, seventeenth-century American architecture requires a fresh appraisal in several comparative areas. None of the resultant "styles" are really primitive in morphological terms, although it is customary for the first century of European colonial buildings transplants to be dismissed or treated lightly as such (fig. 18-5). Each separate colony and nationality bears a somewhat different relation to its progenitors, but collectively they have a special significance due to their mixed ancestry. During the first few generations in America, functional and practical forms acquired connotations and meanings deeper than mere expedients (Mumford 1941, 14–7). On a new expanded land pattern, the same kind of structure, materials, and plan types branched off to form a separate, congruent architectural base in the New World. New roots took hold in the colonies (fig. 18-6).

French to the North

The first builders of New France were not trained in the court style of Paris and Fontainbleau. Champlain's artisans at Québec (1608) and those who followed to establish Montreal (1642) came mostly from the coastal regions of northwestern France. Like the English, they carried rural craft traditions with their medieval kits for design: function, economy, simplicity, along with steep-sloping roofs and stone and timber construction. They also brought, however, a special vintage of Latin sensitivity that in essence is classical.

Like the Spanish, French explorers in America were also soon joined—sometimes led—by zealous mission-building religious orders whose patient efforts with the Indians opened the way for cultural interchange. The native's expertise at inland travel and navigation was skillfully exploited by the *coureurs de bois*, penetrating the

18-5 *Upper and Lower town of Québec, L. J–B. Franquelin, 1688. (Photograph: Service Historique de la Marine.)*

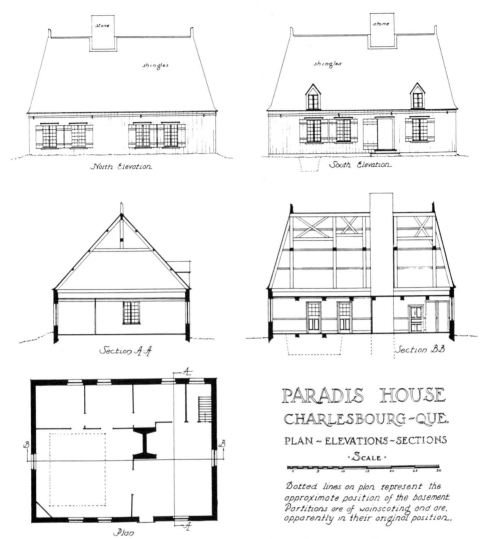

North Elevation.

South Elevation.

Section A-A

Section B-B

Plan

PARADIS HOUSE
CHARLESBOURG-QUE.
PLAN ~ ELEVATIONS~SECTIONS
· Scale ·

Dotted lines on plan represent the approximate position of the basement. Partitions are of wainscoting and are, apparently in their original position.

18-6 **Typical early Québecois house. (Canadian Architecture Collection, Blackades, Lauteman, Library of Architecture & Art, McGill University.)**

wilderness to gain French dominance of the fur trade. The French discovered the Mississippi in 1672 and ultimately claimed the vast province of Louisiana from Fort du Détroit to Nouvelle Orléans, and thence up the river highway to Saint Louis and the tributaries to the west. Names like Pontiac and Cadillac symbolize the mobility link between the canoe and the automobile.

In spite of their common Gothic heritage in building techniques, the early French contrasted in temperament and outlook with the Puritans and Anglicans from across the English Channel who were led to expect "infinite good things of the New World." French colonists, expecting less, accepted the New World environment more philo-sophically and with greater tolerance toward adverse conditions. Their tractability led to working *with* rather than *against* the extremes of climate, the varied nature of the land, and the natives.

On the whole, French settlers were vivacious and voluble; by temperament they were cheerful and used to singing, dancing, and drinking—not only in local taverns but *en famille. La joie de vivre* and *bon vivant* were terms of approbation without pejorative connotations that still linger in English language usage. Such French expressions suggest qualities that are subtly reflected in architecture: a regard for essential space, outside and in, and a greater degree of flexibility in the accommodations for pleasant living.

Québec: A Village on River Below and Cliff Above

Samuel de Champlain's Ville de Québec—the contemporary French counterpart of Spanish Santa Fe and English Jamestown—is the most influential relative of the many former French towns in the United States. Had Québec been closer, more accessible to Europe, not on an icebound route, it might have functioned as effectively in the urbanization of New France as Mexico City did for New Spain. Nevertheless, one must turn to Québec and the St. Lawrence valley for architectural prototypes and comparisons with the work of French colonizers in the Mississippi valley and the Gulf states.

When Renaissance design principles began to be imported from Italy, French architects rejected the flat or low-sloping Italian roofs and retained the traditional pavilion with its familiar "northern" look and function. (Lavedan 1956, 184–5). Their method was to eliminate the disruptive angular gables and to terminate the pitched planes on all four sides with a continuous horizontal cornice line.

In the French method of adding more space, contrary to seventeenth-century practice in English colonies, projecting cross wings and gables were not permitted to interrupt the basic rectangular form or the linear continuity of the original facade. Dormer windows were subordinated to the building block and sat snugly just above the eaves as a logical continuation of the wall plane below; in double-storied attics, the upper tier of dormers was smaller than the lower. Noteworthy too, in view of their Flemish and English popularity, parapet walls were not generally shown on the gables of seventeenth-century buildings in rural New France; for practical reasons the roof overlapped the wall, not vice versa.

French in the South—New Orleans

The exact site for New Orleans was selected on the spot in 1718 by the Canadian Jean Baptiste le Moyne le Sieur de Bienville (fig. 18-7). In March 1721, a permanent plan for the city was urgently needed to head off haphazard building by impatient settlers. A year later, le Blonde de la Tour, Louisiana military engineer-in-chief presented a formal draft of a plan for a town that, with additional tiers of blocks, is the present-day Vieux Carré (Pickens 1974, 240). Like St. Augustine, but unlike Philadelphia, Charleston, and Savannah, the principal plaza at New Orleans opened toward the water and in effect included the quay itself. The site at a bend in the Mississippi commanded the view, as if toward the open sea, with wide-angle (twin Baroque) vistas both up and down the river.

Superficially, the Vieux Carré plan may appear to be only "a certain number of little squares," but its simplicity is deceptive. The studied size and shape of lots within the blocks made possible the palisade-enclosed eighteenth-century gardens, which became the nineteenth-century space for interior courts or patios. Because of them and the central open plaza, a very special style of urban living has continued. Here, we can find a case history of regional mutation: French regional architecture from the frigid St. Lawrence skillfully adapted by humanist planning to the hot, humid climate. After more than two and a half centuries, urban planners can measure the balanced relationship between physical scale, while residents are attracted to fluvial *joie de vivre*.

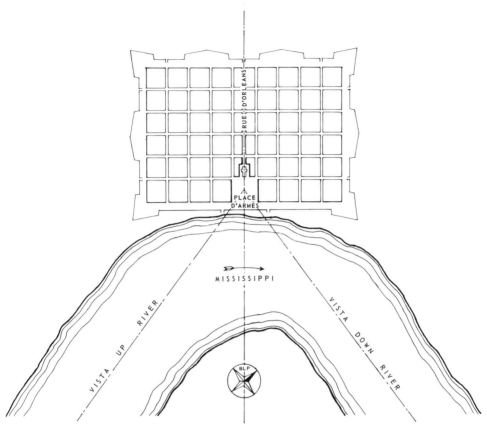

18-7 *New Orleans, emplacement on the river bend. (Drawings: Buford Pickens.)*

The Early Louisiana Plantation House

Beginning in New Orleans when it was a village, a prototype emerged for the free-standing house that was destined to spread along the Gulf Coast and up the Mississippi. Paris archives conserve the 1749 drawings—plan and section—for the Intendance Building (about 34 × 75 feet), open to two-storied, columned galleries across the entire front and back (fig. 18-8).

> Here for the first time a drawing appears for a great house with galleries in the form that was adopted for most of the plantation houses of Louisiana of the subsequent French and Spanish colonial periods. (Wilson 1969, 288–9).

The regional Louisiana house that evolved during the late eighteenth century is always raised above the ground, usually on brick piers (fig. 18-9). (In later one-story variations, the living floor is elevated about 2 feet—enough for air to circulate freely.) But in "classical" larger houses (fig. 18-10) the elevation is from 7 to 8 feet, permitting a full basement story. In addition, the elevation gave to the living floor a better view over the flat landscape and easier circulation of air, aided by high ceilings and windows to the floor (Pickens 1948, 33–6).

Besides the *piano nobile* principle, other features taken *tout ensemble* distinguish the classical Louisiana house:

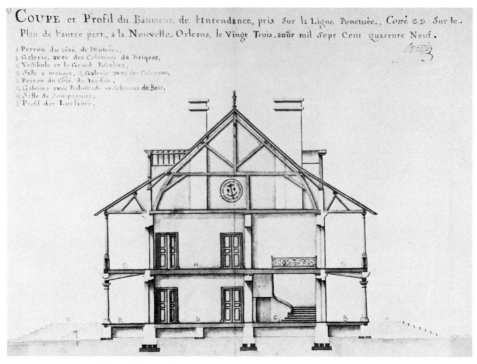

18-8 *Section and profile of the 1749 Intendance Building. [Photograph: Paris, (Document Archives nationales (Centre des Archives d'Outre-mer) La. #100, Broutin.]*

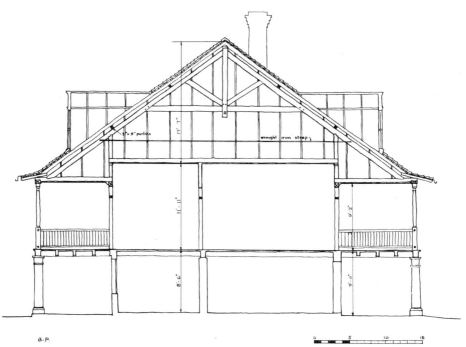

18-9 *Section, Louisiana plantation house. (Drawing: Buford Pickens, after HABS-L.C.)*

18-10 **Parlange Plantation House, New Roads, La. (Photograph: Buford Pickens.)**

- The structurally integrated, open gallery on one or more sides of the building
- The pavilion—hipped roof over the simple rectangular plan, an umbrella-like protection from both intense sun and rain
- The carryover of many traditional elements such as French shuttered windows

Many of the same architectural elements continue to solve regional problems of living with the hot and humid climate along the Gulf from Texas to west Florida and north along the Mississippi to the "Illinois Country" and Ste. Genevieve Missouri (Porterfield 1969, 141–77). They vary in size from the one-story "raised cottage" (Jackson 1985, 1–31) to the (yet-unstudied mutation in) "Greek Revival" mansions. Geographers have identified and traced the cultural pattern and routes of vernacular variations of the Louisiana house types as they encounter Anglo-midwestern influences throughout the state (Kniffen 1936, 179–93), but their derivation from the French Colonial prototype seems to be clear.

Bearing in mind the earlier caveat, we can find two-story galleried building types in many European regions of moderate climate. They also turn up regularly during the late nineteenth century (sometimes with cast iron columns) in tropical French colonies: Haiti, Guadeloupe, Martinique, and even in the far Indian Ocean island of Réunion. "La coincidence ne signifie pas nécessairement une influence" (Lavedan 1954, 275). The two-story building with two-story gallery may well be a universal vernacular type, but as far as the Louisiana region is concerned the original design can be traced to a practical-minded French military architect-engineer, who had surveyed Alsace for three years before his assignment to Louisiana (Grenacher 1964, 65–9).

THE COLONIAL EXPERIENCE: ENGLISH
England and the Lingering Medieval Tradition

The adjustments of the colonists to climate and terrain are more apparent in the great river valleys—the upper Rio Grande and the lower St. Lawrence and Mississippi—where special conditions unlike those of the motherland demanded more careful consideration and greater change. Relatively less architectural challenge was presented to most English colonies, where the new environmental conditions were not greatly dissimilar to those in England. Seventeenth-century builders in Virginia and Massachusetts used similar, uncomplicated geometric forms and functional, practical plans that were understandable to the colonists in the direct terms of technology and materials; not books, but methods that had been tested by tradition, begat the first generation of buildings. All this was soon to change with the "tides of English taste."

The first settlers in New England wee not the King's men or the lords of country manor houses; quite the opposite, they were mainly yeomen, artisans, and tradesmen from rural sections who became the first English colonial builders in the seventeenth century. They brought with them a modernized version of the medieval vernacular—steep-roofed, compact structures that had already begun to change from the traditional Gothic plan (Cummings 1979, 3–39). In a trans-Atlantic recapitulation, we can follow the evolution from their late-Medieval functional form to the Renaissance (provincial Georgian) style. For this purpose the timber-framed buildings of New England provide a convenient starting point.

"A Man's Home Is His Castle"

This famous quotation from the great common-law jurist Sir Edward Coke expresses more than an early seventeenth-century legal opinion; it suggests the Medieval origin of the symbolic image for the house type brought to America by the English colonists. Sir Edward's familiar metaphor conveys the idea of an enclosed sanctuary, protected from external forces of nature. It implies, figuratively, that the threshold of the house is a drawbridge and the interior space a haven of security, warmth, and relative comfort. It expresses man's reaction to a hostile world, and thus it provides a key to the northern European's visual (or psychic) imagery of the ideal house. For him summer is not the major problem; he must build against the caprices of nature that may strike throughout the long months of winter. During this season man needs as much light and warmth as he can get from the sun, and for this reason he is not interested in wide horizontal cornices or in deeply recessed openings in exterior walls.

Without conscious aesthetic implications, this climatic legacy encouraged architectural forms that in their function reinforced common usage:

- Steep-sloping roofs do shed the snow and rain, but they also suggest verticality.
- Not only do chimneys provide the necessary insulation for fireplaces and carry the smoke high above the roof for essential draft, but also by their height and functional repetition they harmonize with the upward thrust of angular roofs and gables.
- Chimneys also connote internal warmth radiating within the circle of space around the family hearth, in contrast to the blustery vastness, dampness, and cold of the external world.
- Rough-textured materials combined with an ample factor of safety in structure give tacit reassurance of permanent qualities that protect life within the house.

After several hundred years in England these preferences in building form set certain limits within which social and economic change could be accommodated under the disciplines of differing regional environments—highlands, lowlands, midlands; basic materials—stone, timber, and clay; and local craftsmen's technology. The resulting visual imagery and the kind of lived-in spaces gradually became the accepted norm, a unifying force behind a harmony of elements in vernacular architecture (figs. 18-11 and 18-12).

A British archaeologist (Barley 1961, 144–5) has traced the English farmhouse and cottage from its legacy in the Middle Ages through a "housing revolution" in their vernacular tradition, from the first phase in 1575–1615 to its ultimate demise in 1690–1725. Some Americans today may be surprised to learn that the timber-framed structures of early New England incorporated several innovations that had just been made in the homeland. We may have assumed that this clapboarded type was a primitive, functional form resulting from the lack of adequate means to build more solidly and with greater sophistication. Even after the legitimate ancestry had been established by Barley, the timber-framed house type was thought to be a reversion to an earlier Gothic form, not a late mutation.

Many medieval features, for the most part structural, were retained: timber frames from earlier "cruck" construction; the lean-to, which was a direct descendant from the single-aisled hall; the venerable steep-gabled roof; and the structural overhang or "jetty." About the latter we read:

> much nonsense has been written about the jetty, which became one feature of the medieval timber-framed house, lasting well into the 17th century. It was *not*

18-11 *View of typical English Colonial timber-framed house. (Courtesy of the Society for the Preservation of New England Antiquites.)*

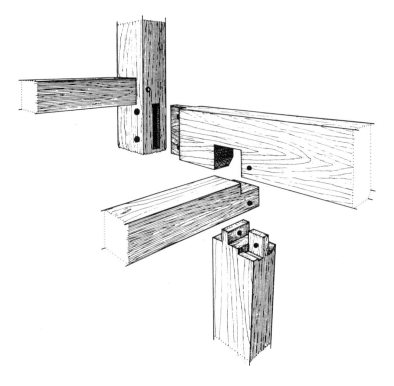

18-12 *Timber corner post assembly, Boardman House, Saugus, Mass. (Drawings: Lawrence A. Sorli. Abbott Lowell Cummings,* The Framed Houses of Massachusetts Bay, 1625–1725. *Harvard University Press. Reprinted by permission.)*

18-13 *Adobe house under construction, exterior, Taos, New Mexico, 1964. (Photograph: Buford Pickens.)*

18-14 *Adobe house under construction, interior, Taos, New Mexico, 1964. (Photograph: Buford Pickens.)*

a sensible way of winning more space for upstairs rooms, . . . the best technical explanation is that the carpenter hit on it as a way of strengthening the frame of the house, for it gave him two places for the junction of ground and upper wall posts with the first [second, in our terms] floor beam (Barley 1961, 14).

Thus the modest jetty illustrates a familiar path in vernacular architecture: first toward a more elegant structure—better use of material, greater precision in detailing and craftsmanship; then to greater visual pleasure and increased cost; and finally to a symbol. For the English colonist, the bulging, tightly clinging effect of overhangs, bays, and lean-tos, which gave his house the look of having been inflated by life from within, helped to express the premium he placed on enclosed space.

Regional forms are those which most closely meet the actual conditions of life and which most fully succeed in making people feel at home in their environment; they do not merely utilize the soil but they reflect the current conditions of culture in the region (Mumford 1941, 30; Bradshaw 1988, 169ff). (See figs. 18-13 & 18-14).

REFERENCES

ALBERTI, LEONE BATTISTA. 1955. *Ten Books on Architecture*, transl. James Leoni, ed. J. Rykwert, London: Tiranti.

BARLEY, M. W. 1961. *The English Farmhouse and Cottage*. London: Routledge & Kegan Paul.

BARTH, PIUS J. 1950. *Franciscan Education and the Social Order in Spanish North America, 1501–1821*. Chicago: DePaul University.

BLUNT, ANTHONY. 1966. *Artistic Theory in Italy, 1450–1600*. Oxford: Oxford University Press.

BRADSHAW, MICHAEL. 1988. *Regions and Regionalism in the United States*. Jackson: University Press of Mississippi.

CUMMINGS, ABBOTT LOWELL. 1979. *The Framed Houses of Massachusetts Bay, 1625–1725*, pp. 3–39, 95–117. Cambridge: Belknap Press/Harvard University Press.

GLASSIE, HENRY. 1968. *Pattern in the Material Folk Culture of the Eastern United States*. Philadelphia: University of Pennsylvania Press.

GRENACHER, FRANZ. 1964. "Current Knowledge of Alsacian Cartography." *Imago Mundi* 18:65–9.

JACKSON, J. B. 1985. "Urban Circumstances." *Design Quarterly* 128:1–33.

KNIFFEN, FRED B. 1936. "Louisiana House Types." *Annals of the Association of American Geographers* 26:179–93.

KUBLER, GEORGE. 1940. *Religious Architecture of New Mexico in the Colonial Period and Since the American Occupation*. Colorado Springs: The Taylor Museum.

_____. 1943. "Two Modes of Franciscan Architecture: New Mexico and California." *Gazette des Beaux-Arts* 23:39–48.

_____. 1948. *Mexican Architecture of the Sixteenth Century*. Vol. 1. New Haven: Yale University Press.

LAVEDAN, PIERRE. 1956. *French Architecture*. Baltimore: Penguin Books.

_____. 1959. *Histoire de l'Urbanism*. Vol. 2. Paris: H. Laurens.

LAYFIELD, JOHN. 1906. Earl of Cumberland, III. Samuel Purchase, B.D. *Purchase His Pilgrimes*. Vol. 16. Glasgow: University Press.

MOHOLY-NAGY, SIBYL. 1957. *Native Genius in Anonymous Architecture*. New York: Horizon Press.

MUMFORD, LEWIS. 1941. "The Basis for American Form." *The South in Architecture*, pp. 12–41. New York: Harcourt Brace.

PEVSNER, NICHOLAS. 1960. *An Outline of European Architecture*. Jubilee ed. Baltimore: Penguin Books.

PICKENS, BUFORD. 1948. Regional Aspects of Early Louisiana Architecture. *Journal of the Society of Architectural Historians* 7(1–2):34–6.

_____. 1974. "Neuf-Brisach, An Alsatian Link Between Louisiana and Vauban, Architect and *Colonisateur*." *Journal of the Society of Architectural Historians* 33(3):240–1.

PORTERFIELD, NEIL H. 1969. "Ste. Genevieve, Missouri." In: *Frenchmen and French Ways in the Mississippi Valley*. ed. John Francis McDermott. Urbana: Univ. Illinois Press.

SCHUETZ, MARDITH. 1983. "Professional Artisans in the Hispanic Southwest |Texas|." *The Americas*. Bethesda, Md.: Academy of American Franciscan History.

WILSON, SAMUEL, JR. 1969. "Ignace François Broutin." In: *Frenchmen and French Ways in the Mississippi Valley*. ed. John Francis McDermott. Urbana: Univ. Illinois Press.

ZAVALA, SILVIO. 1962. *The Colonial Period in the History of the New World*. Abridgement in English by Max Savelle. (Comision de Historia. Publ.No.239). Mexico, D.F.: Instituto PanAmericano de Geografia e Historia.

19 Ritual and Regional Genesis of Architecture

Folke Nyberg • Farouk Seif

The growing alienation of person from place (Relphs 1976) as well as the separation between community and region has caused a reconsideration of regionalism (Frampton 1983). While the traditional relationship between place, work, and people in the region was identified by Frederic LePlay and Patrick Geddes, the significance of ritual in providing the communal representation and affirmation of these relationships should be better understood in architectural terms. And whereas the Renaissance and the Baroque introduced ceremonial aspects of civic design through architectural masques (Bacon 1967), American society has primarily depended on nature and landscape in furthering a common ethos (Shepherd 1967). This aspect of regionalism motivates much of the interest in the Pueblo architecture of the Southwest. The mystique of Pueblo architecture lies in its ability to join living inanimate things in the continuing re-creation of an authenticity of place, not in terms of architectural monuments but as participatory rites. In this chapter we emphasize the importance of rituals in furthering an "ethical imagination" by considering how the physical setting reinforces communal myths through mimetic enactment.

This dimension of regionalism escapes a rational and systematic definition in architectural terms. As Louis Mumford has written,

> Before man could discover and project order outside himself he had first, by constant repetition, to establish it within. In this, the part played by ritual exactitude can hardly be overestimated. The original purpose of ritual was to create order and meaning where none existed; to affirm them when they had been achieved; to restore them when they were lost. What an old-fashioned rationalist would regard as "meaningless ritual" was rather, on this interpretation, the ancient foundation layer of all modes of order and significance (Mumford 1966, 62).

While Western society has developed a Cartesian split between reason and emotion resulting in inauthentic communities alienated from their regional context, the Pueblos have continued to attract the attention of those disenchanted with the demystified societies of western civilization and perhaps best celebrated in the writings of D. H. Lawrence and Vincent Scully.

In considering the ritualistic dimension of Pueblo architecture, we question the primarily stylistic emphasis in the current reconsideration of regionalism, and instead focus on its experiential and communal nature. The edifying function through ritual provides an alternative to the European emphasis on the creation of architectural civic and religious monument.

REGIONALISM AND RELIGION

To understand more fully the essential difference between civic architecture in terms of neoclassical formalism and the definition that is associated with early-twentieth-century Regionalism, Patrick Geddes' work in India is the most enlightening. It is here that Geddes has an opportunity to build on existing cultural tradition, and, unlike

Edwin Lutyens, his proposal for India is not to employ stylistic transformations of architecture to meet regional needs, but instead to have a ritualistic dimension in achieving a religious awareness of the physical environment. Geddes writes:

> Such effective action cannot be brought about simply by a diffusion of scientific knowledge as too many of us still believe, since we were all trained at College and University to be intellect-idolators. Emotion is the vital spark necessary to ignite the cold potentiality of knowledge into the flame and energy of desire, will, resolution, and deed. This unity of thought and feeling, by which an emotionalized idea is clearly imaged into vision and warmed to aspiration and purpose, is the essential of religion; and correspondingly ethics finds its realization when emotion kindles thought or vision to action (Tyrwhitt 1947, 69).

In diagramatic terms Geddes expands LePlay's triad of Place, Work, and Folk to include the essential means to create the energy of desire to bring about active participation. It was Geddes' unique genius to see the trivial housekeeping ritual of "spring cleaning" as having a connection to Easter, the spiritual festival, and inner purification and in turn to draw a parallel with this activity and the Diwali festival in India. Geddes (in Tyrwhitt 1947, 71) also acknowledges that the great masters of religion, "Manu for the Hindus, Tirthankars for the Jains, Zoraster for the Parsees, Mohammed for the Faithful all realized the need for purity of all the elements of air, water, earth and fire and of the human body, or life in relation to these."

In attempting to come to terms with the plague in India, Geddes as a biologist fully realized the scientific origins of the disease, but his insistence on the power of public rituals to "ignite the cold potentiality of knowledge" to achieve lasting civic improvements through the Diwali procession at Indore in 1918 is perhaps the most interesting example of his contribution to implementing regionalism.

Lewis Mumford carried on Geddes' work in the United States, and he was also critical of the theologians who neglected the earthbound origins of ethics. According to Mumford, however,

> among American theologians it has become the fashion to speak of ethics without religion as a mere cut flower, with no roots in the soil of life: beautiful, perhaps, but doomed to winter. But careful historic analysis shows that just the opposite is the truth; for ethics lies in the common earth of life, with roots that go deep into our animal ancestors; while religion, though it takes us to the mountain top and discloses vistas that stretch far beyond our common daily horizon, produces wider ethical imperatives only because it rests securely on an older ethical order (Mumford 1951, 212).

Ritual according to Mumford established a social order that ensured an understanding through participation whereby the enactment of common myths internalized an ethic or what we might term as "ethical imagination." This concentric activity established limits and boundaries of appropriate behavior or decorum as the basis for social order. As Mumford (1966, 67) observes, "Once ritual had been established as a basis for other forms of order, then, apart from the growth of language, the next step was to project a large part of its compulsive mechanism outside the human personality; and that process may well have taken as long as the original translation of actions into meanings."

From these insights by Geddes and Mumford, perhaps the two most able contributors to the definition of Regionalism in the twentieth century, we can conclude that the prerational society always included three aspects of ritual: the sacred acts or events, the sacred place, and the sacred cult leaders. All these aspects developed together for religious function, yet they change rather slowly over time in order to preserve a thread of continuity throughout different changes in the social order and/or the environment.

> If ritual was the earliest form of work, it was sacred work; and the place where it was performed was a sacred place—identified by a spring, a great tree or stone, a cave, or a grotto. Those skilled in the performance of such sacred works developed into shamans, magicians, wizards, finally kings and priests; specialists set apart from the rest of the tribe by their superior talents, their gift for dreaming or interpreting dreams, for knowing the order of the ritual and interpreting natural signs (Mumford 1966, 67).

Once the patterns of ritual were established, they provided the security for a reliable order that primitive man at first did not find in his existential environment. Furthermore,

> Ritual promoted a social solidarity that might otherwise have been lost through the uneven development of human talents and the premature achievements of individual differences. Here the ritual act established the common emotional response that made man ready for conscious cooperation and systematic ideation (Mumford 1966, 63).

It is, however, the loss of the participatory "extasis" as part of the development of an ethical imagination based on rituals that has led to its replacement by a "systematic ideation" that eventually disconnected modern society from experiencing the region in place-specific terms.

REGIONALISM AND MODERNISM

While Geddes and Mumford maintained that regionalism should maintain an intimate relationship with the landscape, the necessity of diverting growth by rational methods would eventually result in a regional planning effort or a "systematic ideation" that we associate with Cartesian rationalism. This denied the religious dimension of regionalism, which sought stewardship rather than management of the natural environment.

This attempt to instrumentalize the work of Geddes without his acknowledgement of the celebrating and ritualistic aspect in the integration of place, work, and folk made all aspects of regionalism logical problems. This emphasis on methods may also be the inheritance of the paralyzing skepticism of New England scientism, which looks to management and control to replace metaphysics. The American adaptation of regionalism eventually leads to the ecology movement, which, when institutionalized, becomes land resource management. Although this approach senses the quality of the environment, it is a quantitative and analytic methodology that seeks the same value-neutrality of all sciences. In short, American regional planning as exemplified by the New York Regional Plan destroyed all possibilities for ontology by its rationalistic and nominalistic methodology. Regionalism in these terms, therefore, continues the Cartesian split, with the analytic intellect dominating and isolating the emotional relationship to the landscape, becoming a voyeuristic and picturesque experience that does little to root understanding in a religious relationship to the earth. Various attempts by so-called countercultures indicate an acknowledged need for this relationship but usually fail to achieve the momentum to go beyond the state of isolated and culturally incomplete cults.

At this juncture the distinction should be made between modernity as the continuation of the rational Enlightenment project and Modernism as the attempted phenomenological understanding that goes beyond an object-oriented rationality.

While it can be argued that Cartesian rationalism with its split between reason and emotion exemplifies the modern condition, it can also be said that Modernism in art and architecture has also sought to use phenomenology to recover the experiential qualities of life. Edmund Husserl and Merleu Ponty are perhaps the best-known philosophers contributing to a new way of "seeing," a "new vision" encouraging a primacy of perception. It is also of interest that Cubism drew directly from so-called primitive art for examples of forms that invited a participatory way of "seeing."

This aspect of modern art exemplifies a similar search to that of phenomenology in representing reality. Through a deconstruction of established conventions our perceptions are engaged in forming a new understanding and the participant experiences perceptual possibilities in a logic of discovery. This emphasis on the generative aspects of form where the observer become participant returns art to an active role rather than continuing it as passive aesthetic consumption.

In this sense Modernism has, through phenomenology, returned art to an engaging and active role, but also to a subjective interpretation that cannot be easily shared or communicated. It is for this reason that Martin Heidegger's work acknowledges phenomenological "seeing" as a creative uncovering that reveals notably the nature of the world in terms of "things themselves," but also in terms of their interrelationships within a common horizon, a region. This requires a poetics that returns us to the origins of meaning and the necessity for ontology of dwelling. Heidegger (1971, 151) writes "In saving the earth, in receiving the sky, in awaiting the divinities, in initiating mortals, dwelling occurs as the fourfold preservation of the fourfold."

Regionalism in these terms of ontology returns us to the significance of mimetic ritual as the means to embody meaning without the split between subject and object that has brought us technological thinking. Heidegger (1977, 48) writes,

> All mere chasing after the future so as to work out a picture of it through calculation in order to extend what is present and half-thought into what, now veiled, is yet to come, itself still moves within the prevailing attitudes belonging to technological, calculating representation. All attempts to reckon existing reality morphologically, psychologically, in terms of decline and loss, in terms of fate, catastrophe, and destruction, are merely technological behavior.

The phenomenology of modernism subscribes to the recovery of immanent experience, which is not subservient to a controlling rationality, and acknowledges the importance of active participation and that object qualities must include the experiential aspects of phenomena.

In rethinking the contribution of Regionalism to a radical ontology and Modernism's relationship to phenomenology, archaic cultures should be reconsidered in their ability to integrate experience through active participation in mimetic rites. In this edifying sense, the relationship between architecture and ritual becomes significant not only in its didactic role, but also in terms of how the "genius loci" is represented.

Dance and building are the two primary arts. While dance is the first art, using the human figure in interpreting life through mime, architecture as an edifice embodies and formalizes mimetic rituals in built form. It can be argued that the forgetfulness of the origins of architecture in these terms has produced an autonomous formalism that no longer is connected to or responsive to the rituals celebrating genius loci. It is with this question in mind that architecture and ritual will be considered in comparing Egyptian architecture and Hopi Pueblo buildings in relationship to regional qualities.

EGYPTIAN ARCHITECTURE AS THE EMBODIMENT OF RITUAL

Two different cultures are chosen here for exploration and examination in terms of the relationship between region and ritual: the culture of ancient Egypt and the Native American tribal culture of the Hopi. Although some speculation about the relationship between Egyptian and South American Indian architecture has been advanced by Thor Heyerdahl, the comparison here will be on how religious rituals relating to regional qualities of place can result in two different manifestations: the symbolic and processional aspects of Egyptian architectural monuments and the Hopi Indians' landscape-oriented and anti-monumental ceremonial dances.

Stability, according to Edward Hall (1976) is an essential quality if human society is to prosper, develop, and evolve to its potential. For the ancient Egyptians, however, regional quality was most desirable and attainable not only through stability, but also through enduringness. Egyptian works were made for eternity; their temples and statues were to last forever, their names were to remain unchanged and enduring. Unfortunately, a popular concept of ancient Egypt typifies Egyptians as being preoccupied with death and tombs. However, it was spiritual instruction that was given the most significance in their architectural representation (Seif 1988).

Unlike the Hopi, ancient Egyptians used architectural monuments as the setting for participatory rites to join living and inanimate things. The function of rituals, which were carried out in the form of processions within temples and sometimes throughout the countryside, was to help the pharaoh perform his duty to administrate and to ensure the well-being of Egypt. The ritual procession serving the god was to harmonize with the movement and the path of the sun; its rising, zenith, and setting. The pharaoh's presence was ensured by the statues and reliefs on the walls of every temple. The participatory rites were performed not only in the ceremonial activities in the temple, but also through the delegation of the Pharaoh's duties. These duties were delegated to priests who were ordinary citizens (serving twice a year for 30 days each time, except for the high priests who served on a full-time basis), which meant that a large number of citizens assumed the duties of priests, a fact that most Egyptology literature ignores (Seif 1988). The social conditions and solidarity of the ancient Egyptians influenced religion as much as, and in many cases maybe more than, religion influenced social conditions. In fact, the spirit and the outward form of religious practices were altered in response to changes in social conditions.

According to the cult of Isis and Osiris, it was the ruler who was sacrificed and put to death in the beginning; later, a symbolic substitution for the ruler was used for this ritual royal sacrifice. The Pharaoh was a dual personality, both god and human. As god he was the giver of all humans, and as a human he was, like other humans, the creation of his own god. "As the king was the embodiment of fertility, he was also the Divine Victim who might be put to death to ensure fertility, when it was expedient that one man should die for the people" (Murray 1964, 110). The ancient Egptian legends show that the sacrifice of the Pharaoh was well known, and it was in "the nature of a rain charm" (Murray 1964, 111).

Egyptian temples included dwellings, workshops, cultivated land, administrative buildings, a school, and a library. This concept of the temple may have been influential in the development of Christian monasteries in the way they functioned as a community. Egyptian forms were based on their symbolic content, and the temples were arranged with regard to ritualistic and mythological needs about which we know little although the architectural forms endure.

The Egyptian temple was not merely a house for the god where he was nourished and protected; it was also the materialization of the celestial horizon from which he appeared or emerged to bring light and energy to the earth. Thus, the temple had to represent both the world and divinity. This sense of wholeness is what the Egyptian sages called the "intelligence of the heart," a cosmic consciousness of the human being. The pharaonic Egyptians utilized symbolism in architecture as an extrarational means of transmitting knowledge for almost 3000 years.

Schwaller de Lubicz (1977) explains that in the ancient temple civilization of Egypt, numbers, our most ancient form of symbol, did not simply designate quantities, but instead were considered to be concrete definitions of energetic formative principles of nature. The Egyptians called these energetic principles *neters*, a word that is conventionally rendered as "gods."

In considering the esoteric meaning of Number, we must avoid the following mistake:

Two is not One and One; it is not a *composite*. It is the multiplying *Work*; it is the notion of the plus in relation to the minus; it is a new *Unity*; it is sexuality; it is the origin of Nature, *Physis*, the Neter *Two*. It is the Culmination (the separating moment of the full moon, for example); it is the line; the stick, movement, the way, Wotan, Odin, the *Neter* Thoth, Mercury, Spirit (Lubicz 1977, 10).

The vital linking up of the mental abstraction of calculation with its counterpart in natural phenomena gave the ancient Egyptian mathematicians a living basis for their science. This science advocated transformations of material existence and considered man as being and containing within himself the entire universe (fig. 19-1). The belief that there will be the inevitable resurrection of the spiritual essence that has involved itself in matter in the form of organic creative energy could only have its source in an agricultural society where the cyclical aspects of life and death were an integral part of existence. The architectural embodiment of this belief necessitated not only symbolic representation, but also a mathematics and geometry that would be integrative and

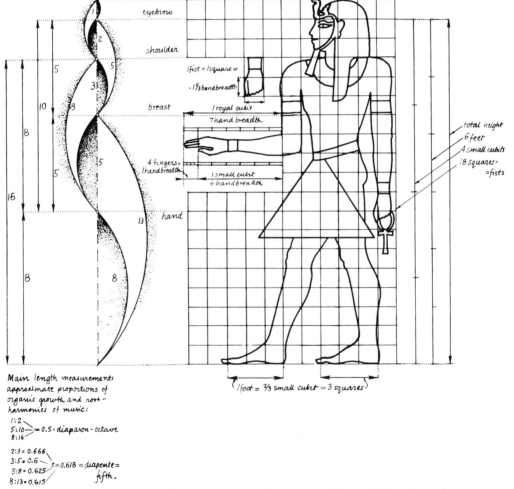

19-1 **Egyptian measures and proportions. Each square of the grid is a fist, corresponding to one-third of a foot. (Source: Gyorgy Doczi 1981, p. 37.)**

transformational in relating the parts to the whole as is the case with the Golden Number (fig. 19-2). While this ordering system and its subsequent use to establish architectural harmony in other periods of architectural history not only show the danger of formal architectural qualities being separated from their origins in a specific culture, it also indicates the possibility of abstraction developing an autonomous existence, like symbols, which can take on a life of their own separate from their original significance. In contrast, Hopi culture, by its emphasis on the immanence of rituals without architectural representation, discouraged a vulgarization of the monumental architectural forms that embodied religious practice (fig. 19-3).

HOPI RITUALS AND THE DEVELOPMENT OF AN ETHICAL IMAGINATION

The centrality of ritual in Hopi culture can be seen in the way buildings are used to frame a plaza in which ceremonial dances are performed. Vincent Scully (1975, 9) draws this conclusion from Benjamin Lee Whorf's study of the Hopi language, where whatever reference there is to words that describe building elements are to an active building usage that does not lend itself to an abstract ordering or architectural space. It is this immanence and analogical relationship between meaning and use that make Hopi

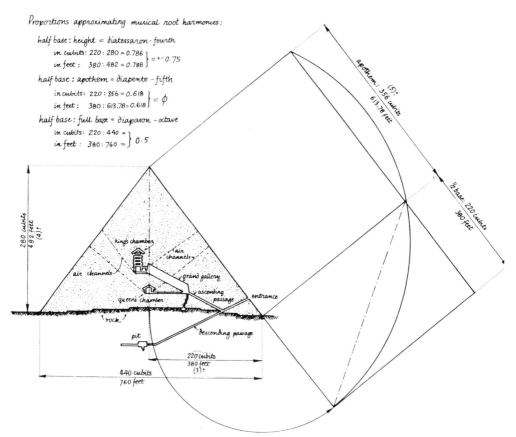

19-2 *Great Pyramid of Cheops at Gizeh. Cross section shows that the apothem and half the base are in golden section relationship. (Source: Gyorgy Doczi 1981, p. 41.)*

building relevant to Modernism's attempt to replace the aesthetic formalism of a rational and categorical ordering of space. Rather than reifying their relationship to landscape, community, and history through architectural monuments or metaphysically categorizing their relationship to their region, the Hopi emphasize the eternal present. By not emphasizing an architectural order of space, they share with archaic Greek religion the mimetic demon dance as the primary means of representing the genius loci.

The importance of the pueblo was therefore not the object qualities of the building, but rather how well it served as the setting for the mimetic enactment of the Hopi relationship to the region that sustains their life. Unlike the highly ordered, abstract, and symbolic architecture of ancient Egypt, which sought permanence in spatial terms, the Hopi emphasized the dance as the means to further a collective ethical imagination.

Bringing order out of the many and diverse sensory impressions of mimetic enactment, the ceremonial plaza was open to the region and its landscape and the focus of communal participation. The ceremonial plaza provided the "primal gathering principle" where the ceremonial event would bring about a collective willing or concentrated prayer force that would align the community with the powers of nature. The religious, in the sense of *religio,* "to bind together," was the central core of Hopi life, and not only buildings but life in general were given an order based on the cyclical

19-3 *Michael Graves, Portland Public Service Building, Portland, Oreg. Fifth Avenue elevation with the pharaoh's head transposed. (Photograph: Farouk Seif 1986.)*

nature of sacred events. In this sense Hopi building was anti-architectural in its denial of any permanent and autonomous form that did not assist in the ritualistic enactment of the community's relationship to the natural world.

The Hopi sense of the immanence and primacy of direct experience is also indicated by the absence of tenses for their verbs. With no past, present, or future in their language, only the eternal present exists, and measurement is not subject to any mechanical notion of time but only to the rhythm of life punctuated and marked by reference to the dance ceremonies held throughout the year (fig. 19-4). In their association with sacred dances, the authority and power of events dominate Hopi life as the open plaza dominates their placement of buildings. These rituals are not only anticipated as an event, but are also preceded by days of preparation in the kiva and followed by several more days of kiva rituals. Indeed rituals are, in D. H. Lawrence's words, "a rhythm of eternity in a rugged, inconsequential life," and in Hopi culture there are seven great ceremonies. All Hopi ceremonies are, in a general sense, for rain, fertility, and growth of crops with the various matriarchal clans in whose hands its principal ceremonies rest. Each clan is to a large extent autonomous, owning its own land and house sites, choosing its own leaders, and transacting its own affairs with a great deal of independence. Such a social system is rather precarious in that the more firmly people adhere to the clan, the weaker must be their village ties.

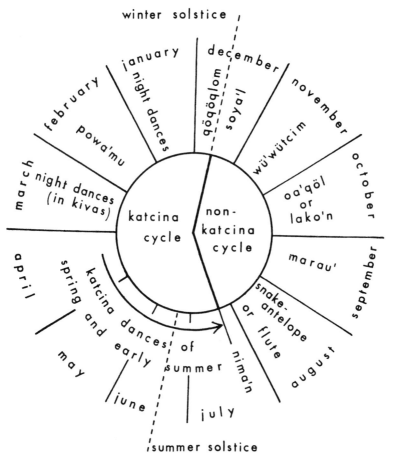

19-4 *Hopi ceremonial cycle. [Redrawn from Wright and Roat (1965), p. 28. Source: Richard Maitland Bradfield (1973), p. 56.]*

Hopi villages could therefore conceivably be in constant danger of dividing into their component parts if it were not for cross-clan marriages and the proper performance of ceremonies, yet another indication of the power that resides in the rituals that require the cooperation between the members of the different clans within the Pueblo. The successful Pueblo is therefore directly related to the cooperative spirit of its clans, which in its social structure are essentially anarchic. Based on cooperative performance and not on codified law, the importance of the representation of common myths that explain the state of things including the emergence of the people from the underworld, the founding of the village, distribution of land, and the establishment of the ceremonial cycle.

In terms of the rites themselves, the Pueblo liturgy includes many elements. Some of them are structures such as the kiva, which serves a dual function as a ceremonial chamber and as a social club, owned by various clans. There are also ritual objects essential to the performance of the ceremony that are kept in the house of the clan that owns the ceremony (fig. 19–5). The preparation includes a sand mosaic at which the prayer sticks or pa'hos will be consecrated. Placed around the sand mosaic in each of the four cardinal directions are form clay stands or patio fields. H. R. Voth, quoted in Bradfield (1973, 76–77), writes about these.

> In these are inserted at one end a small ngolosh-hoya (crook), to which a turkey feather is fastened. The crook is . . . the symbol of life in its various stages. Next to this stands one of the four pa'ho(s), . . . representing corn, the main subsistence of the Hopi. These double pa'ho(s) are sometimes called 'kao (corn ears); and then [carry] a sprig of an herb to which four ququopi, chat (Icteria virens), feathers are tied. Sometimes sikya'tsi (flycatcher) feather are used instead. The herbs differ in the four stands. The one on the north side is a siva'pi [*Chrysothamnus*, or rabbit-brush]; the one on the west a hovak'pi [*Artemisia filifolia*, sand sage] on the south a ho'novi [*Cowania mexicana*, cliff rose], and on the east a maxi siva'pi [another species of *Chrysothamnus*]. These four herbs, and especially; the two varieties of siva'pi, are used in making the wind-breaks in the fields, and their use here signifies a prayer or wish for protection of the plants and corn against the destructive sand storms for which these wind-breaks are made. Next to her herb is inserted an eagle feather, to

19-5 *Powa'lauwn alter [Redrawn from Voth (1910), pl. xliii. Source: Richard Maitland Bradfield (1973), p. 67.]*

which four sikya'tsi (fly-catcher) feathers are tied as a prayer for warm weather when the birds come. As the Hopi use the term sikya'tsi rather promiscuously for different small birds with yellow and greenish feathers, such as the fly-catchers and certain kinds of warblers, it is very probably that feathers of any of these birds are used on this eagle feather. The last object inserted in this pa'ho stand is a short stick called ta'ka pa'ho (man pa'ho), pointed at both ends and made of the stem of tu'mi |*Cleome serrulata*, beeweed|. This stick is colored yellow in the sand on the north side, green on the west, red on the South and white on the east stand. This stick is fastened a yahpa |mockingbird| feather. This pa'ho . . . is said to represent a kaletaka (warrior) standing at the end of the pa'ho stand, keeping watch over and protecting the various objects on the pa'ho stand.

As this detailed description of some aspects of the ritual indicates, both the rites themselves and the preparation for them are based on participation and the furthering of common experience. The ephemeral nature of the religious "altar" as well as other religious objects also indicates the necessity of continuing a practice that has been internalized within each member of the clan.

It is, then, a capability of the Hopi Pueblo to serve as the setting for the furthering of an "ethical imagination" that not only is the basis for the continuance of the community but also binds together (*religio*) the Hopi people with all life, flora as well as fauna, in a continuum that is experienced as an eternal present. The act of making and representing is not based on continuing internalized practices with permanent objects or monuments reifying the religious experience as architecture.

The spiritualization of nature includes, of course, the relationship of the Hopi to the earth and the underworld of origins as well as to the sky and the Cloud People, the dead that serve as beneficial messengers to the deities. There could be no stronger or more completely religious relationship between region and people than that of the Hopi, and it is not surprising that this extension of religious practice to include all of the landscape, animate and inanimate, make them the spiritual guardians of the Southwest.

REGIONALISM IS NOT A STYLE

In considering the parallel development of Regionalism and Modernism, it has been emphasized that both share intentions to further experience in the phenomenological sense by seeking to replace an aesthetic or stylistic emphasis on object qualities with an active and participatory mode of understanding. Religious rituals in the sense of *religio*—to bind together—have provided this spiritualization of nature by sharing the interrelatedness of all things, and the wholeness of this understanding is internalized by participants as religious "practices."

This concentric structure of experience discourages fragmentation and alienation from place through the development of an "ethical imagination" that sees all things as ultimately related. That this wholeness, where the parts are continually reintegrated with the whole through ceremonies, can be thought of as style indicates formalistic misunderstanding and a reification of existence where architecture becomes inauthentic in its forgetfulness of its archaic beginnings. In this sense the archetype degenerates quickly into sterotypes and by simulacra replaces the original ontological role that building can provide in bringing about dwelling.

The "mystique" of Pueblo buildings is the harmony they reveal in relationship to the landscape and in the appropriate response they invite among their dwellers. This authenticity is ontological in providing a setting for a continuum of affirmation of origins and relationships that are sustained through religious practice. In this sense the region is bounded and circumscribed by the space that is consecrated by these rites and the understanding that is granted to the participants.

In comparing ancient Egyptian architecture and the Pueblo building, it is understandable why Egyptian architecture has been more influential in the development of an architectural form language. It is also apparent that it has not been possible to recover the underlying religious origins of the forms as completely as the architectural manifestations of temples and pyramids. That these forms are now once again entering into the architectural form language is a tribute to the autonomous integrity of their form, but, as with style, the symbolism used is no longer binding in the religious or edifying sense. From this perspective, Modernism's critique of the misuse of style is still valid, and it is hoped that Modernism's contribution to the recovery of the spiritual in art will not be lost as has been the case with other efforts that emphasized the immanent over the monumental. Regionalism in this sense can remain authentic only as long as the "ethical imagination" is nurtured through an enactment of rituals that unite the "intelligence of the heart" of the community participants with an understanding of their needs and the ability of the land to sustain them. This continuing reinterpretation of community origins and relationship to the natural landscape reaffirms the primacy of dance as the mimetic representation that precedes built form, making architecture secondary as the setting for participatory rituals in the Hopi culture.

REFERENCES

BACON, EDMUND. 1967. *The Design of Cities*. New York: Viking Press.

BRADFIELD, RICHARD MAITLAND. 1973. *A Natural History of Associations, A Study in The Meaning of Community*. London: Duckworth.

CENIVAL, JEAN-LOUIS DE. 1964. *Living Architecture: Egyptian*. New York: Grosset & Dunlap.

DOCZI, GYORGY. 1981. *The Power of Limits: Proportional Harmonies in Nature, Art & Architecture*. Boulder, Colo.: Shambhala Publications, Inc.

FRAMPTON, KENNETH. 1983. "Prospects for a Critical Regionalism." *Perspecta 20*. Cambridge, Mass.: MIT Press.

HALL, EDWARD T. 1976. *Beyond Culture*, Garden City, N.Y.: Anchor Press/Doubleday.

HEIDEGGER, MARTIN. 1971. *Poetry, Language, Thoughts*. Trans. Albert Hofstadter. New York: Harper & Row.

_____. 1977. *The Question Concerning Technology*. Transl. William Lovitt. New York: Garland.

LUBICZ, R.A. SCHWALLER DE. 1977. *The Temple in Man, The Secrets of Ancient Egypt*. Trans. R. & D. Lawlor. Brookline, Mass.: Autumn Press.

MUMFORD, LEWIS. 1951. *The Conduct of Life*. New York: Harcourt, Brace.

_____. 1966. *The Myth of the Machine, Technics and Human Development*. New York: Harcourt, Brace & World.

MURRAY, MARGARET A. 1964. *The Splendor That Was Egypt*. New York: Frederick A. Praeger.

RELPHS, E. 1976. *Place and Placelessness*. London: Pion.

SCULLY, VINCENT. 1975. *Pueblo: Mountain, Village, Dance*. New York: Viking Press.

SEIF, FAROUK. 1986. "At Home—Away From Home." Working paper.

_____. 1988. "Ethics and Ritual as a Dual Necessity for Regional Reality." Paper submitted to Regionalism Seminar, University of Washington, Seattle.

SHEPHERD, PAUL. 1967. *Man in the Landscape*. New York: Knopf/Random House.

TYRWHITT, JACQUELINE. 1947. *Patrick Geddes in India*. London: Humphries.

20   On Regions and Regionalism

Amos Rapoport

Having been asked to address regionalism in general, I will approach it broadly.

WHAT IS REGIONALISM?

I have long argued that built environments are more than buildings. They comprise those *systems of settings* within which people live, act, and behave [cf. Rapoport 1977, 1980a, 1982b, 1985a, 1986a, in 1989]. These in turn comprise *cultural landscapes*, which now include most landscapes; all, even "natural" settings, have been greatly modified by human action. The study of regionalism in environmental design, therefore, concerns the properties of cultural landscapes of regions rather than buildings.

What, then are regions?

The View from Different Disciplines

"Region" originally referred to political control (from the Latin *regere*, to rule or govern). It is still used in political science and international relations to refer to the territorial basis of government, but it has also been used to study the arts and aesthetics (Odum and Moore 1938, 167–8). There are "regional painters," such as Curry, Wood, and Benton in the United States (Liffring-Zug 1977; Czestochowski 1981), and the relation of paintings to regional landscapes has been studied (Klitgaard 1941). Natural regions have been defined on the basis of climate, vegetation, and soils, and their landscapes have been related to geomorphology and regional geology.

While the concept of "region" has proved useful in many disciplines, it has been basic to one—geography. It has been said that all geography is either *systematic* (dealing with systems) or *regional*, and there are even textbooks on regionalism (Zimolzak and Stansfield 1983; de Blij and Muller 1986). The concept of cultural landscape also comes from geography.

Strangely, while geography is concerned with "landscape and the geography of culture" (de Blij and Muller 1986, Ch. 4), regional landscapes have been neglected. For one thing, natural regions based on climate, vegetation, geomorphology, geology, and so on, have not been integrated with human geography and social science. Between the 1930s and 1970s the emphasis was primarily on economic regions. Only since the 1970s has there been interest in social and cultural aspects of regions (Gastil 1975; Jordan 1978; Zelinsky 1980; Rooney et al. 1982). The emphasis has still not been on cultural landscapes.

Studies have referred to data needed but still missing, among them data on funeral practices, folk medicine, festivals and holidays, handicrafts, and myths, legends, and proverbs (Rooney et al. 1982).

Certain single attributes of cultural landscapes have been used: settlement forms and patterns, house styles, barns and other structures, ruins, land subdivision, and place names. Important components of cultural landscapes such as spatial character (Siksna 1981), planting, and vegetation in private gardens and urban public spaces (as opposed to fields) (E. H. Rapoport and Lopez-Moreno 1987, 46–50, 63–6; references to Kimber, Anderson, and others in Rapoport 1977, 1982a; articles in the journal *Urban Ecology*, etc.) have been neglected. Different plantings can result in very different cities [e.g., Tucson vs. Phoenix (cf. Jackovics and Saarinen 1978)] and regions. Even more serious has been the neglect of cultural landscapes as a whole.

The criteria used have resulted in maps with different numbers of regions or subregions, such as the Southwest, New England, and the Midwest; the Mormon and Pennsylvania cultural regions; the Sunbelt, Frostbelt, and Rustbelt; the "frontier" and the "Bible belt," and so on (Gastil 1975; Zelinsky 1980; Rooney et al. 1982; Glass 1986).

Clearly, an infinite number of regions are possible, depending on what is being analyzed. This means that in mapping exercises there is no right or wrong way to define regions (Gastil 1975, 39; Zelinsky 1982). Typically, more than one attribute has been used, so that regions are based on multiple attributes. Thus a recent major atlas of North American regions (Rooney et al. 1982) uses twelve major categories of attributes to produce 387 maps of the United States and Canada.

There are genuine cultural regions where a number of attributes do coincide. One example is a region based on the congruence between dialects, place-names, religion, ethnicity, architecture, diet, and political behavior (Zelinsky 1982, Fig. 1-3). Another is the definition of the Pennsylvania cultural region based on the barn forebay, which agrees with the definitions based on farmhouses and farmsteads, settlement form, street patterns, and others from six independent studies. The barn forebay then becomes a *diagnostic feature*, a surrogate for a larger set, more easily used in mappings (Glass 1986).

In such cultural regions there is a relative uniformity of cultural traditions and practices that results in areas of distinctive material culture. The more congruence between those, the greater the redundancy and the more distinctive the region and its boundaries (Rapoport 1977, 1982a). Old World regions are more distinct than North American regions, because such distinctiveness is related to tradition and opposed to and by modernism; in that sense regional is traditional, hence often rural rather than urban, local as opposed to cosmopolitan or international, peripheral as opposed to "of the center" (Rapoport 1988b).

The role of redundancy in strengthening distinctiveness introduces the notion of *emic* definitions of regions. The studies discussed have been *etic*: regions have been defined and mapped by researchers, scholars, governments, businesses, and the like. There is a small body of work on vernacular or popular regions, those based on the public's perception (Jordan 1978; Zelinsky 1980; Rooney et al. 1982, Chs. 1 and 13).

The importance of emics is generally well established (Rapoport 1977, 1980a, 1980b, 1982a). For regionalism this importance is twofold. First, etic and emic definitions often differ. Thus there seem to be popular "misconceptions" about the attributes of the Pennsylvania cultural region; even painters and writers depict it "wrongly"; that is, the public uses attributes different from those used by Glass (1986, 229–30). This means that the perceived (emic) landscape is likely to be very different from the analytic (etic) one. For example, insiders and outsiders perceive different attributes of urban areas, rank them differently in importance, and evaluate them differently (Brower 1985).

There is a second reason why emic definitions are important. This relates to the role of noticeable differences with respect to the congruence of attributes and redundancy. While there are an infinite number of etic regions, there are fewer emic regions. In effect there is less choice—they are either perceived or not. This makes them more "natural," less arbitrary, and thus easier to define.

Commonalities Among the Views of Different Disciplines

All disciplines seem to agree that regions (and hence regionalism) involve *diversity at the areal level* and hence *distinctiveness*. This may be why regional architecture is often identified with the vernacular, implying a combination of "local" and "traditional" (or indigenous) architecture.[1] I define "vernacular," whether referring to language, art, poetry, or architecture, as belonging to, developed by, and used by people of a particular locality or region. This implies some identity, *some recognizable qualities or uniqueness that make it different from other places*.

An informal analysis of a list of twenty-eight definitions of "region" from a variety of disciplines (Odum and Moore 1938) shows similar commonality: differences among areas that are homogeneous in terms of activities, behavior, demographics, psychology, and culture interacting with natural characteristics and economics result in regions.

In effect, regions are useful concepts because the world is not uniform: they help to describe, understand, and control place-to-place differences. *A region, then, is any portion of the earth's surface that stands apart in terms of a given characteristic or set of characteristics* (Zelinsky 1982). Regionalism thus involves two ingredients: the intellectual concept of "region" and the concrete manifestations of distinctive areas differing in the attributes that characterize them. These attributes are relatively uniform or homogeneous, so that the differences within a region are less than those among regions [analogous to group differences (Rapoport 1980b, 1989)].

A region is thus homogeneous only taken as a whole in comparison to other regions. Internal variability is overlooked, and lesser irregularities are ignored. Regions are areas *reasonably* lacking in internal differences, with recognizable and mappable limits, and differing significantly from other cultural regions (Zelinsky 1982). The result is a distinctive *personality*,[2] *character*, or *ambience*, often noticed or felt when crossing regional boundaries.

All this makes "region" both a relative and highly generalized concept—often overgeneralized and hence *too large*. This process of generalizing the character of regions into stereotypes or icons that are attached to regional landscapes and their people (Jakle 1987, 241–2) is important, however. It creates expectations about regions and their inhabitants that play a role in people's reactions to regions.

Also common to the various approaches is the view that regionalism implies the existence of different, identifiable cultural groups occupying distinct areas. The attributes that characterize a region typically involve, at least initially, groups and the boundaries between them, so that regions as geographically identifiable entities are related to *identity in areas of various scales*. The question of scale thus requires discussion.

I have already suggested that most U.S. geographical regions seem too large. Thus Gastil (1975) divides the United States into thirteen regions; Zelinsky in his earlier work identified five first-order regions within which were to be found second- and third-order regions. But clearly "the South" or "the West" are far too large. Philip Lewis has shown that Wisconsin alone has seventeen or eighteen distinct natural landscapes. Significantly, the few emic studies lead to smaller regions. Zelinsky (1980) finds fourteen U.S. regions, while Jordan (1978) identifies twenty-nine regions in Texas alone.

The scale of regions is ambiguous. "Regional" is sometimes contrasted with "local" (Vink 1983, 232), but the distinction is unclear. A sequence exists, starting with the earth, through continents, subcontinents, countries, through regions, cities, and neighborhoods, to smaller entities. Intuitively regions imply the *mesoscale*, but this also is ambiguous. Clearly, regions involve both *scale* and *character* or *ambience*; while the latter is my main concern, the former cannot be ignored.

Regions in Environmental Design

For the present purpose, the earlier definition of region can be restated as follows:

> *A region is any portion of the earth's surface that stands apart from others in terms of that set of perceptible characteristics (in all sensory modalities) that produce a cultural landscape with a distinct character or ambience.*

Several points need emphasis.

1. Only some of the many attributes used to define regions are relevant—those that directly or indirectly affect cultural landscapes.
2. These attributes need to form sets that describe ambience.
3. My emphasis is not on mapping regions but on their perceptible character; this implies emic regions. Thus regionalism is part of environmental perception and cognition (Rapoport 1977); the distinctive ambience of regions is a function of *noticeable differences* (Rapoport 1977, 1982a, 1983a.)

Etic attributes remain useful, and both types of definitions need to be compared. Also, etic attributes, if potentially significant but not noticed, can suggest planning or design interventions to make them noticeable.

The concept of landscape that distinguishes among regions is relatively recent, traceable to the Renaissance. It has also changed recently; rather than referring to artistic and literary representations of the visible world, as it did through the nineteenth century, it has come to refer to the integration of natural and human phenomena on a portion of the earth's surface (Cosgrove 1984; Jackson 1984; Meinig 1979). In this view, landscapes are taken to be intimately related to human life and are primarily for living and working in rather than just for looking at. They are also always symbolic; that is, they have meaning (Rapoport 1982a).

The emphasis on the perceptible character of such landscapes means that the impact of human action is most important—and that occurs over time, so that a cultural landscape is the result of a complex history (Yates 1985). As a result, cultural landscapes often have significant historical continuities, so regions have historical roots related to the groups that have occupied them. The cultural landscape of regions is the result of the interaction of physiographic regions, resources, populations and their cultures, and history. It follows that cultural landscapes become the property of groups and help to identify them and distinguish among them. In this way regions are linked to culture; they describe bundles of traits that seem to hang together and identify groups and areas over time (Gastil 1975, 47).

Since present cultural landscapes are the result of the sum total of human activities over time, one needs to consider how they come to be and also how they change.

I have previously drawn attention to a most important characteristic of cultural landscapes. While they are the result of innumerable independent decisions by many individuals and groups over long periods of time, they take on highly recognizable form; in effect, they produce a style (Rapoport 1972, 1977, 1981a, 1984, 1986b).

Two important inferences follow. The first is that the people involved in making decisions *must share schemata*. The second is that these schemata, often embodying ideal landscapes, are expressed through the application of *systems of rules*, which provide the frameworks within which the independent decisions "add up." Both schemata and rules, in turn, are linked to life-styles, values, world views, and, ultimately, culture. Their role, through systematic choices, in achieving the level of distinctiveness of an area that is a regional landscape implies both sociocultural homogeneity and residential clustering.

In general, the persistence of strong cultural orders depends on conservatism, that is, tradition-oriented people unwilling to alter that which has worked and is time-honored (Glass 1986; Hakim 1986; Rapoport 1988b.) As tradition weakens or disappears, so do the degree of sharing of schemata, the strength of rules, and hence regional differences.

Before these matters can be discussed, however, it is necessary to identify the attributes of regions.

WHAT ARE THE ATTRIBUTES OF REGIONS?

From the present perspective, there are several problems with the attributes generally identified in the study of regions. The concern has been primarily with etic attributes that can be mapped rather than with publicly perceptible, or emic, attributes. Clearly, no single attribute can account for the character of a region; there must be many attributes working together.

Let us derive a set of attributes that might describe the character of regional landscapes. The outcome will be a lexicon of likely potential attributes that characterize cultural landscapes and describe the ambience of regions. Although in principle these attributes must be noticed and used, even if only subliminally, at this stage our question cannot be answered, since there is no work on the emics of cultural landscapes. However, a number of ways of studying such questions have been developed (Low and Ryan 1985; Groat 1986).

I am not suggesting that cultural landscapes are identified in this way; they are not. Usually one perceives a total gestalt or ambience intuitively and affectively. It can, however, then be checked in terms of multiple attributes and their specific profiles [Rapoport 1988b, in press (b)]. Only these attributes that influence the perceptible character of regions directly or indirectly need to be considered.

In this chapter I combine all sensory modalities. I distinguish among natural components of landscapes, those modified by human action, and man-made elements. I also distinguish between fixed, semifixed, and nonfixed features (Rapoport 1977, 1982a).

My main purpose is to show the number and variety of attributes that comprise the character of regions on the basis of cultural landscapes rather than building styles. Eventually, using the idea of profiles analogous to those I have suggested for environmental quality and life-style (Rapoport 1985a; 1985b), it should be possible to describe the ambience of regions.

A very large set of potentially noticeable attributes are needed to characterize the ambience of cultural landscapes and distinguish among regions.

I have already suggested that, for example, in the case of vernacular design or tradition one must move away from ideal-type definitions or characterizations based on single attributes or small sets of them [Rapoport 1982c, 1988a, 1988b, in press (b)]. Rather, one must use sets of multiple attributes. In such cases, not every member of a type must have all the qualifying attributes; one finds a range of variations within defined limits so that each member of the type possesses many of the attributes, and each attribute may be shared by many members of the type. Thus no single attribute (or even a small set of attributes) is both sufficient and necessary for membership in the type.[3]

It follows that regional character will also have to be defined by a large number of attributes, not all of which will necessarily play a role in any given case. Rarely can all attributes be present and congruent in any given case, although redundancy is possible and desirable. The result will be a profile of attributes that may communicate ambience.

CAN THESE ATTRIBUTES BE USED, AND IF SO, HOW?

I have previously suggested that four attitudes are possible regarding vernacular design [Rapoport 1982c; in press (b)] or traditional built environments (Rapoport 1983a, 1983b). Designers can ignore, reject, or copy them—or try to learn from them. I have argued that neither ignoring nor rejection can be justified. Copying fails because the results are often rejected by users (Rapoport 1983b, especially p. 253); more important, the results tend to be unsatisfactory. Thus vernacular design and traditional settlements must be analyzed and principles and lessons applicable to planning and design derived. This also applies to regional cultural landscapes; they must be analyzed into potentially relevant attributes that might be usable, although consider-able interdisciplinary research will be needed for this approach to become useful.

To understand how such attributes should be used, it is useful to know how they should *not* be used. Consider another example of copying. It concerns a "Maine style" in domestic architecture, discussed in a special issue on shelter in the regional (!!) magazine *Down East* (1986).[4] There is one photograph of a unique local farm—a connected farm (Hubka 1984) and a few examples of past architects' work that hardly seem unique to Maine. A few architectural elements, arbitrarily selected, then sup-posedly influence some designs. Those could, in fact, be anywhere and are justified in terms of general architectural rationales. Moreover, not only can the designs not be linked to local examples, but most seen antithetical to them. More serious, however, is the neglect of the cultural landscape. Some of its natural attributes are seen in a photograph of Southwest Harbor, Maine (Jakle 1985, 208); no buildings are shown, but the rockbound coast and vegetation are distinctive. Other natural features and Maine buildings, roads, settlements, fields, semifixed elements, the relationships among them, and so on may also be distinctive. By generating an attribute list of the Maine cultural landscape, a possible Maine style, if there is one, might be found. Such an analysis needs to be done over time, because different elements change at different rates (Rapoport 1983b).

This suggests an important general point: *not all elements, settings, buildings, or parts of the cultural landscape are equally likely to retain regional character, or equally capable of being made "regional."* Note that this differentiation into many specialized settings is very different from traditional built environments (Rapoport 1988b; 1989).

It may thus be that "regional character" may be differentially relevant to different parts of the cultural landscape: to parks and gardens more than fields; to pedestrian streets more than freeways; to housing and neighborhoods more than banks. More-over, for any given environment, there may be important differences in housing and neighborhoods for different groups, for example, science vs. humanities buildings in a university.

There are also other reasons why regional character cannot be achieved by copying elements of buildings. Even when clear-cut stylistic and material attributes can be identified and are applied to appropriate settings (e.g., the new parliament in Denpasar or the new tourist hotel at Nusa Dua, both in Bali), they may not work. The scale may be wrong, or the relationships among the elements—among the buildings or between buildings and the larger landscape. In general, shared schemata are more likely and easier to use at relatively small scales; regions will be correspondingly small. In cities, for example, only small areas can be preserved, and often with difficulty.

The key to retaining regional character is the cultural landscape, but it is not enough merely to inventory its attributes. In order to preserve, control, or develop its character one needs to consider and understand its nonfixed features, its people and their culture, behavior, and so on. Although one cannot control them, one can plan for their clustering and homogeneity (Rapoport 1977, 1980/81, 1982a). More can be done with the semifixed and fixed feature elements, modified by human action and man-made, and their relationships to the natural landscape as well as the meaning these have for people (Rapoport 1982a). It is also important to understand the relation of the cultural landscape to the culture that created it, particularly the process of their creation, how the values, ideals, schemata, and rules used in the choice process that is design lead to the systematic choices that produce style or character.

The design of specifics will rarely help retain or strengthen important attributes. After all, as we have seen, cultural landscapes are never, or hardly ever, "designed." A more fruitful approach seems to be to understand the ordering principles, the rule systems that produce frameworks that allow many independent design decisions to cohere and the critical attributes to emerge. The goal may be to "design" regulations, codes, or controls that lead to the desired or appropriate attributes and thus preserve and strengthen the existing cultural landscapes of regions.

SOME EXAMPLES

By and large the three examples discussed in this section try to identify the important attributes of the places in question, although none study emics—those attributes that are noticed and communicate appropriate meanings, that is, regional identity (cf. Low and Ryan 1985). All examples go beyond architectural style and deal with the cultural landscape. They also go beyond mere copying, as found in the neovernacular of Great Britain or the new tourist towns of the French Riviera. All try to preserve regional character by making new development fit in, and all adopt an approach based on developing a rule system embodied in codes or regulations.

The three examples to follow are concerned with context and continuity, with fitting new development into the fabric of a cultural landscape, either an existing or created landscape. Here again, if things are to fit, one must identify the emics of the attributes of both the existing fabric and new work (Groat 1986). None of the three examples do that.

The first example is the San Francisco Planning Code, which dates from 1978. It covers 70 percent of the city area, trying to make new development achieve the distinctive character of the urban landscape (Vernez Moudon et al. 1980; Vernez Moudon 1986). This code was based on an etic analysis of the unique urban fabric of San Francisco (Vernez Moudon 1986). Among the attributes identified are the fine grain and scale of dwellings resulting from the original land subdivision (narrow and deep lots); the three-dimensional additive quality; the resulting complexity; how dwellings meet the ground; rhythms; solid–void relations; responses to topography; and so on.

The second and most recent example is the work of Duany and Plater-Zyber (*Lotus International* 1986; Leigh Brown 1988). An analysis of traditional small towns is used to derive their critical attributes. Codes are then produced to guide development, leading to urban landscapes with the "look and feel of a traditional town" (Leigh Brown 1988). As in the other cases I am less concerned with whether the attempts (in Town of Lakes Inn, Seaside, and Kentlands) are successful and with whether the attributes identified are valid than with the approach. As usual, there is an attempt to identify important attributes, although in addition to the usual lack of emic analysis there may also be too much generalization: too diverse a set of towns is analyzed, and regional issues are neglected. Then too there is an emphasis on rules rather than on design per se.

The earliest and still the most comprehensive example of the applied analysis of regional attributes is the Essex *Design Guide* (Essex County Council 1973). This was an attempt to preserve the traditional cultural landscape of an English county through a code controlling new residential development. It was meant to preserve attributes identified as constituting the distinctive cultural landscape of Essex. A large set of attributes were identified and illustrated, both in a traditional version and through examples of new development.

It is significant that all three of these attempts to maintain a region's architectural identity begin by identifying multiple attributes of the cultural landscape and then devise guidelines and regulations rather than designing elements. They thus depend on rule systems to ensure systematic choices and to create frameworks within which many independent design decisions will cohere into distinctive cultural landscapes. Whether they actually do, whether the attributes are correct, whether the public would agree and so on is not the point. What is important is the commonality among these attempts and their link to what seems to be the most critical aspect of cultural landscapes from an analytic viewpoint.

Since shared schemata and clustering of homogeneous groups are both declining, the approach taken, based on rules, may be the only one feasible. But is it useful to try?

WHY REGIONALISM?

I have assumed that concern about regional character is sensible. It needs to be discussed, however, because regionalism seems to be weakening. Schemata are less shared; homogeneous groups cluster less—and find it more difficult. In the past, regional distinctiveness defined groups; since the populations in the examples just discussed are all heterogeneous, the distinctiveness sought may no longer be appropriate. With modernization, regional differences weaken, because material culture in traditional societies varies in space, and in modern societies, over time (Glassie 1968). The clearest regional landscapes are thus found in traditional societies (Rapoport 1988b; Glass 1986; Nemeth 1987; Hakim 1986; Al Sayyad 1987). The "natural" development is thus away from regionalism. This is aided by the increasing dominance of central governments, egalitarian policies, administrative changes, national statistics, mass marketing and consumption, national and international brands and media, and mobility; all tend to weaken regional life-styles and landscape and reduce regional distinctiveness.

But these are countertrends. Interest in regionalism and its use to organize knowledge have had ups and downs generally, in geography, in environmental design, and so on. Thus, loss of salience is not always permanent. Many aspects of regionalism still seem important. "Sense of place" and identification with areas survive, even if the distinctiveness is less and boundaries uncertain. There are even arguments for the growing importance of regions; at the very least there has been less decline than expected. Regional differences persist in North America (Jakle 1985, 193), and predictions about the loss of regional accents, food, the look of buildings, and so on have been exaggerated (eg., see *Congressional Quarterly* 1980).[6] Life-styles still vary, even between northern and southern California; interest in regional cooking is growing, and regional differences in preferences persist and affect advertising and marketing.

The persistence of regions resembles that of urban neighborhoods (Rapoport 1977; 1980/81), which may, in fact, be getting stronger.[7] While no longer the setting for the whole of life, they are important intermediates between the metropolis and the individual. As institutions become larger and societies more pluralistic and fragmented in terms of life-styles, ethnicity, and such, intermediate or mediating structures become more important; this can be seen, for example, in developing countries (Berger 1981; 1983). Such structures often need supportive built environments, one aspect of which may be distinctive cultural landscapes. These can then be justified because they are supportive in various ways, such as instrumentally, in terms of meaning, identity, and defensive structuring. This suggests that regional attributes, including those of architecture, have meaning and can become important for symbolic and political purposes. Thus regional landscapes are not only nostalgic but also symbolic; meaning is central but has been neglected (Rapoport 1982a; 1988c).

Many arguments in favor of regional distinctiveness of built environments ultimately relate to one theme—"sense of place" (Eyles 1985; Jackovics and Saarinen 1978), or *genius loci*—a concept already emphasized in the 1950s by Gordon Cullen and the English Townscape group, who, in effect, tried to identify the attributes of townscapes.[8]

These concepts are taken to have value in themselves, because they preserve the knowledge and experience incorporated in them (Rapoport 1978; 1980b) and because of the complexity generated by transitions among distinct areas (Rapoport 1977). This has implications for tourism.

The attributes of distinctive regional character often identify preferred landscapes. These can be found by content analysis of writings, paintings, films, photographs, postcards, posters, guidebooks, and tourist literature (Rapoport 1969; 1973a; 1977; 1982a). The attributes of preferred landscapes can also be revealed by the extent of tourism. In addition to these possible relationships between tourism and regionalism, there are also possible links related to the feasibility of preserving regional identity.

The various possible reasons for preserving regional identity discussed so far are all based on fairly abstract concepts difficult for decision makers to accept. However, a case could be made for the instrumental importance of preferred landscapes and the complexity due to transitions among distinct regions, that is, for the instrumental importance of environmental regionalism for tourism.

Tourism is becoming ever more important (cf. Hart 1975, 171; MacConnell 1976) and "is going to be the No. 1 industry in the world by the year 2000" (*New York Times* 1988b). Tourism also often leads to the loss of regional identity. Awareness that this loss is an economic as well as cultural or aesthetic problem may help reverse it.

We have seen that there are ways to identify the attributes of places that attract tourists. For example, one could identify the attributes that make New Mexico a "Land of Enchantment." Identity and distinctiveness are certainly important—and clearly related to regionalism. It is significant that many years ago Aldo Leopold suggested that uniqueness was a major characteristic of natural landscape value. Also, as early as the nineteenth and early twentieth century, many travelers commented negatively about the sameness of North American cultural landscapes (Jakle 1985, 200). The successive tourist "invasions" of Europe, Latin America, Asia, Africa, even Antarctica, strongly suggest a search for experience and authenticity (MacConnell 1976). Tourists are in search of a system of attractions that includes natural, cultural, and technological aspects of landscapes as well as museums; they go to see a society, its life and works, even if they are not consciously aware of doing so (MacConnell 1976, 15, 23, 78, 88). Clearly, the attributes I have identified include all of those.

"Tourists," however, is clearly an overgeneralization. Tourists vary, and different types of tourists—for example, those with a high need for authenticity as opposed to those with a low need—will seek out different experiences and hence evaluate different types of tourist space very differently (Cohen 1979). There is thus a need for a variety of equivalent regional landscapes.

In their search for experience, tourists look for folk music, costumes, art, decor, handicrafts, food—and clearly also buildings and cultural landscapes, particularly premodern ones, that emphasize what modernity is not (MacConnell 1976, 8–9), one aspect being clear regional differences (Rapoport 1988b).

This search begins with schemata. As always, people match their expectations against reality (Rapoport 1977). Validating expectations by matching them with reality is particularly important in tourism. Jakle (1985, 40) cites Gunn (1972), who, in a work on designing tourist regions, suggests a three-phase process of such place validation.

- First, *hypotheses* or expectations about the qualities of places are developed, based on information from newspapers, novels, films, television programs, posters, slides, guidebooks, and so on.
- *Input*, the direct immediate perception of the attributes of a place (in all sensory modalities) follows.
- Third, there is *checking*, the evaluation of expectations against perceived reality.

When expectations are inflated, there is disappointment; when actuality exceeds expectations, there is exhilaration (Jakle 1985).

Tourist environments that are thus experienced fit within a range of scales, from interiors and buildings, sites, scenic vantage points, and natural features; through neighborhoods, cities, and regions; to countries and continents (Pearce 1982, 99; MacConnell 1976, 50). Regional landscapes can become objets d'art (Pearce 1982, 82); they can be "museumized" (MacConnell 1976, 8–9).

In all this, the ambience or personality of regional cultural landscapes, including people and their actions, their distinctiveness, vividness, and colorfulness, and the unpredictability of unfamiliar orders (Rapoport 1984) all play an important role. Regions themselves become attractions (Jakle 1985, 199–224), and as a concept they help organize the diversity of attributes encountered in travel (if these are noticeable). It follows that homogenization, which destroys regional distinctiveness, reduces those qualities and makes tourism less interesting and more *commonplace* (Jakle 1985, 193)—a term Jakle rightly prefers to Relph's "placelessness."

We have seen the role that the testing of schemata, stereotypes, or readily recognized icons plays in travel, and these are based on the attributes that differentiate regions. These can be elusive, so that people tend to look for the obvious and ignore subtleties, and redundancy leading to noticeable differences is important for tourist regions.

History plays an important role in regional distinctiveness and character and is an attraction in itself (MacConnell 1976; Jakle 1985, 286; Rosenow and Pulsipher 1979); tourists look for "living reminders of the past" (Pearce 1982, 88). Tourists' sense of history may be inaccurate, but it is important to travel; many tourist attractions involve the past. Each place, at whatever scale, has a specific past and elements that symbolize it. Since cultural landscapes are inherently historical, so are many of the attributes that make them distinct.

Diversity among places is therefore essential in the new tourism, which depends on successful preservation of the identity and character of places and the attributes of cultural landscapes. Since this has clear economic benefits, *tourism can play a role in helping to preserve such diversity* (see, e.g., Rosenow and Pulsipher 1979). Because it becomes useful to preserve the distinctive attributes of areas, the needs of tourism and regionalism tend to coincide. The former may help the latter by giving it a *raison d'etre* that is culturally and politically appropriate and acceptable, particularly since it also involves some of the other rationales already discussed.

A case can thus be made that regions and regionalism are still worth preserving.

THE FUTURE

Prediction is risky. Also, the future of regionalism generally, and of environmental design specifically, depends not only on unpredictable broad social and cultural developments but also on economic and political aspects of implementation. A few observations may be useful, however.

In the previous section I discussed trends toward both the persistence and decline of regional differences. The future depends on which prevails.

Regional survival has been greater than expected, and the leveling tendencies exaggerated. Even mobility does not necessarily reduce regional differences. The differential attraction of the attributes of different regions, that is, habitat selection, tends to maintain and recreate regional differences, as it does neighborhood distinctiveness (Rapoport 1977; 1980/81). In many countries regions are becoming more important. Hardly a day goes by without news of major conflicts all over the world and, on July 5, 1988, the Soviet Union decided to "create conditions for the greater independence of regions" (*New York Times* 1988a). Regional differences in culture, language, religion, and so on are thriving, and the future of groups seems guaranteed.

Diversity and pluralism characterize most countries. There are also calls for understanding regional variations and using regions in planning and policy evaluation; these emphasize that by building on existing spatial cultural variations, the quality of life can be improved. The revival of regional awareness is worldwide. Interest in folk art, crafts, and food; tourism in search of differences; and the normative arguments of scholars and planners suggest a sound future for regionalism generally.

The future of regional cultural landscapes may be more problematic. Growing group diversity is not reflected in cultural landscapes, either because groups do not cluster, because of lagging planning and design responses (Rapoport 1985a; 1985b), or because of unpalatable ideological implications (Rapoport 1986b). This may, however, be changing.

There are advantages to standardization and good reasons for uniformity such as easy communication and greatly increased predictability (Rapoport 1973c, 1982a). Hotel and restaurant chains possibly neither should nor can be regional, or only to a limited extent, which may already exist. While research is needed, for example, on regional differences among franchise food operations or roadside strips, this possibility relates to my discussion of the possible differential appropriateness of regional character in different settings.

Clearly, different types of tourists (cf. Cohen 1979) expect and prefer different degrees of standardization, but two of the five major components of tourist attractiveness discussed earlier (Pearce 1982, 5) may threaten regional character. Two, in fact, help the survival of regional distinctiveness (natural and historical attributes) and often receive protection. Another ("social indices") refers to nonfixed feature attributes and can help preserve regional character. Two seem to be threats but need not be, given awareness of the value of distinctive places. For example, there is room for both standarized shopping areas and local versions, such as outdoor markets or bazaars; the same applies to recreation. The infrastructure for tourist comfort seems the biggest threat to regional character, but alternatives exist. Thus, it proved possible to combine a standard tourist hotel program with the vernacular regional landscape of the Greek island of Ios by identifying and making use of its attributes (Evrenoglou 1981).

Regions may also offer more suitable ways to respond to diversity than do groups themselves. The proliferation of groups may entail dangers by disrupting larger structures and being divisive. Actions on a regional basis can by community-forming rather than divisive (Gastil 1975). Not only do residents identify with cultural landscapes of regions, but by choosing where to live, and hence clustering by habitat selection, newcomers also identify with these landscapes, even though they reflect earlier patterns. Starting with regions a new synthesis becomes possible, and material cultural attributes of newly arrived or newly assertive groups can be incorporated, particularly through semifixed elements. Change and innovation can occur within the regional framework, and variety and diversity can survive. Things will change, but because of different starting points and different trajectories they will change differently. Among the many attributes of each region, emphasis may be on natural features, ecological complexes, festivals and parades, architecture, landscaping, different great or lesser cultural traditions, and so on. *The different combination of different traits* should lead to varied regional landscapes without their being frozen or copied or becoming museums. Once the important attributes, both existing and new, have been identified, appropriate rules can produce frameworks within which individual decisions will "add up," resulting in the desired regional character. Habitat selection from among the increased diversity will further tend to reinforce this, partly through clustering.[9]

There is thus at least a possible future for regional cultural landscapes, although their likelihood of survival is uncertain. There are discouraging signs in housing. We have seen that the past is often explicitly rejected in developing countries (Rapoport 1982a; 1983b; 1986b); implicit rejection is also found. In Indonesia, Corinthian precast columns are sold everywhere and widely used; "Spanish-style" houses are extremely popular and are found even in spontaneous settlements. In Bangkok, English castles, Mediterranean terraces, Bavarian half-timbered cottages, and Roman villas are extremely popular among those who can afford them—a symptom of a "penchant for European exotica" (*Milwaukee Journal* 1988). While I have also discussed the search for a national architecture, the outcome for a regional architecture seems problematic. Regional cultural landscapes, however, may have a better chance. These usually have subsystems that change more slowly; they also provide many more potential attributes and thus also many more possibilities.

NOTES

1. These are the references to it in the *Art Index*.

2. A term introduced by Carl Sauer in 1941.

3. More technically, this is a *polythetic* rather than a *monothetic* approach, although I do not, in fact, use it here [Rapoport 1982c; 1988a; and, especially, in press (b)]. Note that for mapping culture regions etically, single diagnostic traits can occasionally be found; the barn forebay for the Pennsylvania cultural region (Glass 1986) or Batik designs for certain Indonesian culture regions (Zimolzak and Stansfield 1983, 217) can be used as surrogates for the larger set. They are most unlikely to work emically or for cultural landscapes where high redundancy among multiple attributes is needed.

4. This was drawn to my attention, and the magazine lent to me, by Tom Hubka.

5. This work was first drawn to my attention by Jim Shields.

6. There have been recent radio and television programs on the persistence of regional accents in the United States.

7. I cannot review the recent evidence for this here.

8. Although this is intimately related to the current interest in "place," that is a concept of little use at the moment and will therefore not be discussed here (cf. Rapoport 1985c).

9. Note that, once again, I am ignoring issues of feasibility, implementation, education, the perceived roles of various actors, and so on.

REFERENCES

AL SAYYAD, N. 1987. "Space in the Islamic City: Some Urban Design Patterns." *Journal of Architecture and Planning Research*, 4 (2):108–19.

ARREOLA, D. D. 1981. "Fences as Landscape Taste: Tucson's Barrios." *Journal of Cultural Geography*, 2(2):96–105.

———. 1984. "House Color in Mexican American Barrios." Paper presented at the Built Form and Culture Research Conference, Lawrence, Kansas. October. Mimeo.

BARNARD, B. 1984. *Cultural Facades: Ethnic Architecture in Malaysia*. UFSI Reports (1984/ No. 5, Asia). Hanover, N. H., Universities Field Staff International.

BERDOULAY, V., and M. PHIPPS. 1985. *Paysage et Systeme*. Ottawa: Editions de L'Université d'Ottawa.

BERGER, P. L. 1981. "Speaking to the Third World." *Commentary*, 72 (4):29–36.

———. 1983. "Democracy for Everyone?" *Commentary*, 76 (3):31–6.

BLIZNAKOV, M. 1987. "Architecture of the Totalitarian State." Paper presented at session on "The Architectural Environment as Administered Space". American Political Science Association Annual Meeting, Chicago, Ill. September. Mimeo.

BRANCH, M. C. 1988. *Regional Planning (Introduction and Explanation)*. Westport, Conn.: Praeger.

BRONNER, S. J., ed. 1985. *American Material Culture and Folklife: A Prologue and Dialogue*. Ann Arbor, Mich.: UMI Research Press.

BROWER, S. 1985. *Design in Familiar Places*. Report to NEA, Baltimore, School of Social Work and Community Planning, University of Maryland at Baltimore. May.

COHEN, E. 1979. "Rethinking the Sociology of Tourist Research." *Annals of Tourism*, Vol. 6.

CONGRESSIONAL QUARTERLY (Editorial Research Reports). 1980. American "Regionalism: Our Economic, Cultural and Political Makeup." Washington, D.C.: Editorial Research Reports.

COSGROVE, D. E. 1984. *Social Formation and Symbolic Landscapes*. London: Croom-Helm.

CRAIK, K. H. 1972. "Appraising the Objectivity of Landscape Dimensions." In: *Natural Environments: Studies in Theoretical and Applied Analysis*, ed. J. V. Krutilla, pp. 292–346. Baltimore, Md.: Johns Hopkins Univ. Press.

CZESTOCHOWSKI, J. S. 1981. *John Stewart Curry and Grant Wood: A Portrait of Rural America*. Columbia, Mo.: Univ. Missouri Press.

DANSEREAU, P. 1975. *Inscape and Landscape: The Human Perception of Environment*. New York: Columbia Univ. Press.

DE BLIJ, H. J., and P. O. MULLER. 1986. *Culture, Society and Space*. 3rd ed. New York: John Wiley.

DESPRES, C. 1987. "Symbolic Representations of the Suburban House: The Case of the Neo-Quebecois House." In: *Public Environments* (EDRA 18), ed. J. Harvey and D. Henning, pp. 152–9. Washington, D.C.: EDRA.

DOWN EAST (The Magazine of Maine). 1986. 32 (7) (February).

ESSEX COUNTY COUNCIL. 1973. *A Design Guide for Residential Areas*. Chelmsford: Essex C. C. Planning Department.

EVRENOGLOU, V. 1981. *A Contextual Approach to Resort Hotel Design: A Cycladic Example*. M. Arch. Thesis. University of Wisconsin—Milwaukee, Department of Architecture (unpublished).

EYLES, J. 1985. *Senses of Place*. Warrington, Eng.: Silverbrook Press.

FOOTE, K. E. 1983. *Color in Public Places*. Research Paper No. 205. University of Chicago, Department of Geography.

FORMAN, R. T. T., and M. GODRON. 1986. *Landscape Ecology*. New York: John Wiley.

GASTIL, R. D. 1975. *Cultural Regions of the United States*. Seattle: Univ. Washington Press.

GLASS, J. W. 1986. *The Pennsylvania Culture Region: A View from the Barn*. Ann Arbor: Univ. Michigan Research Press.

GLASSIE, H. 1968. *Pattern in the Material Folk Culture of the Eastern United States*. Philadelphia: Univ. Pennsylvania Press.

GORDON, M. M. 1978. *Human Nature, Class and Ethnicity.* New York: Oxford Univ. Press.

GROAT, L. N. 1986. *Contextual Compatibility in Architecture: An Investigation of Non-Designers' Conceptualizations.* Milwaukee: School of Architecture and Urban Planning, University of Wisconsin—Milwaukee.

GUNN, C. A. 1972. In: *Vacationscape: Designing Tourist Regions.* Austin: Univ. Texas, Bureau of Business Research.

HAKIM, B. S. 1986. *Arabic-Islamic Cities: Building and Planning Principles.* London: KPI.

HART, J. F. 1972. *Regions of the United States.* New York: Harper and Row.

_____. 1975. *The Look of the Land.* Englewood Cliffs, N.J.: Prentice-Hall.

HIGUCHI, T. 1983. *The Visual and Spatial Structure of Landscapes.* Cambridge, Mass.: MIT Press.

HOUSTON, J. M. 1967. *The Western Mediterranean World: An Introduction to Its Landscapes.* New York: Praeger.

HUBKA, T. C. 1984. *Big House, Little House, Back House, Barn: The Connected Farm Buildings of New England.* Hanover, N.H.: Univ. Press of New England.

JACKOVICS, T. W., and T. F. SAARINEN. 1978. "The Sense of Place: Impressions of Tucson and Phoenix, Arizona." April. Mimeo.

JACKSON, J. B. 1951. "Chihuahua—As We Might Have Been." *Landscape,* 1(1): 16–23. Reprinted in Yates 1985, p. 67.

_____. 1984. *Discovering the Vernacular Landscape.* New Haven, Conn.: Yale Univ. Press.

JAKLE, J. A. 1985. *The Tourist: Travel in Twentieth-Century North America.* Lincoln: Univ. Nebraska Press.

_____. 1987. *The Visual Elements of Landscape.* Amherst: Univ. Massachusetts Press.

JORDAN, T. G. 1978. "Perceptual Regions in Texas." *Geographic Review,* 68(3): 293–307.

KLITGAARD, K. 1941. *Through the American Landscape.* Chapel Hill: Univ. North Carolina Press.

LEIGH BROWN, P. 1988. "In Seven Days, Designing a New Traditional Town." *New York Times,* June 9.

LEIGHLY, J., ed. 1967. *Land and Life: A Selection from the Writings of Carl O. Sauer.* Berkeley: Univ. California Press.

LIFFRING-ZUG, J. 1977. *This is Grant Wood Country.* Davenport, Iowa: Davenport Municipal Art Gallery.

LITTON, R. B. JR. 1982. "Visual Assessment of Natural Landscapes." In: *Environmental Aesthetics: Essays in Interpretation,* ed. B. Sadler and A. Carlson. Western Geographical Series, Vol. 20, pp. 97–115. Victoria, B.C.: Univ. Victoria.

LOTUS INTERNATIONAL. 1986. No. 50.

LOW, S. M., and W. P. RYAN. 1985. "Noticing Without Looking, A Methodology for the Integration of Architectural and Local Perceptions in Oley, Pennsylvania." *Journal of Architecture and Planning Research,* 2:3–22.

MAB. 1977. *Guidelines for Field Studies in Environmental Perception.* Paris: UNESCO.

MACCONNELL, D. 1976. *The Tourist: A New Theory of the Leisure Class.* New York: Schocken.

MACSAI, J. 1985. "Architecture as Opposition." *Journal of Architectural Education,* 38(4): 8–14.

MEINIG, D., ed. 1979. *The Interpretation of Ordinary Landscapes; Geographical Essays.* New York: Oxford Univ. Press.

MILWAUKEE JOURNAL. 1988. "English-Castle Look Wins Favor in Bangkok." June 17.

MURRAY, P. 1984. "Style and Regionalism in Malaysia." *RIBA Journal*, 91(11):20–5.

NEMETH, D. J. 1987. *The Architecture of Ideology: Neo-Confucian Imprinting on Cheju Island, Korea*. University of California Publications, Geography, Vol. 26. Berkeley: Univ. California Press.

NEW YORK TIMES. 1988a. July 5, p. 9.

———. 1988b. July 6, p. 32.

ODUM, H. W., and H. E. MOORE. 1938. *American Regionalism: A Cultural-Historical Approach to National Integration*. New York: Henry Holt.

OSTROWETSKY, S., and J. S. BORDREUIL. 1980. *Le Neo-Style Regional: Reproduction d'une Architecture Pavillonnaire*. Paris: Dunod.

PARKES, D., and N. THRIFT. 1980. *Times, Spaces and Places*. Chichester: John Wiley.

PEARCE, P. L. 1982. *The Social Psychology of Tourist Behavior*. Oxford: Pergamon.

POLYTECHNIC OF NORTH LONDON. 1978. *Historic Landscapes: Identification, Recording, Management*. Dept. of Geography, Occasional Paper.

PRESTON, D. A. 1984. *The Rise and Fall of Regional Studies*. School of Geography, University of Leeds, Working Paper 381, January.

PRICE, E. I. 1968. "The Central Courthouse Square in American County Seats." *Geographical Review*, 57(1):30–6.

RAPOPORT, A. 1969a. *House Form and Culture*. Englewood Cliffs, N.J.: Prentice-Hall.

———. 1969b. "An Approach to the Study of Environmental Quality." In: *EDRA 1*, ed. H. Sanoff and S. Cohn, pp. 1–13. Raleigh, N.C.

RAPOPORT, A. 1972. "People and Environments." In: *Australia as Human Setting*, ed. A. Rapoport, pp. 3–21. Sydney, Australia: Angus and Robertson.

———. 1973a. "Some Thoughts on the Methodology of Man-Environment Studies." *International Journal of Environmental Studies*, Vol. 4.

———. 1973b. "The City of Tomorrow, the Problems of Today and the Lessons of the Past." *DMG-DRS Journal*, 7(3): 256–9.

———. 1973c. "Images, Symbols and Popular Design." *International Journal Symbology*, 4(3): 1–12.

———. 1975. "Toward a Redefinition of Density." *Environment and Behavior*, 7(2): 133–58.

———. 1976. "Socio-cultural Aspects of Man–Environment Studies." In: *The Mutual Interaction of People and Their Built Environment*, ed. A. Rapoport, pp. 7–35. The Hague: Mouton.

———. 1977. *Human Aspects of Urban Form*. Oxford: Pergamon.

———. 1978. "Culture and Environment." *The Ecologist Quarterly*, 4:269–79.

———. 1980a. "Towards a Cross-Culturally Valid Definition of Housing." In: *Optimizing Environments (EDRA 11)*, ed. R. R. Stough and A. Wandersman, pp. 310–16. Washington, D.C.: EDRA.

———. 1980b. "Cross-Cultural Aspects of Environmental Design." In: *Human Behavior and Environment*. Vol. 4. *Culture and Environment*, ed. I. Altman, A. Rapoport, and J. Wohlwill, pp. 7–46. New York: Plenum.

———. 1980/81. "Neighborhood Homogeneity or Heterogeneity." *Architecture and Behavior*, 1(1):65–77.

———. 1981a. "Vernacular Design and the Cultural Determinants of Form." In: *Build-*

ings and Society: Essays on the Social Development of the Built Environment, ed. A. D. King, pp. 283–305. London: Routledge and Kegan Paul.

———. 1981b. "Identity and Environment: A Cross-Cultural Perspective." In: *Housing and Identity: Cross-Cultural Perspectives*, ed. J. S. Duncan, pp. 6–35. London: Croom-Helm.

———. 1982a. *The Meaning of the Built Environment: A Nonverbal Communication Approach*. Beverly Hills, Cal.: Sage.

———. 1982b. "Urban Design and Human Systems—On Ways of Relating Buildings to Urban Fabric." In: *Human and Energy Factors in Urban Planning: A Systems Approach*. Nato Advanced Institute Series D: *Behavioral and Social Sciences*, No. 12, ed. P. Laconte, J. Gibson, and A. Rapoport, pp. 161–84. The Hague: Nijhoff.

———. 1982c. "An Approach to Vernacular Design." In: *Shelter: Models of Native Ingenuity*, Consulting ed. James M. Fitch. Katonah, N.Y.: Katonah Gallery.

———. 1983a. "Environmental Quality, Metropolitan Areas and Traditional Settlements." *Habitat International*. 7(3/4):37–63.

———. 1983b. "Development, Culture Change and Supportive Design." *Habitat International*, 7(5/6): 249–68.

———. 1984. "Culture and the Urban Order." In: *The City in Cultural Context*, ed. J. Agnew, J. Mercer, and D. Sopher, pp. 50–75. London: Allen and Unwin.

———. 1985a. "Thinking About Home Environments: A Conceptual Framework." In: *Home Environments, Human Behavior and Environment*. Vol 8. ed. I. Altman and C. M. Werner, pp. 255–86. New York: Plenum.

———. 1985b. "On Diversity" and "Designing for Diversity." In: *Housing Issues, Vol. I. Design for Diversification*, ed. B. Judd, J. Dean and D. Brown, pp. 5–8; 30–36. Canberra: Royal Australian Institute of Architects.

———. 1985c. "Place, Image and Placemaking." Keynote paper presented at the PAPER 85 Conference on Place and Placemaking. Melbourne, Australia, June 19–22. Mimeo.

———. 1986a. "The Use and Design of Open Spaces in Urban Neighborhoods." In: *The Quality of Urban Life: Social, Psychological and Physical Conditions*, ed. D. Frick, pp. 159–75. Berlin: de Gruyter.

———. 1986b. "Culture and Built Form—A Reconsideration." In: *Architecture in Cultural Change: Essays in Built Form and Culture Research*, ed. D. G. Saile, pp. 157–75. Lawrence: Univ. Kansas.

———. 1987. "Pedestrian Street Use: Culture and Perception." In: *Public Streets for Public Use*, ed. A. Vermez Moudon, pp. 80–91. New York: Van Nostrand Reinhold.

———. 1988a. "Spontaneous Settlements as Vernacular Design." In: *Spontaneous Shelter*, ed. C. Patton, pp. 51–77. Philadelphia: Temple Univ. Press.

———. 1988b. "On the Meaning of Traditional." Invited Keynote Paper given at International Symposium on Traditional Dwellings and Settlements, Berkeley, Cal. April.

———. 1988c. "Levels of Meaning in the Built Environment." In: *Crosscultural Perspectives in Nonverbal Communication*, ed. F. Poyatos, pp. 317–36. Gottingen: Hogrefe.

———. 1989. "Systems of Activities in Systems of Settings." In: *Domestic Architecture and Use of Space—an Interdisciplinary Perspective*, ed. S. Kent.

———. In press (b). "Defining Vernacular Design." In: *On Vernacular Architecture: A Collection of Essays*, ed. M. Turan.

RAPOPORT, E. H., and I. R. LOPEZ-MORENO, eds. 1987. *Aportes a la Ecologia Urbana de la Ciudad de Mexico*. Mexico, D. F.: Editorial Limusa.

ROONEY, J. F., JR., W. ZELINSKY, and D. R. LOUDER, general eds. 1982. *This Remarkable Continent. An Atlas of United States and Canadian Society and Cultures*. College Station: TX Texas A&M Univ. Press. Published for SNACS.

ROSENOW, J. E., and G. L. PULSIPHER. 1979. *Tourism: The Good, The Bad and The Ugly*. Lincoln, Neb.: Century Three Press.

SADLER, B., and A. CARLSON, ed. 1982. *Environmental Aesthetics: Essays in Interpretation*. Western Geographical Series, Vol. 20. Victoria, B.C.: Univ. Victoria.

SIKSNA, A. 1981. "Understanding Australian Urban Space: The Lesson of Country Towns." *Proceedings, 1981 Conference of Australia and New Zealand Archaeological Science Association*, Canberra, pp. 121–7.

TUNNARD, C. 1978. *A World With a View: An Inquiry into the Nature of Scenic Values*. New Haven, Conn.: Yale Univ. Press.

UNIVERSITY OF WISCONSIN—GREEN BAY. 1970. *The Concept of Region and Regionalism—Functions and Delineations*. Proceedings of a seminar. Green Bay: Univ. Wisconsin.

VERNEZ MOUDON, A. 1986. *Built For Change: Neighborhood Architecture in San Francisco*. Cambridge, Mass.: MIT Press.

VERNEZ MOUDON, A., D. SOLOMON and R. OKAMOTO. 1980. "The Development of San Francisco Zoning Legislation for Residential Environs." In: *Optimizing Environments* (EDRA 11), ed. R. R. Stough and A. Wandersman, pp. 22–35. Washington, D.C.: EDRA.

VINK, A. P. A. 1983. *Landscape Ecology and Land Use*. London: Longman.

VLACH, J. M., and S. J. BRONNER, ed. 1986. *Folk Art and Art Worlds*. Ann Arbor, Mich.: UMI Research Press.

VOGT, E. 1955. "American Subcultural Continua as Exemplified by Mormons and Texans." *American Anthropologist*, 57:1163–73.

WAGSTAFF, J. M., ed. 1987. *Landscape and Culture: Geographical and Archaeological Perspectives*. Oxford: Blackwell.

WENER, R., and F. SZIGETI, ed. 1988. *Cumulative Index to the Proceedings of EDRA (Vols. 1–18) (1969–1987)*. Washington, D.C.: EDRA.

WEST, R. C. 1974. "The Flat-Roofed Folk Dwelling in Rural Mexico." In: *Man and Cultural Heritage. Papers in honor of Fred B. Kniffen*, Geoscience & Man, Vol. V, eds. H. J. Walker and W. G. Haag, pp. 111–32. Baton Rouge: Louisiana State Univ.

WIDMAR, R. 1986. "Participation Based Pattern-Generation for Regional Character Planning." In: *The Costs of Not Knowing* (EDRA 17), ed. J. Wineman, R. Barnes, and C. Zimring, pp. 291–7. Washington, D.C.: EDRA.

YATES, S. A., ed. 1985. *The Esssential Landscape: The New Mexico Photographic Survey, with Essays by J. B. Jackson*. Albuquerque: Univ. New Mexico Press.

ZELINSKY, W. 1973. *The Cultural Geography of the United States*. Englewood Cliffs, N.J.: Prentice-Hall.

———. 1980. "North America's Vernacular Regions." *Annals, Association of American Geographers*, 70(1):1–16.

———. 1982. Chapter 1 in *This Remarkable Continent*. J. F. Rooney, Jr., W. Zelinsky, and D. R. Louder, gen. eds. College Station, Texas: Texas A&M Univ. Press.

ZIMOLZAK, C. E., and C. A. STANSFIELD, JR. 1983. *The Human Landscape: Geography and Culture*. Columbus, Ohio: C. E. Merrill.

Pueblo Images in Contemporary Regional Architecture: Primal Needs, Transcendent Visions

Glade Sperry, Jr.

Pueblo style is not a style, it is a way of life shaped by a reaction to the desert climate, available building materials, and cultural and mythical forces. It is also an alluring trap for those of us who must create in the shadow of its force.

Although it is possible to build anew in the materials that have been used in this region for hundreds of years, it seems somehow limiting—a narrow view of the possibilities. The architecture of this place is truly a part of this place; it seems to be rooted in the land in a primal way. Forms are not manipulated; they grow in response to a sense of organization that has much to do with survival in the desert.

The softly focused adobe walls, hand-carved vigas, and patterned brick floors entice you with a familiarity that can deaden creative thought. They do not portend new opportunities for the spaces we inhabit. To replicate the evidence of the cultures that came before dooms the culture of the present. The timeless nature of Anasazi forms signifies that there are elemental forces of spirit that pervade the architecture of this place and offer a typology in which all things are possible.

The work of my firm in Albuquerque, Westwork Architects, takes measure of the issues that can choke the growth of new meanings in the architecture of this region and attempts to offer some thoughtful responses. The fundamentally significant issue that we deal with is shelter, but our formal constructs are also one of the means to our social and cultural evolution.

Our early thoughts on the meaning of this place were concerned with the significance of the formal language of regional architecture and its interpretation. In these projects we reacted not so much against an existing architectural value system as in response to the fulfillment of a perceived need for a richness in content and a sense of belonging. These thoughts took form in such projects as the field office for the State Department of Human Services in Bernalillo, New Mexico, and the Duncan Residence in the Village of Los Ranchos de Albuquerque.

The Human Services field office (1984) is a literal synthesis of archetypal forms of the small villages and towns of New Mexico (fig. 21-1). This project houses social programs for the residents of the area and speaks in direct allusion to these neighbors. A freestanding colonnade (fig. 21-2) signifies the welcoming entry portal of the traditional hacienda, and flat-roofed masses of the building are a universal response to vernacular Pueblo form. In symphony with these images are shed-roofed spaces clad in bright metal roofing, mindful of the rhythms of New Mexican villages both in silhouette and as formal object.

Glass block is borrowed directly in intent from a local dance hall and signifies the introduction of modern materials to the local vernacular building vocabulary. A classical element in the form of a colossal keystone surmounts the entry to an outdoor courtyard and encapsulates the uneasiness of an architectural language that is not born of the emotional and cultural forces of this place.

The Human Services office in Bernalillo spoke to a sense of place and was expanded upon at the Duncan Residence (1984) in the Village of Los Ranchos de Albuquerque. Situated in a rich agricultural setting paralleling the Rio Grande, the temporal functions of this home are introduced to an overlay of mystery in ritual form

21-1 *Human Services Field Office, exterior. (Westwork Architects. Project Team: Glade Sperry, Jr. AIA, Stanley G. Moore AIA, and Lawrence W. Licht AIA. Photograph: Joshua Freiwald.)*

(fig. 21-3). Here the sheltering tranquility of the archetypal hacienda courtyard had to be achieved first by passage through the arid and protective forecourt and the ritual journey through the quasi-religious temple form of the entry (fig. 21-4). Once informed by this sequence, the visitor is absolved and refreshed by the water flowing into a pool from a bright turquoise beam that points the way to the tranquil view of the nearby

21-2 *Human Services Field Office, entry colonnade. (Westwork Architects. Project Team: Glade Sperry, Jr. AIA, Stanley G. Moore AIA, Lawrence W. Licht AIA. Photograph: Joshua Freiwald.)*

21-3 *Duncan Residence: exterior view at courtyard side. (Westwork Architects. Project Team: Glade Sperry, Jr. AIA, Cindy A. Terry. Photograph: Kirk Gittings/ Syntax.)*

mountains. The stepping beam forms that are repeated in silhouette and in relief are borrowed directly from native crafts and send a cultural message not to be missed. Color cues respond to this place simply and directly with hues of cultural and ritual meaning: brown signifying earth as primogenitor, and turquoise acting as a cultural symbol of good omen and signifying sky. The brighter colors added to this palette recall memories of sunsets and desert rock strata and act as counterpoints.

At the Duncan Residence, as in the Human Services office, a place was marked and a language spoken. The language, however, seemed too complex—too many verbs and too much sentence structure. The establishment of a linkage with the timelessness of the desert landscape would require closer contact with the myth and mystery of this place. A sense of place must be concerned less with the interpretation of indigenous built evidence and respond more to the environmental forces and spirit that shape that place if we are to expand the meaning of our architecture and mirror the achievements of our culture.

The Center for Non-Invasive Diagnosis (1986) at the University of New Mexico in Albuquerque presented an opportunity for the science-fiction nature of the technical processes housed there to provide symbols for interpretation of meanings much the same as the rituals of Pueblo life informed their spaces (see fig. 21-5, the jacket cover photo for this book, and fig. 42 on p. 332). The rite of passage into the Center celebrates the culture that has achieved these highly technical processes by elevating their materials and techniques to iconic status. A stainless steel column stands sentry and marks the beginning of the entry sequence with its cool shimmering form both attractive and aloof—an analogy to our love–hate relationship with technological progress. The colonnade of exposed sandblasted reinforced concrete signifies strength and permanence and conjures primal notions of stone monoliths. An overhead trellis that provides shade and spatial definition is rendered in steel shapes that are a direct reflection of the technical processes that created them. High-performance reflective glass panes are set within the grid of standard glazing in a gesture reminiscent of the stained glass windows of cathedrals.

The mystery of the imaging process suggested the forms of the main building. Stripped bare to unload all extraneous meanings, these forms begin to touch the spirit

21-4 *Duncan Residence: entry court. (Westwork Architects. Project Team: Glade Sperry, Jr. AIA, Cindy A. Terry. Photograph: Kirk Gittings/Syntax.)*

and power of this place and project their own air of mystery. Other aspects of this hidden agenda of myth and mystery shaped a group of related projects that followed: the Friedman Residence, the Crystal Growth Research Facility, and the Nelson Residence.

As a metaphorical ship in the desert, the Friedman Residence (1987) comes to rest between two rugged granite outcroppings in the foothills of a mountain range (fig. 21-6). The power of this landscape is overwhelming, and the air of mystery in this place is charged by the presence of megalithic granite boulders that dominate and shape

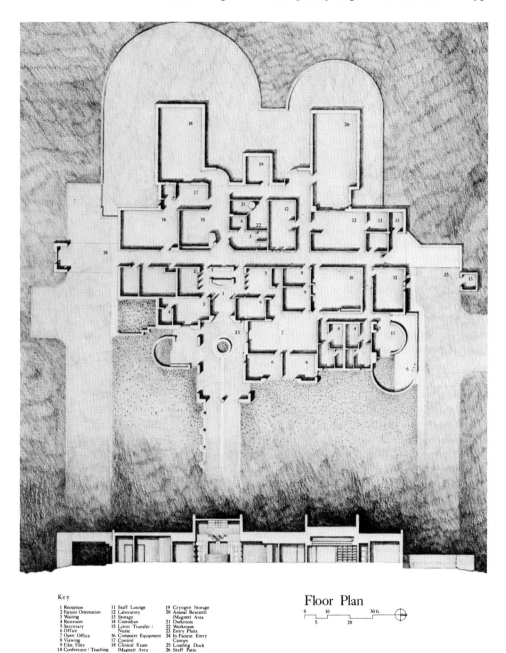

Key

1 Reception	11 Staff Lounge	19 Cryogen Storage
2 Patient Orientation	12 Laboratory	20 Animal Research
3 Waiting	13 Storage	(Magnet) Area
4 Restroom	14 Custodian	21 Darkroom
5 Secretary	15 Litter Transfer /	22 Workroom
6 Office	Nurse	23 Entry Plaza
7 Open Office	16 Computer Equipment	24 In-Patient Entry
8 Viewing	17 Control	Canopy
9 Film Files	18 Clinical Exam	25 Loading Dock
10 Conference / Teaching	(Magnet) Area	26 Staff Patio

Floor Plan

0   10   30 ft.

5   20

21-5 *Center for Non-Invasive Diagnosis: floor plan. (Westwork Architects. Project Team: Glade Sperry, Jr. AIA, Cindy A. Terry. Photograph: Kirk Gittings/Syntax.) See photograph portfolio (Part VII) for additional photos of CNID.*

much of the terrain (fig. 21-7). The ritual need to touch this landscape and form a bridge to it is acknowledged in the entry ramada that fingers out into the site. The tracery of the entry element is in counterpoint to the simple massive forms of the dwelling (fig. 21-8). The architecture here draws its power not from its own formal hierarchy but from the timeless ritual of its surroundings. The drama of the light entering the interior

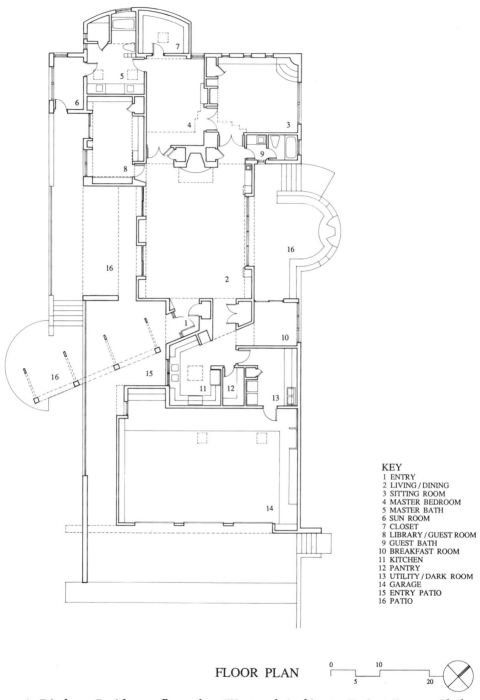

FLOOR PLAN

0   10
5   20

KEY
1 ENTRY
2 LIVING / DINING
3 SITTING ROOM
4 MASTER BEDROOM
5 MASTER BATH
6 SUN ROOM
7 CLOSET
8 LIBRARY / GUEST ROOM
9 GUEST BATH
10 BREAKFAST ROOM
11 KITCHEN
12 PANTRY
13 UTILITY / DARK ROOM
14 GARAGE
15 ENTRY PATIO
16 PATIO

21-6 *Friedman Residence: floor plan. (Westwork Architects. Project Teams: Glade Sperry, Jr. AIA, Cindy A. Terry. Photograph: Kirk Gittings/Syntax.)*

21-7 *Friedman Residence: exterior. (Westwork Architects. Project Team: Glade Sperry, Jr. AIA, Cindy A. Terry. Photograph: Kirk Gittings/Syntax.)*

21-8 *Friedman Residence: exterior. (Westwork Architects. Project Team: Glade Sperry, Jr. AIA, Cindy A. Terry. Photograph: Kirk Gittings/Syntax.)*

295

21-9 *Friedman Residence: living/dining. (Westwork Architects. Project Team: Glade Sperry, Jr. AIA, Cindy A. Terry. Photograph: Kirk Gittings/Syntax.)*

spaces heightens the sense of mystery as shafts of light enter from unseen sources in homage to religious architecture of the region (fig. 21-9).

At the Crystal Growth Research Facility (1987) for the University of New Mexico, as at the Center for Non-Invasive Diagnosis, a place was marked by direct reference to the mystery of the processes housed within. Here this notion is further abstracted and the formal language is even more reductivist. This building houses complex equipment used to grow fragile crystals for use in lasers and other scientific applications. The bipartite plan of this structure houses the crystal growing area in a simple rectilinear

21-10 *Crystal Growth Research Facility: exterior massing. (Westwork Architects. Project Team: Glade Sperry, Jr. AIA, Cindy A. Terry. Photograph: Kirk Gittings/ Syntax.)*

form and places the support spaces, which are the realm of the scientists, in the softer geometric shape (fig. 21-10 and 21-11). Mediating between these two zones is a stepped wall that slices into the building mass and emerges as a soft focus curve at the opposite end of the plan. This wall can be seen as a meeting between the vernacular forms of the ancient ones and the new regions being explored in current technologies.

21-11 *Crystal Growth Research Facility: exterior massing. (Westwork Architects. Project Team: Glade Sperry, Jr. AIA, Cindy A. Terry. Photograph: Kirk Gittings/ Syntax.)*

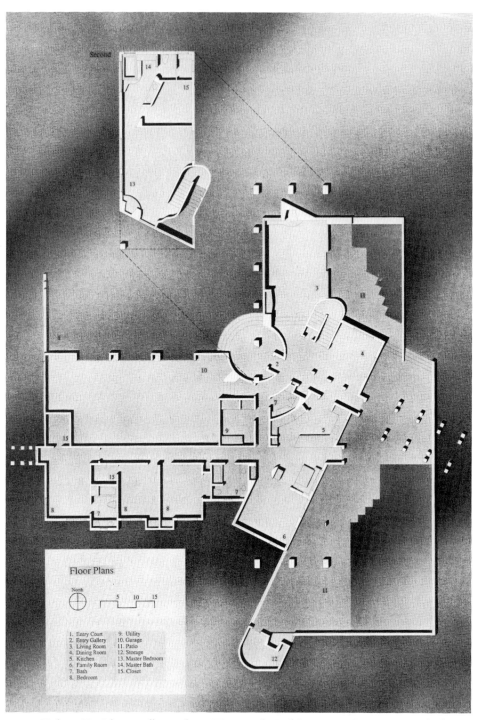

21-12 *Nelson Residence: floor plan. (Westwork Architects. Project Team: Glade Sperry, Jr. AIA, Cindy A. Terry. Photograph: Kirk Gittings/Syntax.)*

298

21-13 *Nelson Residence: courtyard. (Westwork Architects. Project Team: Glade Sperry, Jr. AIA, Cindy A. Terry. Photograph: Kirk Gittings/Syntax.)*

The Nelson Residence (1988) derives meaning from a response to its site. Set in the foothills above Albuquerque, the house assumes two postures in relation to its surroundings. The face presented to the city is ordered and orthogonal, while the side that responds to the natural precinct of the mountains becomes fragmented and irregular. Two major axes organize the plan (fig. 21-12). The entry axis points the way to a nearby canyon and terminates in a shade structure that bridges over the perimeter wall in a move that signifies an open-ended connection between the house and nature (fig. 21-13). This connective link itself can also be read as a forest transformed into lithic permanence. The second plan axis is orthogonal to the city grid and finds its beginning as a skeletal framework of columns emerging from the site (fig. 21-14 and 21- 15). At the spiritual center of the plan is a small entry court carved out as a circular space that turns in on itself and focuses the energy of this place (fig. 21-16).

21-14 *Nelson Residence: front elevation. (Westwork Architects. Project Team: Glade Sperry, Jr. AIA, Cindy A. Terry. Photograph: Kirk Gittings/Syntax.)*

21-15 *Nelson Residence: interior at plan axis. (Westwork Architects. Project Team: Glade Sperry, Jr. AIA, Cindy A. Terry. Photograph: Kirk Gittings/Syntax.)*

Lessons learned from this group of projects pointed the way to a new understanding of the possibilities that exist for an architecture that could expand our thinking. This would be an architecture shaped by place, function, and the technological and cultural messages to be sent by the current inhabitants and not by reliance on a regional style. This architecture would be based on the principles that shape the indigenous forms of this place, but this new regionalism would also expand to include the region of the mind. In this realm, architecture would speak to a place and then transcend it. The

21-16 *Nelson Residence: entry court. (Westwork Architects. Project Team: Glade Sperry, Jr. AIA, Cindy A. Terry. Photograph: Kirk Gittings/Syntax.)*

intent would be timeless work, a chance to unlock new myths and mysteries. This transcendant regionalism would honor the heritage of its place not be replicating its built forms but by capturing the spirit that brought them into being.

The Duncan Barn (1987) was conceived as an ode to this passage into a new region. This small outbuilding takes form as a commentary on this journey (fig. 21-17). It begins with the emergence of a fragmented element from its agricultural setting. This geologic piece represents primal form and is transformed into a pure white plane in recognition

21-17 *Duncan Barn: plan. (Westwork Architects. Project Team: Glade Sperry, Jr. AIA, Cindy A. Terry. Photograph: Kirk Gittings/Syntax.)*

of man's attempts to tame nature (figs. 21-18 and 21-19). This plane slices through the barn structure, an archetypal Pueblo form, and signifies the collision between the need to explore new architectural meanings and the desire to retain a sense of place. The barn structure splinters as a result of this collision and produces an enigmatic triangular form as well as an arbor structure in recognition of the importance of man-made landscapes in the desert.

In a current project, the Erna Fergusson Branch Library for the City of Albuquerque, the physical forms of the buildings are a representation of the journey to knowledge

21-18 *Duncan Barn: exterior. (Westwork Architects. Project Team: Glade Sperry, Jr. AIA, Cindy A. Terry. Photograph: Kirk Gittings/Syntax.)*

21-19 *Duncan Barn: exterior. (Westwork Architects. Project Team: Glade Sperry, Jr. AIA, Cindy A. Terry. Photograph: Kirk Gittings/Syntax.)*

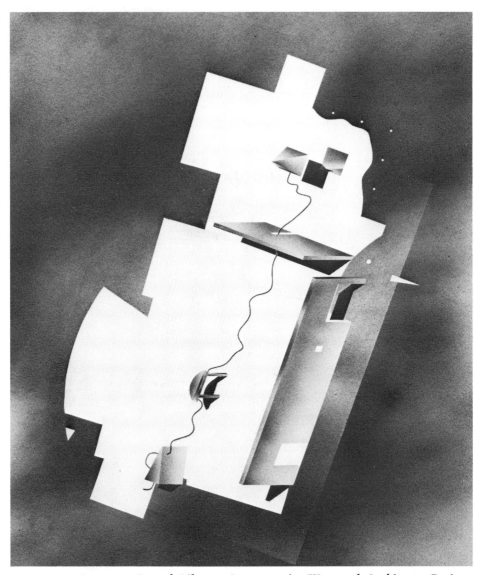

21-20 *Erna Fergusson Branch Library: Axonometric. (Westwork Architects. Project Team: Glade Sperry, Jr. AIA, Cindy A. Terry. Photograph: Kirk Gittings/Syntax.)*

embodied in the library. In this project, associations to place are implicitly suggested by forms that are logical in the environment of its site and therefore aim to surpass time (fig. 21-20). A wedge of polished black granite rises up out of the ground plane at the beginning of the entry sequence and signals the possibilities of new experiences to be had at this place. Walls of granite echo the permanence of the nearby mountain range and shut out the heat and glare of the desert sun and the noise from the adjacent strip traffic (fig. 21-21). A polished metal tube that appears on the interior restates the notion of journey as it emerges from a black granite wedge and traverses the length of the space to spiral up toward the sky into a pyramidal form at the children's program area. The "spirit trail" formed by the path of the shimmering tube has parallels in

21-21 *Erna Fergusson Branch Library: entry elevation. (Westwork Architects. Project Team: Glade Sperry, Jr. AIA, Cindy A. Terry. Photograph: Kirk Gittings/ Syntax.)*

Native American weavings. Navajo mythology holds that the "spirit trail", a line woven into the border of a rug, allows the spirit of the rug to come and go as it pleases. The weavers of these textiles believe that they have put good spirits into their designs and that these woven trails allow those spirits to escape and inspire the weaving of future rugs. The scattered forms of the exterior are enigmatic and respond to this place in a series of isolated dramatic statements (fig. 21-22).

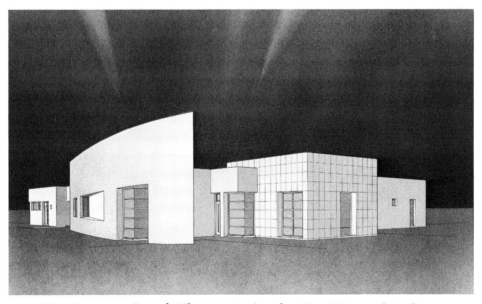

21-22 *Erna Fergusson Branch Library: exterior elevation. (Westwork Architects. Project Team: Glade Sperry, Jr. AIA, Cindy A. Terry. Photograph: Kirk Gittings/ Syntax.)*

As we explore the connection of our work to the primal aspects of shelter, we are tapping a source of energy to drive future creative intentions. We look not to freeze the cultural and social traditions of this place but to follow a process of evolution that comes from the recognition of the concerns of its present inhabitants. A sense of place and belonging is essential and self-renewing. This architecture of transcendant vision must challenge present notions but still be grounded in the history of its place. Myth and mystery, the hidden agenda of architecture, can breathe spirit into our surroundings and bring new meaning to the spaces we inhabit.

VII

Photograph Portfolio

The following portfolio depicts a chronological sequence of photographs tracing the history of architecture in New Mexico. The foundations of this regional architecture were born in the cultural substance of the native peoples of the area. The remains of Anasazi structures at Chaco Canyon and the edifices of their descendants, the Pueblo people, are shown in photographs 1–6.

Photographs 7–10 are of Spanish mission churches constructed at the Indian pueblos. One of the first tasks of the Spanish colonials was to build mission churches, convents, and rectories at existing pueblo sites.

Photographs 11–20 depict Spanish village churches and buildings. These structures are those that the Spanish settlers constructed in establishing their own communities in the region. Most edifices date from the 1700s and 1800s, when Spanish colonization truly flourished.

Photographs 21–27 show the early phases of a revival of the pueblo and Spanish styles of building, but as applied to early twentieth century construction. Santa Fe—the old capital city—along with the University of New Mexico campus were the birthplaces of the revival. Both places had developed during New Mexico's Territorial period with popular Eastern—primarily Victorian—brick structures. The Pueblo-Spanish style revival was an effort to re-establish an architecture more meaningful to the history and culture of the region.

Photographs 28–42 show how that early initiative towards a regional architecture revival took root. These photographs show the development of "the Pueblo Style" from the 1930s and 1940s to present-day interpretations which are interesting extrapolations of the original idea.

307

1 *Doorways, Pueblo Bonito Ruins (ca. 1050–1300 A.D.), Chaco Canyon, N. Mex.*
Photograph: Kirk Gittings/SYNTAX (1988).

2 *Elevated view of Pueblo Bonito Ruins (ca. 1050–1300 A.D.), Chaco Canyon, N. Mex. Photograph: F.D. Reeve, courtesy UNM Special Collections, Zimmerman Library, neg. no. #000-158-0032.*

3 *North Building, Taos Pueblo, Taos, N. Mex. Photograph: John K. Hillers (1880), courtesy N.M.S.P.A., neg. no. 16096.*

4 *Acoma Pueblo, Acoma, N. Mex. Photographer unknown, courtesy N.M.S.P.A., neg. no. 90919.*

5 *Walpi Pueblo, Hopi, Ariz. Photograph: William Henry Jackson (1875), courtesy N.M.S.P.A., neg. no. 87582.*

6 *Pueblo Bonito Ruins (ca. 1050–1300 A.D.), Chaco Canyon, N. Mex. Photograph: Kirk Gittings/SYNTAX (1988).*

7 *San Felipe Mission Church (1736), San Felipe Pueblo, N. Mex. Photograph:*
T. Harmon Parkhurst (ca. 1945), courtesy N.M.S.P.A., neg. no. 3391.

8 *San Esteban Mission Church (ca. 1641), Acoma Pueblo, N. Mex. Photographer*
unknown, courtesy N.M.S.P.A., neg. no. 1982.

9 *San José Mission Church (1706), Laguna Pueblo, N. Mex. Photographer unknown, courtesy N.M.S.P.A., neg. no. 55496.*

10 *San Jeronimo Mission Church (1726), Taos Pueblo, N. Mex. Photograph: Wyatt Davis (ca. 1945), courtesy N.M.S.P.A., neg. no. 111108.*

11 *Rear view, San Francisco de Asis Church (1818), Ranchos de Taos, Taos, N. Mex. Photograph: Kirk Gittings/SYNTAX (1988).*

12 *Santa Cruz Church (ca. 1744), Santa Cruz, N. Mex. Photograph: William Henry Jackson (1881), courtesy N.M.S.P.A., neg. no. 14351.*

13 *San Francisco de Asis Church (1818), Ranchos de Taos, Taos, N. Mex. Photograph: T. Harmon Parkhurst (ca. 1935), courtesy N.M.S.P.A., neg. no. 9729.*

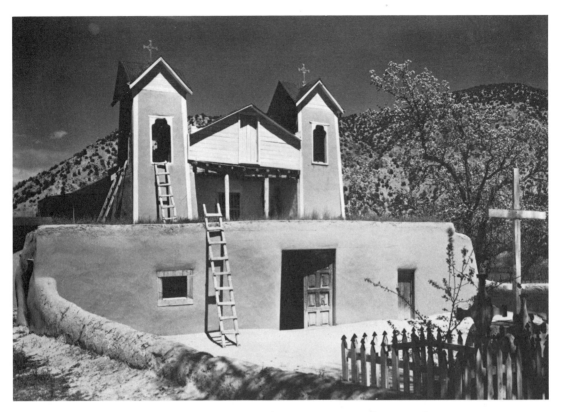

14 *Santuario de Chimayo (1823), Chimayo, N. Mex. Photograph: T. Harmon Parkhurst (ca. 1935), courtesy N.M.S.P.A., neg. no. 11531.*

15 *Church, Cordova, N. Mex. Photograph: T. Harmon Parkhurst (ca. 1935), courtesy N.M.S.P.A., neg. no. 9729.*

16 *Palace of the Governors (1706), portal (1913), Santa Fe, N. Mex. Photograph: Ferenz Fedor (ca. 1946–1952), courtesy N.M.S.P.A., neg. no. 100676.*

17 *Interior of San José de Gracia Church (1760), Las Trampas, N. Mex. Photograph: T. Harmon Parkhurst (ca. 1935), courtesy N.M.S.P.A., neg. no. 11531.*

18 *Interior of Santuario de Chimayo, Chimayo, N. Mex. Photograph: Jesse L. Nusbaum (ca. 1912), courtesy N.M.S.P.A., neg. no. 13754.*

19 *Martínez Hacienda (1818), Taos, N. Mex. Photograph: Anthony Richardson/ SYNTAX (1988).*

20 *San José de Gracia Church (1760), Las Trampas, N. Mex. Photograph: Anthony Richardson/SYNTAX (1988).*

21 *Carlos Vierra House (1915), Santa Fe, N. Mex. Photograph: Wesley Bradfield (1921), courtesy N.M.S.P.A., neg. no. 51927.*

22 *Kwataka Dormitory (1906), University of New Mexico Campus, Albuquerque, N. Mex. Photographer unknown (ca. 1907), courtesy N.M.S.P.A., neg. no. 30987.*

23 *Hokona Hall (1907), University of New Mexico Campus, Albuquerque, N. Mex. Photographer Mr. Walton (ca. 1917), courtesy N.M.S.P.A., neg. no. 52012.*

24 *Sigma Tau Fraternity Building (1906), formerly President's House, University of New Mexico Campus, Albuquerque, N. Mex. Photographer unknown (ca. 1917), courtesy N.M.S.P.A., neg. no. 987.*

25 *Fine Arts Museum (1917), Santa Fe, N. Mex. Architects: Rapp & Rapp.
Photograph: Kirk Gittings/SYNTAX (1988).*

26 *La Fonda Hotel (1920), Santa Fe, N. Mex. Architects: Rapp & Rapp. Photograph: J. Gans (1923), courtesy N.M.S.P.A., neg. no. 40752.*

27 *Old Post Office (1920), Santa Fe, N. Mex. Architects: U.S. Department of the Treasury Staff. Photograph: Anthony Richardson/SYNTAX (1988).*

28 *Interior of Cristo Rey Church (1940), Santa Fe, N. Mex. Architect: John Gaw
Meem. Photograph: Tyler Dingee (ca. 1955), courtesy N.M.S.P.A., neg. no. 31493.*

29 *La Fonda Hotel, Phase II (1929), Santa Fe, N. Mex. Architect: John Gaw Meem. Photograph: T. Harmon Parkhurst (ca. 1935), courtesy N.M.S.P.A., neg. no. 10690.*

30 *Scholes Hall, Administration Building (1936), University of New Mexico Campus, Albuquerque, N. Mex. Architect: John Gaw Meem. Photographer unknown, courtesy N.M.S.P.A., neg. no. 52015.*

31 *Zimmerman Library (1936), University of New Mexico Campus, Albuquerque, N. Mex. Architect: John Gaw Meem. Photograph: Ernest Knee, courtesy N.M.S.P.A., neg. no. 19651.*

32 *Eddy County Courthouse (1938), Carlsbad, N. Mex. Architects: F. W. Spencer & K. W. Vorhees. Photograph: Anthony Richardson/SYNTAX (1988).*

33 *Hallenbeck House (ca. 1932), Santa Fe, N. Mex. Architect: John Gaw Meem.*
Photograph: Anthony Richardson/SYNTAX (1988).

34 *Doña Ana County Courthouse (1937), Las Cruces, N. Mex. Photograph: Anthony*
Richardson/SYNTAX (1988).

35 *Laboratory of Anthropology (1936), Santa Fe, N. Mex. Architect: John Gaw Meem. Photograph: Anthony Richardson/SYNTAX (1988).*

36 *Cristo Rey Church (1940), Santa Fe, N. Mex. Architect: John Gaw Meem. Photograph: Anthony Richardson/SYNTAX (1988).*

37 *McKinley County Courthouse (1938), Gallup, N. Mex. Architects: Trost and Trost. Photograph: Anthony Richardson/ SYNTAX (1988).*

38 *La Luz Condominium (1973), Albuquerque, N. Mex. Architect: A. Predock. Photograph: Anthony Richardson/SYNTAX (1988).*

39 *Fine Arts Building (1962), University of New Mexico Campus, Albuquerque, N. Mex. Architects: Hooker/Hollein/Buckley. Photograph: Anthony Richardson/ SYNTAX (1988).*

40 *Humanities Building (1974), University of New Mexico Campus, Albuquerque, N. Mex. Architect: W. C. Krueger. Photograph: Anthony Richardson/SYNTAX (1988).*

41 *Center for Non-Invasive Diagnosis, front entrance (1986), University of New Mexico Campus, Albuquerque, N. Mex. Architect: Westwork Architects. Photograph: Kirk Gittings/SYNTAX (1988).*

42 *Exterior of the Center for Non-Invasive Diagnosis (1984), University of New Mexico Campus, Albuquerque, N. Mex. Architect: Westwork Architects. Photograph: Kirk Gittings/SYNTAX (1988).*

Index